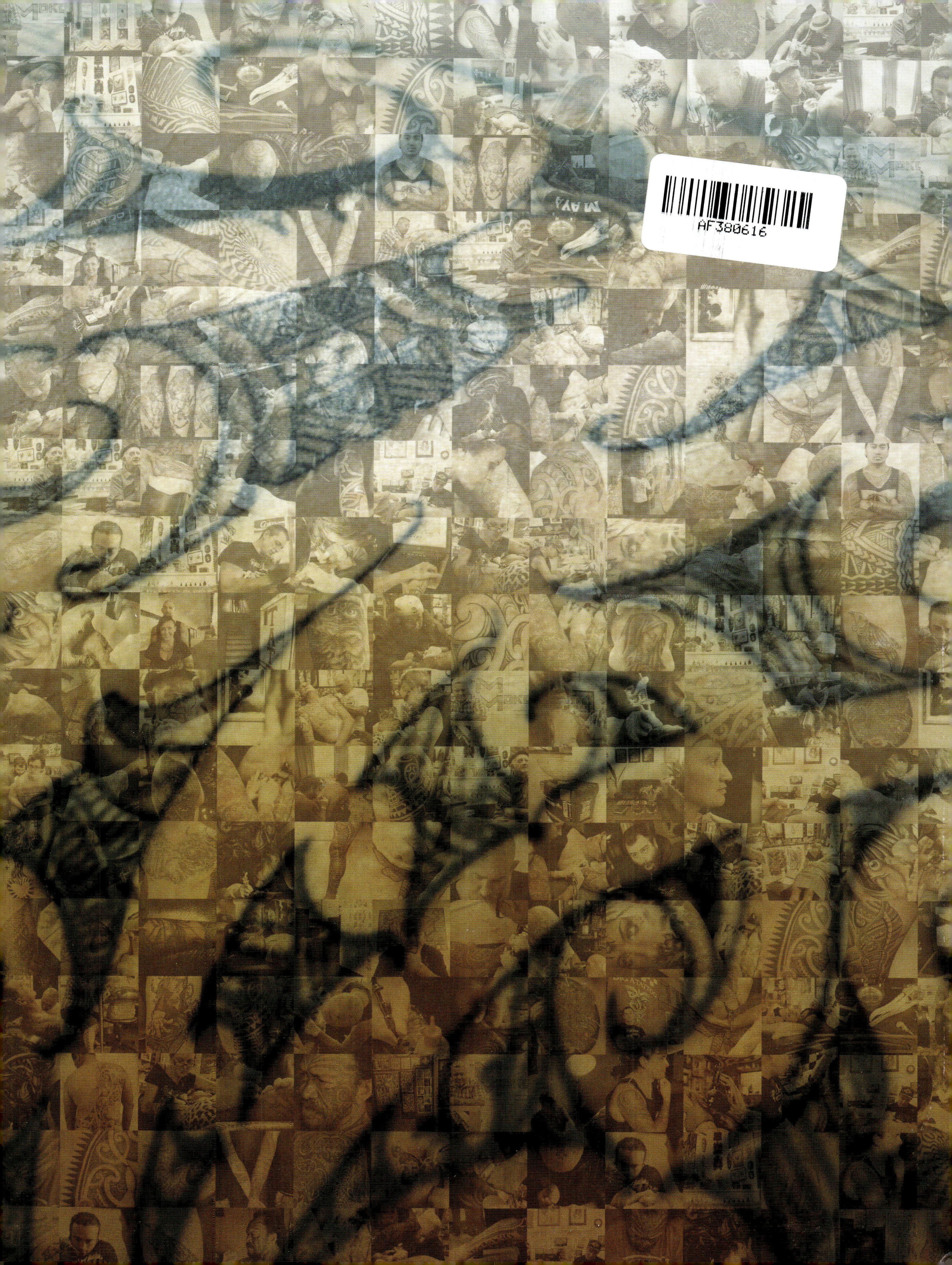

NEW**ZEALAND**TATTOO

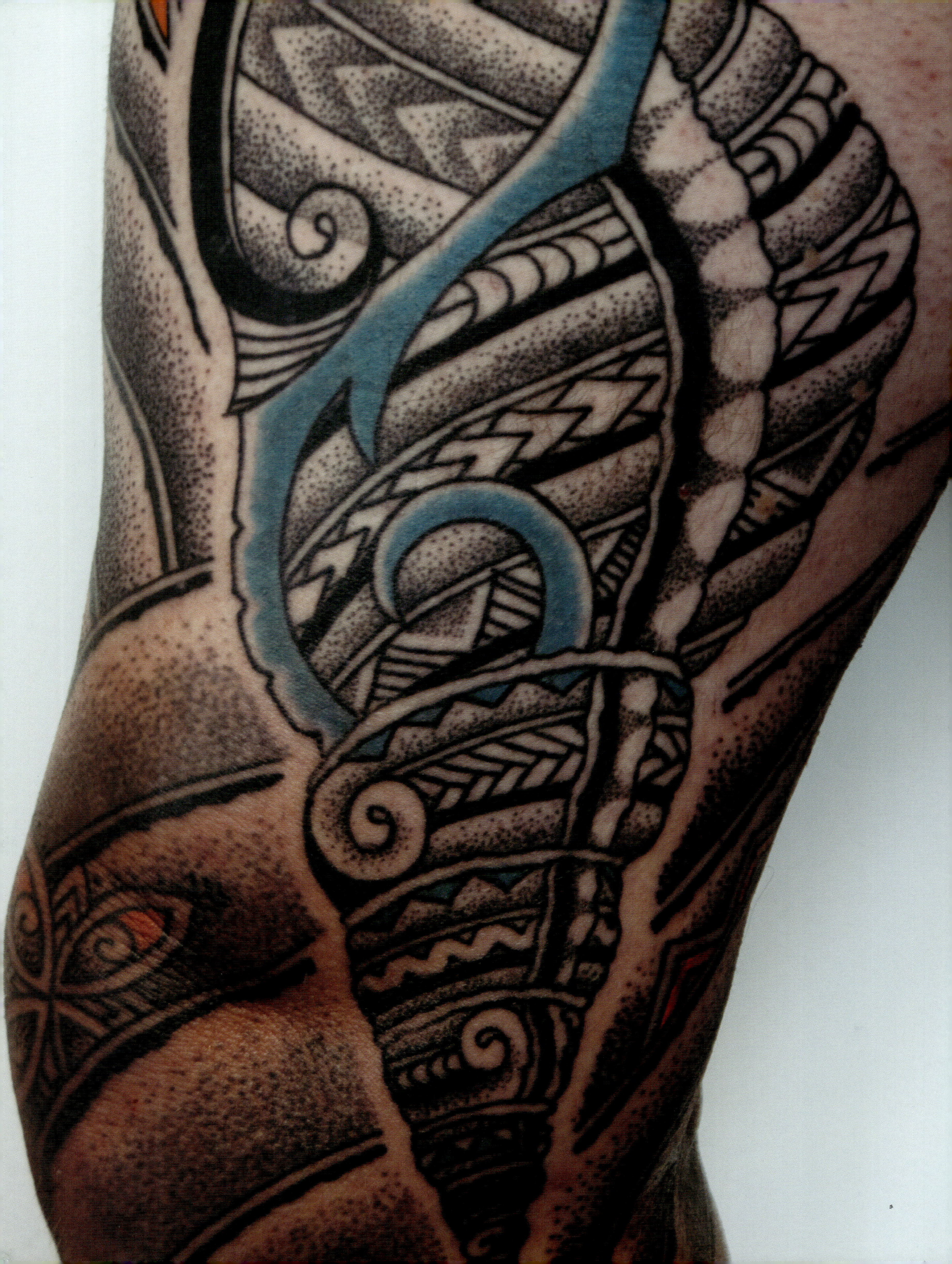

NEW**ZEALAND**TATTOO
IN THE HOME OF THE TATTOOIST'S ART

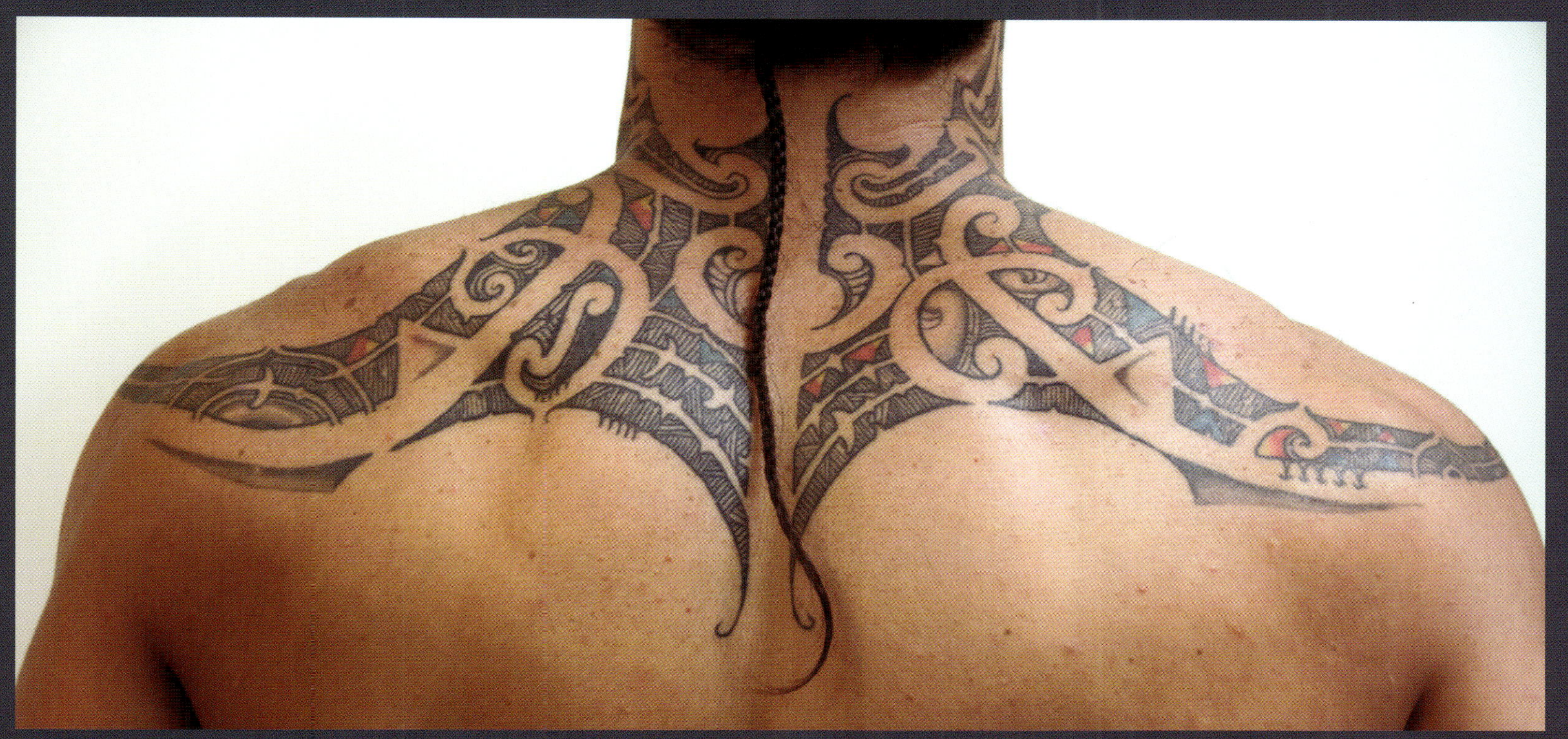

CHRIS **HOULT**
TEXT BY STEVE FORBES

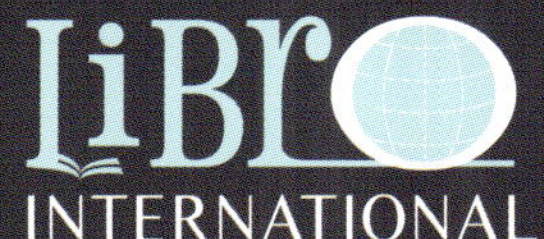

LiBRo
INTERNATIONAL

Published by Libro International, an imprint of Oratia Media Ltd (www.librointernational.com).

The publishers extend their gratitude to all of the tattooists and tattooed who agreed to be interviewed and photographed. The art works represented are meant to inspire, not to be copied.

ISBN 978-1-877514-47-0

Edited by Peter Dowling and Carolyn Lagahetau
Copy edited by Mike Bradstock, Bradstock & Associates
Designed by Cheryl Rowe, Macarn Design

Cover image: Danny Haimona (Dam Native), tattoo by Turumakina Duley, tiki by Leon Kipa.
Back cover: Merv O'Connor.
Feature images, works by: p.2: Tim Hunt; p.3: Daniel (Raniera) McGrath; p.6 Riki Manuel;
p.8: Andy Swarbrick; p.176: Steve Ma Ching's studio door.

Set in Latinia 8.5pt/14pt

First published 2012
Printed in China by Nordica

CONTENTS

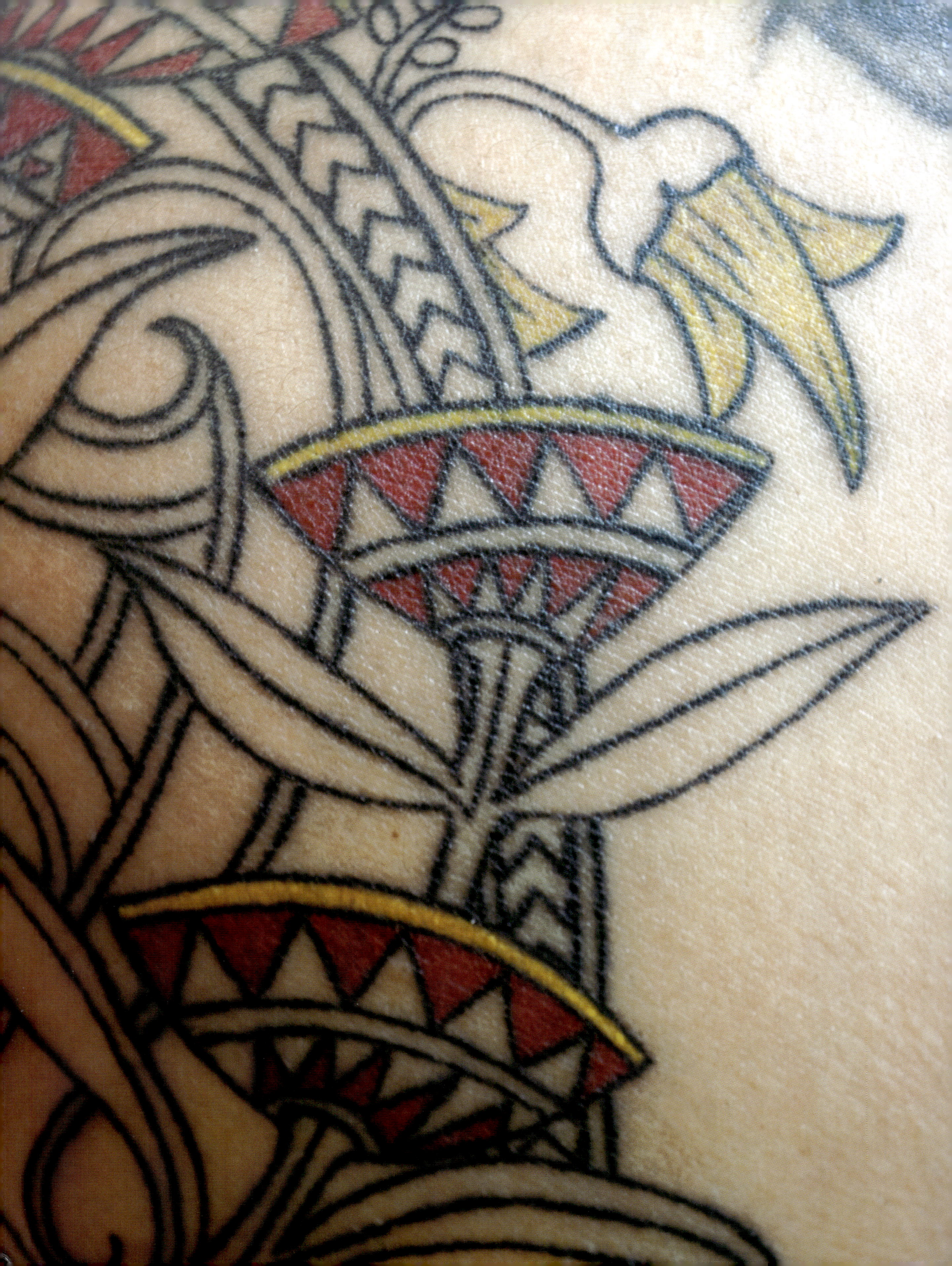

MIHI

Nā Mataora i ako

Te mahi a Uetonga,

Te mahi tā moko.

It was Mataora who taught

The art of Uetonga,

The art of tattooing.[*]

* In Maori oral history, Mataora learned the art of tattoo from Uetonga, father of his wife Niwareka, when Mataora pursued her to the underworld.

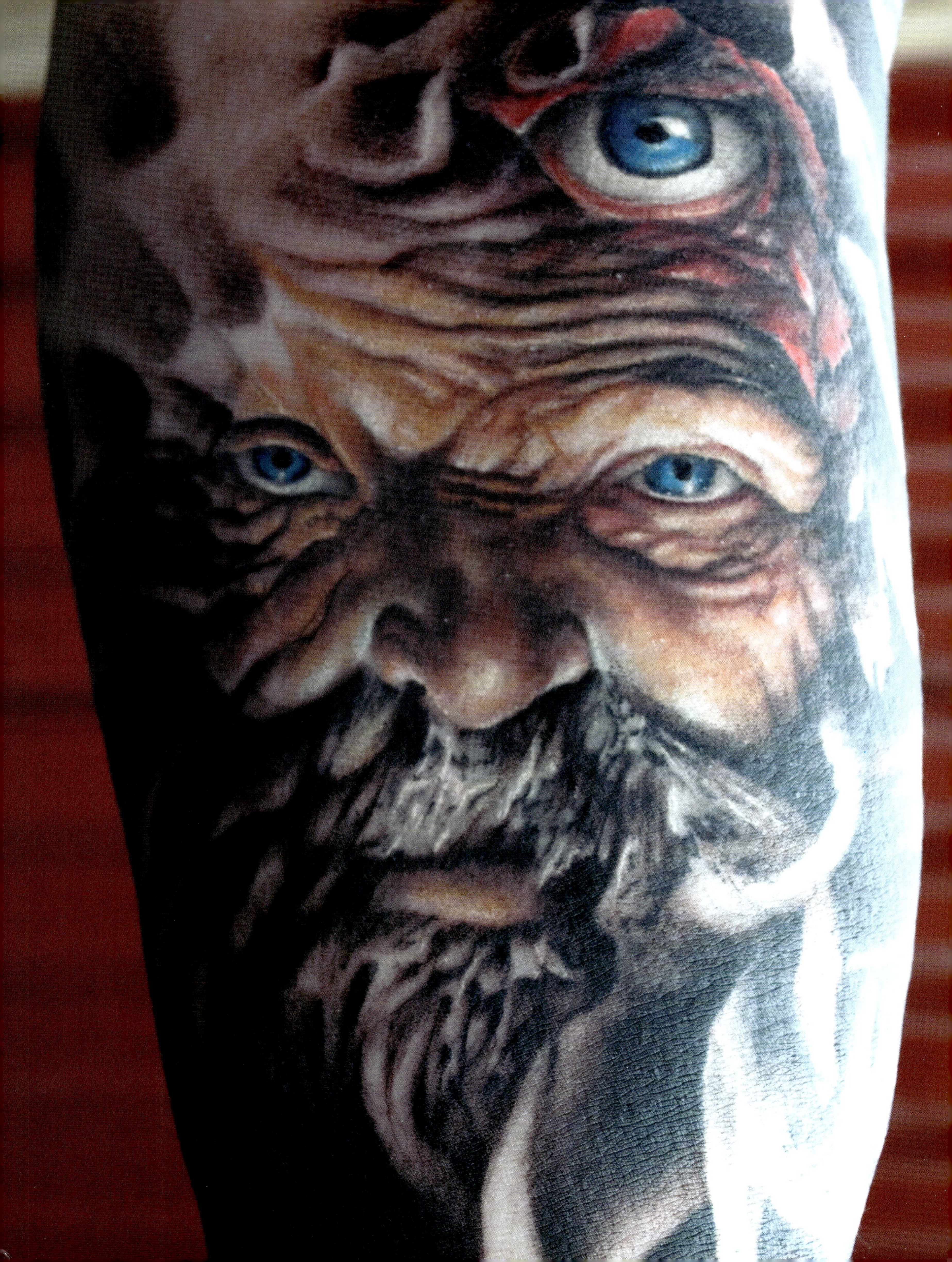

FOREWORD

New Zealand Tattoo does not set out to be a definitive work on New Zealand tattooists. It represents a snapshot, if you will excuse the pun, of the tattoo scene as writer Steve Forbes, publisher Peter Dowling and I experienced it in 2011 and 2012.

I admit to some hesitation when we embarked on the book. After all, what I knew about tattooing was derived mostly from growing up in Levin in the 1960s where, with apologies to a significant proportion of my family and friends, if you had a tat you were classified as a hoon, on the fringe of society and a little bit dangerous. It was a far cry from today, where tattoos are very much part of the mainstream.

How would the tattooists and their patrons react to one of the great 'uninked' (I have no tattoos) daring to make a book on their art form? I needn't have worried: we could all learn some lessons from tattooists! Unlike some other segments of the population, they are totally accepting of those who are different. To use a well-known quote — 'The only difference between tattooed people and non-tattooed people is that tattooed people don't care if you aren't tattooed'.

Not only do we have a thriving tattoo industry but the quality of that work is world renowned. Only some of New Zealand's gifted tattooists are featured in this book; our aim was not to cover all artists at work today. We did, however, try to include a fair representation of styles and traditions — ta moko, tatau and tattoo.

By taking a succession of road trips to different parts of the country, and meeting the artists in their studios, we have tried to convey *their* views of the tattoo world here in Aotearoa. Our heartfelt thanks to the tattooists and their clients featured in these pages, to the many others who gave their time and advice, and to everyone who supported us on the road. Hopefully we have helped in some small way to dispel the misconceptions that still surround this art form.

Chris Hoult, 2012

NEW ZEALAND TATTOOING: A BRIEF HISTORY

The styles and methods of tattooing in 21st century New Zealand are extremely diverse. From the traditional Maori and Pacific Island techniques to the various mainstream popular styles, the range available is wide. But the oldest form of tattooing in New Zealand is ta moko. It is hard to establish exactly when and where the practice first started because Maori didn't have a formal written language. Instead, to understand ta moko prior to colonisation, historians have had to rely on archaeologists and the personal accounts of the first Europeans to arrive in the country.

According to Dr Ngahuia Te Awekotuku, tattoo chisels have been found at some of the oldest excavated sites in New Zealand. Many of the tools found have wide combs, suggesting a link to those used in Samoa. In her essay 'Ta moko: Maori tattoo' (in Roger Blackley, *Goldie*, 1997, p. 109), she states: "Ta moko is related to the tatu of Eastern

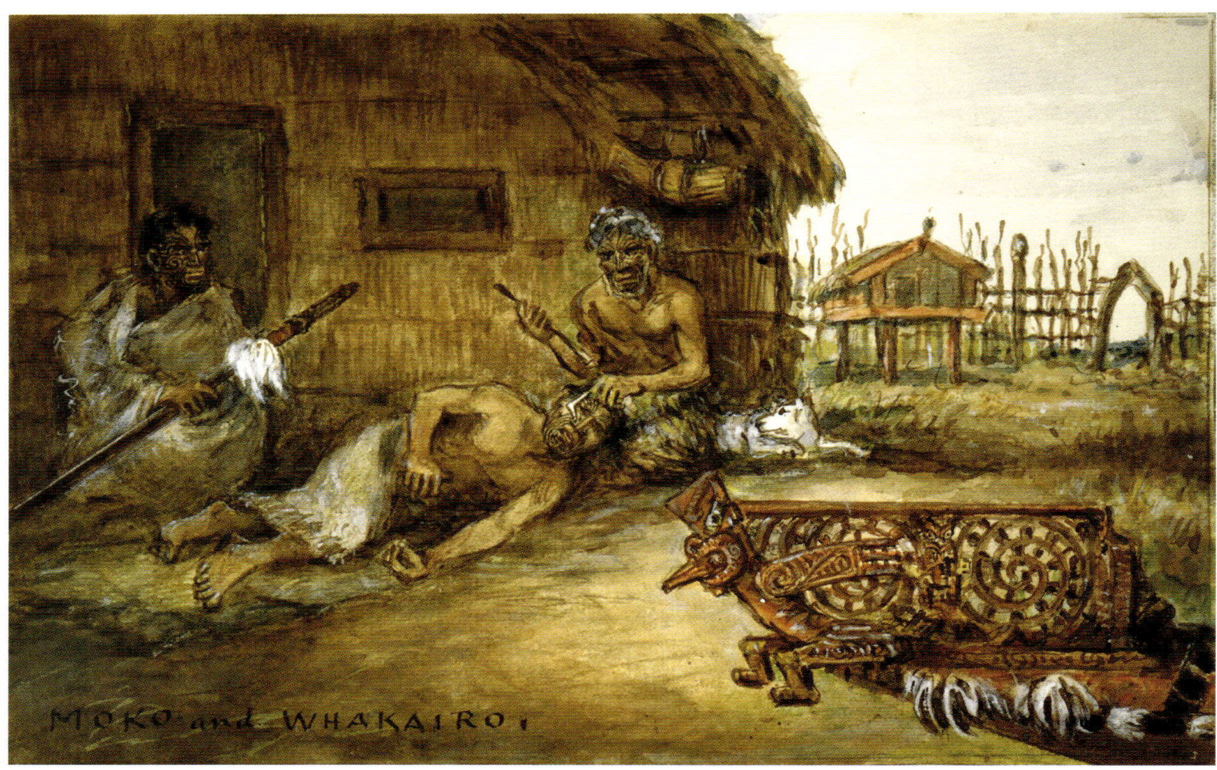

Moko and Whakairo, a scene depicting Maori chisel tattooing with carving in the mid-19th century.
(Horatio Gordon Robley, 1864 or later; Ref: A-080-012, Alexander Turnbull Library, Wellington, New Zealand)

Polynesia, and the uninterrupted, superlative tatau of Samoa. Though the patterns taken by the skin vary dramatically from one island group to another, the technique of rhythmically tapping a bone chisel lashed to a small wooden haft remains the same."

Some of the earliest written accounts of tattooing here were by Sydney Parkinson, an artist aboard Captain James Cook's ship *Endeavour* when it first landed in New Zealand at Poverty Bay in 1769. Parkinson was employed by botanist and natural historian Joseph Banks, and sketched thousands of drawings of the plants and animals Banks and his assistant Daniel Solander collected. Parkinson also painted and sketched images of local Maori displaying their impressive moko, and described in detail the different styles and patterns that he saw. Many of these were included in his book *Journal of a Voyage to the South Seas, in His Majesty's Ship the Endeavour*, published in 1773.

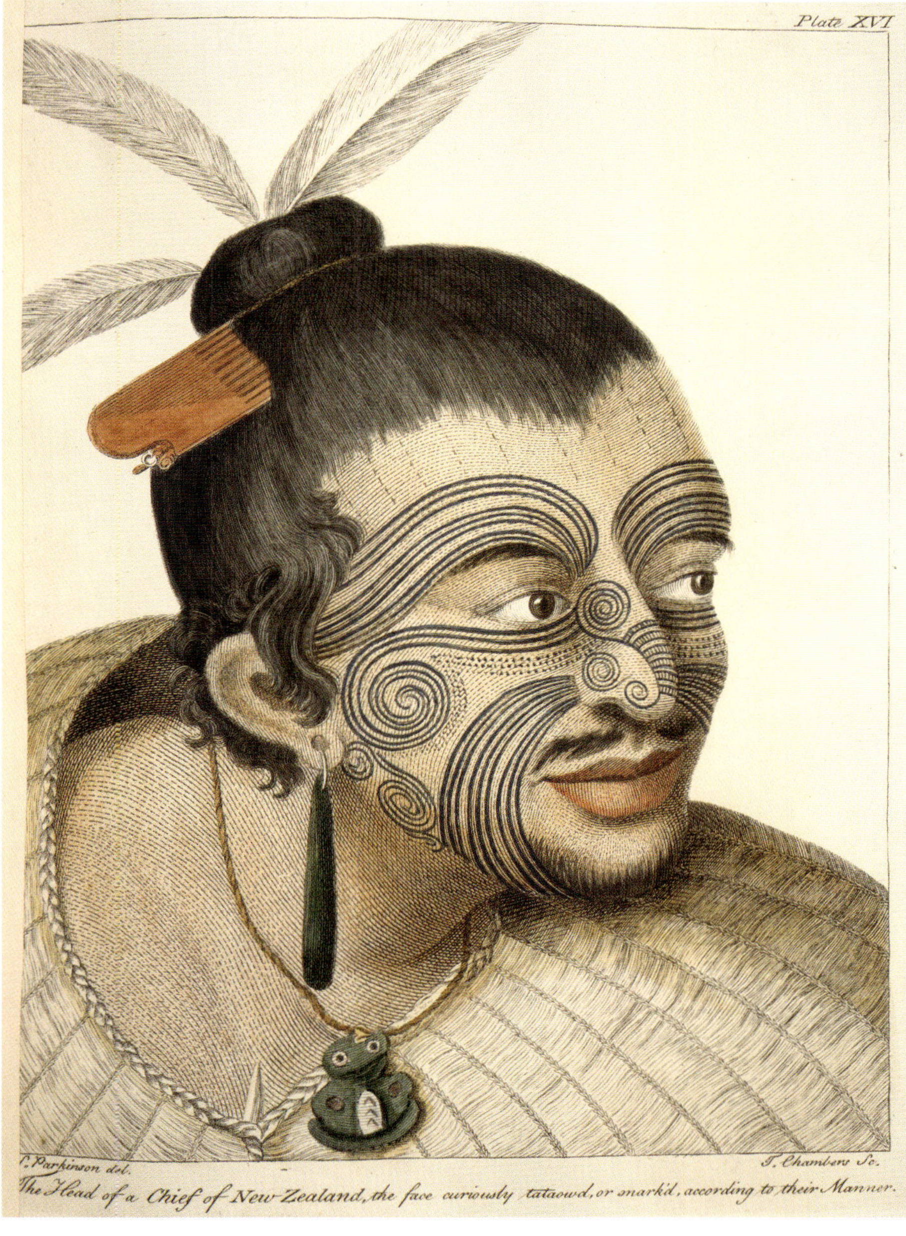

Sydney Parkinson's journal entry of 12 October 1769 was accompanied by this image (Plate XVI), captioned "The head of a chief of New Zealand, the face curiously tataow'd, or marked according to their manner."

(Sydney Parkinson, 1784; Ref: PUBL-0037-16, Alexander Turnbull Library, Wellington, New Zealand)

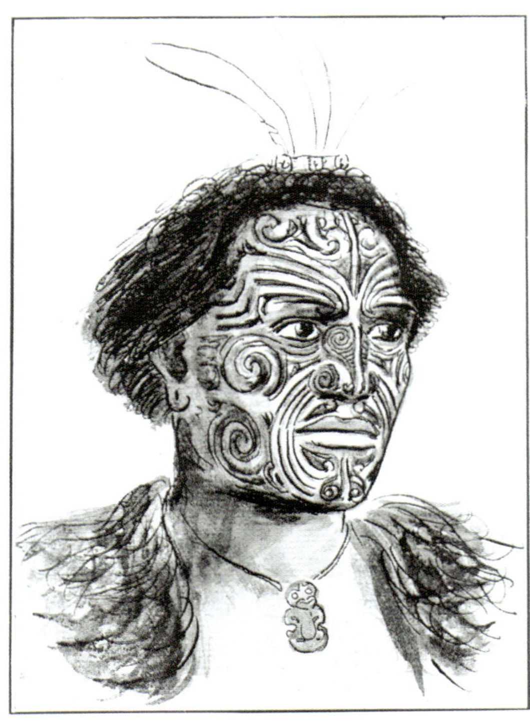

Hongi Hika.

(Horatio Gordon Robley, 1923; Ref: PUBL-0067-154, Alexander Turnbull Library, Wellington, New Zealand)

On 12 October 1769 Parkinson described in his journal Maori on the east coast of the North Island: "Their faces were tataowed, or marked either all over, or on one side, in a very curious manner; some of them in fine spiral directions like a volute, (see pl. XVI) being indented in the skin very different from the rest: and others had their faces daubed over with a sort of red ochre."

Many of the sailors who came to the Pacific in the 18th century on these early voyages returned home with tattoos, helping to strengthen the tradition of tattooing among sailors.

During the early 19th century missionaries made regular contact with Maori and attempted to convert them to Christianity. Ngapuhi chief Hongi Hika went with a group of missionaries to England in 1820, where he helped with the first English–Maori dictionary. Hika met King George IV of England and was rewarded for his efforts. He exchanged his gifts for muskets and ammunition in Sydney on the way home, and then launched raids against other Maori tribes in the North Island.

During the ensuing troubles, known as the Musket Wars, some Maori discovered Europeans would trade weapons, powder and shot for tattooed preserved heads, or mokomokai. Some tribes began to raid other tribes solely to collect and preserve their tattooed heads as macabre items of commerce. Many of these were sold to museums and collectors.

Major General Horatio Robley was a member of the British Army and fought in the New Zealand land wars during the 1860s. After he retired and returned to England he collected tattooed heads, many of which are now in the American Museum of Natural History in New York. He also wrote *Moko, or Maori Tattooing,* which described the art form.

In 1840 the British Crown signed the Treaty of Waitangi wtih Maori. Many of the Maori chiefs who signed this founding document used drawings of their distinctive moko patterns instead of written signatures. By the mid-19th century many of the traditional materials used to make ta moko chisels, such as human and albatross bone, were being replaced by iron and metal.

In 1874 the Czech artist Gottfried Lindauer came to New Zealand and over a 40-year period painted many intricate portraits of the country's tattooed Maori elders. Many of these works are now in the Auckland Art Gallery and have helped influence modern ta moko artists.

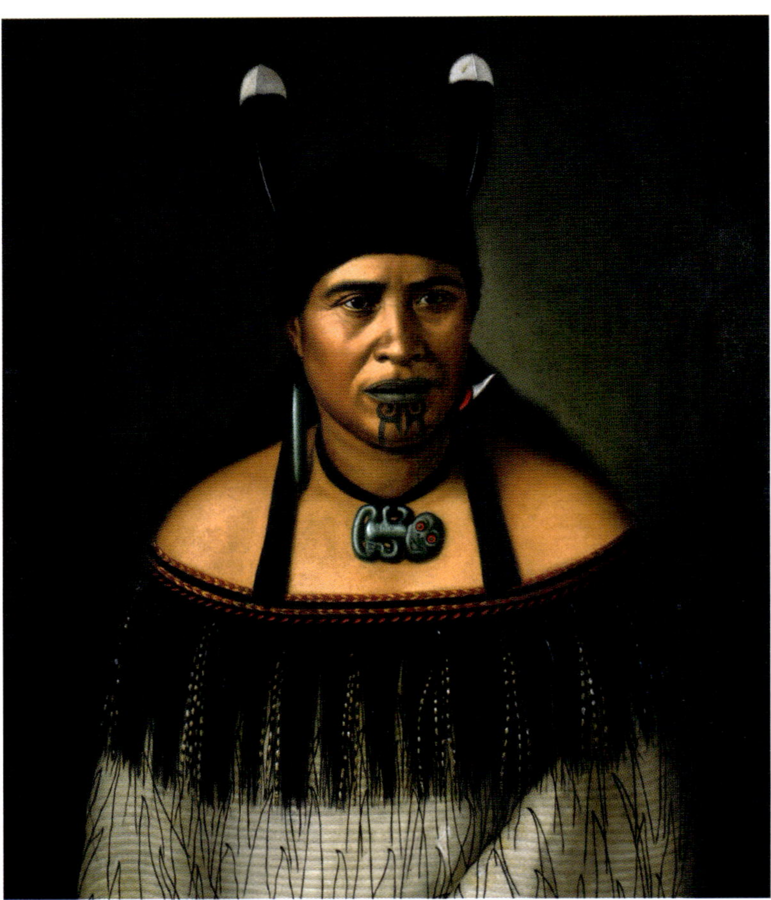

Female use of the chin moko helped sustain traditional tattooing through the turn of the 20th century, and Gottfried Lindauer's paintings of Maori elders were important source material in its revival. This is Lindauer's portrait *Hinepare of the Ngati Kahungunu tribe of Taakitimu fame.*

(Gottfried Lindauer, ca 1890; Ref: G-516, Alexander Turnbull Library, Wellington, New Zealand)

By the early 1900s the traditional art form was dying out under
the growing influence of Christian missionaries. However, Maori
carvers continued to use the ancient patterns and designs on wood,
stone and bone. According to tattooist Gordon Toi, the only people
who continued to wear moko were the female elders in some of the
country's more isolated communities: "Our last bastion for the survival
of the art form was the women, the kuia, who wore the chin moko."

The first seeds of modern tattooing had been planted in the United
States in the mid-1800s, and in 1891 Samuel O'Reilly patented the first
tattoo machine. But tattooing remained on the fringes of society and
was still seen as the domain of outlaws, circus freaks and sailors.
This only added to its appeal to outsiders as a badge of honour.
New Zealand in the early 1900s was no different. Some of the
country's first tattoo parlours were established in the rougher areas
of cities — often near the wharves where clientele such as sailors
were readily available.

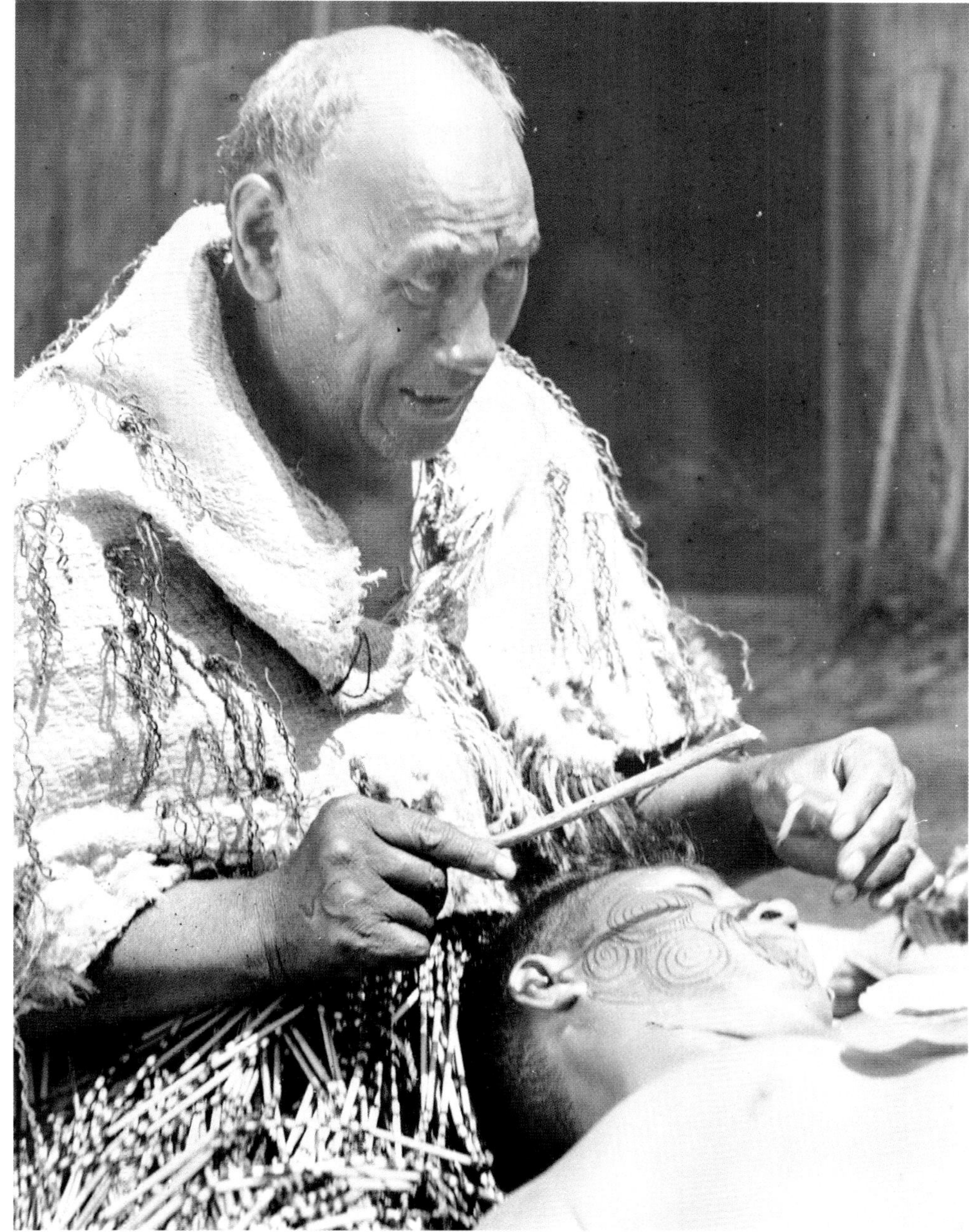

Ta moko refused to disappear;
here an unidentified Maori man
tattoos the face of another with
traditional implements, possibly
in the Rotorua district, in the
1930s.

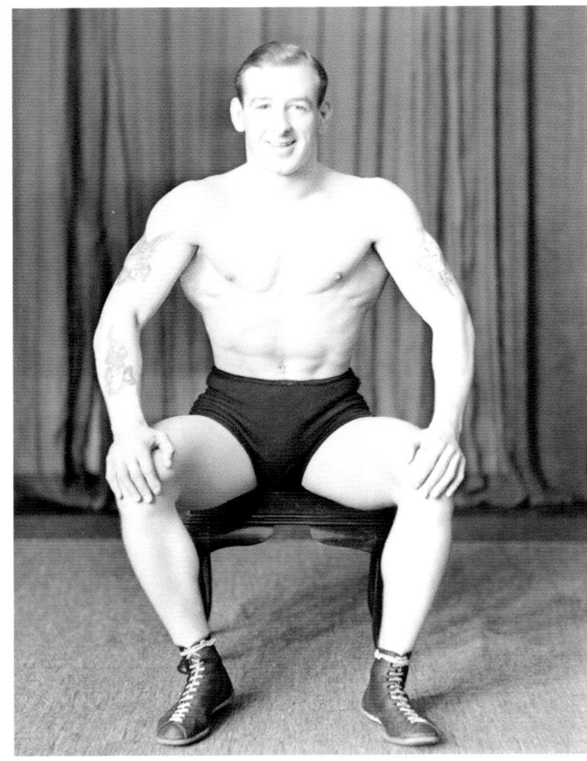

Until the mid-20th century tattooing was confined to the margins of society, although those with a passion for the art were not afraid to show it – as in this 1937 image of *Wrestler, Mr H Bartlett, with tattoos*.

(Crown Studios Ltd: Negatives and prints; Ref: 1/1-033242-F, Alexander Turnbull Library, Wellington, New Zealand)

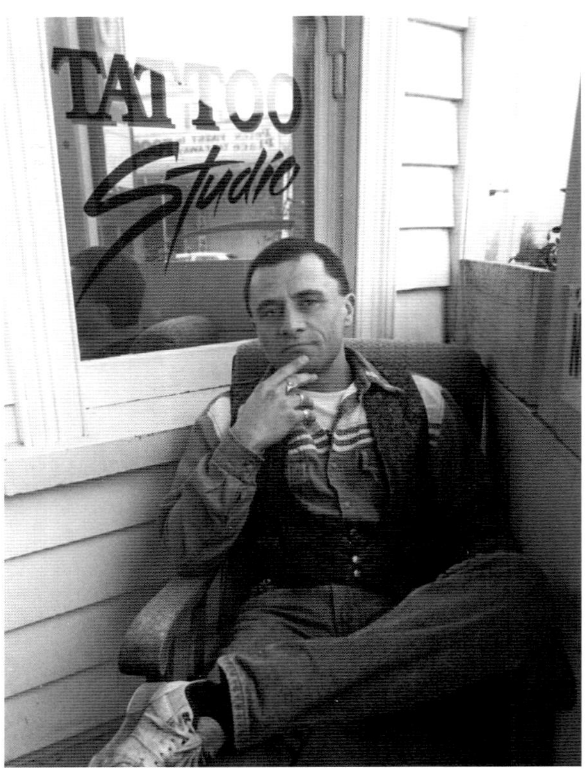

Phill Matthias, who opened Dermagraphic Tattoo on Auckland's College Hill in 1984, was a driving force in making tattooing acceptable to mainstream New Zealand up until his untimely death in 2005.

(Chris Hoult)

Things started to change towards the mid-20th century. Many men returned from the Second World War with tattoos, and by the 1950s and 1960s the art form had become more common than ever. Auckland tattooist Merv O'Connor is one of the only artists from that era who is still working. He was first exposed to tattooing as a child by his father, a returned serviceman who tattooed his mates in the New Zealand Army during the Second World War. Merv himself took up tattooing in his teens, during the late 1950s: "It was a very closed shop in those days. To get into tattooing you had to know a tattooist or be heavily tattooed yourself." He recalls there were only about three other professional tattooists in Auckland at the time: Tiger Mitchell, Joe Hood and Bill Grey.

By the mid-1960s there was a noticeable increase in the number of immigrants coming to New Zealand from Samoa, Tonga, the Cook Islands and other Pacific Island nations, and many of these people continued their traditions such as tatau. In *Tatau: Samoan Tattoo, New Zealand Art, Global Culture* (pages 18–19), Sean Mallon states: "Samoan migration to New Zealand was at its peak in the 1960s and 1970s. It is not surprising that tattooing, like language, went with these people.

"Samoans were staking out new social and cultural territory for themselves. They were establishing crucial links for sustaining a burgeoning tattooing practice and a thriving community life an ocean away from home."

In the 1970s the proliferation of ethnic gangs in New Zealand saw an increase in members with facial tattoos. Some attempted to recreate traditional moko patterns. According to Gordon Toi, this led to a resurgence of tattooing and helped raise the public's awareness of the practice.

Mainstream tattoo artists such as Merv O'Connor and Roger Ingerton also played a part in the revival of ta moko through their use of its patterns and designs. From the 1970s a cultural renaissance in kapa haka saw competitors wearing painted-on moko patterns at Maori cultural events. This had a flow-on effect, with more people becoming interested in ancient styles of tattooing.

In 2000 a group of ta moko artists formed Te Uhi a Mataora, a national collective to preserve, enhance and develop the art form. Its members include senior artists Derek Lardelli, Richard Francis, Mark Kopua and Patrick Takoko, along with emerging talents like Daniel (Raniera) McGrath and Taryn Te Uira Beri. Since the group's formation there has been a growth in well-known figures from around the world wearing ta moko designs, including musician Ben Harper, singer Robbie Williams and former world heavyweight boxing champion Mike Tyson. Toi says this has led to a lot of debate about non-Maori wearing ta moko. True moko is considered tapu (sacred) to Maori and the patterns and designs represent the genealogy and status of the person wearing them.

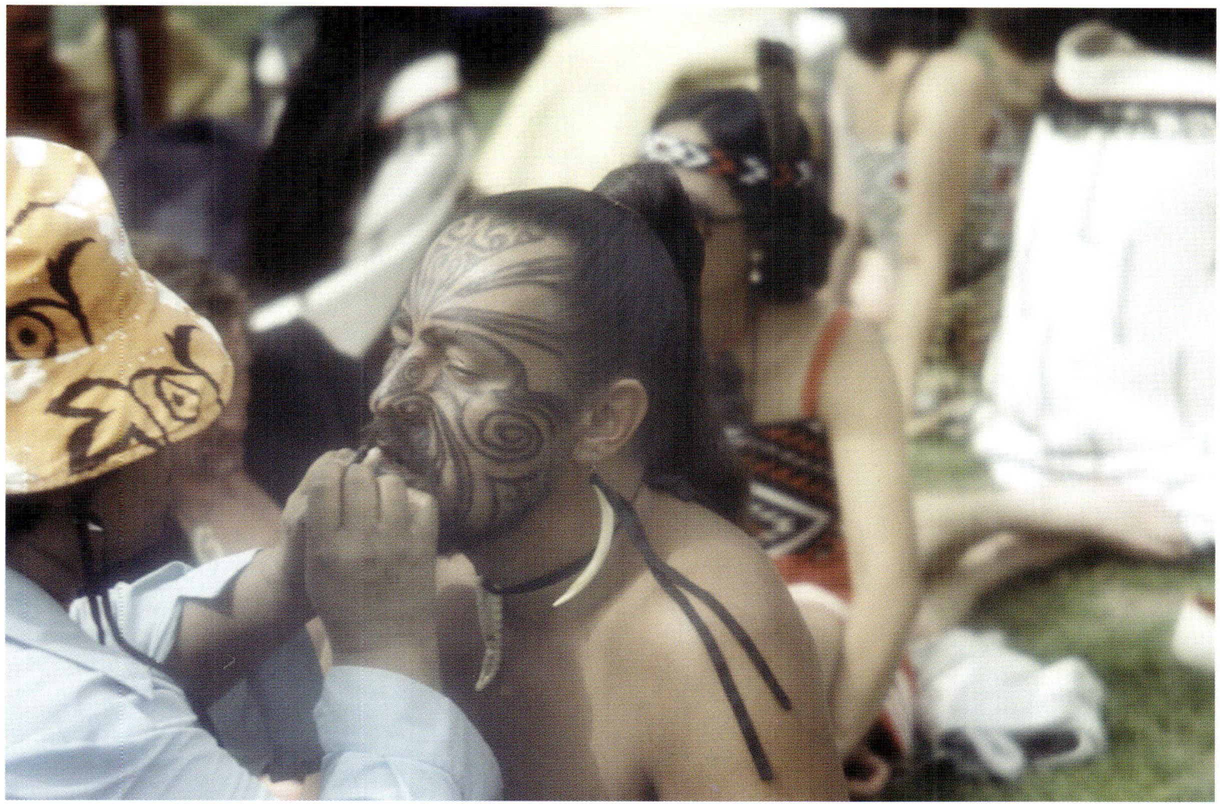

A woman pens a moko for a Maori performer in the 1970s.

(Keith Woods: Photographs relating to dance in New Zealand; Ref: PA12-7109-01, Alexander Turnbull Library, Wellington, New Zealand)

Auckland International Tattoo Convention director Pip Russell says that in New Zealand tattoos are now more popular than ever: "It's far more socially acceptable than it is in other countries." And she says the number of artists in the industry is increasing as well. Growing numbers of sporting heroes wearing tattoos have also influenced the mainstream acceptance of the art form.

According to a poll by UMR Research in 2009, New Zealand is the most tattooed country in the world, with one in five Kiwis wearing ink. And attitudes towards tattoo are changing as well. The survey found that New Zealanders under the age of 30 are more likely to have a tattoo than any other age group, and more women were wearing tattoos than ever. In fact women outnumbered men, with 22 percent wearing them compared to 17 percent of men.

Further reading

Steve Gilbert, *The Tattoo History: A Source Book*. New York, powerHouse Books, 2000.

Dean Johansson, *Wearing Ink: The art of tattoo in New Zealand*. Auckland, David Bateman Ltd, 1994.

Sean Mallon, 'Samoan Tattooing, Cosmopolitans, Global Culture', in Mark Adams (photographs) with essays by Sean Mallon, Peter Brunt and Nicholas Thomas, *Tatau: Samoan Tattoo, New Zealand Art, Global Culture*. Wellington, Te Papa Press, 2010, pp. 18, 19.

Anne Nicholas, *The Art of the New Zealand Tattoo*. Auckland, Tandem Press, 1994.

D.R. Simmons, *Ta Moko: The Art of Maori Tattoo*. Auckland, Reed, 1999.

Ngahuia Te Awekotuku, *Mau Moko: The World of Maori Tattoo*. Auckland, Viking, 2007.

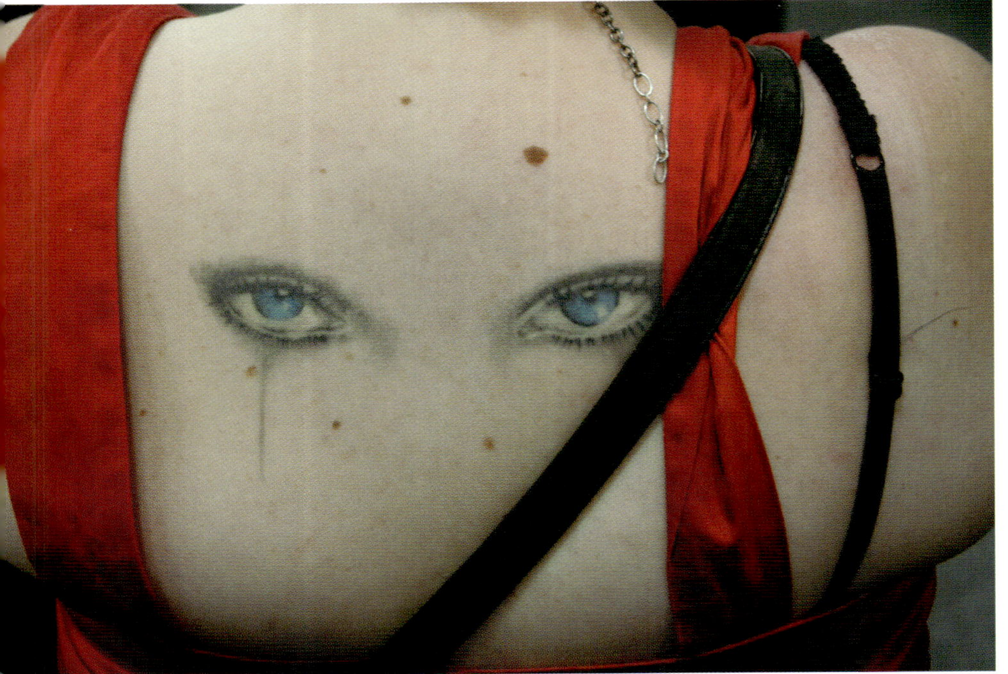

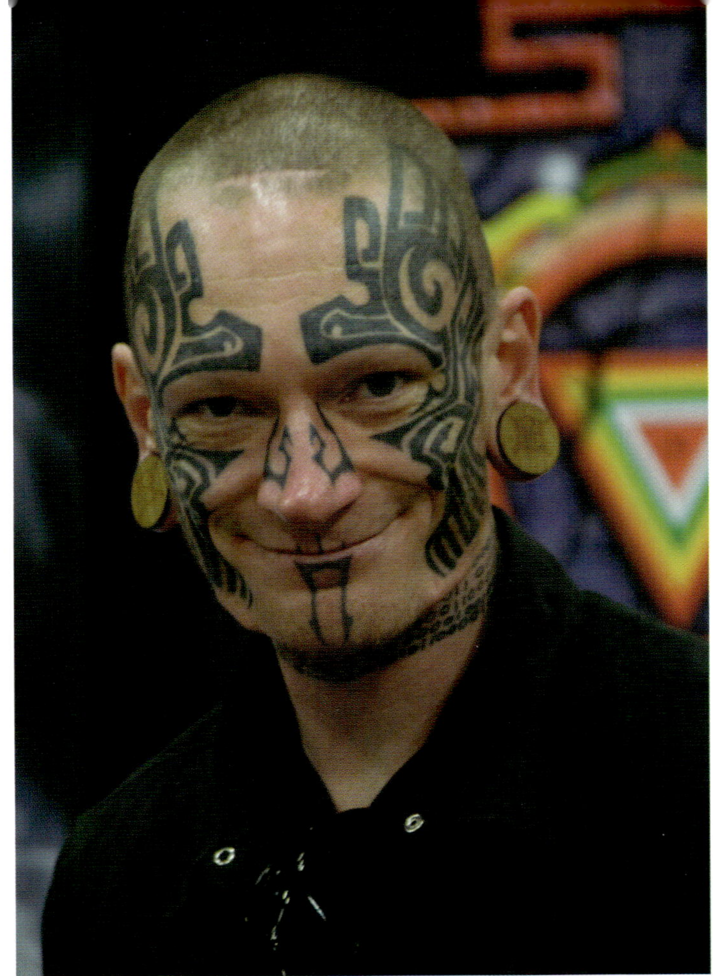

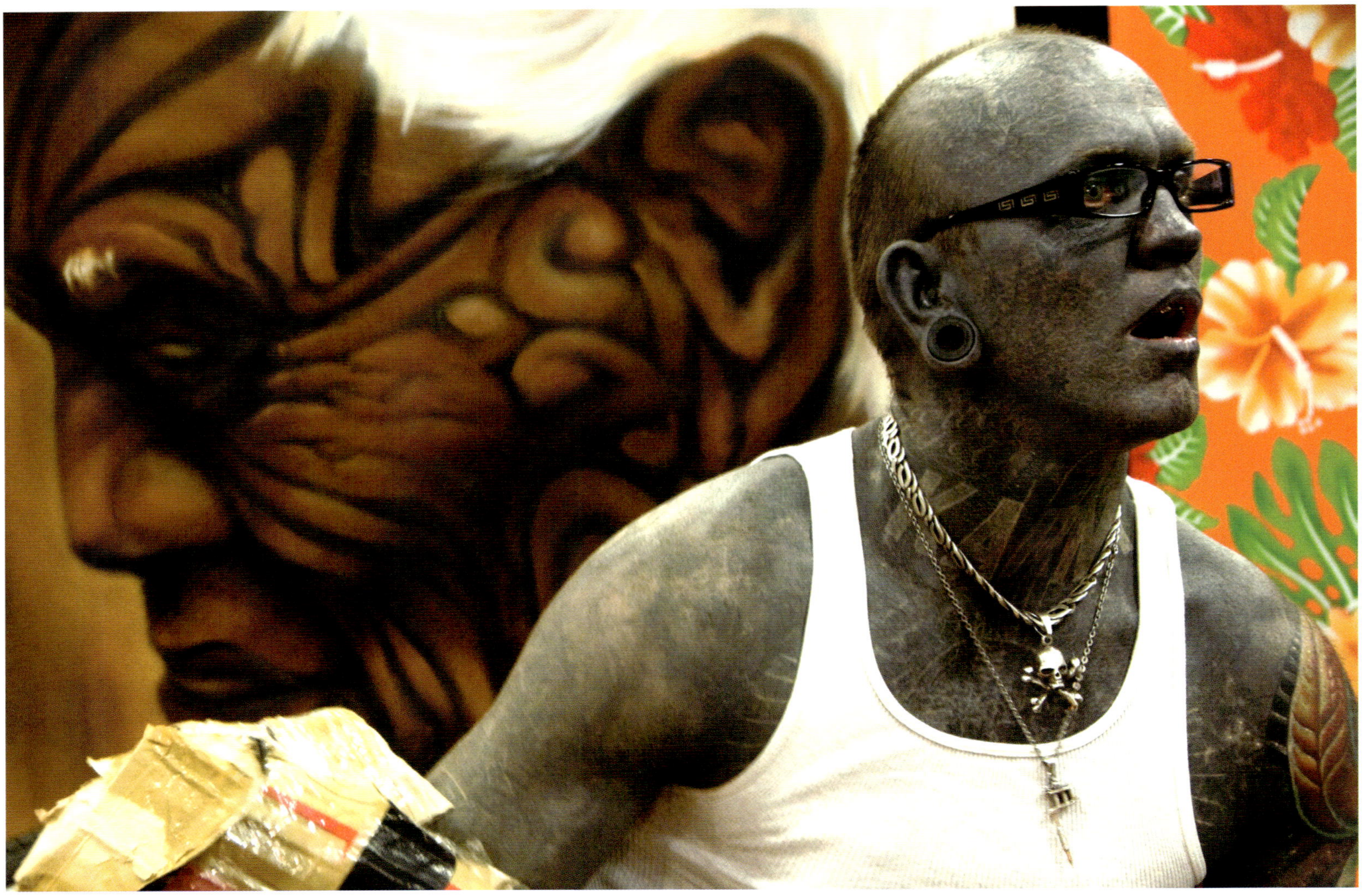

Lucky Diamond Rich.

AUCKLAND INTERNATIONAL TATTOO CONVENTION

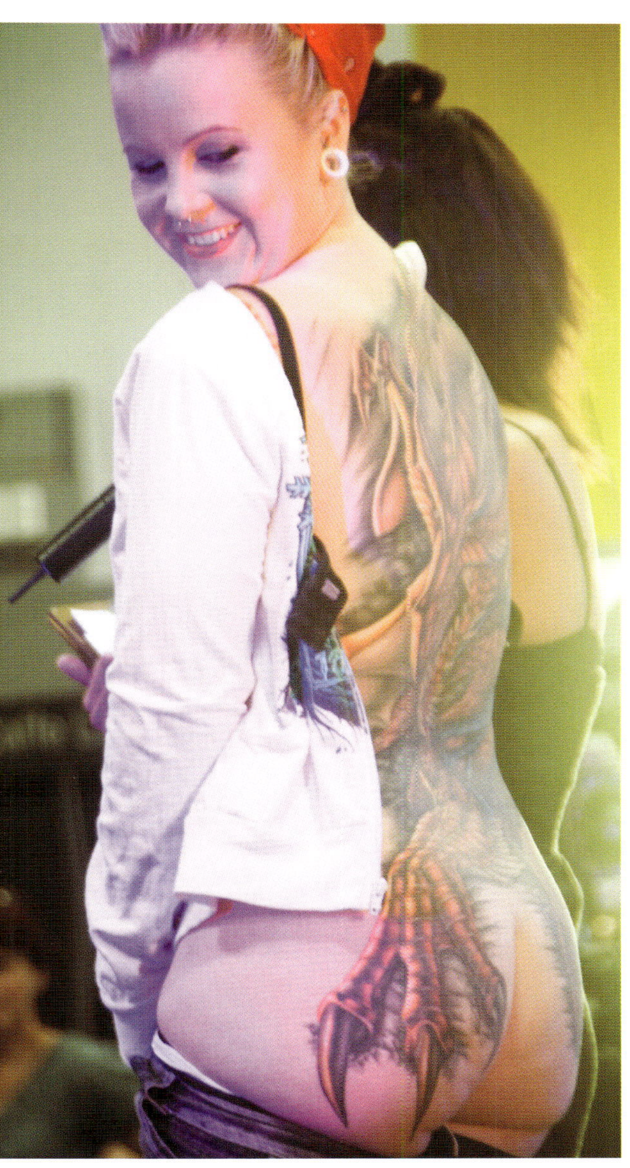

The Auckland International Tattoo Convention is one of New Zealand's premier tattooing events and is a true exchange of cultures, according to director Pip Russell.

The country's special place in the history of tattoo is a major drawcard for artists who come from around the world to attend the biennial event. "For them it's like checking out the roots of tattooing," Pip says.

Pip's at the ASB Showgrounds where the 2011 Auckland International Tattoo Convention is being held. She's flat out dealing with media requests and trying to make sure everything runs smoothly.

The convention centre is humming with artists from England and the US to South Korea and Samoa, busy tattooing those who want a memento of their visit. There are displays and demonstrations for those attending to take in, including ta moko and tatau tattooing with hand tools. The two-day convention also features a packed schedule of entertainment, from the Tongan Kalia dance troupe and some of Auckland's finest DJs, to burlesque dancing.

English tattooist Craigy Lee says it's great to be at the event: "A lot of tattooists like to come here because the traditional tattooing is so old, whereas in Europe it's only been around for about 150 years. It's still pretty new compared to here in New Zealand."

Bill Funk, owner of the Body Graphics Tattoo shop in Philadelphia and secretary of the US-based National Tattoo Association, has come specially. It's his first time in New Zealand and he's keen to check out some of the ta moko artists attending the event. "You can meet some new friends and run into some old ones."

His wife Anna Paige runs Skin Deep Tattoo in Waikiki in Hawaii and is with him at the Auckland convention. "I've worked with some artists from New Zealand but I've never been here before. So I had to come and see for myself," she says.

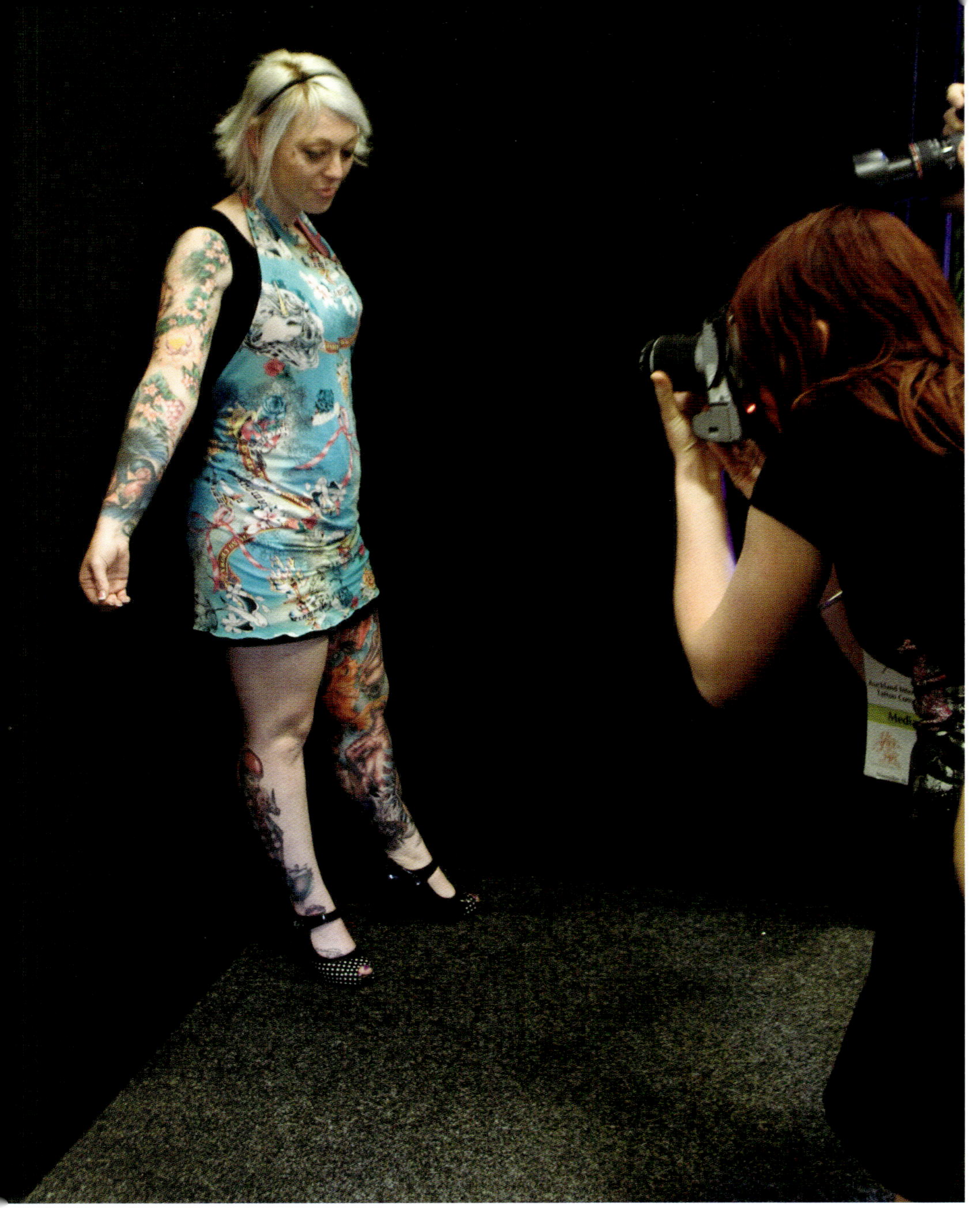

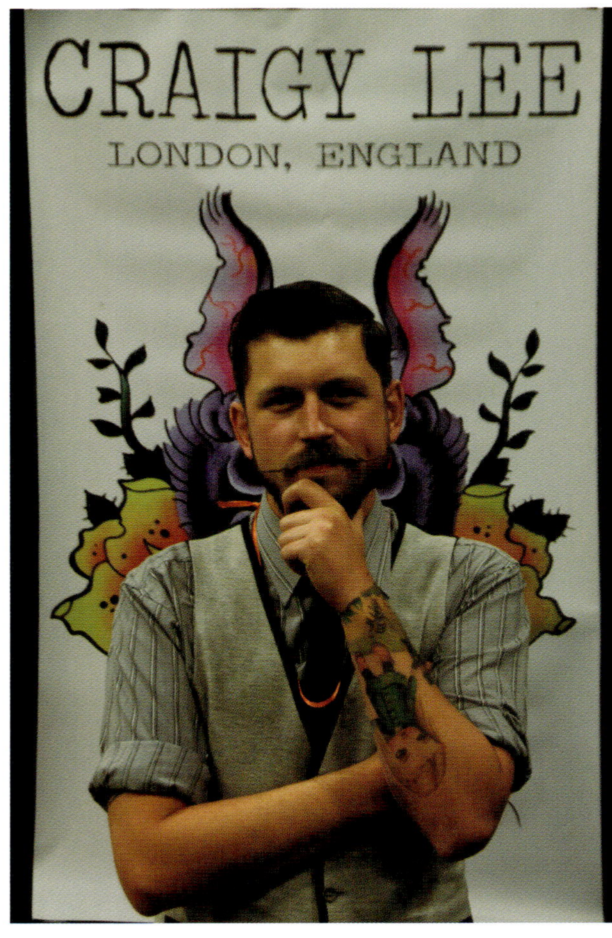

New Zealand-born tattoo artist Sam Rulz is happy to be back after travelling around the world for the past year. When she's back in the country she often does a guest spot at the Two Hands Tattoo studio in Auckland. "Most of the people here I've met before, but it's really good to catch up with them and see what they are doing."

New Zealand-born Lucky Diamond Rich has the illustrious title of being the world's most tattooed man, and has ink covering his entire body, from inside his mouth and his ears to his nether regions. These events are his bread and butter: "I *live* at conventions." But the Auckland event has a special significance for him: "The people who run it are good friends of mine and it's a real celebration of the art form."

The first Auckland International Tattoo Convention was held in 1999 at the University of Auckland. The idea of holding the convention originally came from the late great Samoan tatau artist Paulo Suluape. "Paulo was organising a convention in Samoa at the time and he said we should put on a show in Auckland because all the artists were going to come through New Zealand," Pip recalls. He saw the convention as a way to bring together the artists from the tattoo, tatau and ta moko worlds. Sacred Tattoo, Artrageous and Moko Ink were also vital to getting that first convention off the ground.

And there was a bigger goal behind the event: "In the beginning it was about trying to educate some of the international tattoo artists about Maori culture. People from overseas were using the ta moko patterns, but they didn't realise what they meant — they were copying them from Goldie and Lindauer paintings." But she says the international tattooists also had a lot to teach the New Zealand artists in terms of the technical side of tattooing and the latest developments in sterilisation.

Two years later when the next convention was held they got government funding through Creative New Zealand. By 2009 the event was marking its tenth anniversary. These days it is run by the Ta Moko Tatau Tattoo Trust. Pip is on the board, along with Nehe Reuben, Paul Peachey (who owns the Artrageous Tattoo Studio in Auckland), and artist Corinna Hunziker. Nehe says it's amazing to consider the impact the event has had since it first started in 1999.

"It's lifted the quality of the young tattooists coming through and now you can see the results of that everywhere," he says. "A lot of the international tattooists help fill the booths, but the quality of the New Zealand tattooists is right up there."

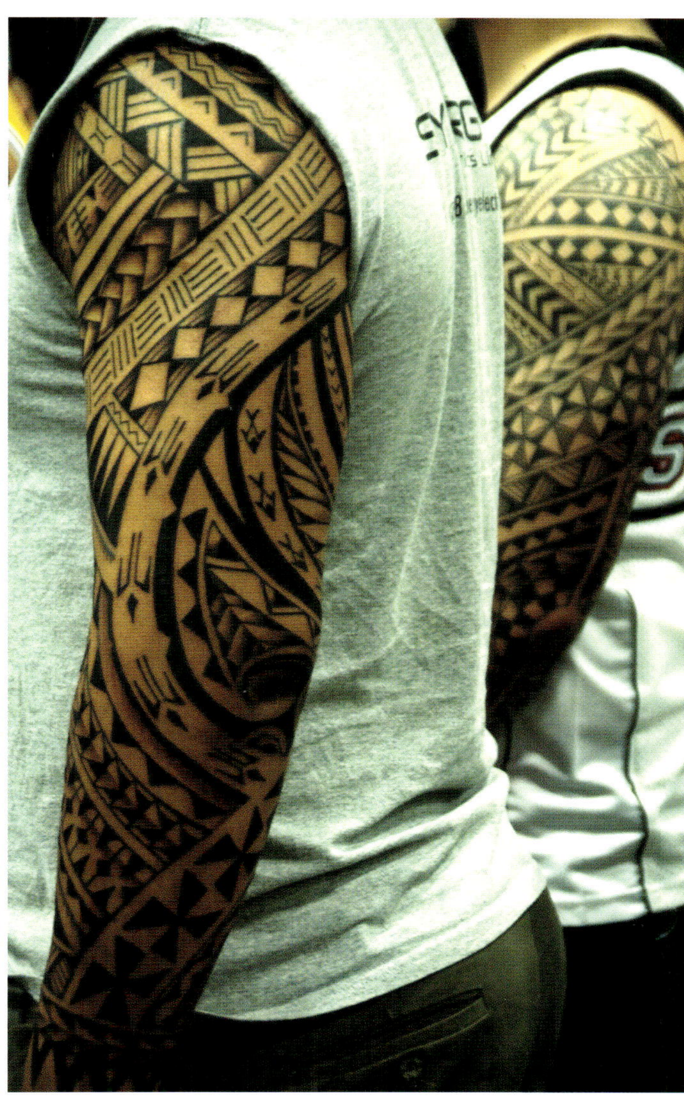

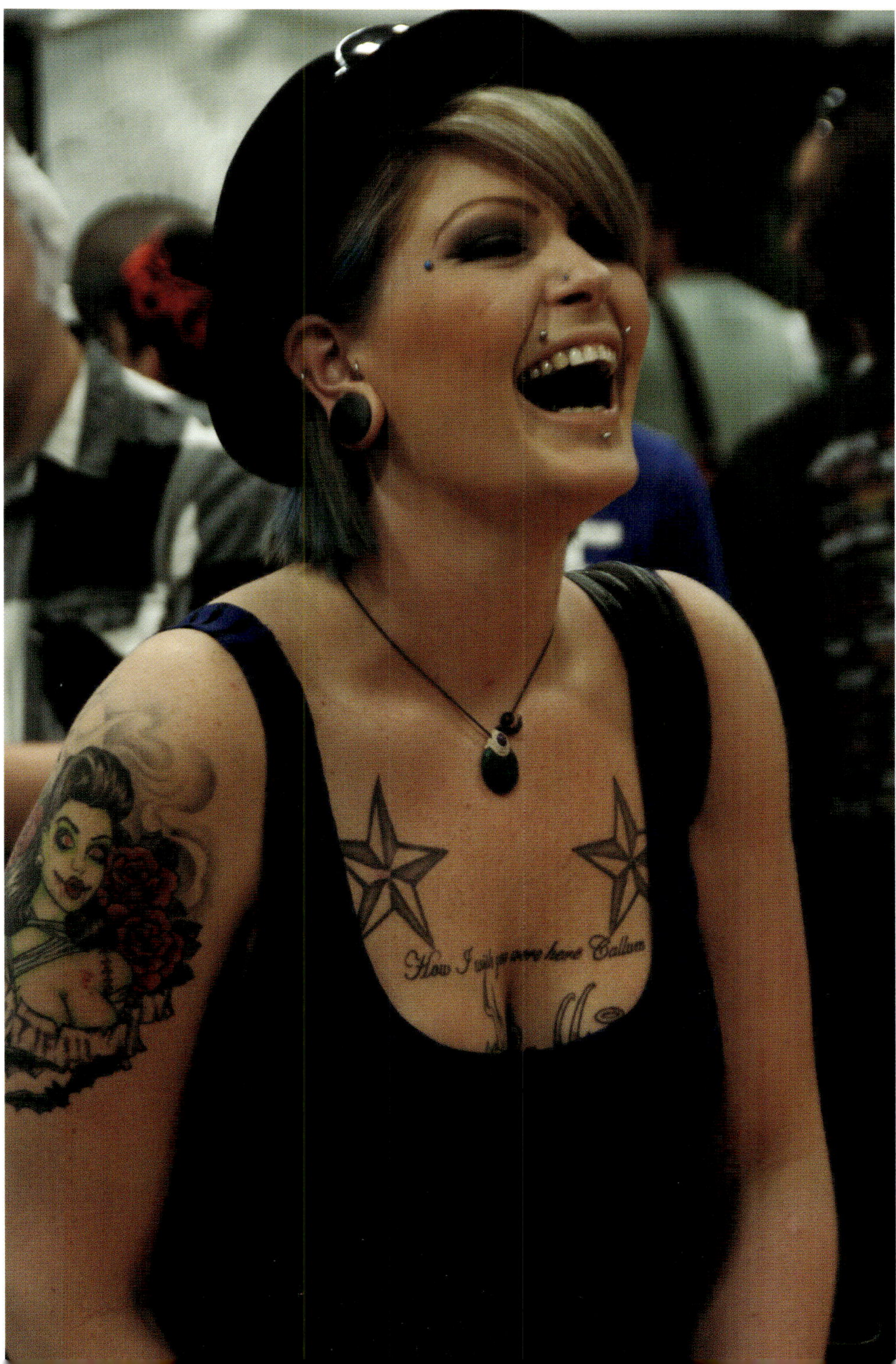

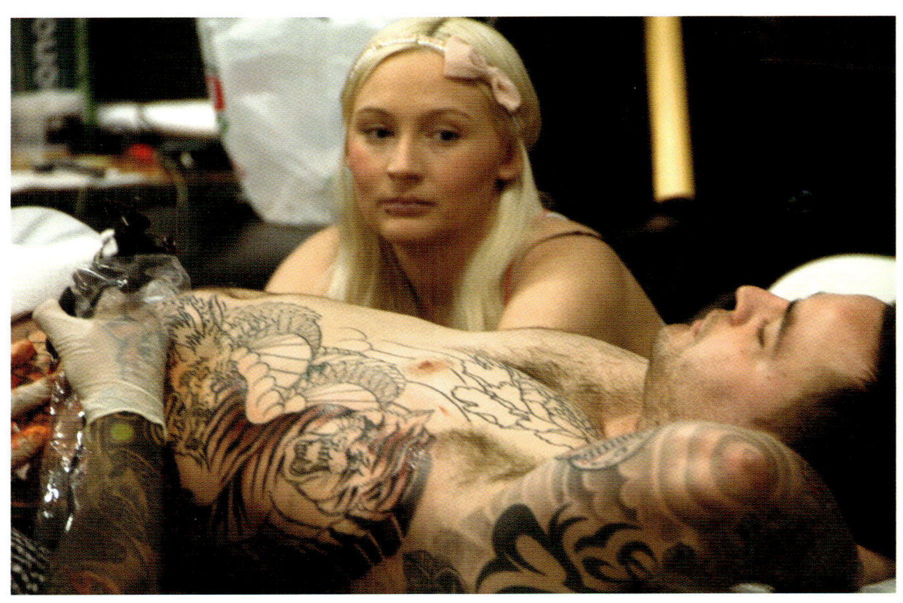

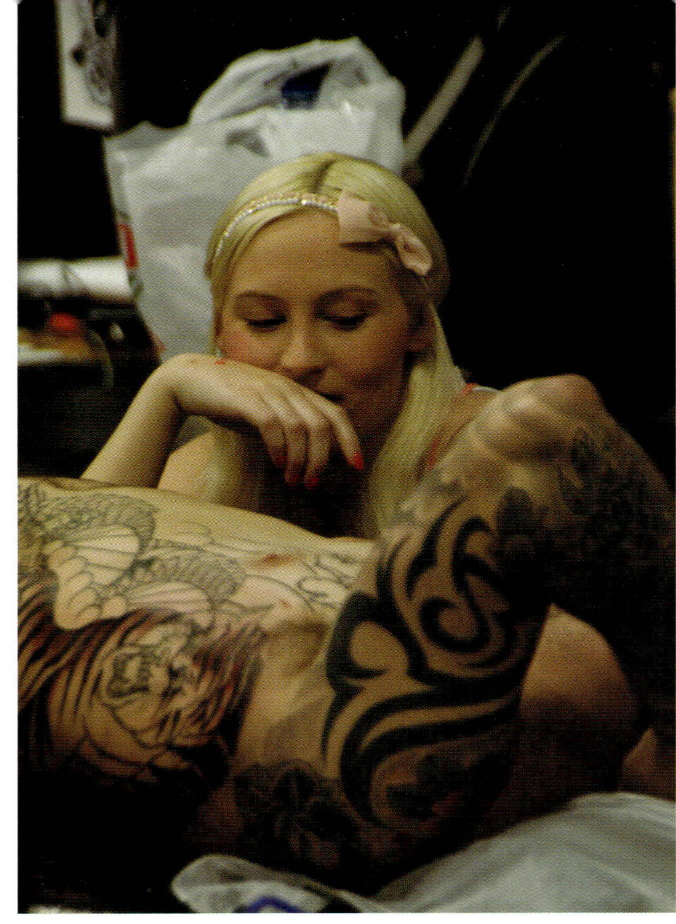
WWW.THETATTO

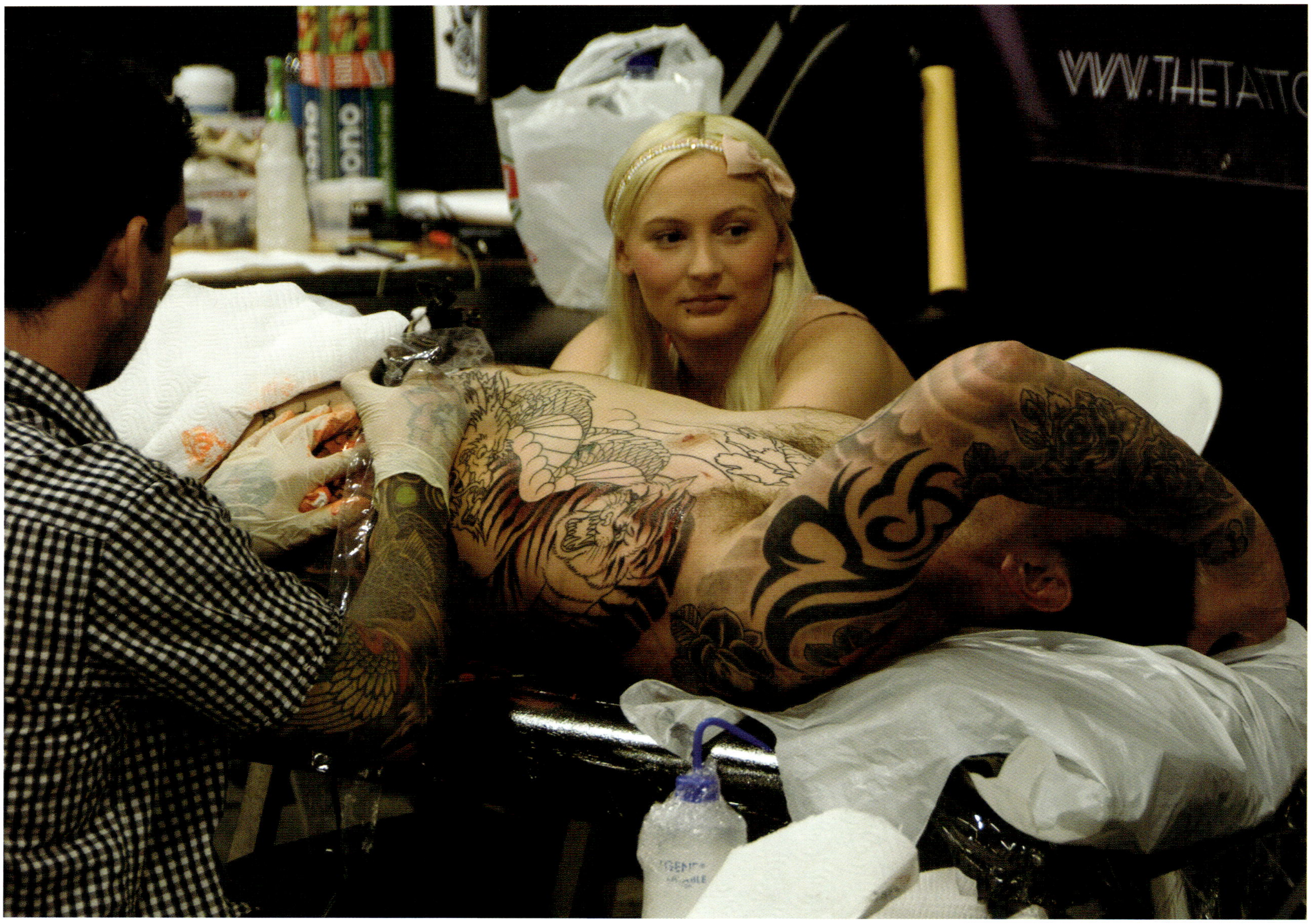

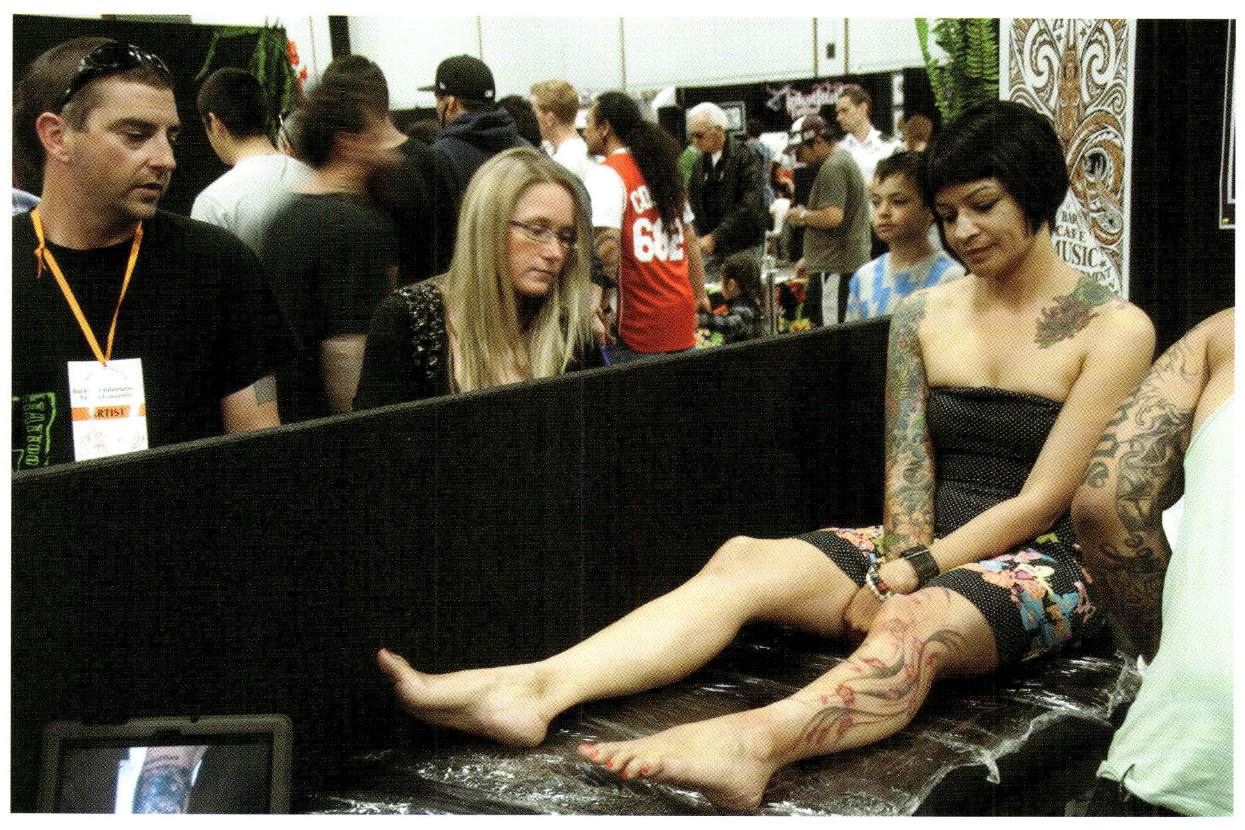

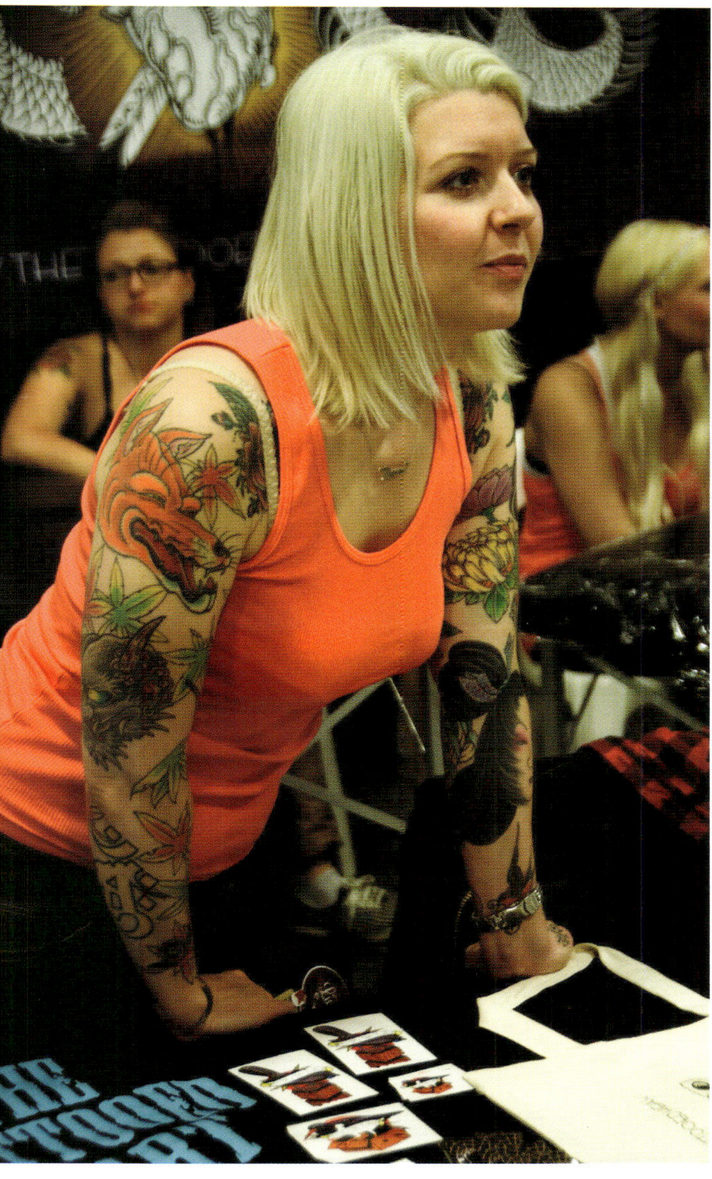

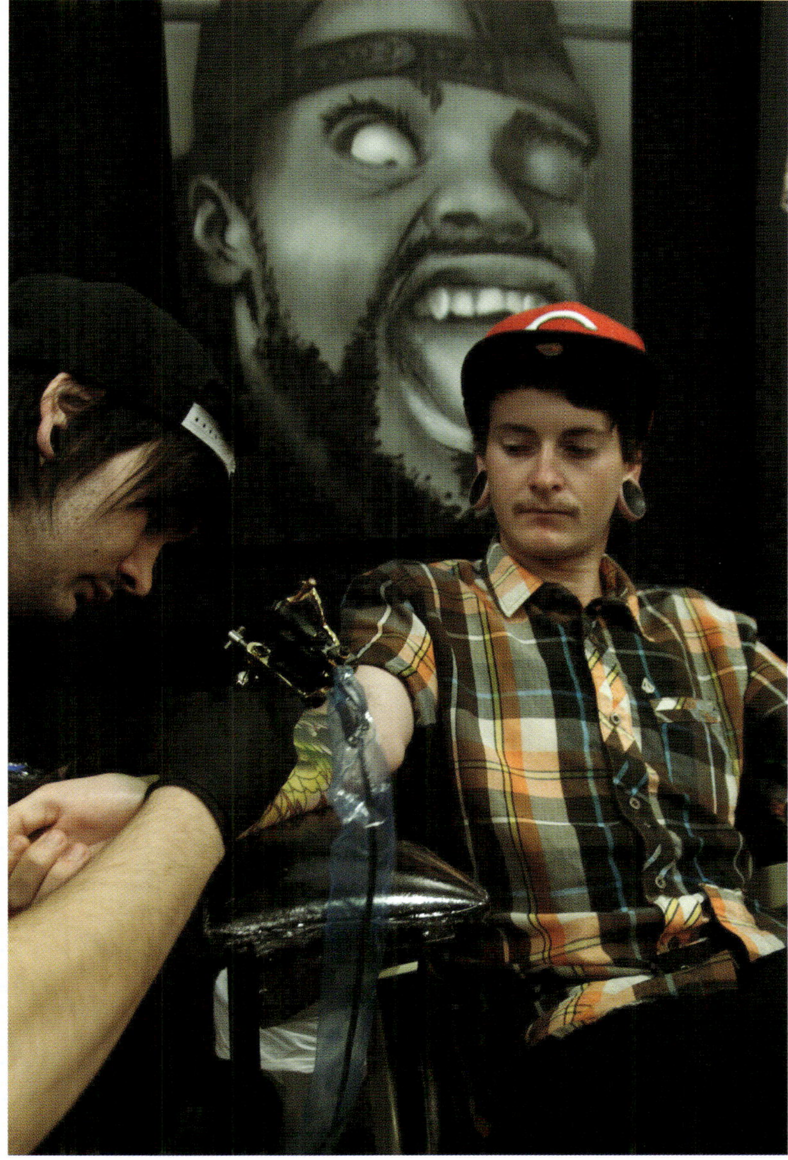

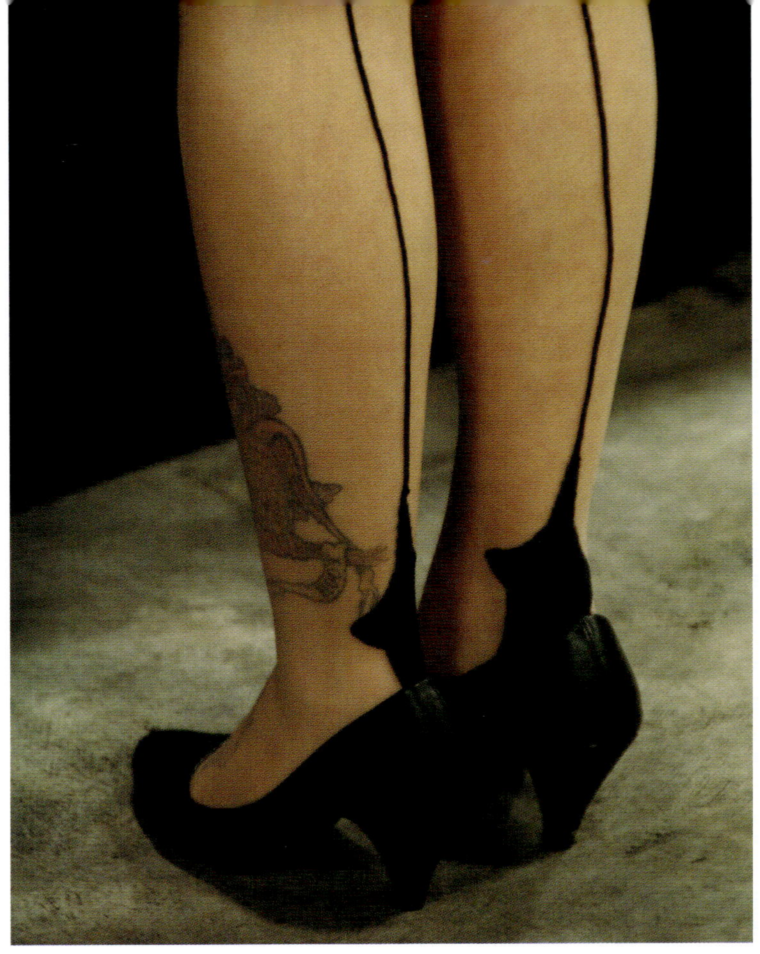

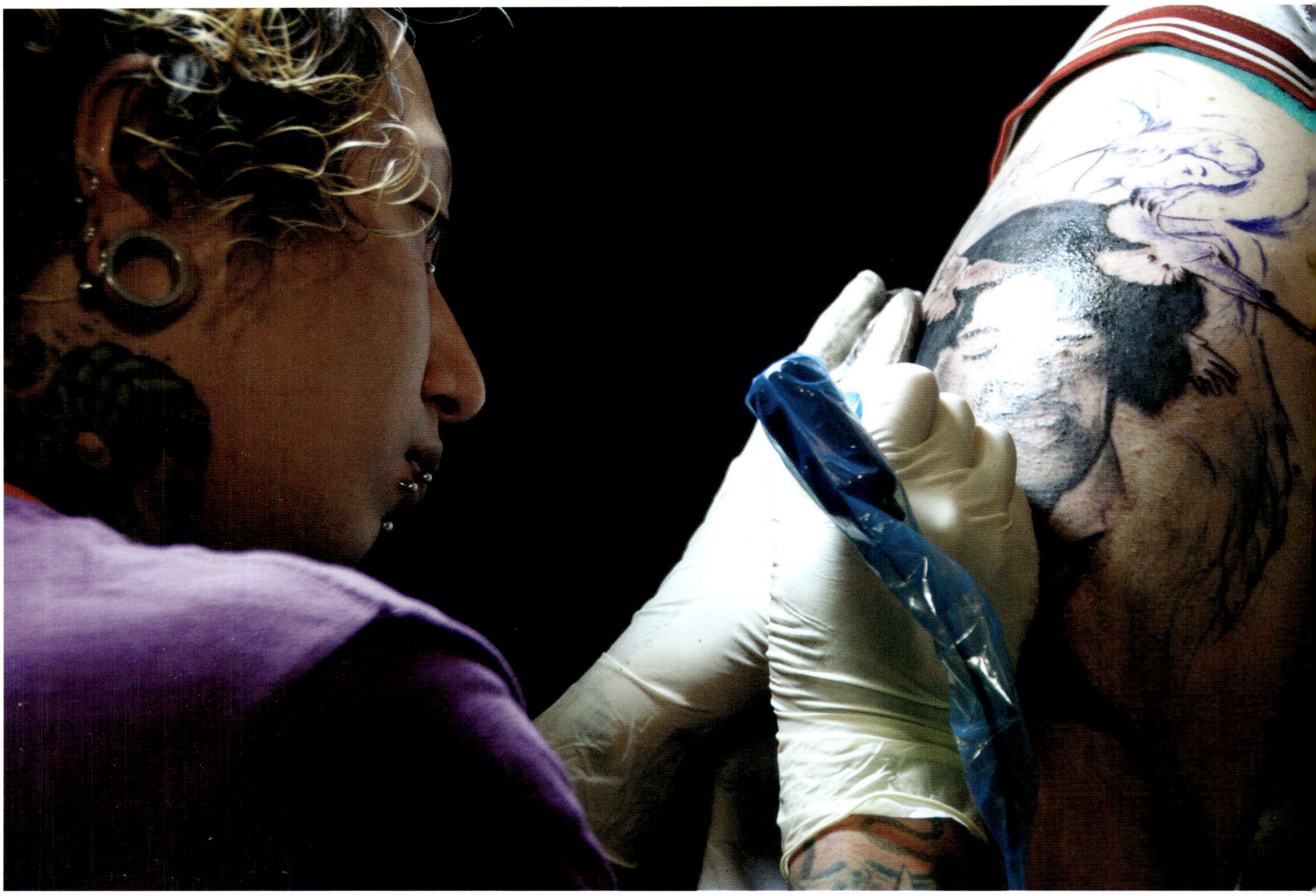

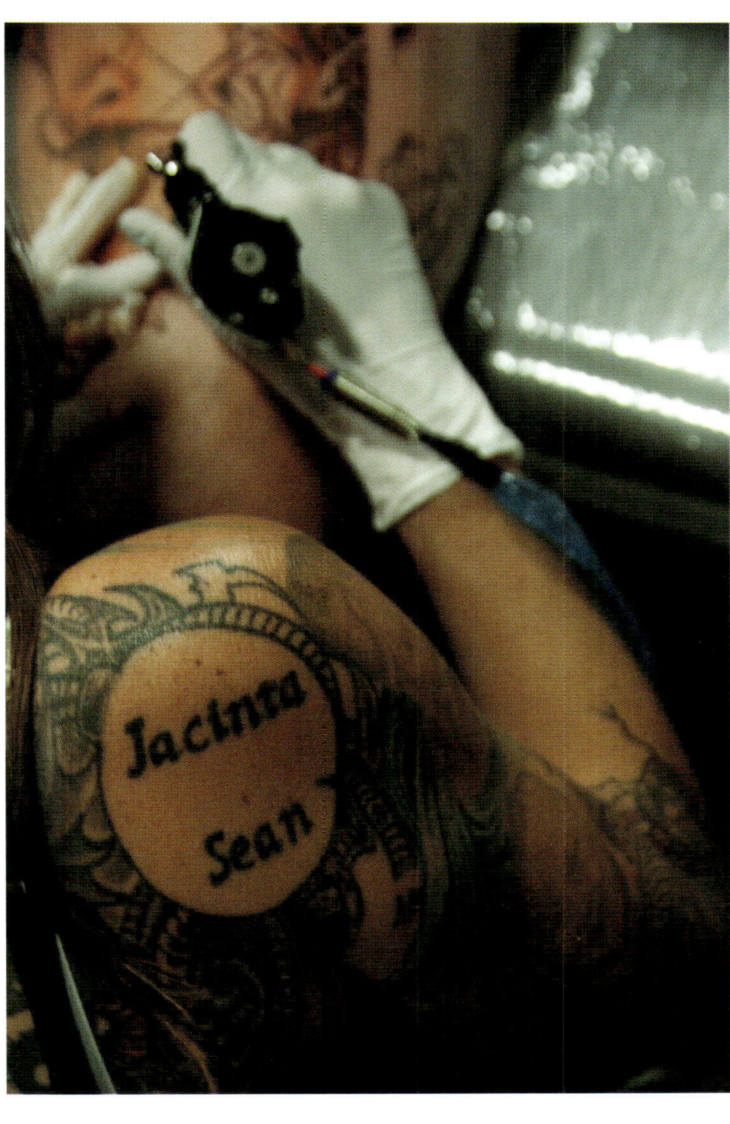

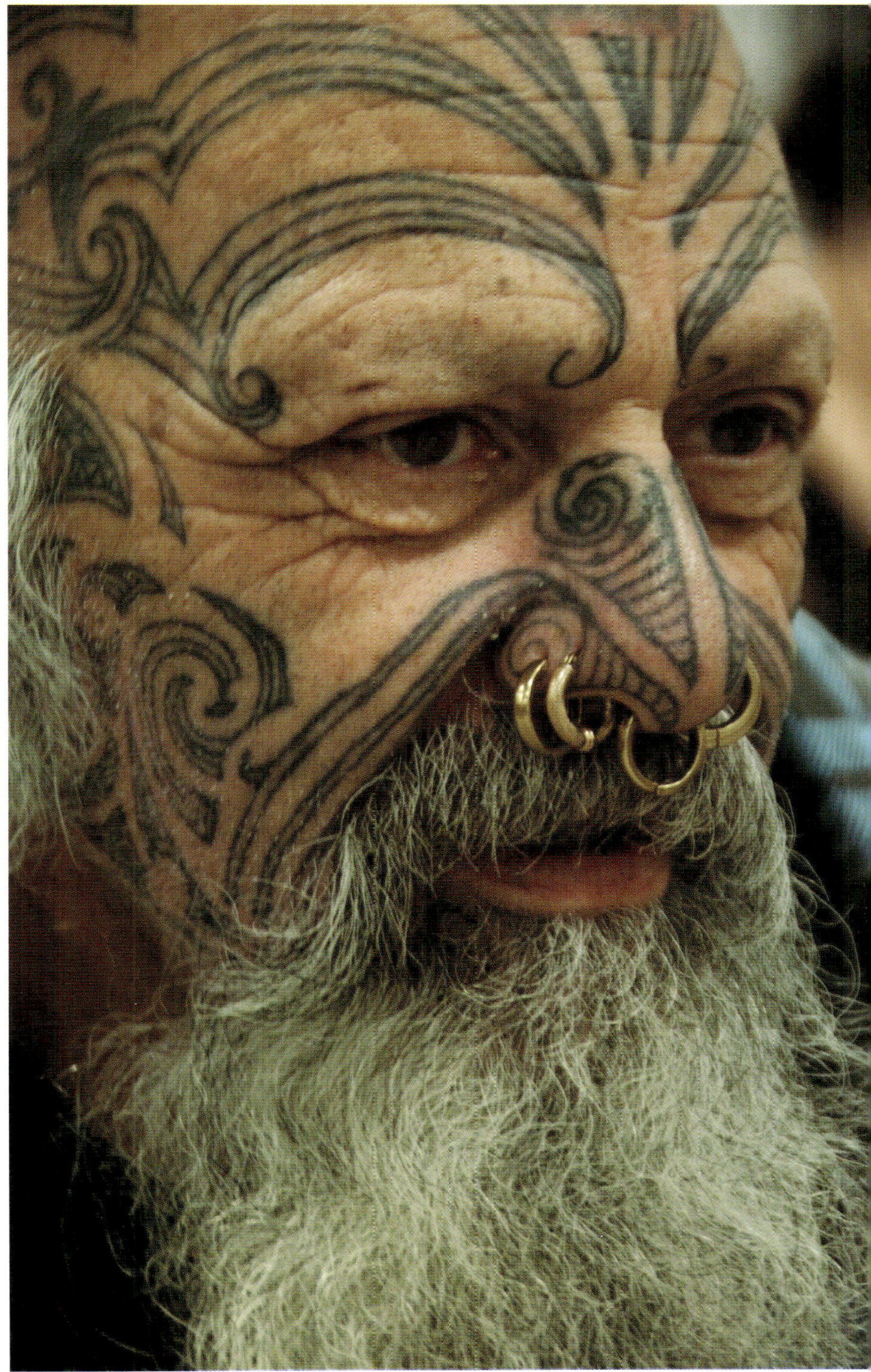

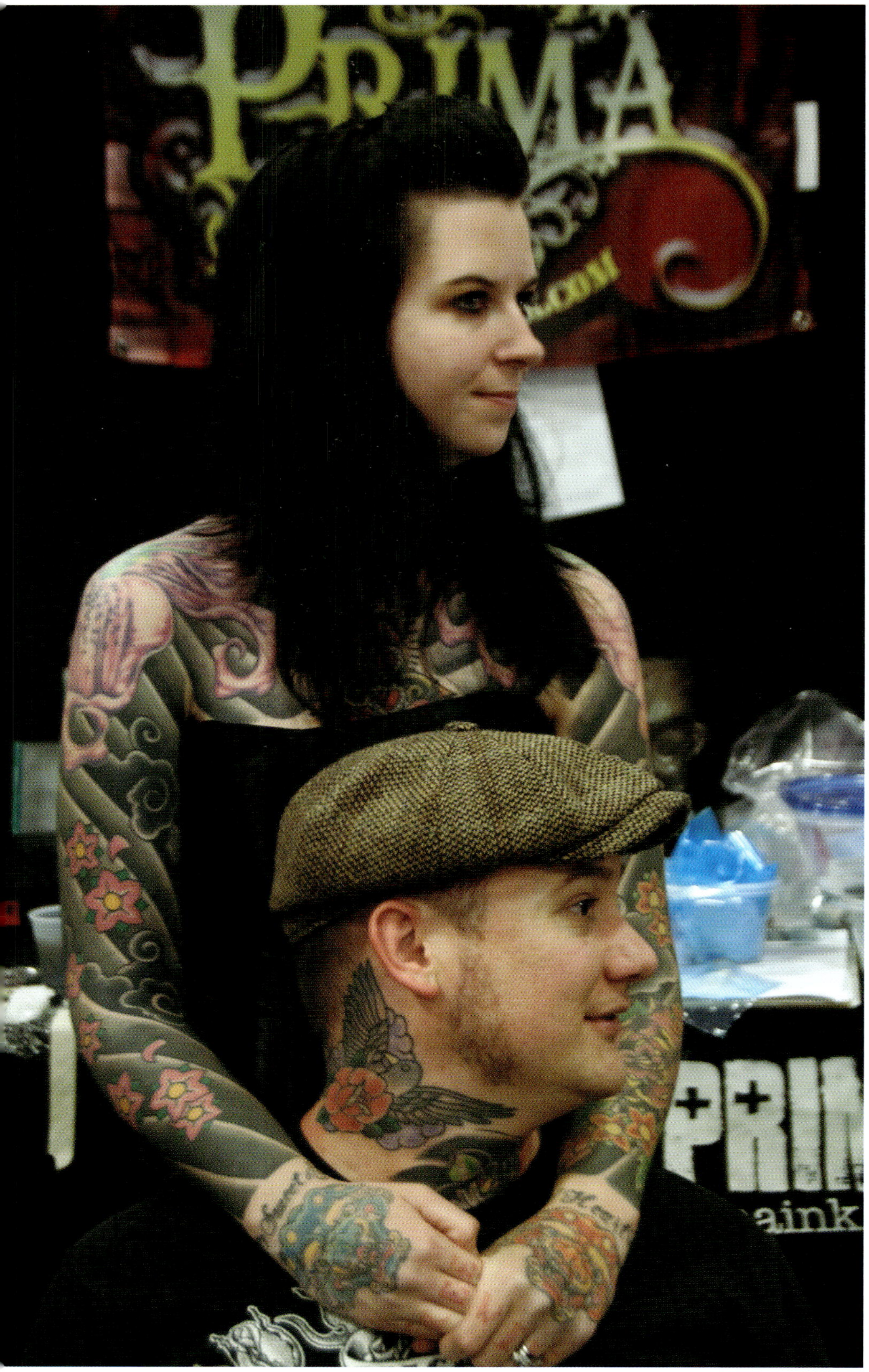

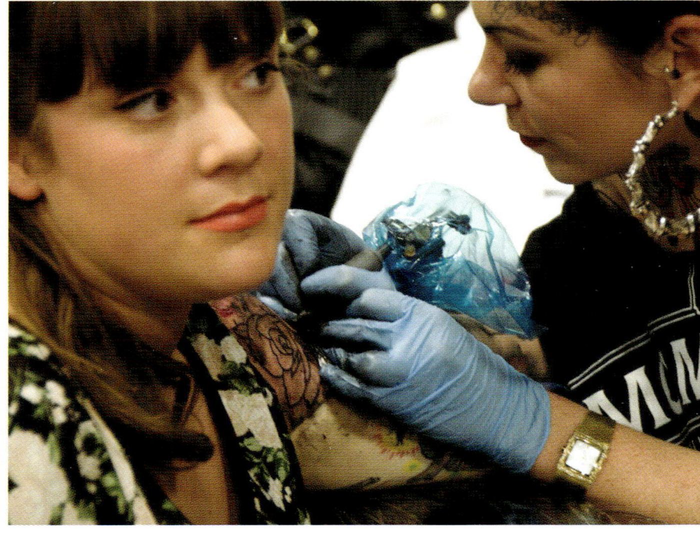

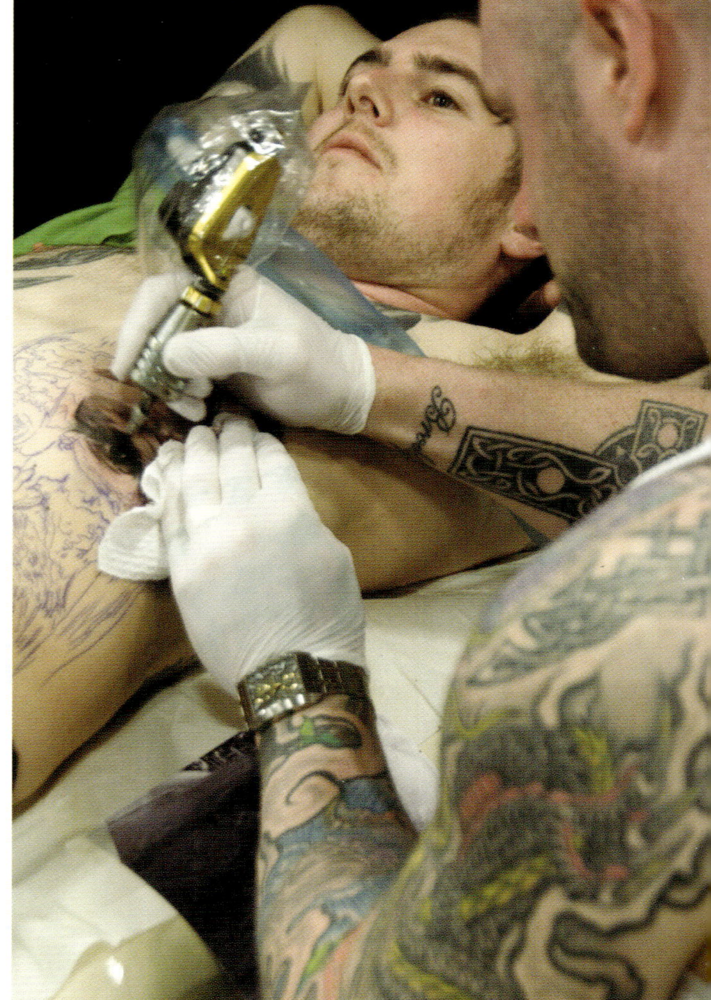

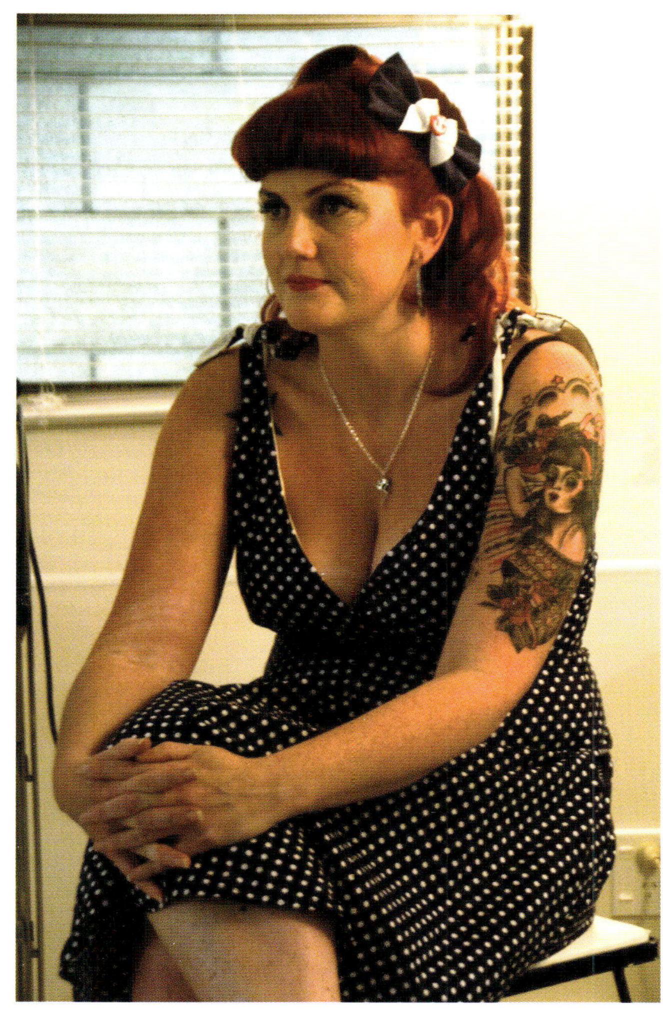

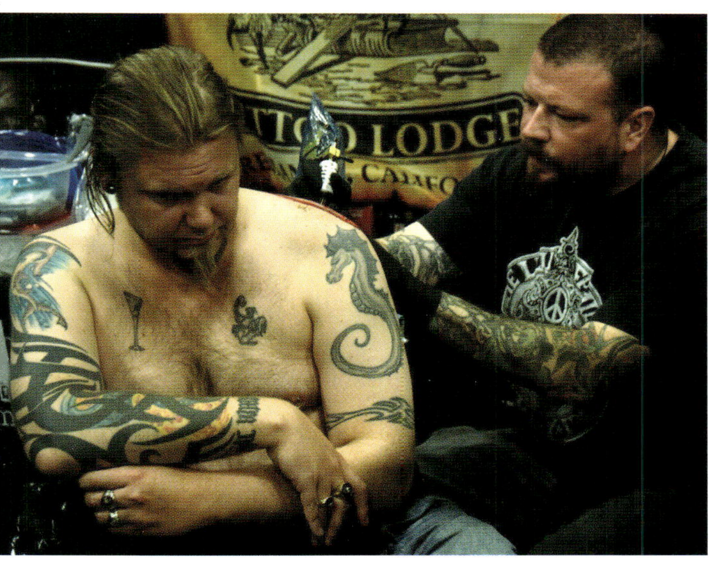
TATTOO LODGE

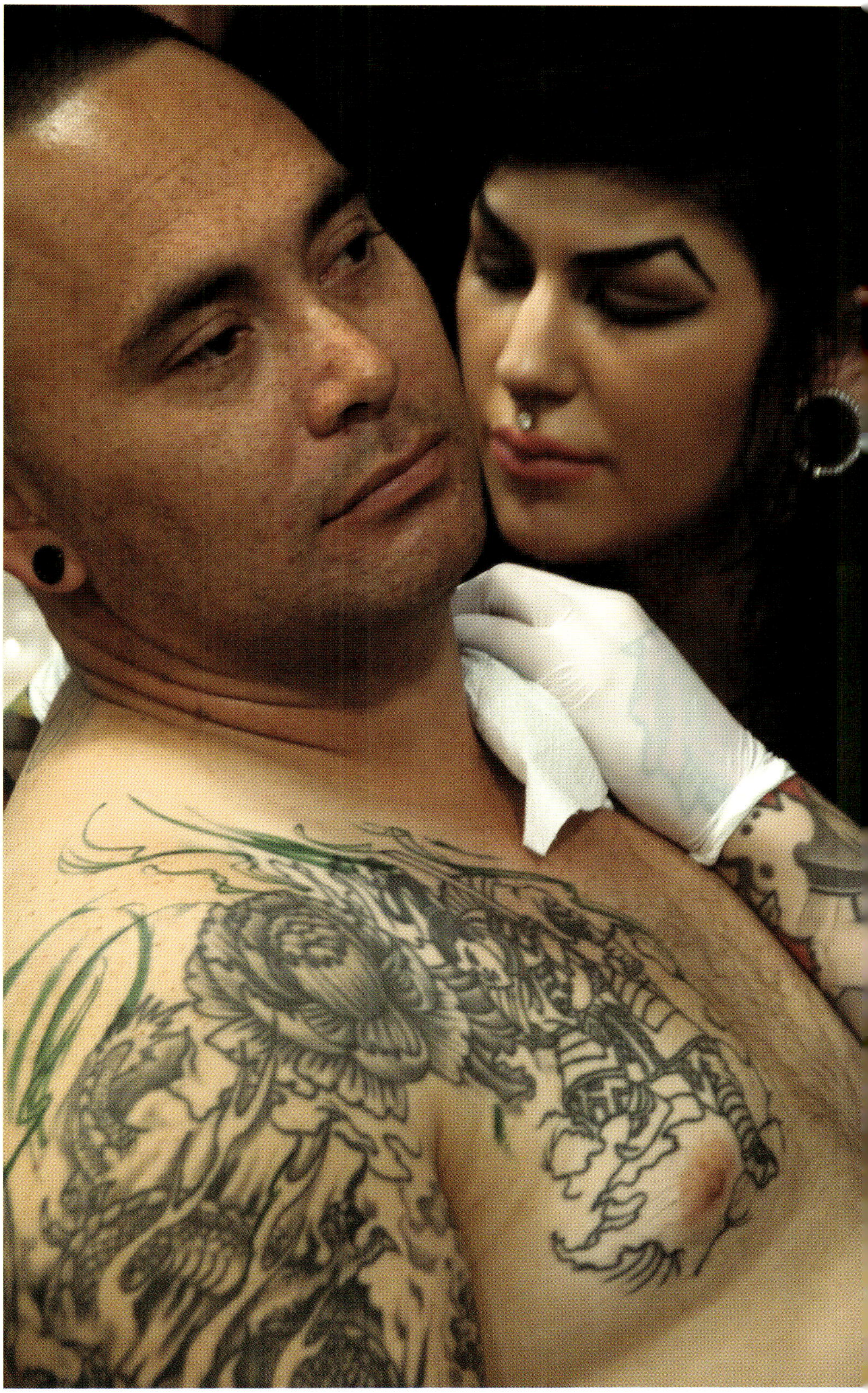

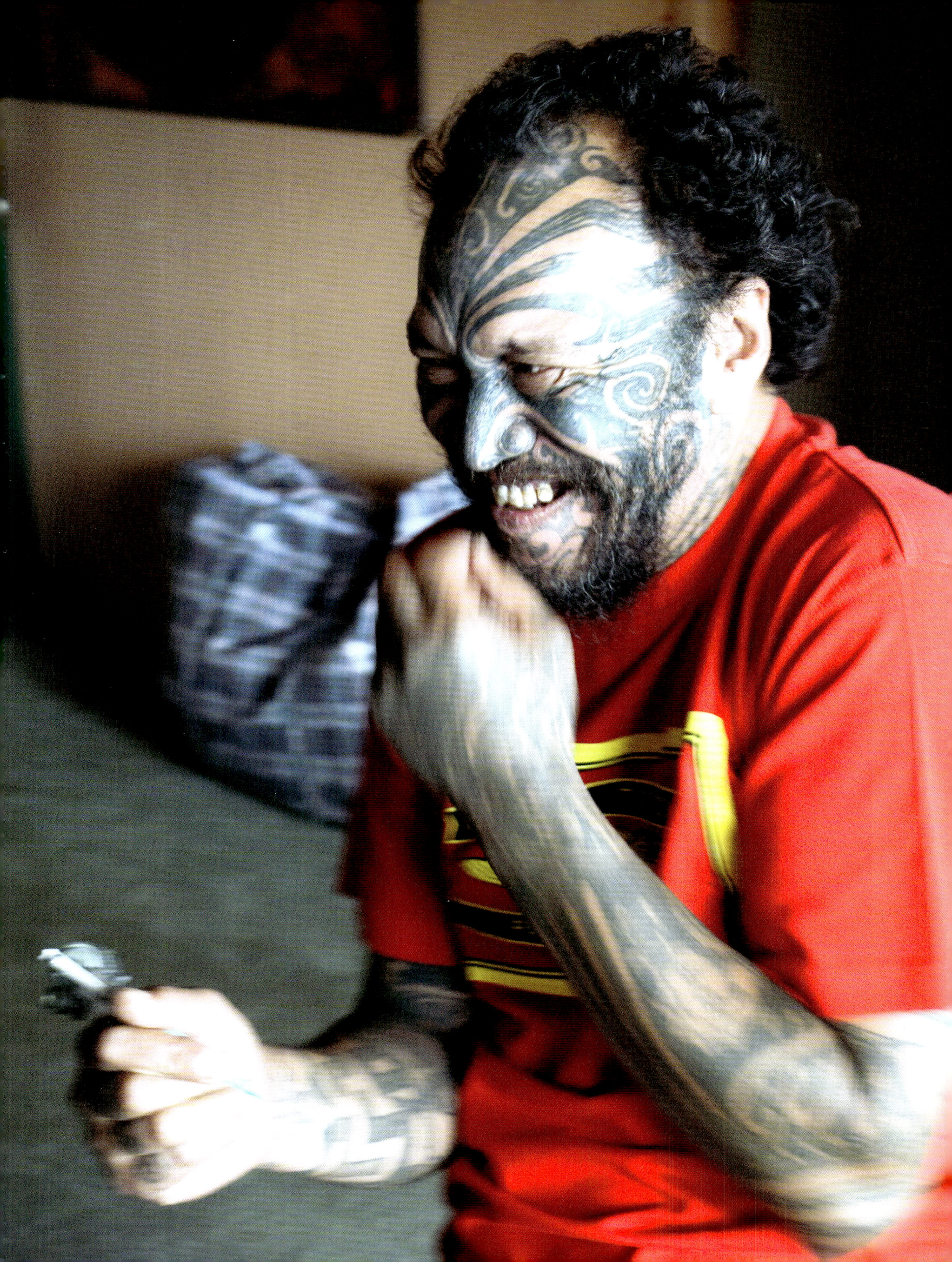

NEHE **REUBEN**

Ruatoria in the late 1980s was a town in crisis. A Rastafarian sect was wreaking havoc in the area with churches, a police station and a court all burned down in a string of arsons. Its followers wanted to extinguish the influence of Christianity in the small East Coast town and see it returned to its pre-colonial roots. The events culminated in December 1990 when Rastafarian leader Chris Campbell was shot and killed.

It was during this period that Nehe, who was part of the group, first turned his hand to tattooing. He'd been carving since he was a child and ta moko had always fascinated him. "I first started when I was about 25 years old. No one was doing it at the time. It was a sacred subject and nobody wanted to talk about it. But I was looking for the answer. Why didn't we still look like that?"

The only people maintaining the tattoo traditions were the women in isolated parts of the country who continued to wear the chin moko. "Back in Ruatoria there was a resistance to ta moko. But that was influenced by non-Maori. So it was about changing their mind-sets. We had to show our people, we had to kick that imaginary door down."

Because young ta moko artists had no one to teach them, the intricate carvings that adorn meeting houses at marae around the country were their only points of reference. "Those centre poles in marae are a memorial to an ancestor and if they wore tattoos that's on the carving. There weren't many ta moko artists around, so those carvings were our library."

Since machines weren't readily available, Nehe started making his own. Using a rotary motor from an electronic toy train set, some batteries, a pen and a needle, he would use this kind of homemade machine for over ten years, tattooing from his home in Ruatoria.

But there were still a lot of negative forces at play in the small East Coast town following the tensions from the late 1980s, and by 1999 Nehe decided to move to Auckland. There he met Inia Taylor, who had recently opened his own studio, Moko Ink. Nehe offered to work for him voluntarily, and joined other tattooists at the studio including Pip Russell, Tim Hunt and Haki Williams. "I'd been tattooing for 11 years by then." Moving from Ruatoria to the big city was a bit of a culture shock: "When I first came up to Auckland I couldn't get into bars — the doormen would look at me sideways because I had tattoos."

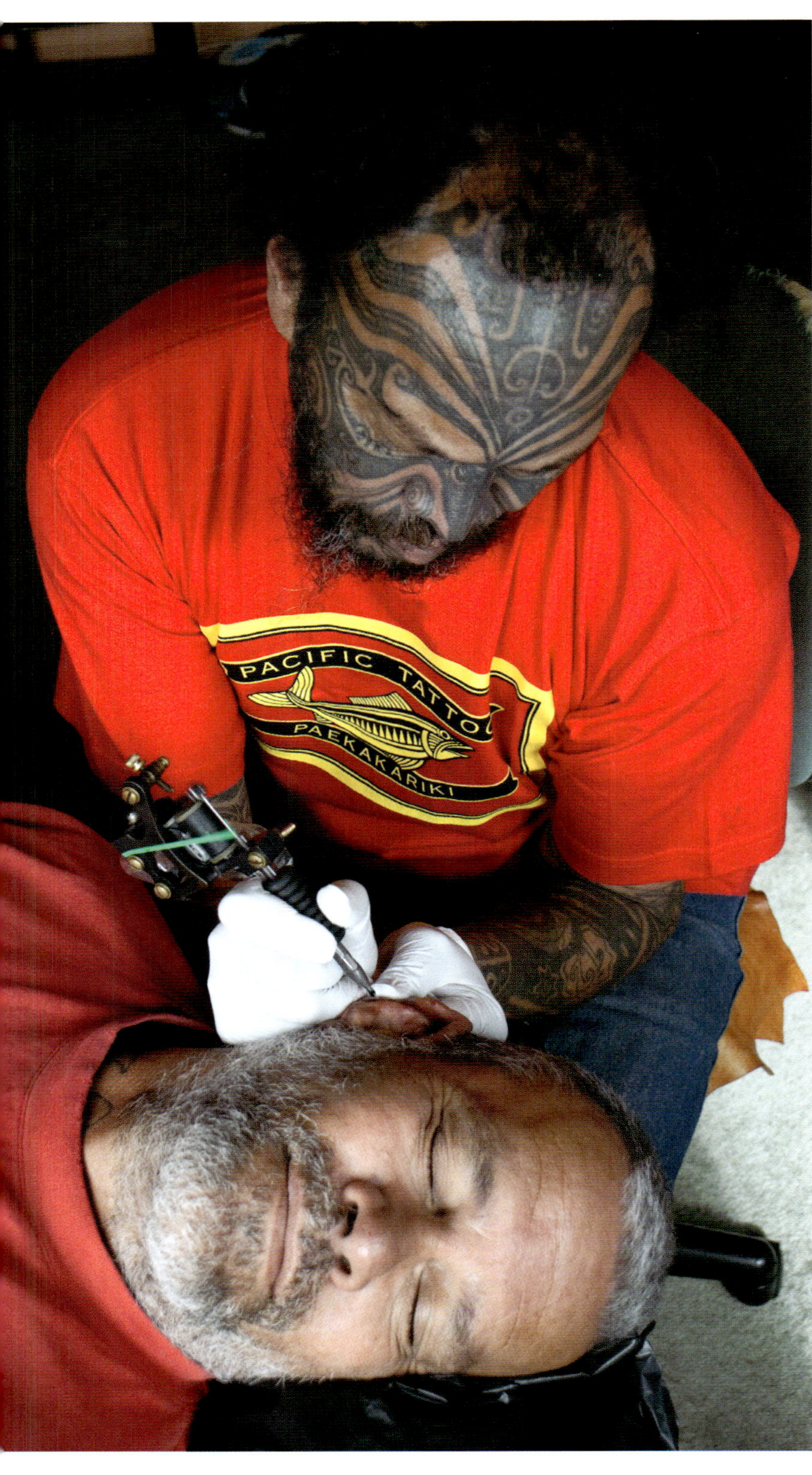

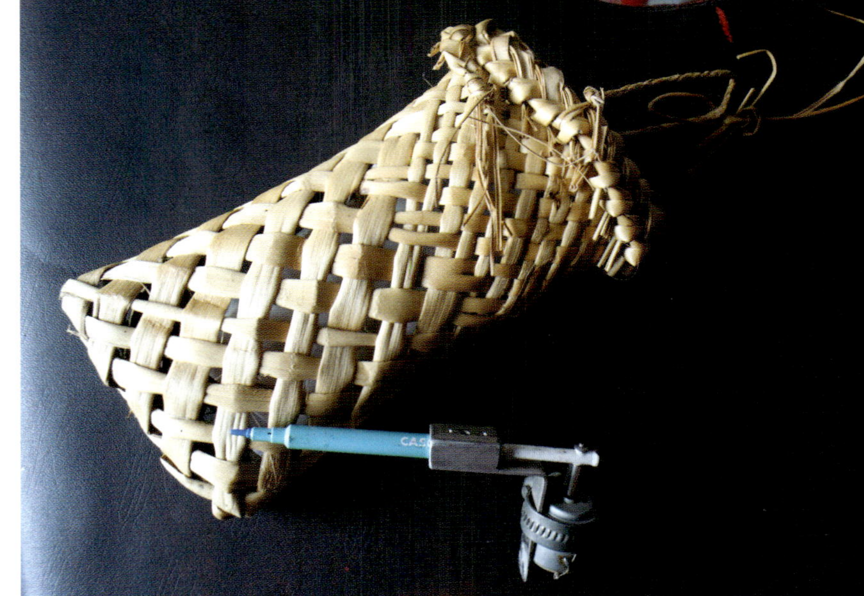

After six months at Moko Ink he went out on his own. He and then partner Pip Russell opened a small studio at their home in the suburb of Te Atatu. In 2001 he met Dutch tattooist Rinus Souisa, president of the Dutch Union of Tattoo Artists, who had come to attend a convention in Christchurch organised by Riki Manuel. Invitations to Europe followed and from then until 2007 Nehe made an annual pilgrimage to the continent, spending time in Germany, Switzerland and the Netherlands.

The travel exposed him to better machines and inks, and he learned to tattoo faster and make his handiwork last longer. "They treat you with so much respect over there, but you are only as good as your last tattoo wherever you are."

These days he lives near Waitakere township, west of Auckland, where he tattoos and carves. A commission from a Ponsonby café explains the large totara post on his deck; Nehe will spend about three months completing the detailed woodwork.

Occasionally he still uses the traditional ta moko tools when tattooing. "It's not something you do every day. Not many people come to me to get that work done. But whether it's the hand tools or the machine — it's just an extension of my hand to draw and write the message. That's what a moko is."

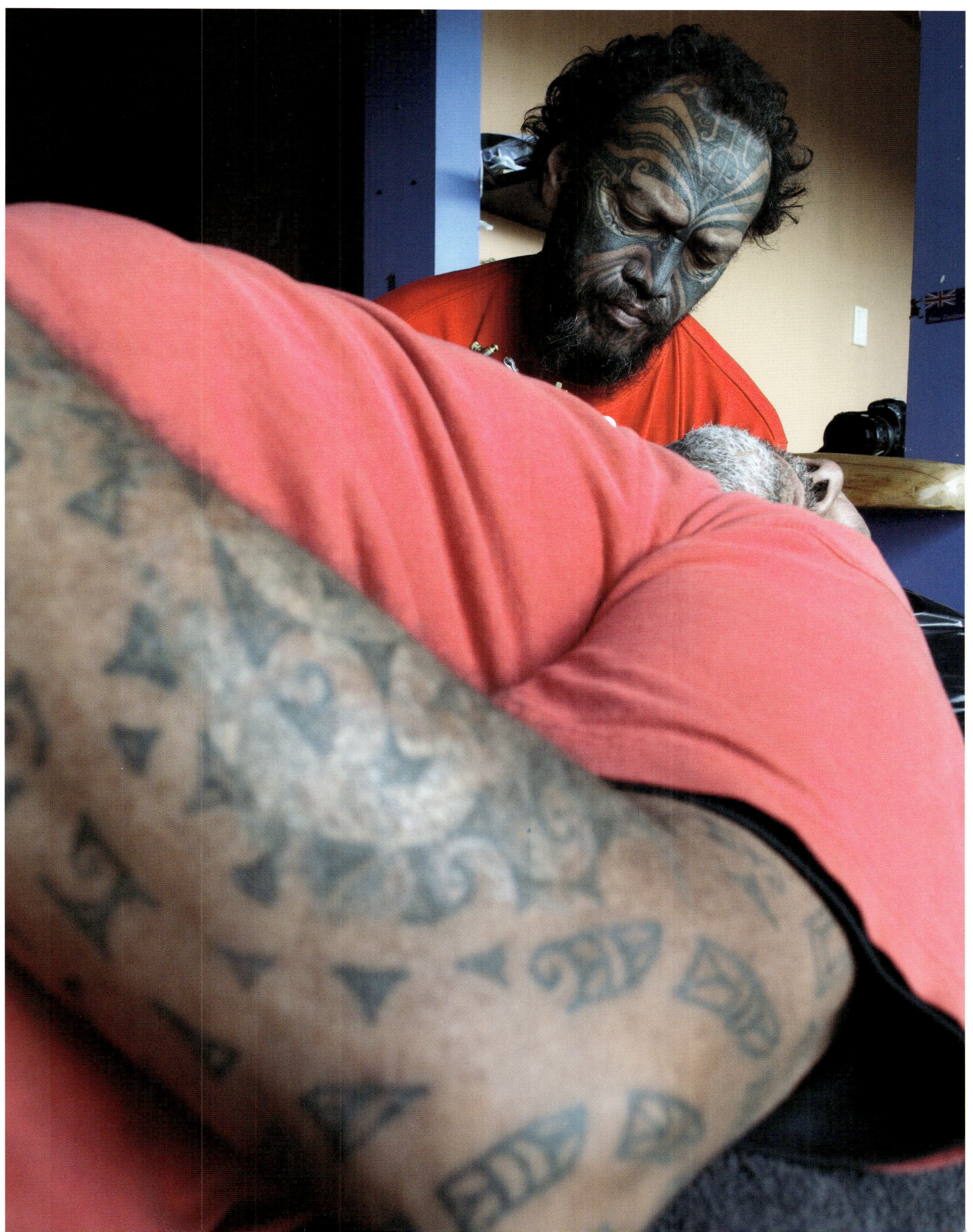

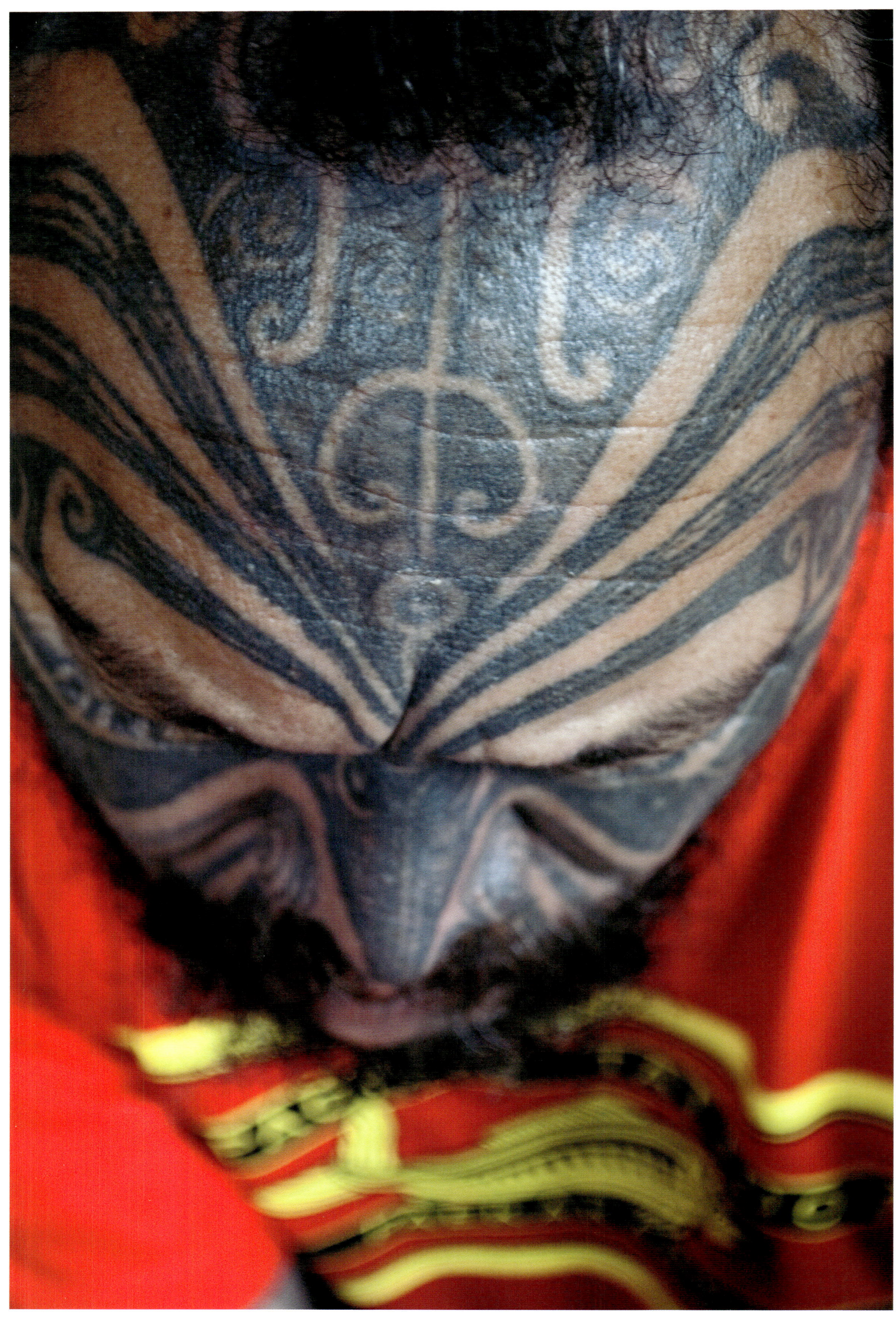

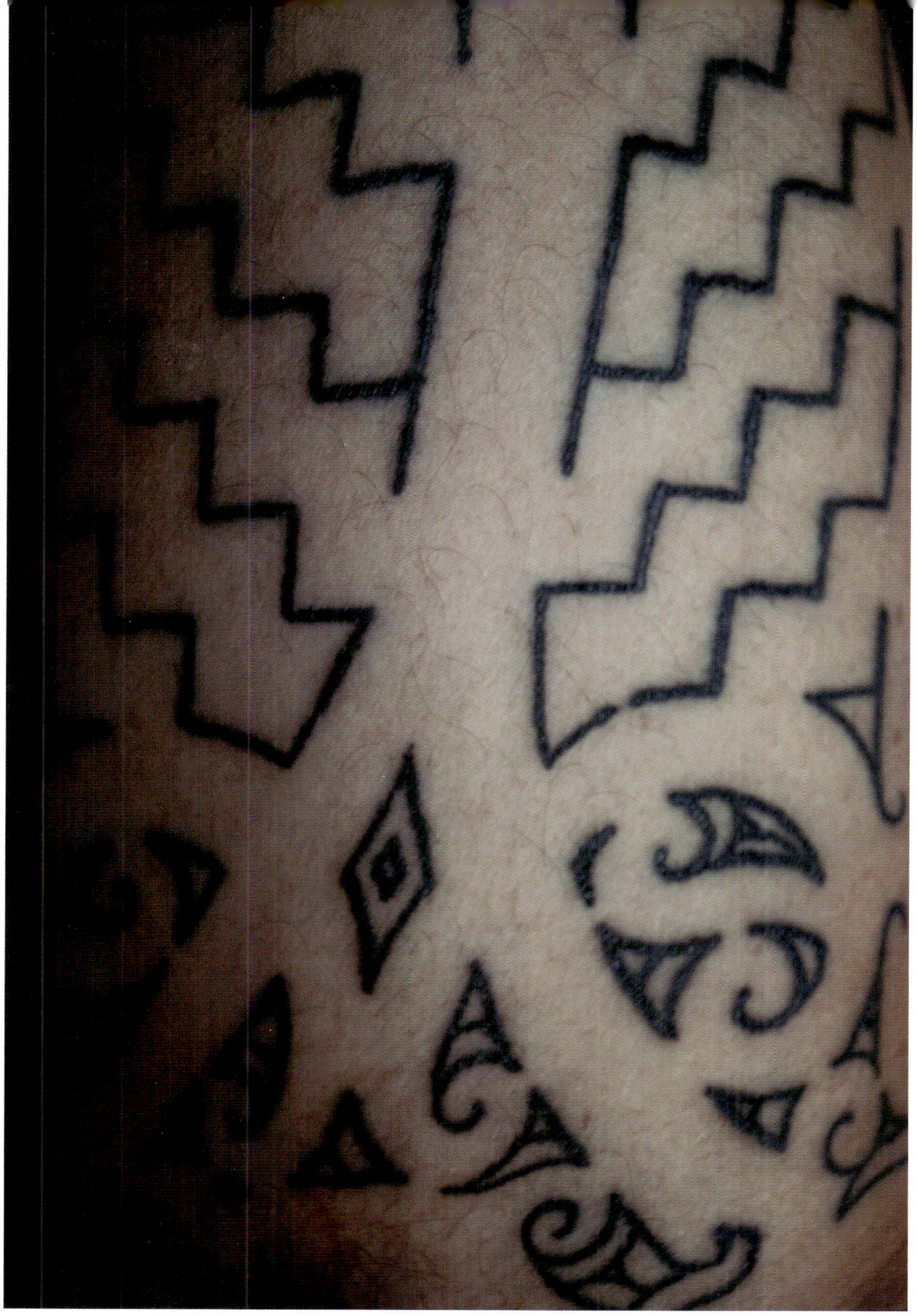

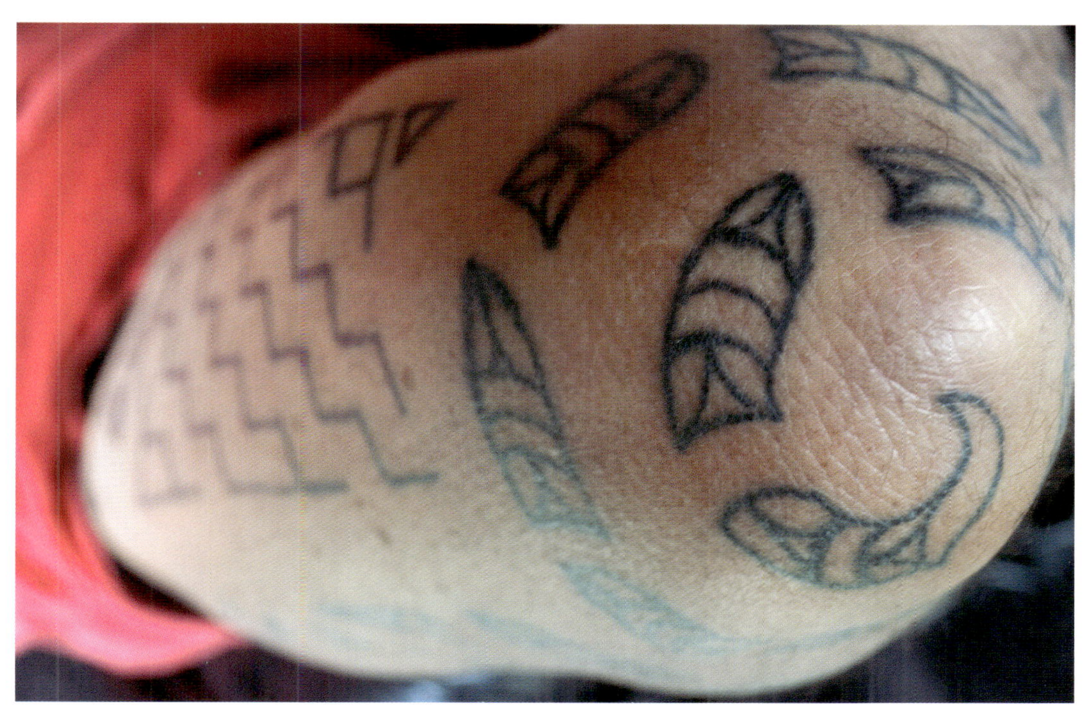

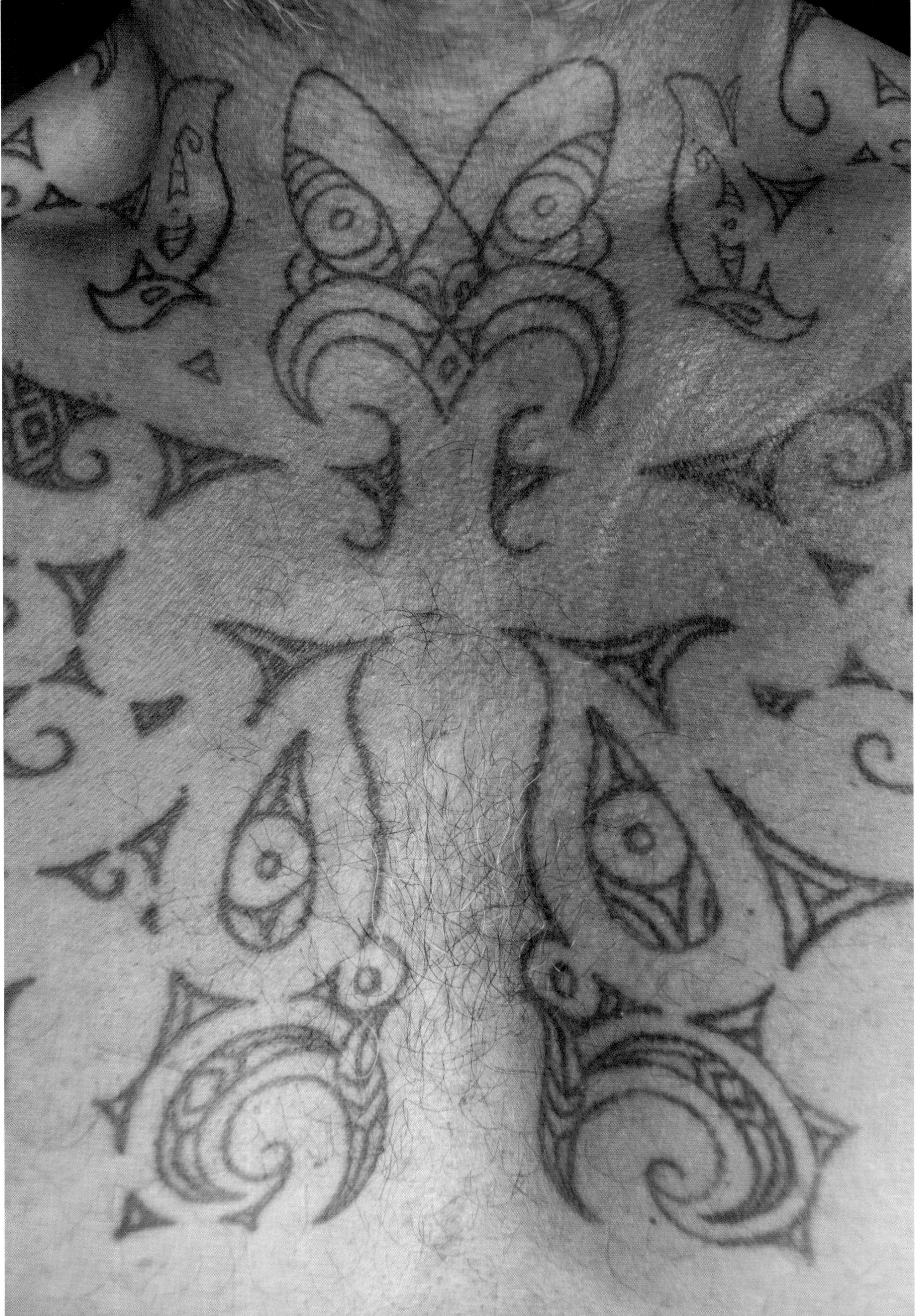

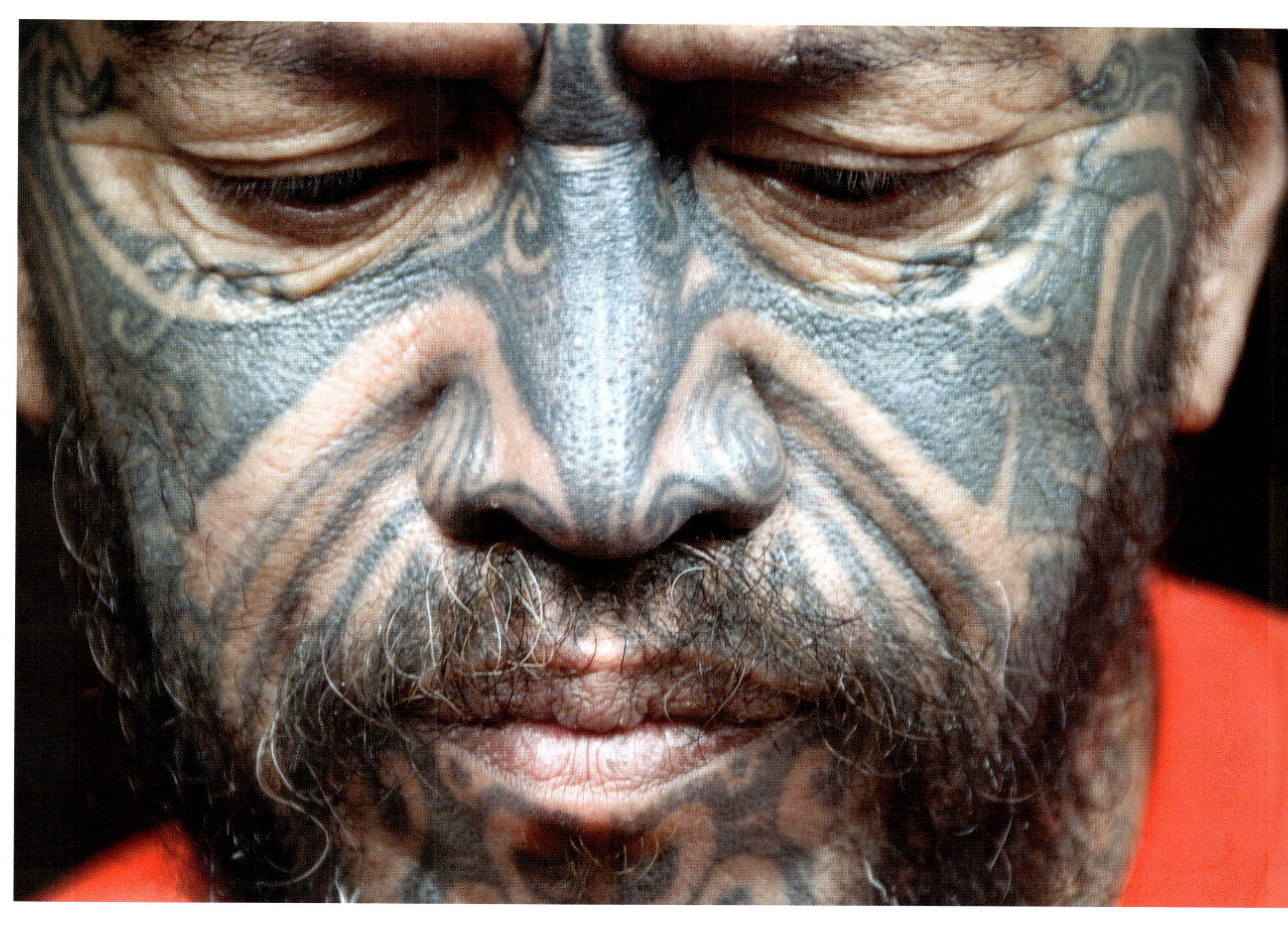

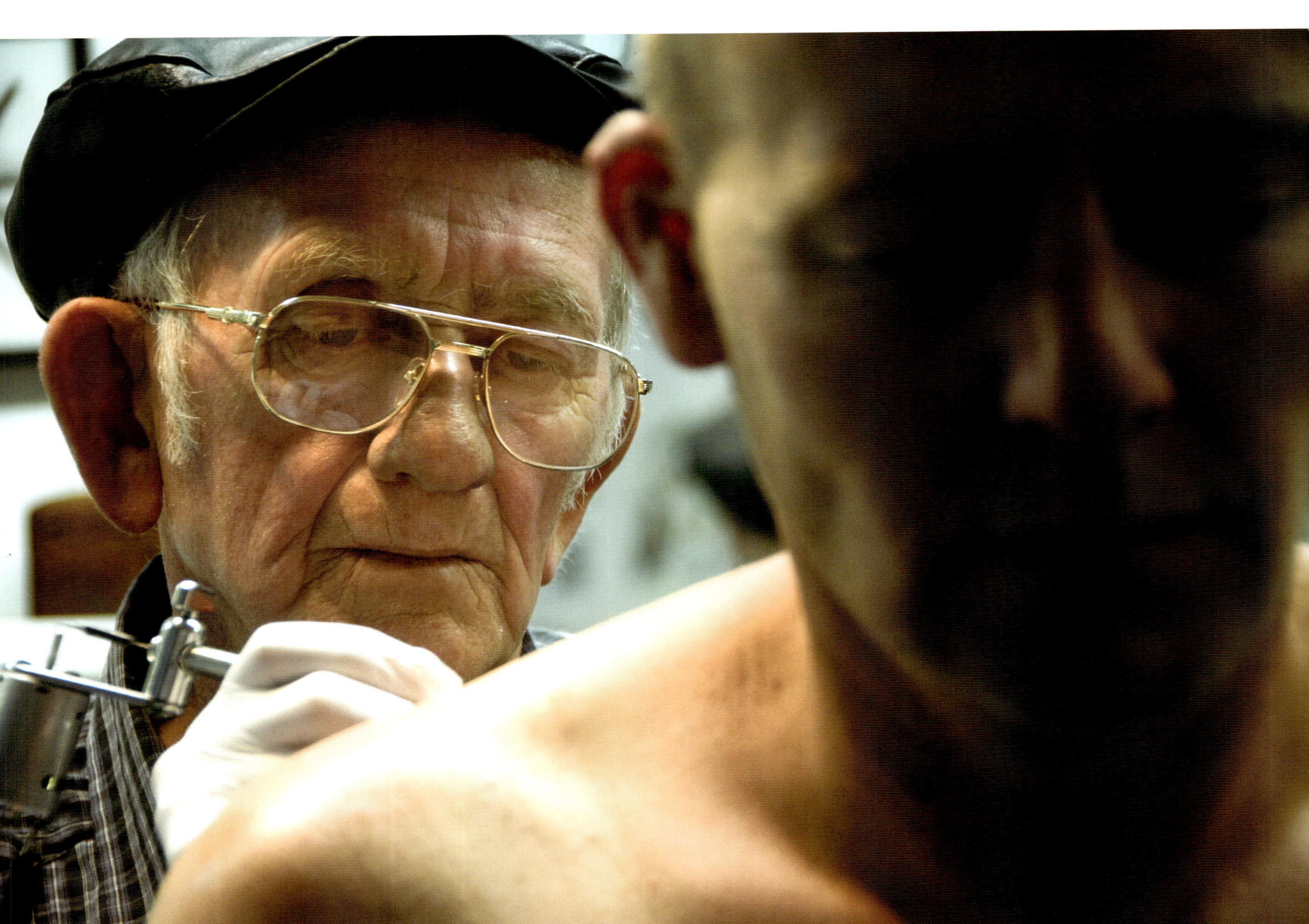

MERV **O'CONNOR**

AUCKLAND TATTOO STUDIO

Merv O'Connor is a New Zealand tattooing icon. He's been in the business for over 55 years and for the past two decades been based at the Auckland Tattoo Studio on Ponsonby Road. It's an old-school parlour, complete with designs people can choose off the wall: "I prefer the walk-up customers," Merv says.

It's a Saturday afternoon and he's got the horseracing running on a small television in the background. He looks across to the set every now and then to keep up with the day's race meeting: "I've still got an interest in a couple of horses, but I'm not a gambler. I saw too many guys lose a lot of money when I was a jockey."

Merv was first exposed to the art of tattooing by his father when he was just eight years of age. His parents had split up when he was young and he was sent to live with his grandmother, who ran a boarding house. When his dad came to visit one day, one of the young boarders noticed his father's tattoos and asked him where he'd got them done. He said he'd done them himself and he used to tattoo his mates in the army.

Then the young man asked Merv's dad if he would tattoo him. "So my father sent me to the shop to get some Indian ink, beading needles and tracing paper. When I got back I watched him sketch the piece on the tracing paper and bind three needles on the end of a peg. Then I watched him do the tattoo and it really blew me away.

"I was pretty good at art and when I was about 11 years old I started tattooing some of my friends at school." But it didn't go down too well with some of the subjects' parents. His first tattoo, consisting of the letters 'NZ', dates from that time — and he did it himself. Merv motions to his forearm: "It's in there somewhere."

At 13 he went to work in the stables to become a jockey and four years later moved to Wanganui to start a five-year apprenticeship. Merv says his tattooing career started to gather momentum at the same time.

"Bev Robinson, who everyone knew as Cindy Ray, was married to Danny Robinson, a really good Australian tattooist. I bought some tattooing equipment from her."

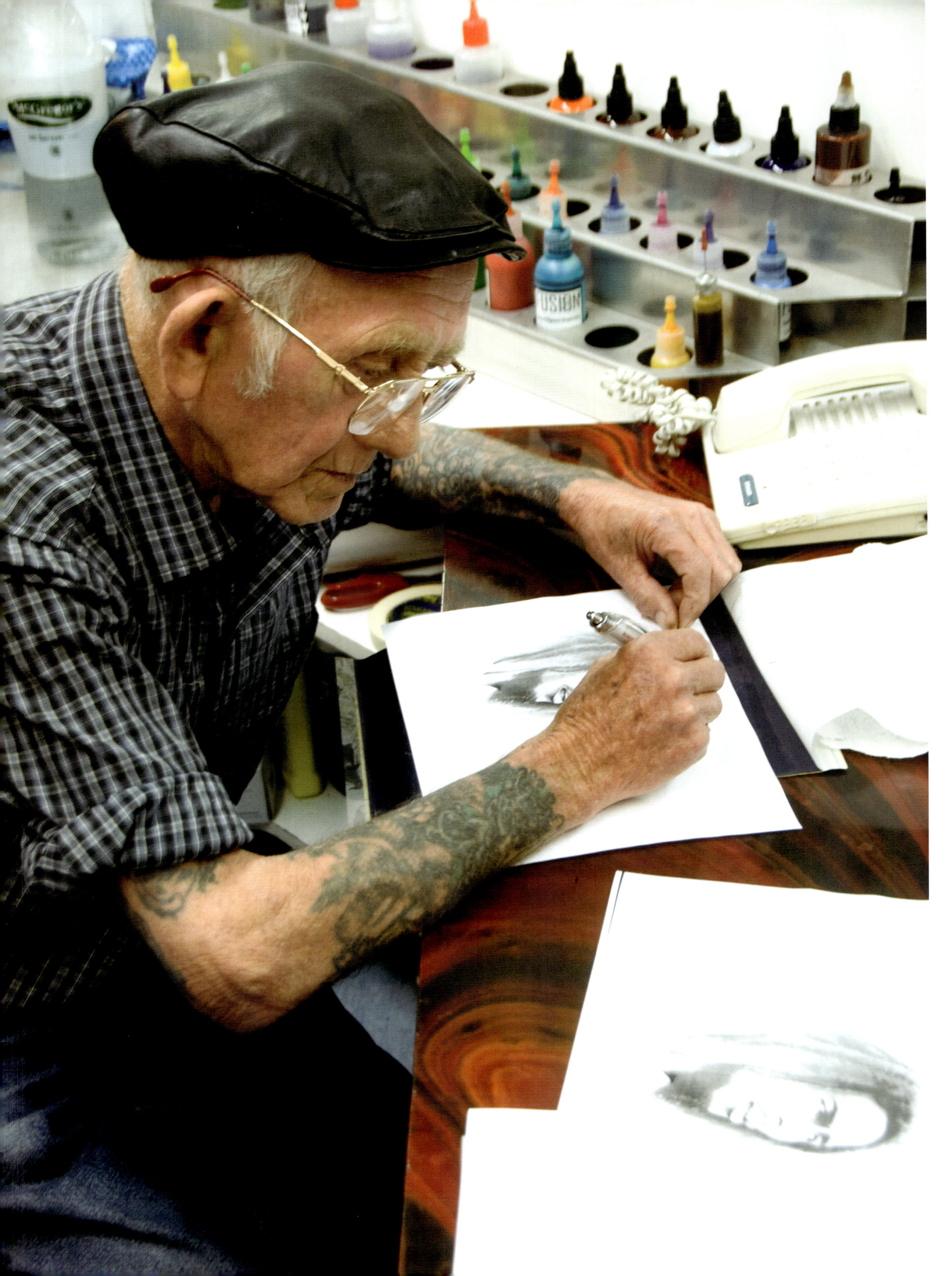

In between his time at the racetrack Merv would do the rounds of freezing works in the North Island, including Patea and Foxton, to tattoo the workers. At one of the freezing works he met Wellington tattooist Kevin Grice. "He had a studio down there and gave me a few tips about tattooing; and I gave him a few tips on the horses."

But he finally turned his back on the racing industry after a series of injuries and moved to Auckland in late 1969, opening his first studio that year. "After a couple of years I shifted to Karangahape Rd, where I stayed for about 10 years. Then I bought a shop in Richmond Rd about 25 years ago because I knew the inner-city rents were going to get too high." Merv moved to his current shop in Ponsonby Road in the early 1990s.

The tattooing industry was totally different in those days: he remembers "Even getting the equipment was really difficult, whereas nowadays you can get top-notch machinery on the Internet. But now the conventions have really opened it up for a lot of people."

Although Merv has seen various trends and styles come and go, he's not above admiring some of the young tattooists of the modern era: "Some of the work being done today is wonderful: the colours, the machinery. There are some amazing young artists out there."

Merv doesn't claim a particular style, but can turn his hand to anything — and he does. On most days you can bet Merv will be waiting at the Auckland Tattoo Studio for one of the many walk-up customers he still gets: "I'm here six days a week from 10 till 5."

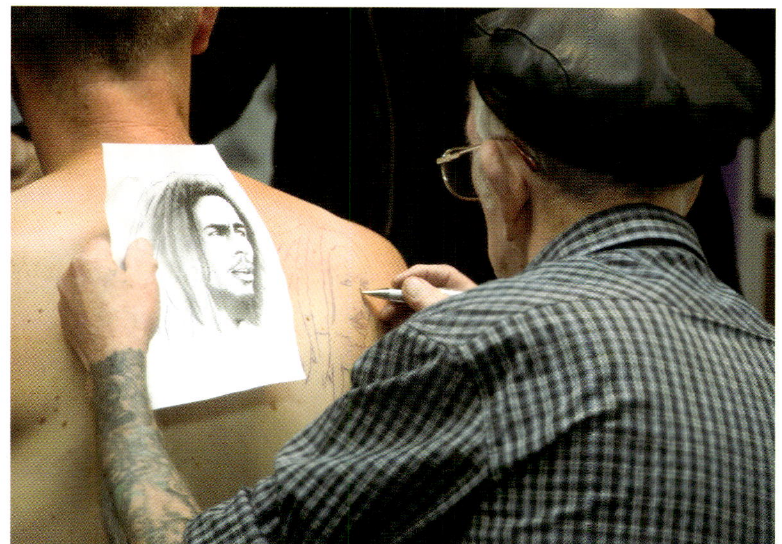

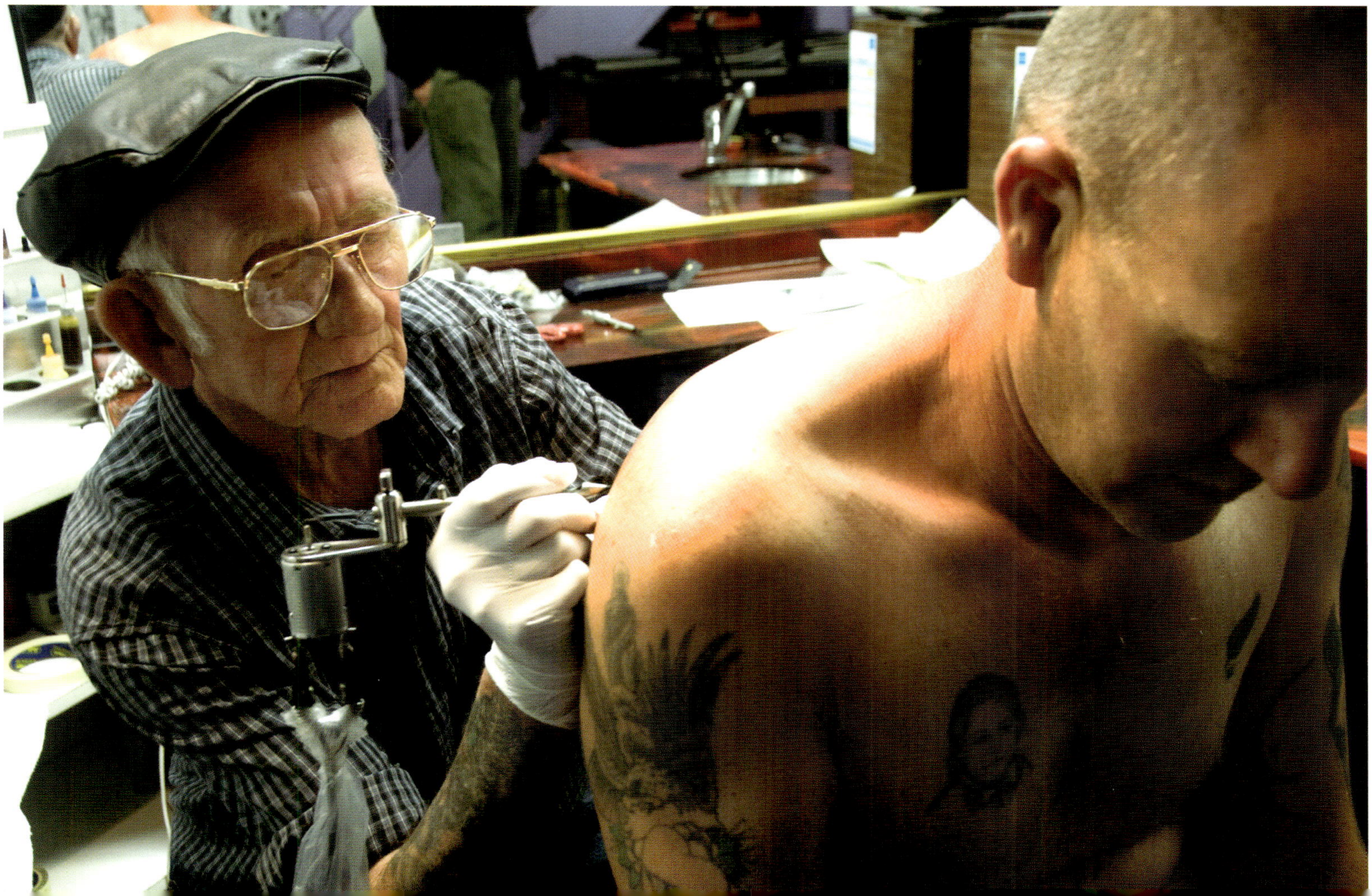

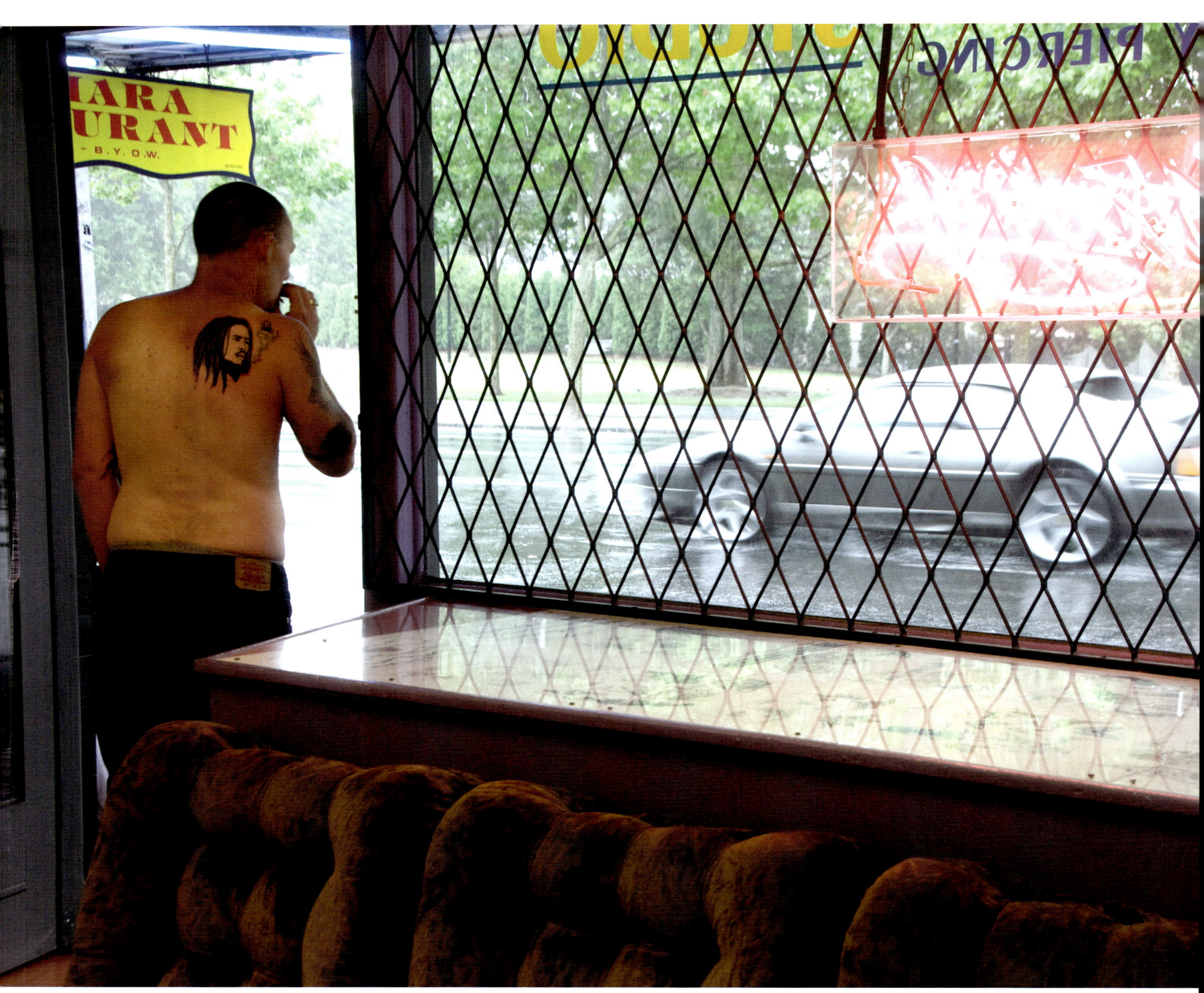

HARA
URANT
B.Y.O.W.
PIERCING

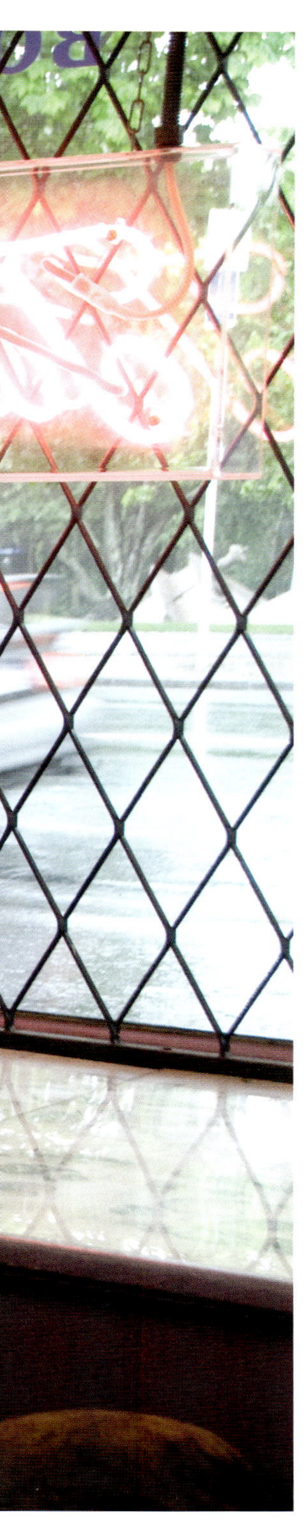

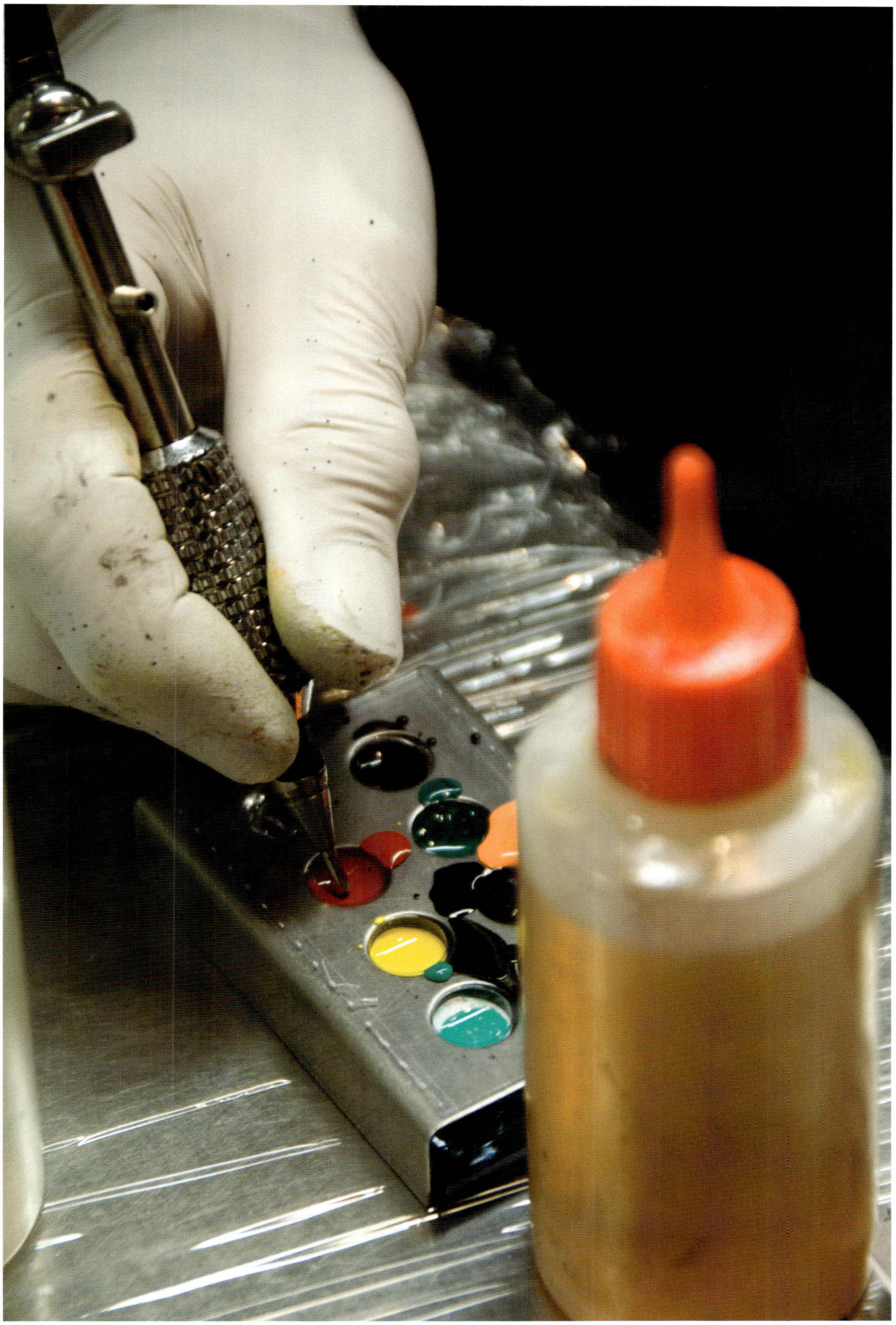

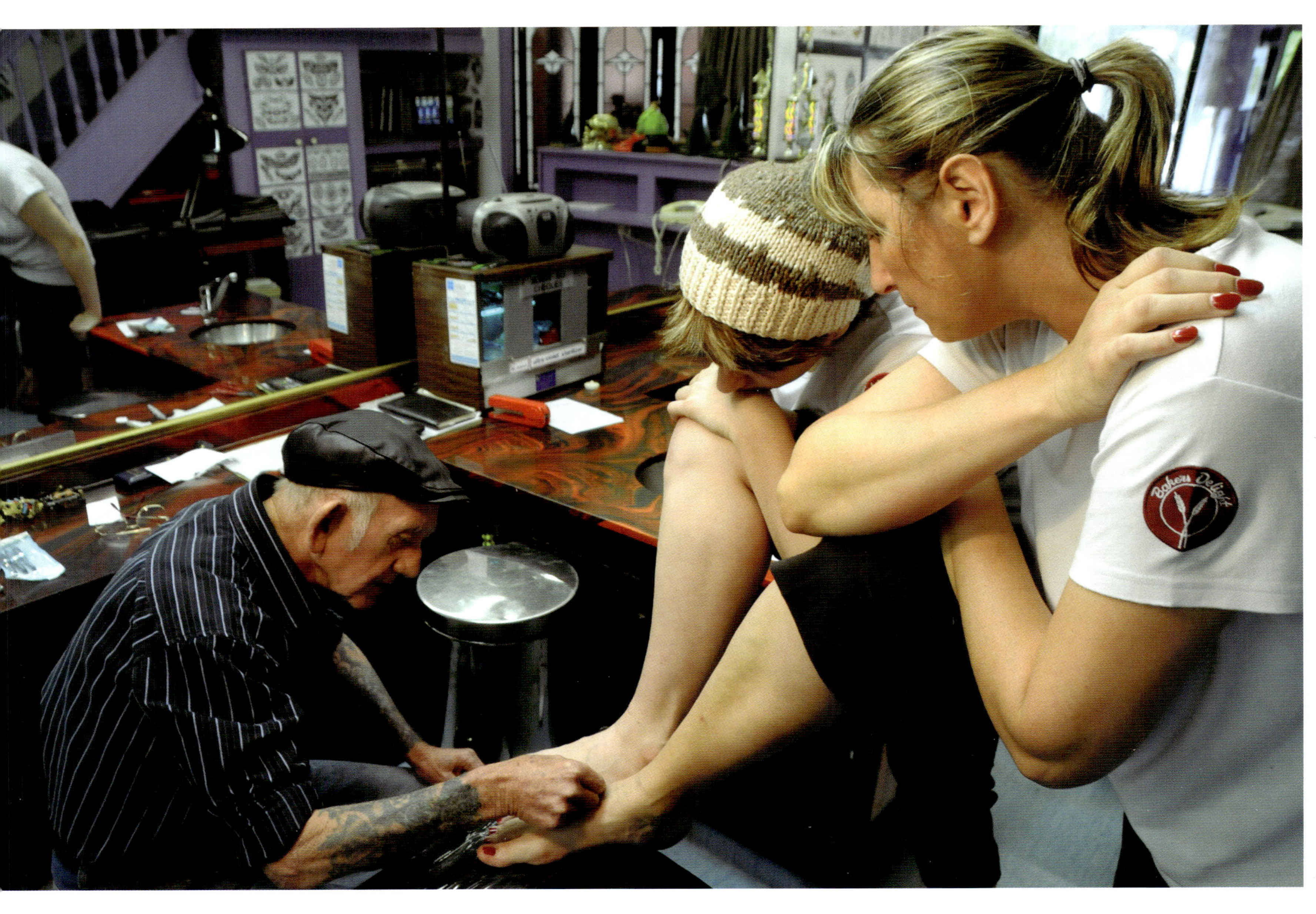

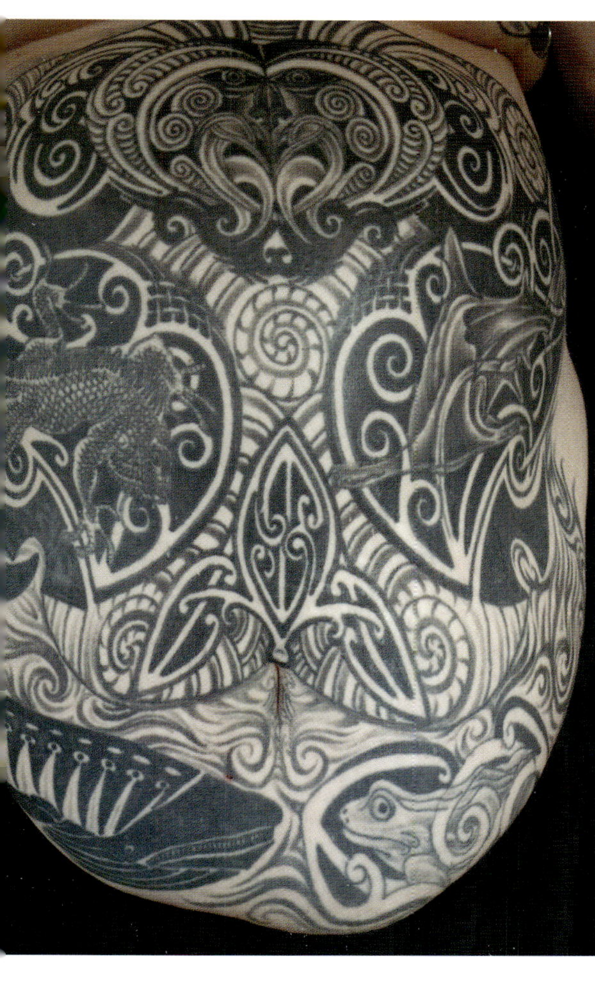

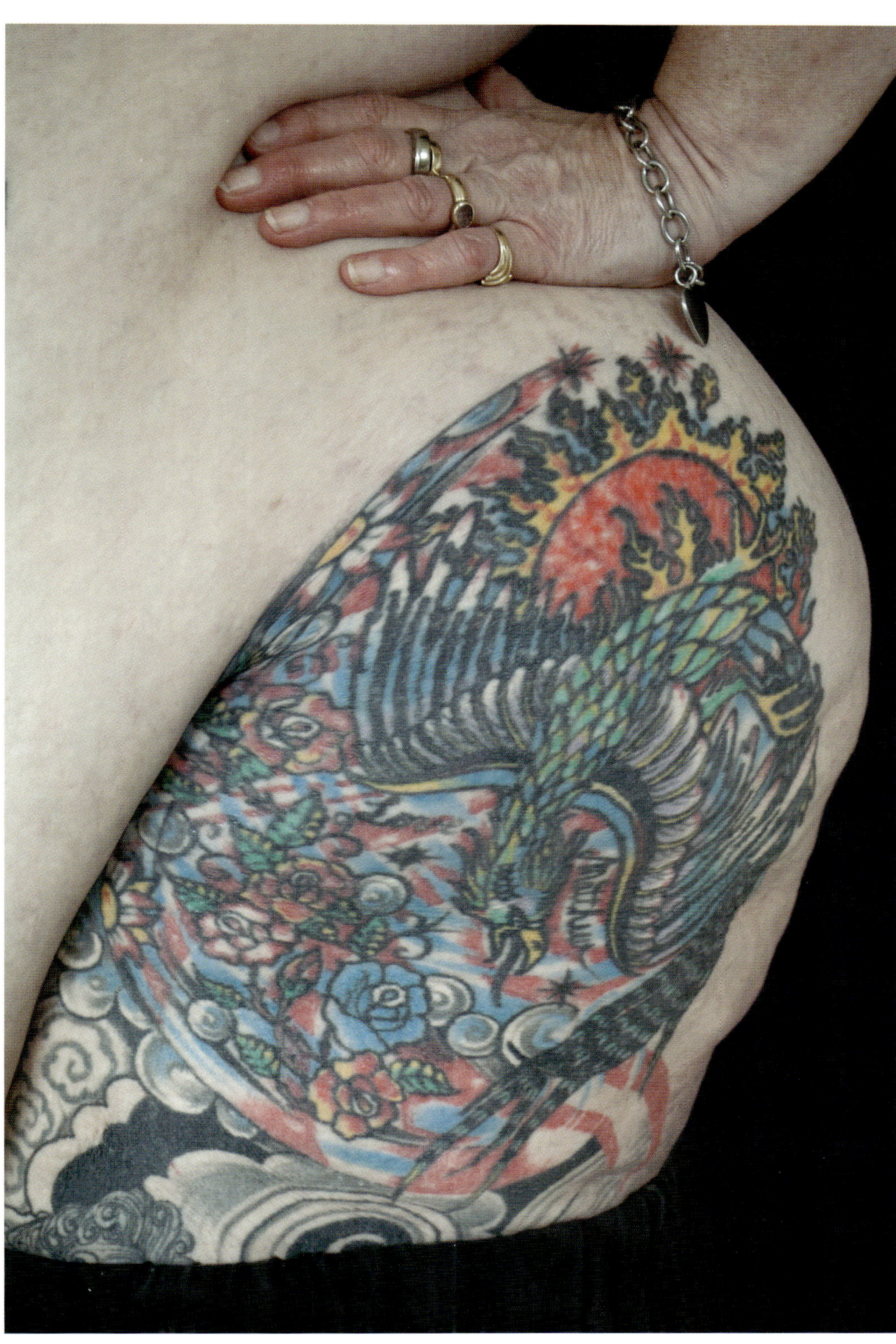

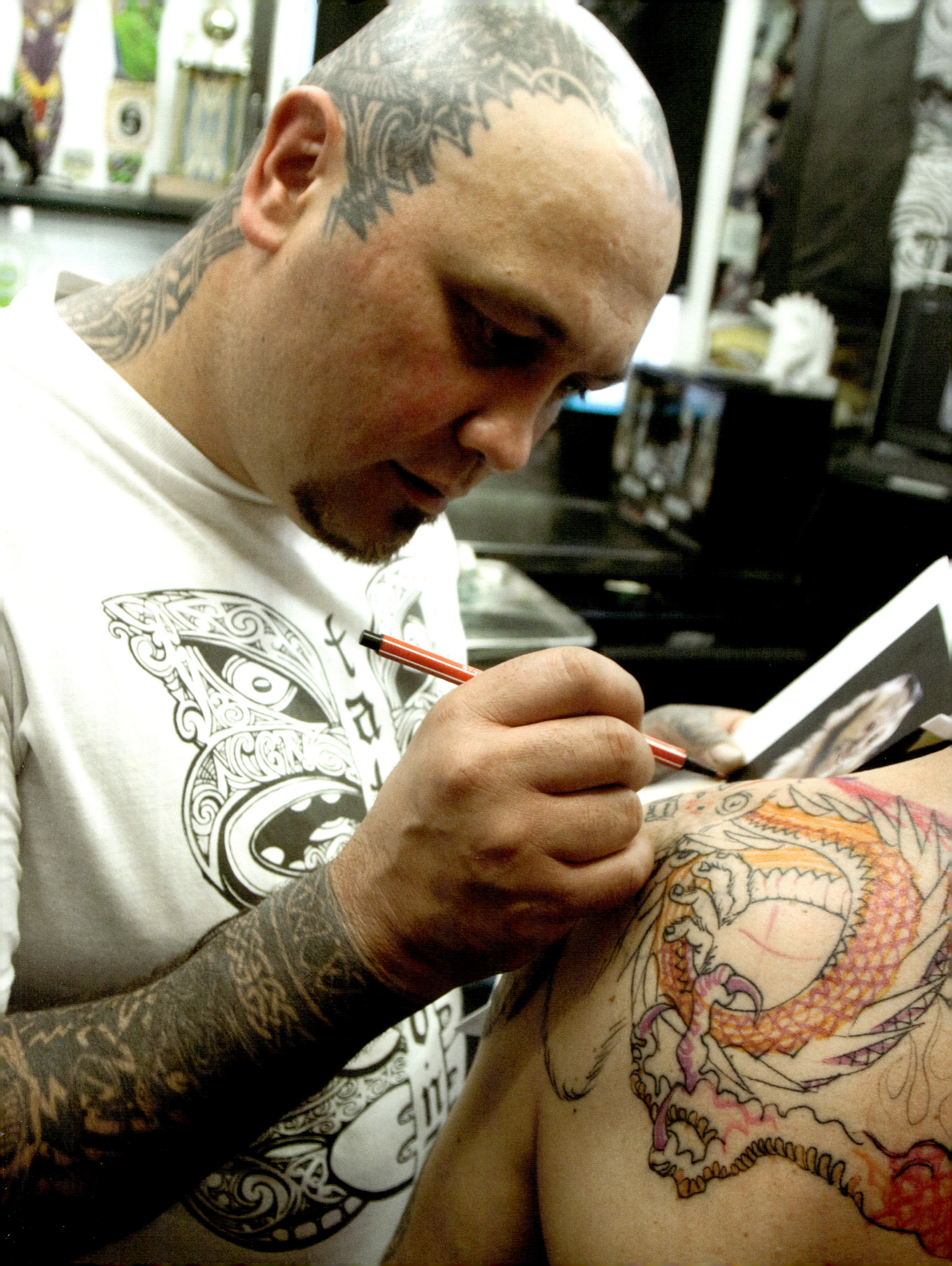

STEVE **MADDOCK**

Although he'd already been tattooing for over a decade, Steve Maddock's first attempt at doing it professionally came when he opened his Wellington studio, Underground Arts, in 1994. Steve had tattooed his mates as a teenager and made his first tattoo machine when he was just 14. But it was through a friend that he really learned the art form. "My mate the Artful Dodger was a master at it. He taught himself in jail and knew how to make a machine using a 0.5 pen."

Steve does most forms of tattooing, but his main focus is freestyle original. "The only things I transfer are portraits, coats of arms and cars. I don't like to use transfers. If you put it on the wall people will ask for it, but any tattooist can do that. I would rather do something other tattooists can't." And he's always up for a challenge. "I don't think there's anything that's impossible to tattoo. It's all just a question of scale."

He's constantly studying what other tattooists are doing in New Zealand and around the world. "It's one of those professions where if you are smart you are learning every day." Wellington artist Roger Ingerton is one of his favourites: "Roger's always been a gentleman in the tattooing profession, very humble, and what I like about him is he's always freehand-drawn everything he's done."

Looking at tattooing today, Steve summarises: "The artists have improved, the equipment has improved, and the tattoos have improved." But there are some things he sees that he doesn't like, such as the growing use of transfers and "cookie-cutter" generic designs. "The mainstream has re-established the old-school as a valid style. For me, if I can turn that work away I do."

Steve opened the National Tattoo Museum in November 2001. These days it's located in the same Vivian Street building as Underground Arts. He came up with the idea after hearing about the Amsterdam Tattoo Museum in Holland. "Tattooing is a quality art form that is too often ignored by the mainstream art world. So when I first heard about the Amsterdam Tattoo Museum I thought it was a great idea. I thought somebody should open something like that in New Zealand." He visited Amsterdam in 2011, and while he was there he visited Hanky Panky's historical treasure trove and spoke to the man himself.

The National Tattoo Museum is spread over two rooms and features hundreds of pictures of indigenous and contemporary tattooing, as well as carvings and oil paintings. Entry is free and Steve funds the museum himself with money from the studio. However, the museum has moved twice since it first opened, owing to problems with funding.

But with the increasing number of people making a pilgrimage to New Zealand to get inked he's not short of tourists who are keen to see the museum. Some of his most prized items in the collection are traditional tattooing tools he's collected from around the world — from Maori ta moko chisels to Samoan tatau tools and utensils from Burma.

He had to downsize the museum when he relocated it to Vivian Street in April 2010. "We've got a lot of photos and videos in our archive but we're now transferring them to digital format because we don't have the room for them all."

Despite the fact he doesn't make a lot of money out of the museum, for Steve it's a way of celebrating tattooing. "Tattooing is a perishable art. So that's why you need a museum to save the art and history. I still do walk-up customers and if I'm not tattooing I'm working in the museum."

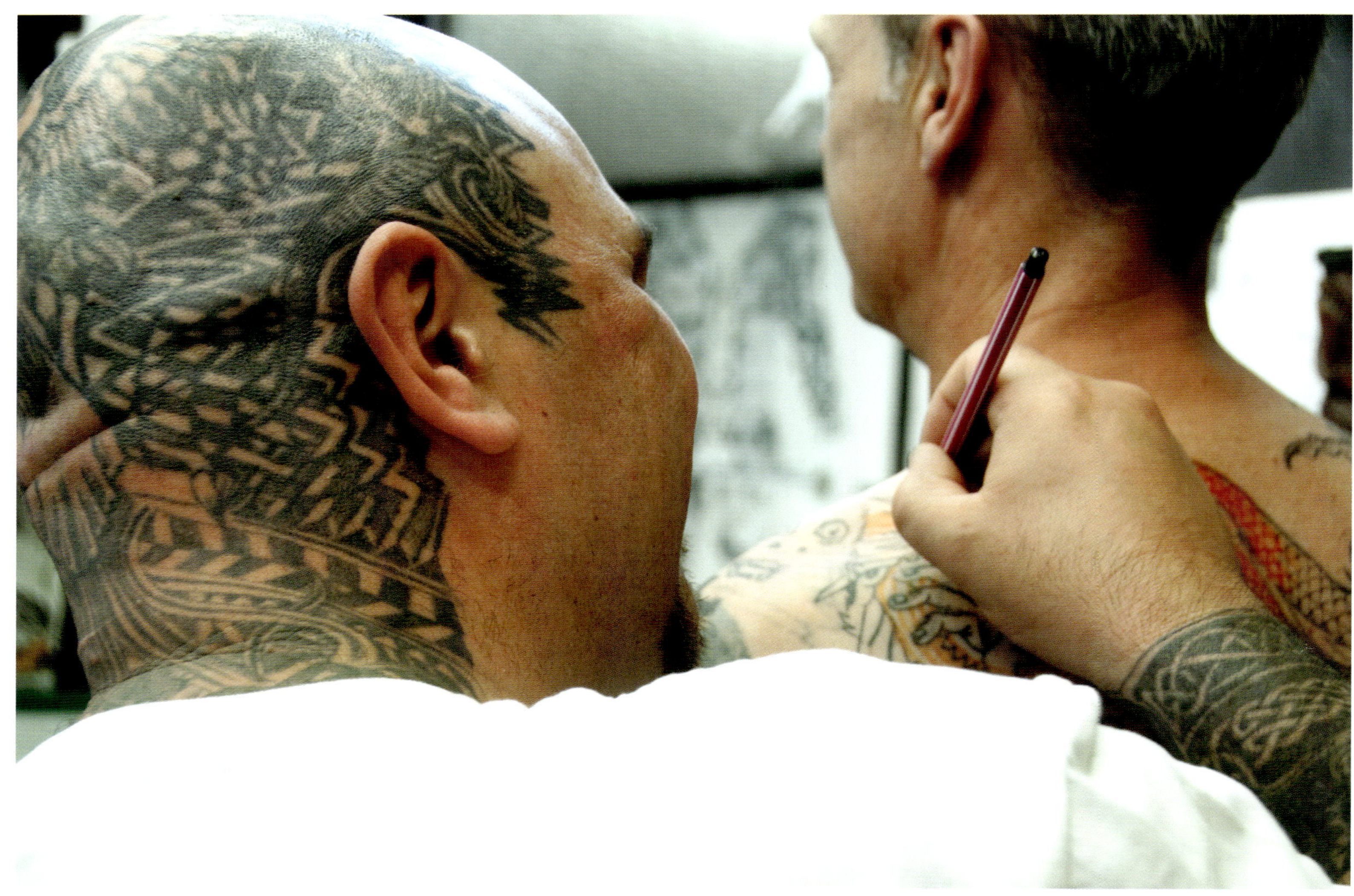

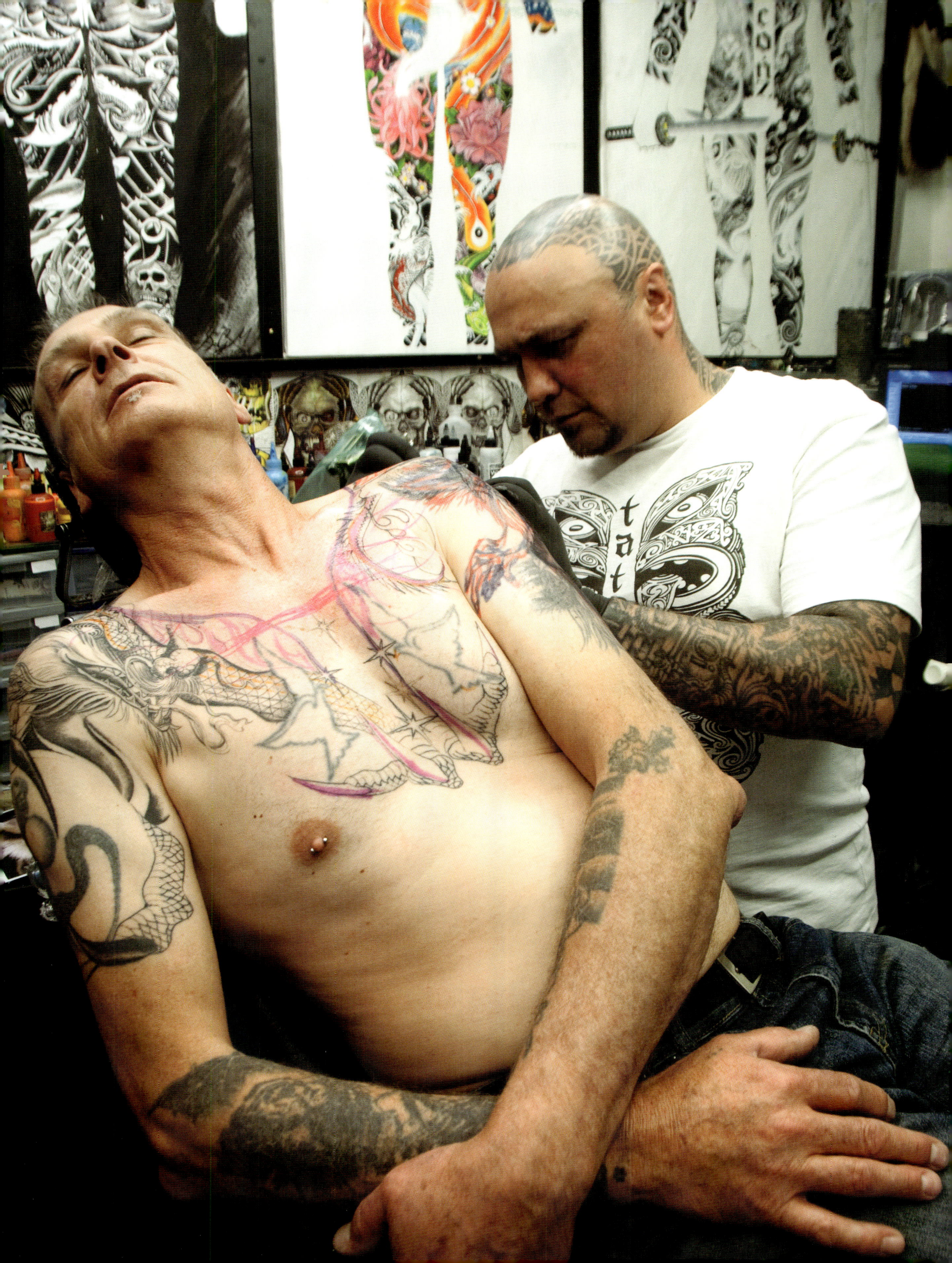

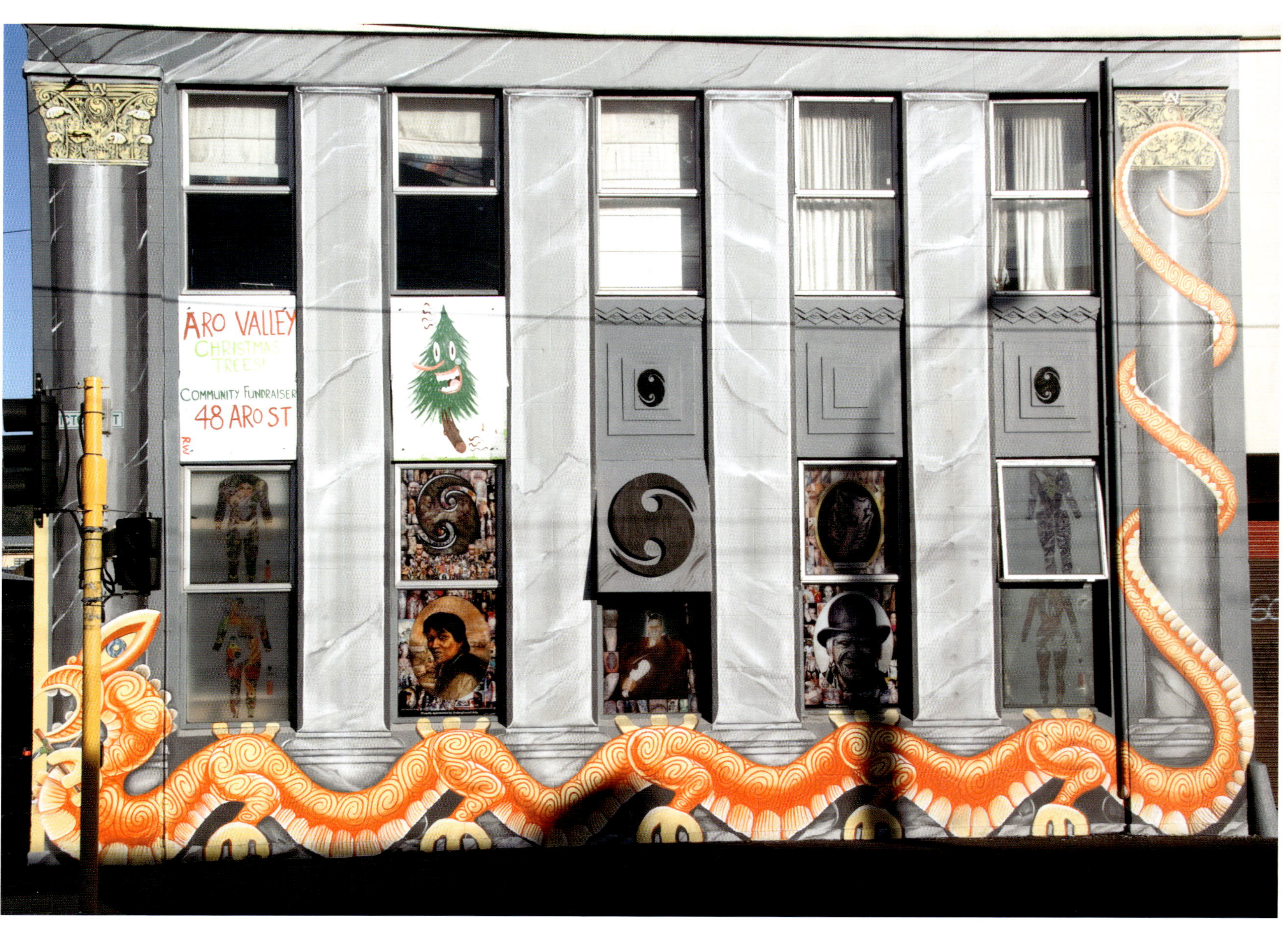
ÁRO VALLEY
CHRISTMAS
TREES!
COMMUNITY FUNDRAISER
48 ARO ST

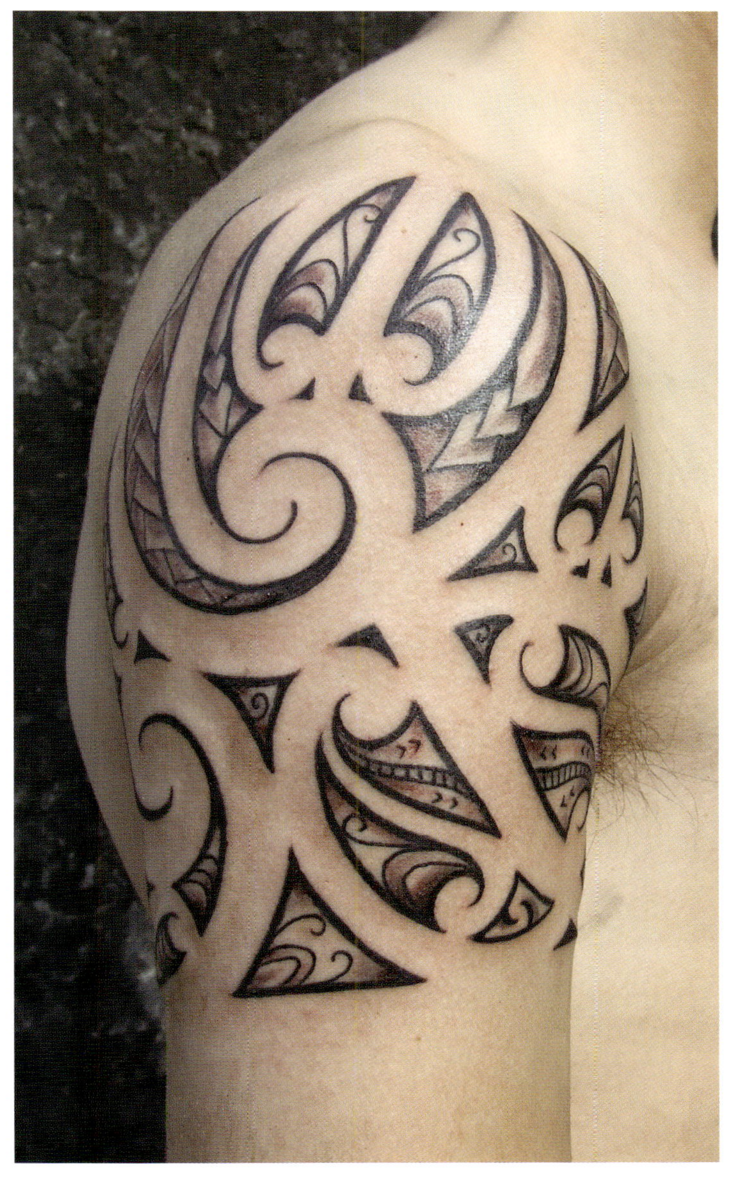

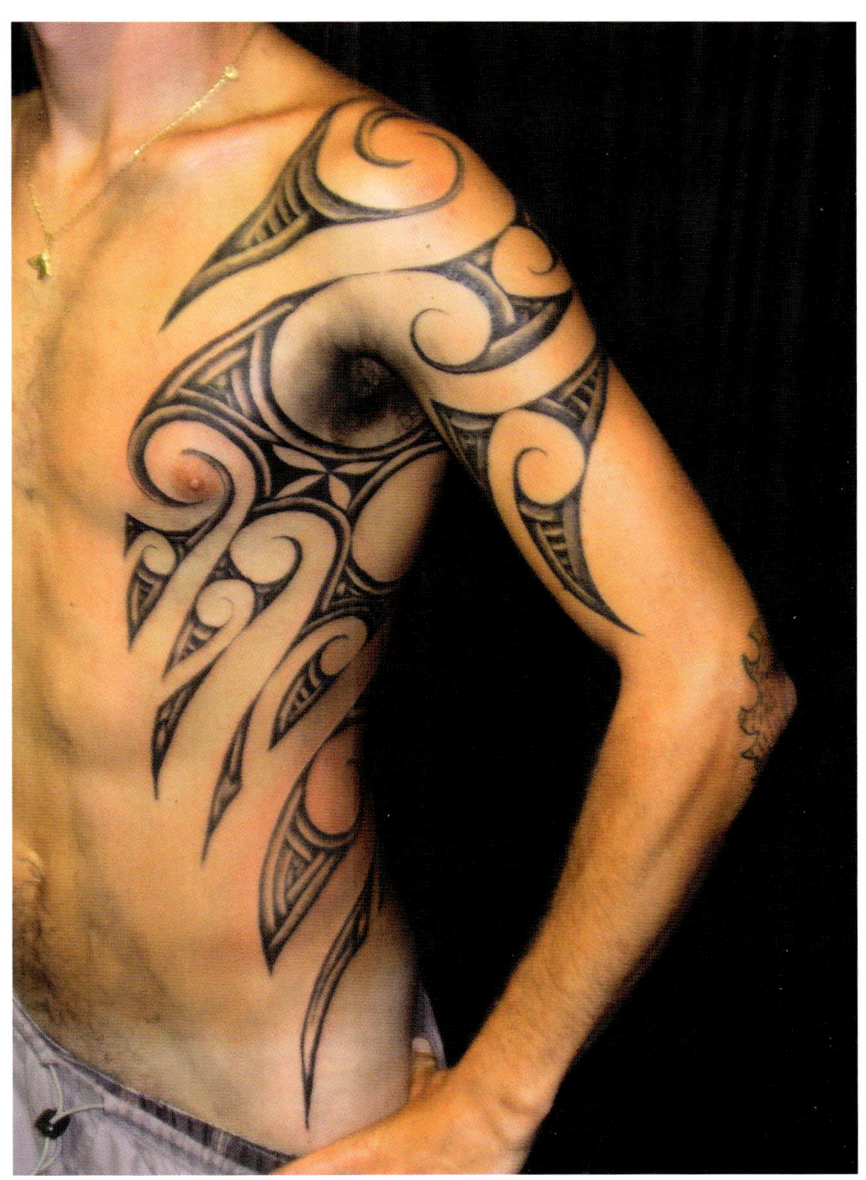

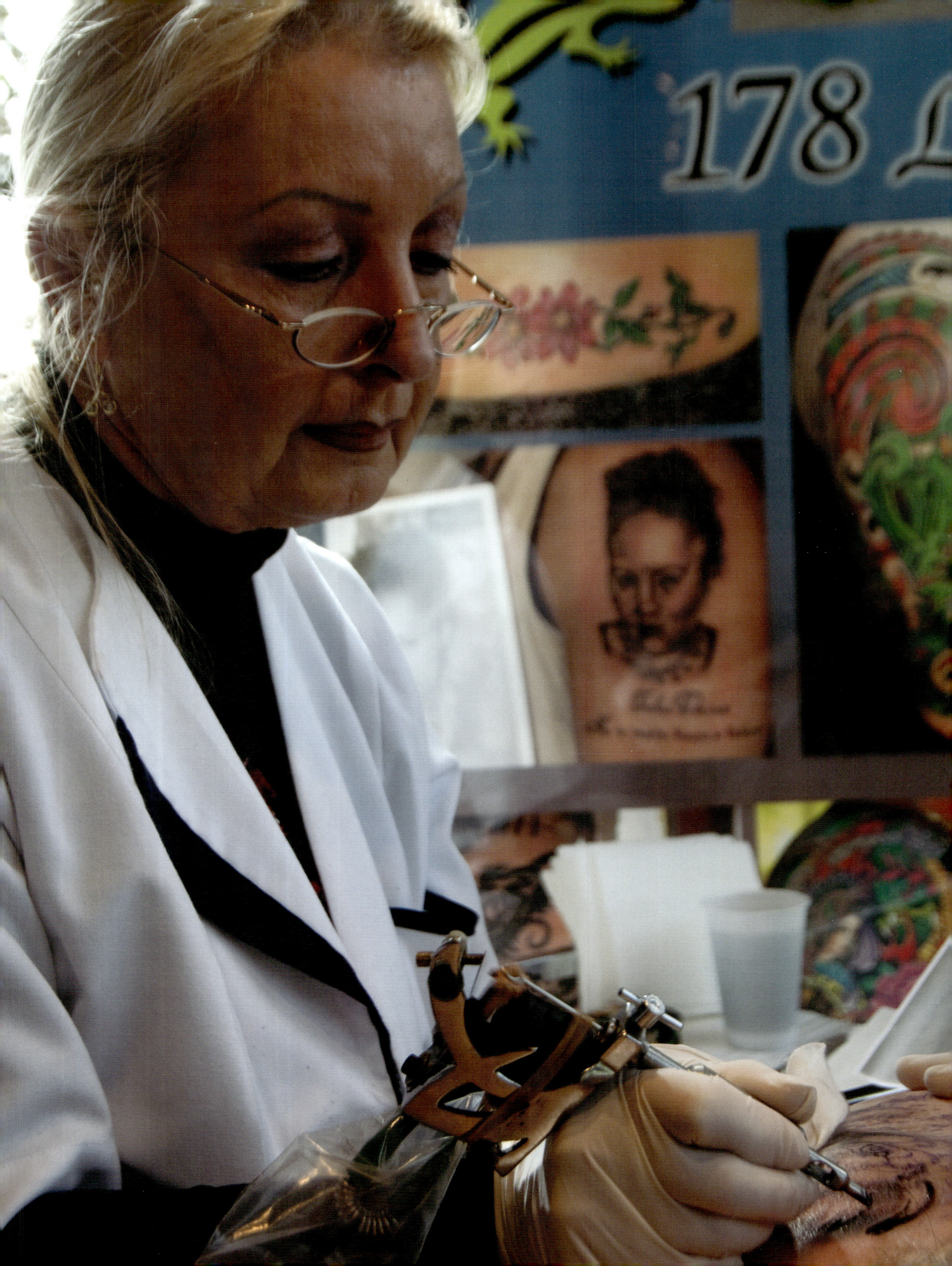

MONIQUE **MATAGA**

After almost two decades' tattooing in Europe, Monique Mataga was planning to retire from the industry when she emigrated to New Zealand from Germany. Instead she ended up opening a new shop on busy Lincoln Road in West Auckland, where she's been for the past 14 years. "When you are a tattooist you never really retire," she says.

Monique comes from a background as a commercial artist, where she did everything from airbrush work and oil painting to sculpture. She went to live in Australia in the 1960s, and a chance visit to a Sydney tattoo parlour with a friend in the early 1970s opened her eyes to the world of tattooing. It was her first time in a tattoo studio and she was fascinated by what the artist could do and felt inspired to try her hand at it.

"However, 35 years ago the industry was dominated by men and no one wanted to teach me. It was very difficult for women to break into the scene. But the more I got knocked back the more I wanted to do it."

Monique started doing cover-ups as a hobby, then when she returned to live in Germany in the early 1980s she opened a studio in her home town of Wiesbaden. She tattooed in Germany for 16 years, and says Germans and Kiwis are poles apart in their attitudes: "It's a totally different scene. Here in New Zealand everyone's got a tattoo, whereas in Europe it's seen as something different."

Nowadays she works with her daughter Buzzy, her partner George Mataga and grandson Hans, all of whom are tattooists, while her son-in-law Charlie takes care of the piercings.

After 35 years as a tattooist Monique knows what she likes: "I prefer doing one-offs, but I can do anything, it doesn't matter what it is. I also do a lot of portraits." Monique enjoys living in New Zealand. "And I really like the Maori and Pacific tattoo art — it's amazing."

But there are some facets of the tattoo industry she doesn't like. Top of the list is the high number of backyard operators that are still commonplace in New Zealand. "There are far too many of them. Coupled with the cheap inks and machines that are pouring into the country, it's a serious issue that has to be addressed."

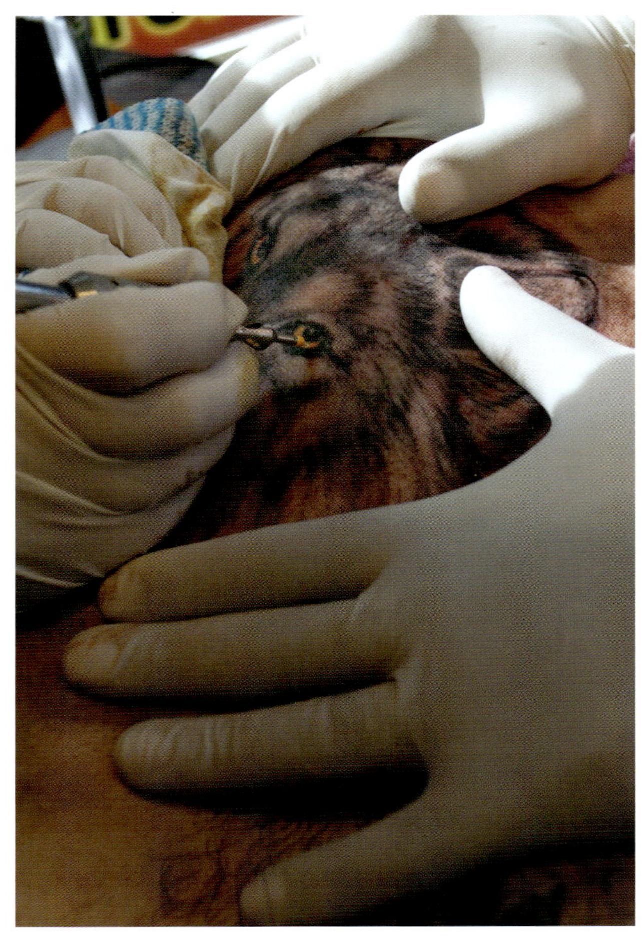

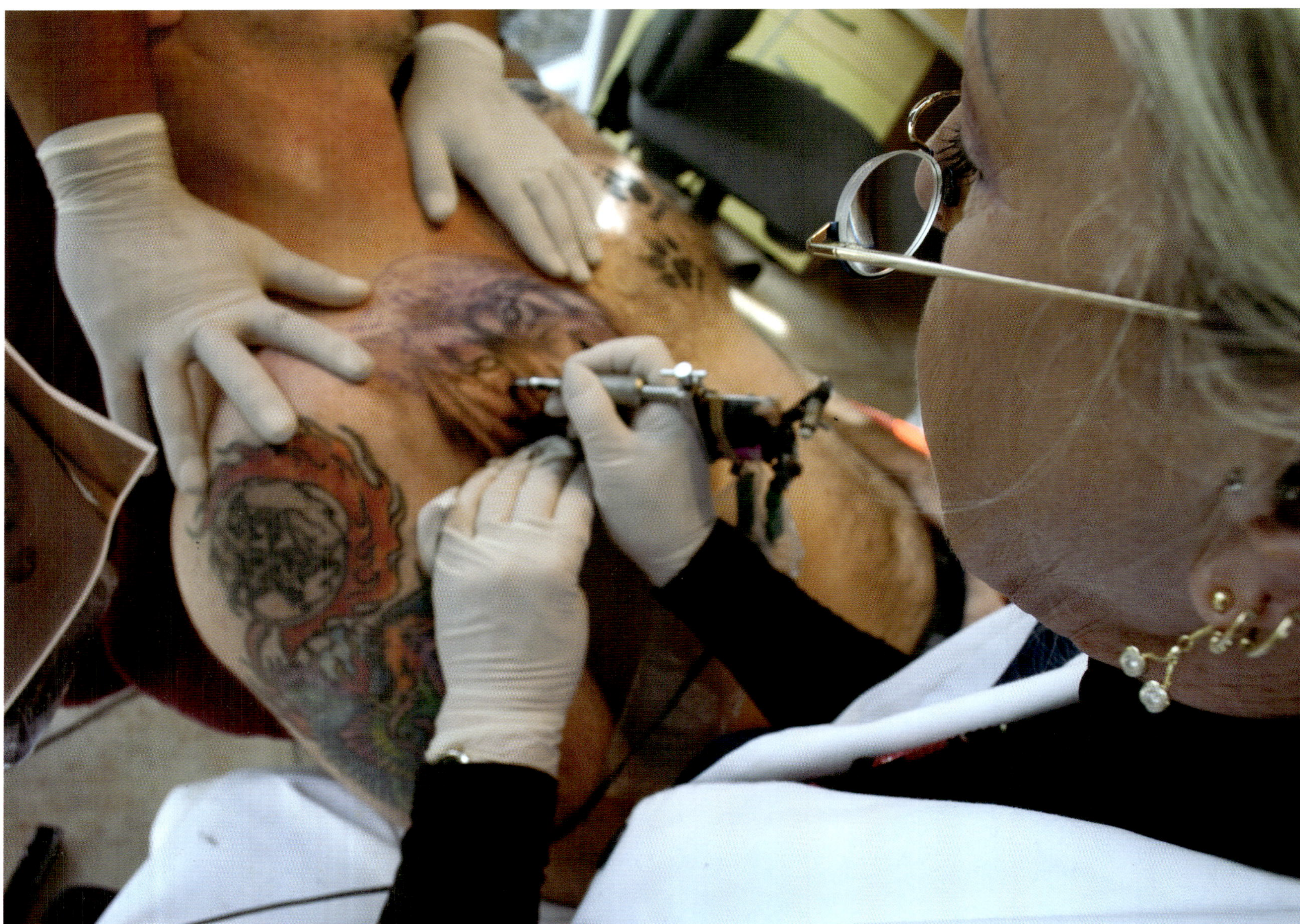

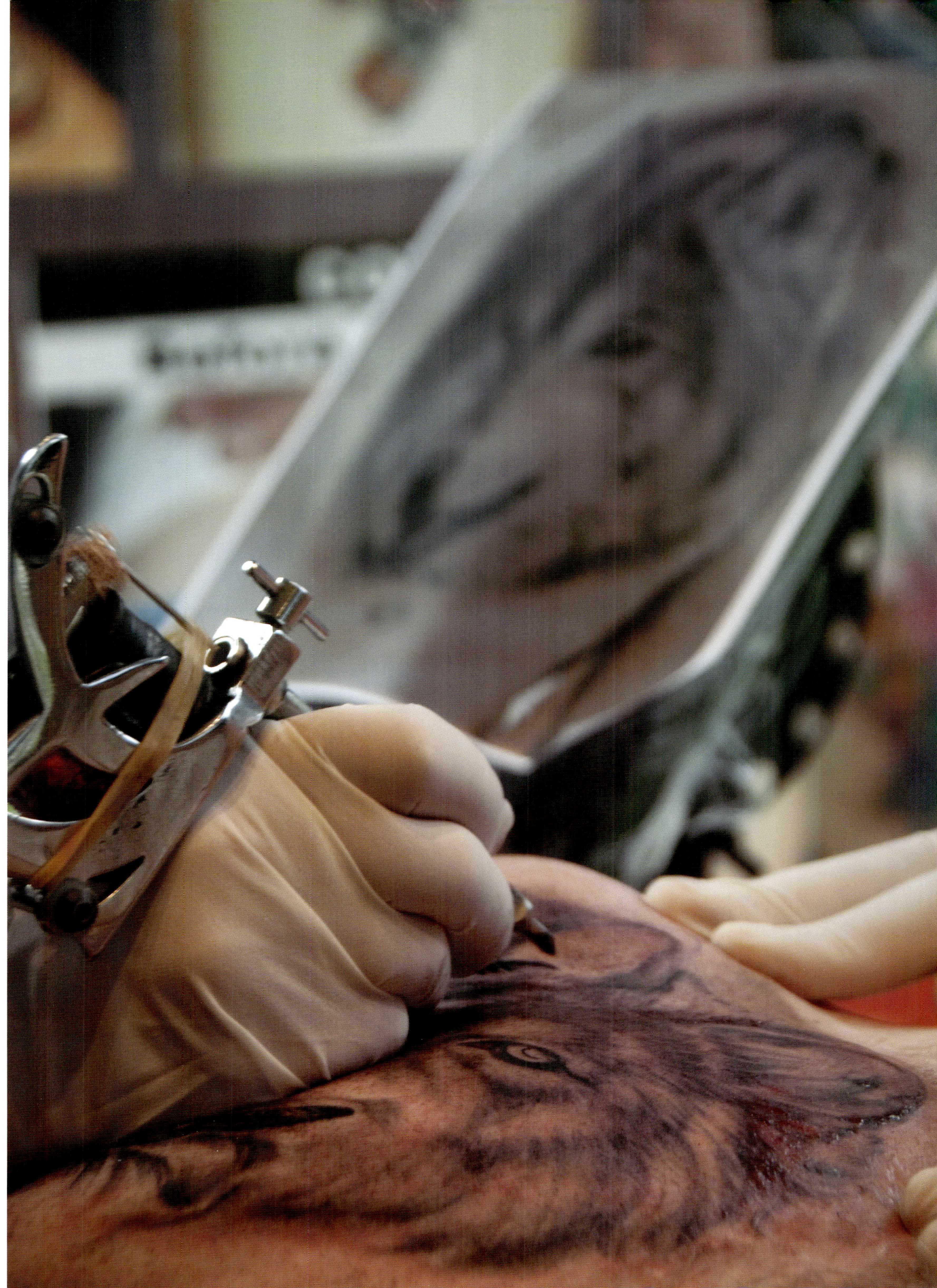

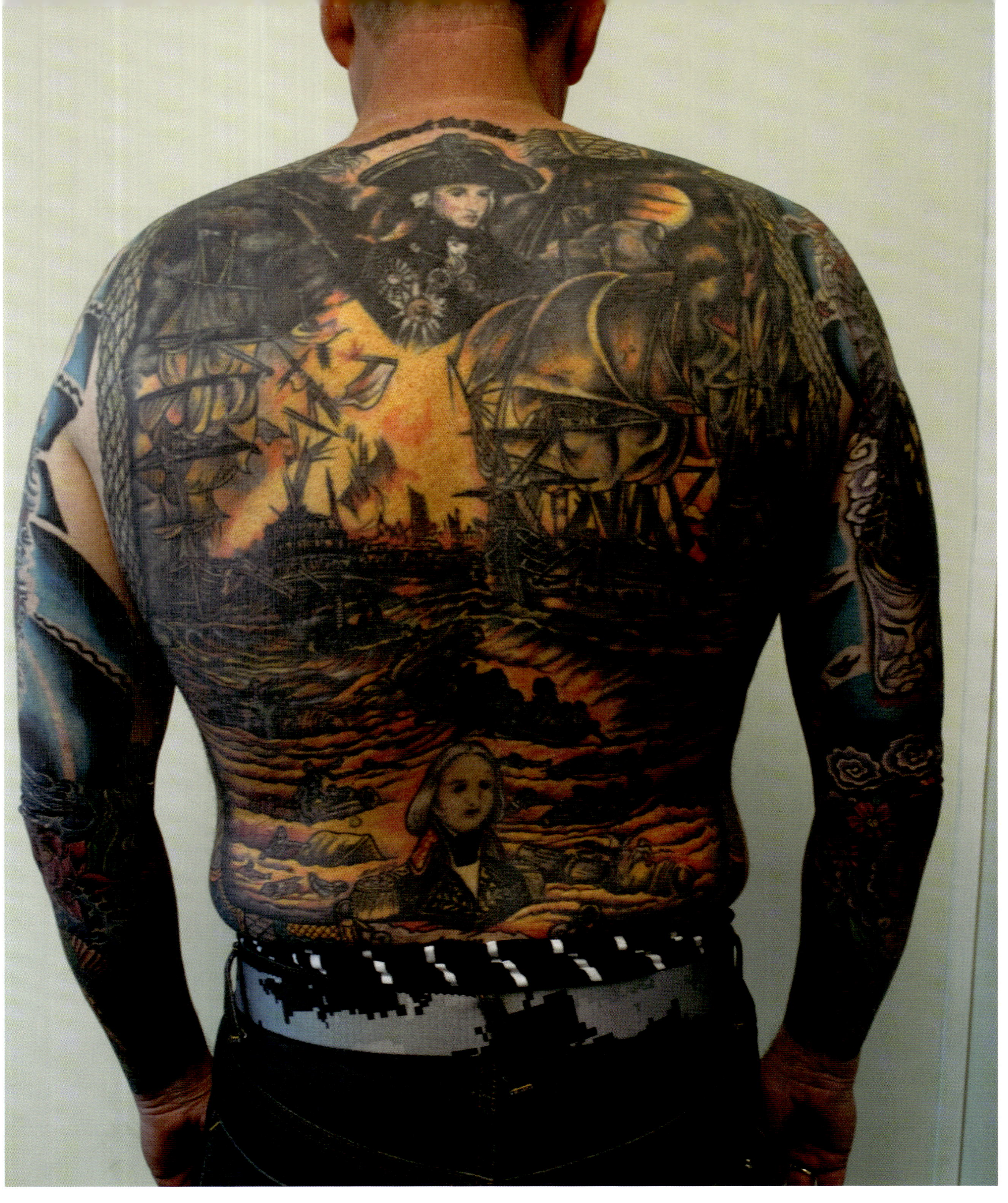

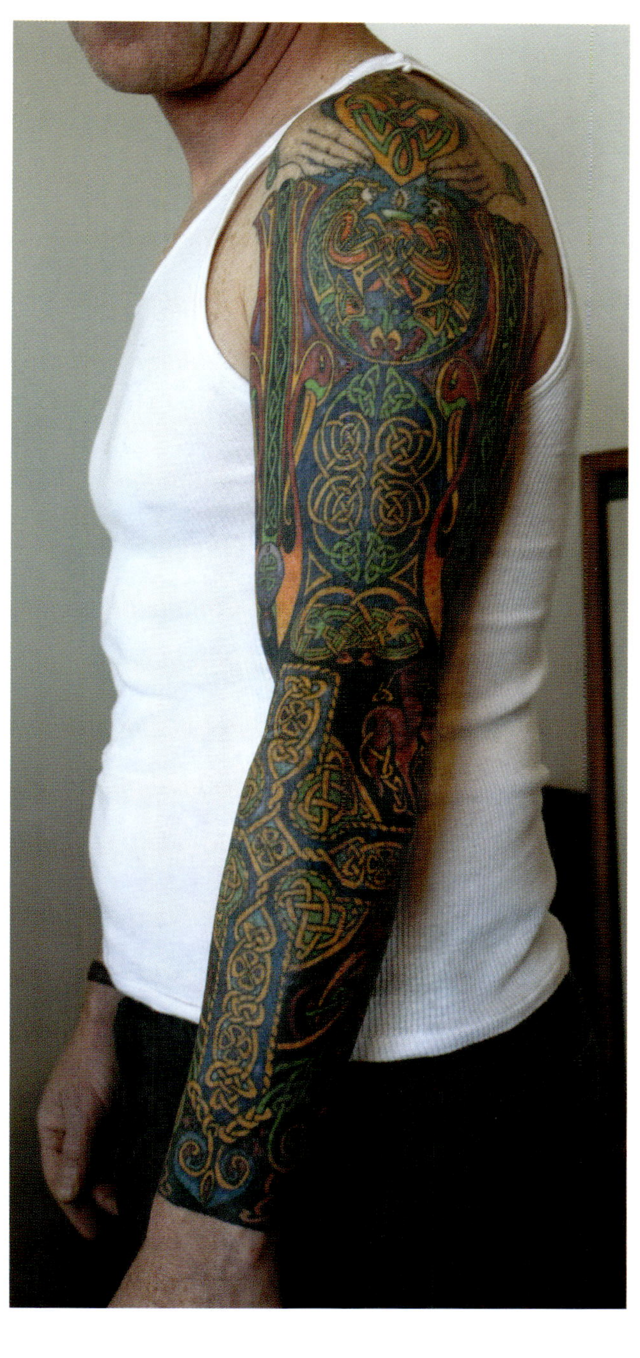

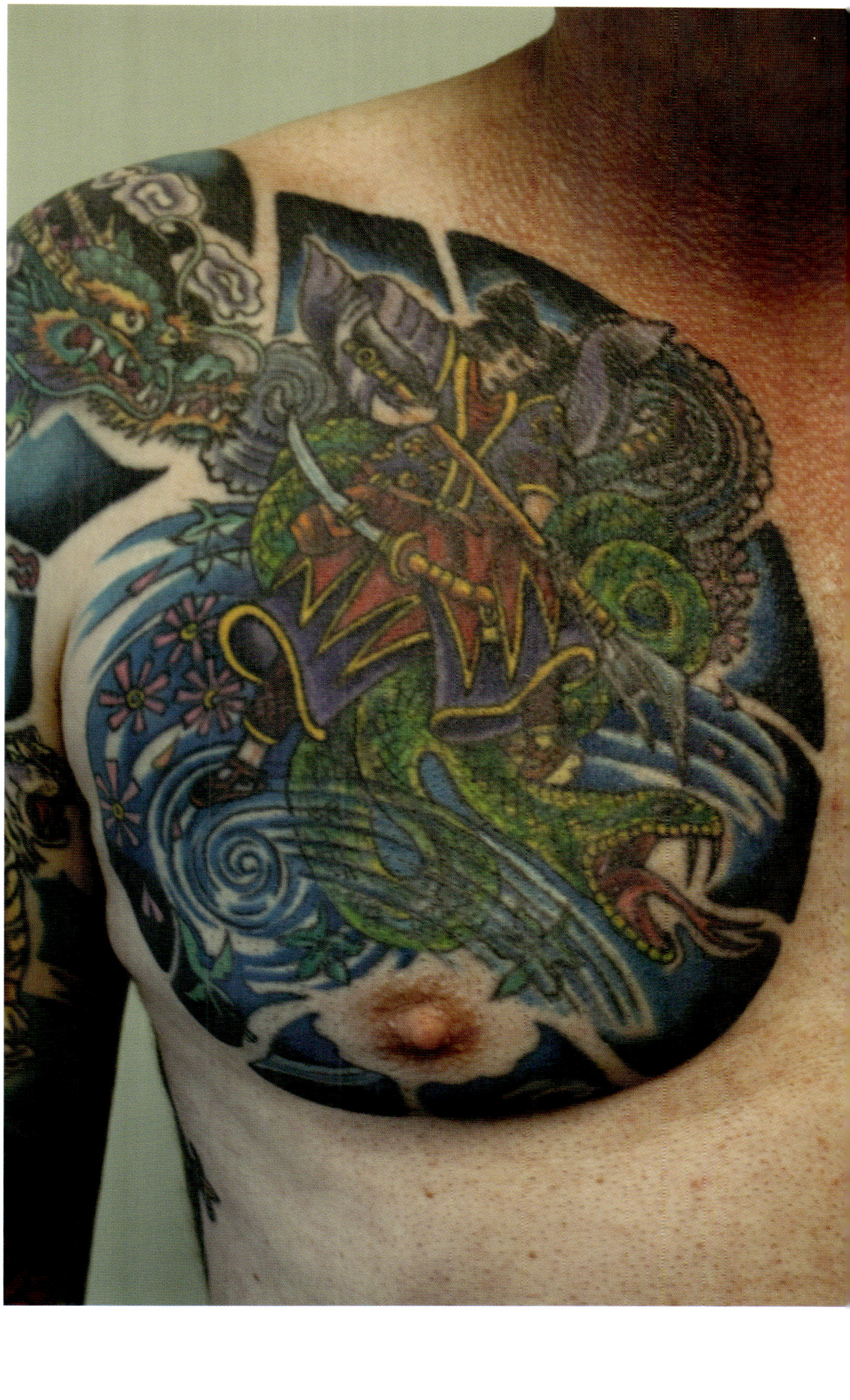

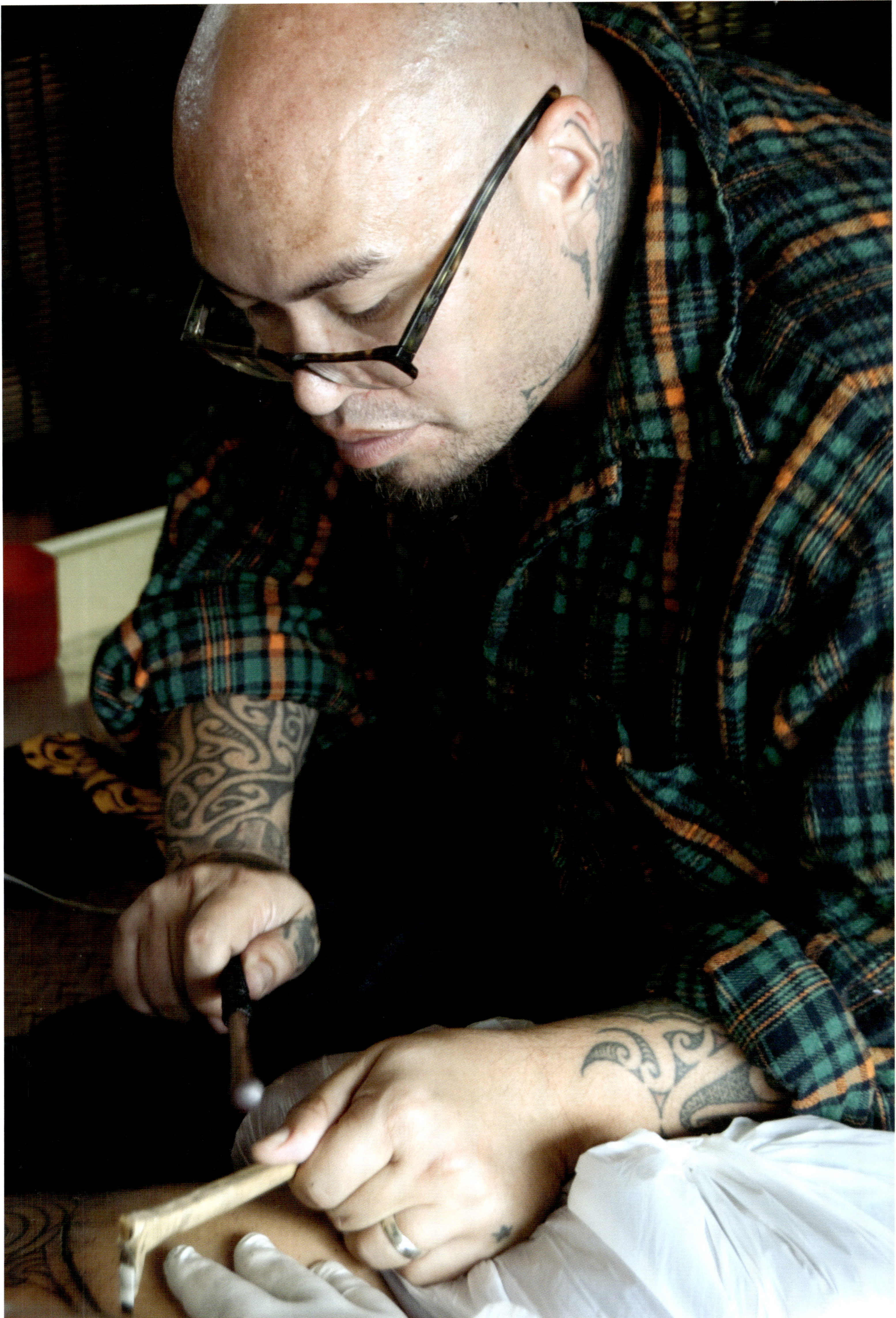

TE **RANGITU** NETANA

Te Rangitu Netana's skills in ta moko have taken him around the world and seen him tattoo a number of famous people. Despite the bright lights and the big cities he's seen, he's returned to his roots and is now living in Kerikeri, in New Zealand's Far North. His family is from Kaikohe, a small Northland town with a history of producing creative people, including renowned artist Ralph Hotere.

Te Rangitu says he got into tattooing after his family moved to Auckland when he was about 17. "We moved to the city when my dad became sick, and I started hanging out at the tattoo parlours." One of those was the Dermagraphic Tattoo Studio, owned by the late Phill Matthias. Te Rangitu started off drawing designs and it wasn't long until he was taken on as an apprentice and given the task of dealing with cover-ups, learning along the way how to make his own tattoo machines.

"An apprenticeship in those days was a lot more in-depth — but it also came with a lot more attitude. I was there about four years and then Rick Lockett started Primal Tattoo in Fanshawe Street. I helped manage that shop and finished my apprenticeship with him. It was a crazy time; it was like living with a bike gang. As a young guy it taught me what not to be like."

But he was already looking at heading in a new direction: "I knew what I wanted to do was ta moko — Maori tattooing. But I knew I couldn't do it around them so I walked away.' Despite the tough lessons he learned, he had at least mastered the art of tattooing. And it wasn't long until he met Laurie Nicholas and Gordon Hatfield, two master carvers who were teaching people at different marae around the country about ta moko. "Their job was to talk about moko and I would talk about sterilisation and how to prevent infection. I worked with them for two or three years doing that." Although the two men were relatively new to the world of tattooing, they had excelled as carvers, and had worked with Roger Ingerton.

In the mid-1990s Te Rangitu met Samoan tatau artist Paulo Suluape. Through Paulo he met other artists from Tahiti, Samoa and Tonga. Suluape talked about creating a worldwide movement of traditional tattooists, and encouraged Te Rangitu to think about the wider ties between Maori and other South Pacific cultures.

In the late 1990s he went to Europe for five years, including a 12-month stint in Amsterdam where he worked at Hanky Panky Tattoo and the Amsterdam Tattoo Museum. "I was still using the machine and trying to find myself in my own style. But the good thing was I was away from the influences back here." It made him realise how archaic tattooing was in New Zealand, with most artists still using single needles and rotary machines.

Te Rangitu also spent time in the UK, where he worked at Temple Tattoo in Brighton and did various guest spots and conventions. "It was fun there. They're very creative and always pushing the envelope. It was a good place to work. It also made me look into my Maori roots."

Through Paulo Suluape he met the legendary Hawaiian tattooist Keone Nunes while he was in the UK, and asked the master to teach him how to use traditional tools. He then spent a few months in Hawaii with Keone, and says they still keep in regular contact and discuss the art form.

During his time as a tattooist Te Rangitu has had some famous clients including Cypress Hill's DJ Muggs, Sonique and Robbie Williams. Despite all he has achieved he's still aiming for higher goals. "To be fully traditional I need to drop the machine that I've used for the past 22 years. The machine for me is a man-made thing and it creates egos. The mana of the person is in the person's hands.

"With the uhi, or chisel, the mana is separate. You tattoo someone and they become like family. You've got more responsibility as an artist because you are dealing with their families' stories, with their whakapapa. When I started doing it there was talk about it being tapu, you should leave it alone, are you the right people to be doing it? But someone had to do it. We went to Europe to try and educate them on how sacred it is."

But there are still realities he has to face on a day-to day-basis when deciding whether to use a conventional tattoo machine or the uhi, he accepts. "One pays the bills and the other one everyone is scared of."

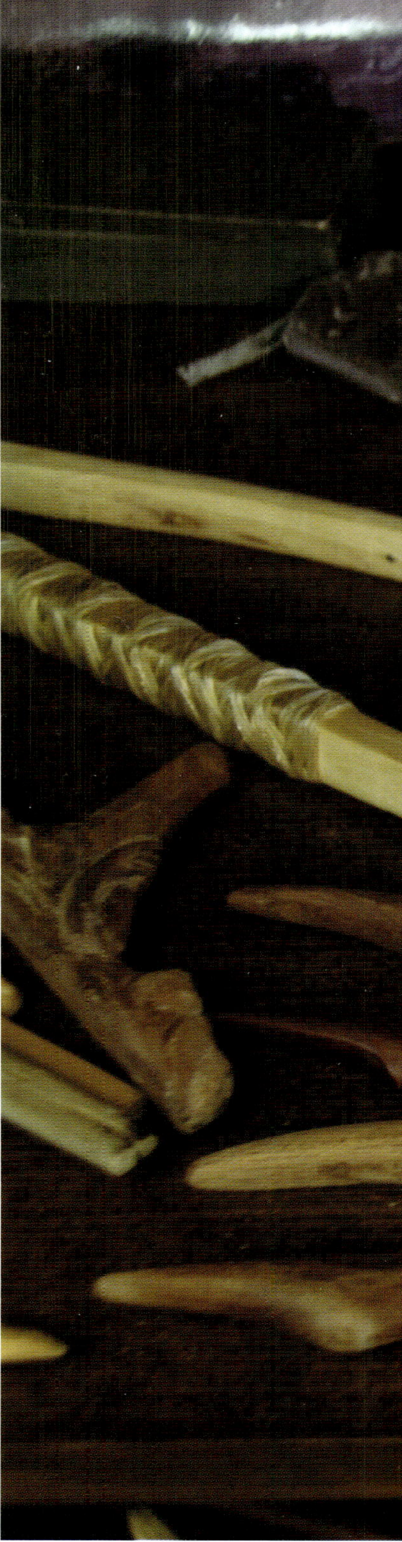

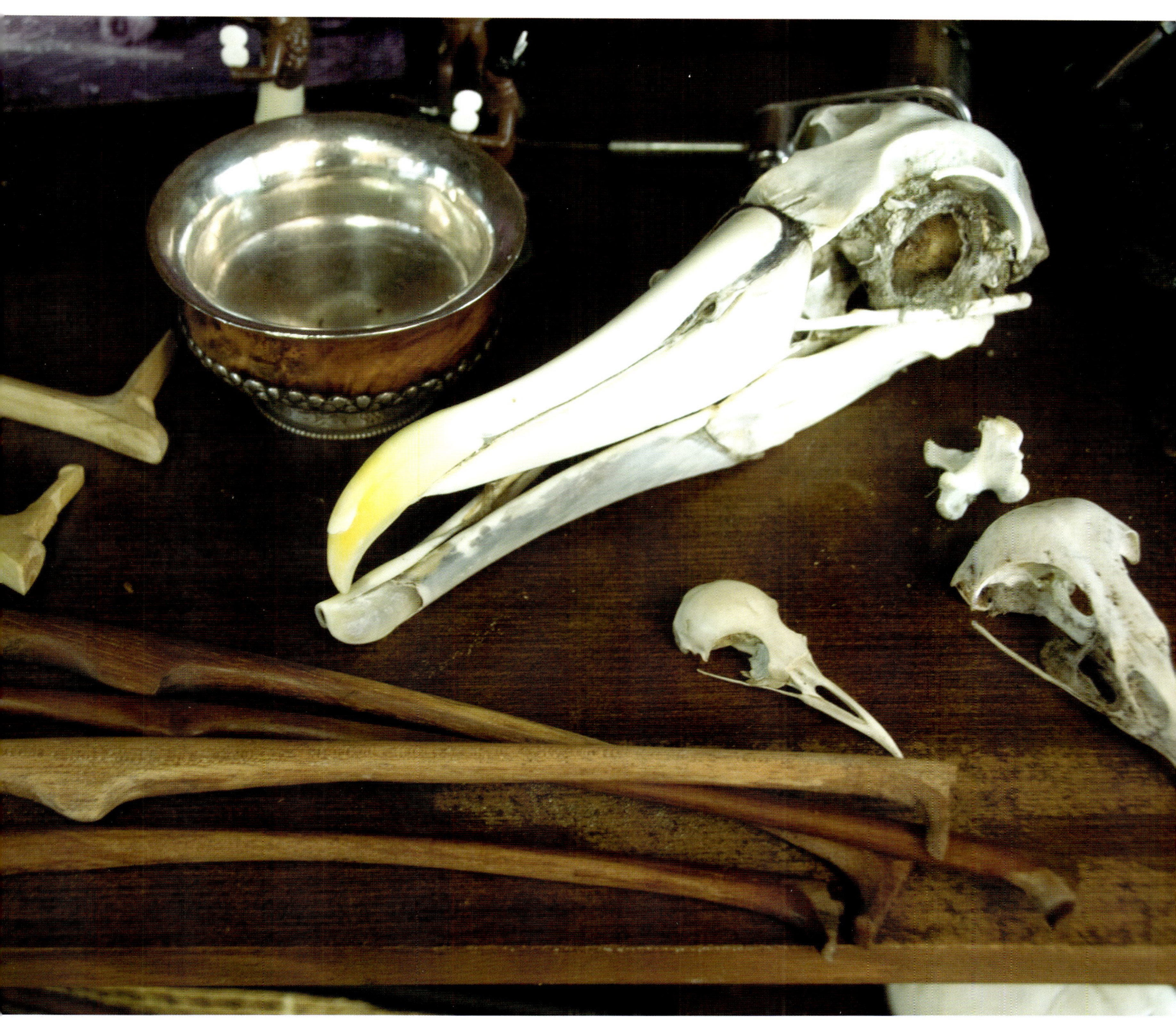

Traditional uhi, made from toroa (albatross) bone.

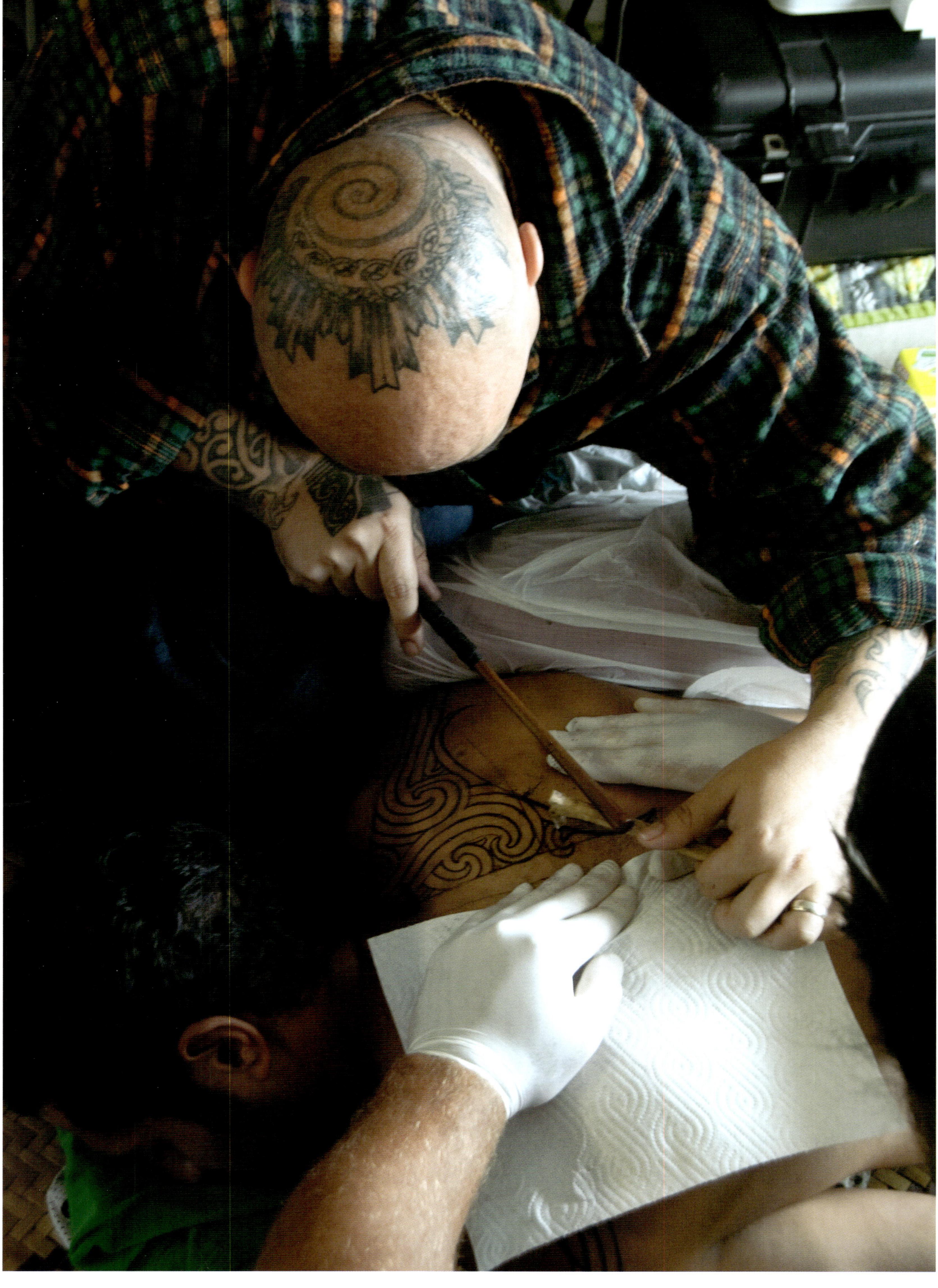

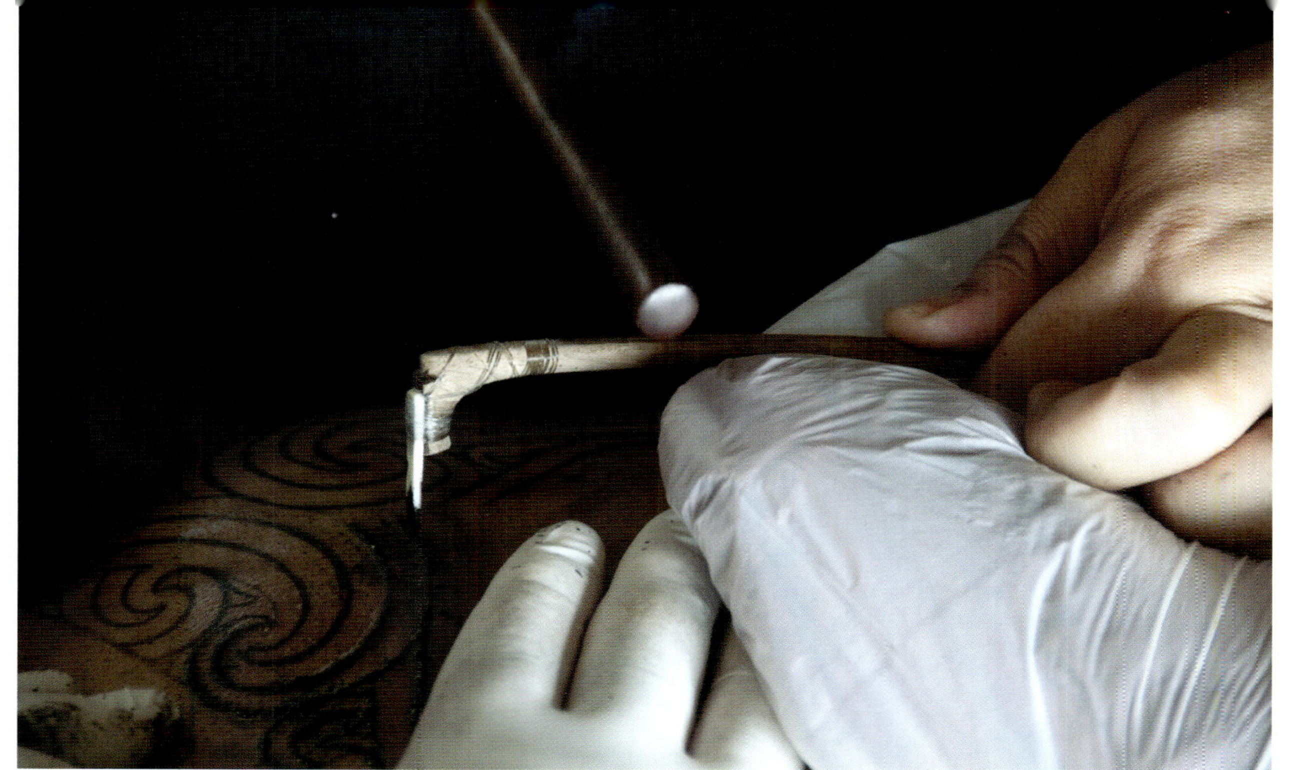

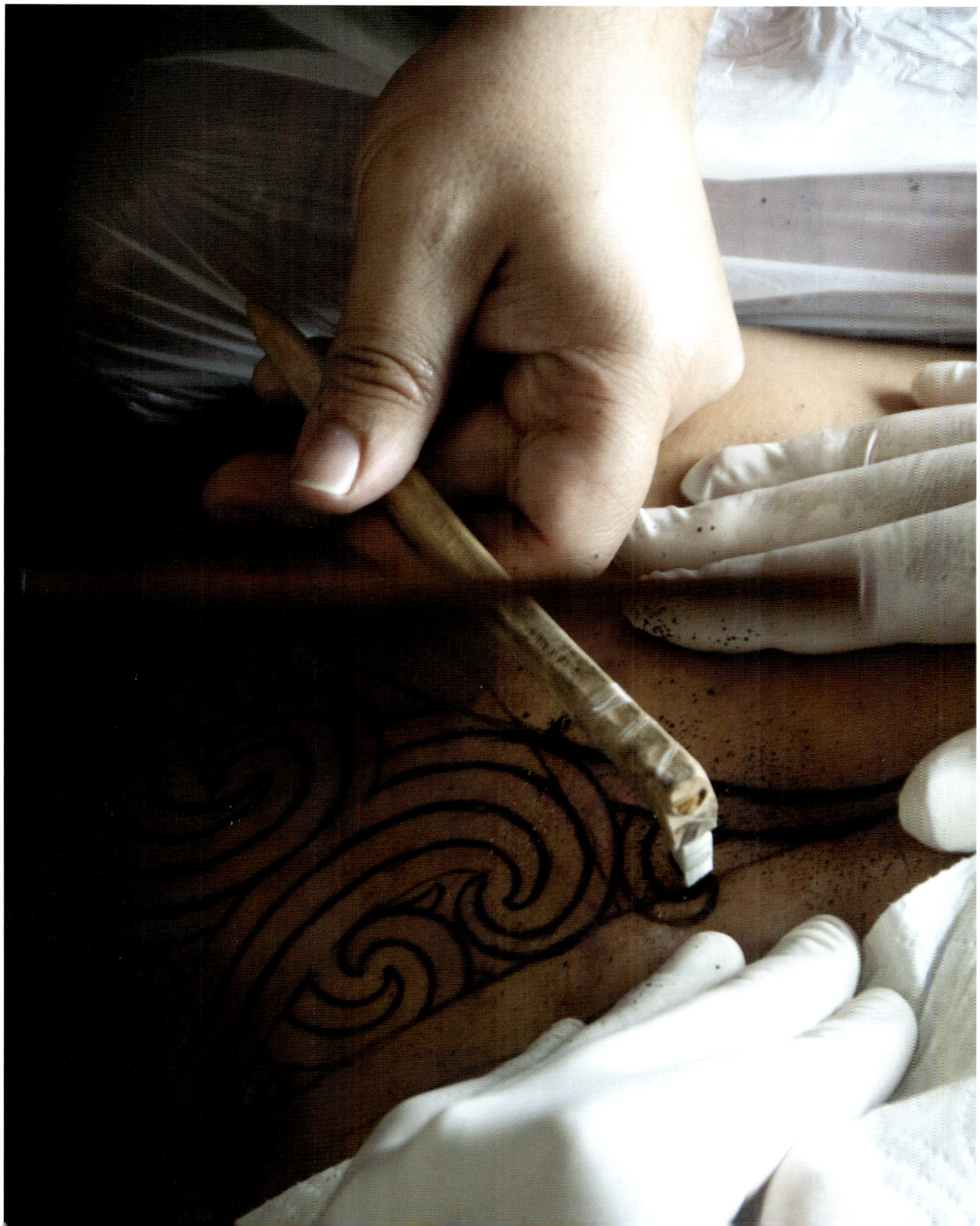

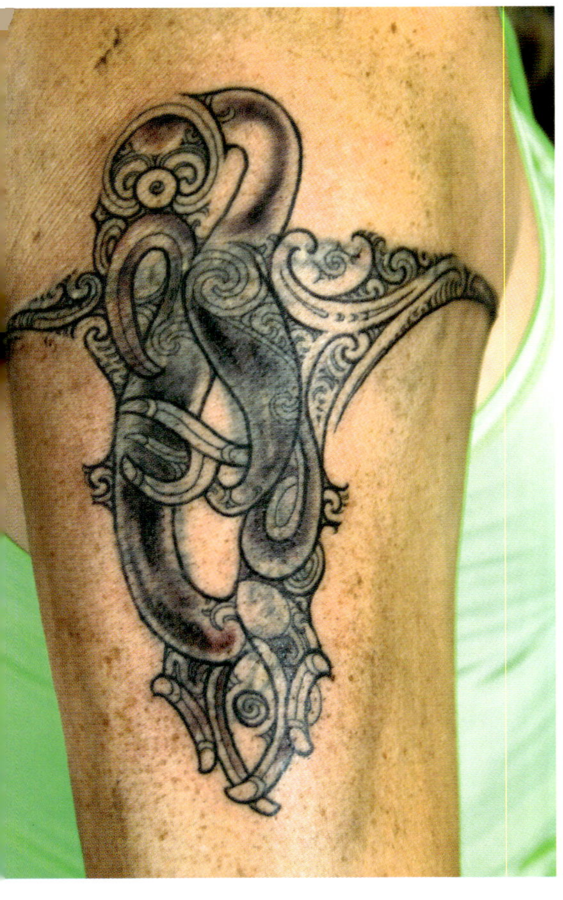

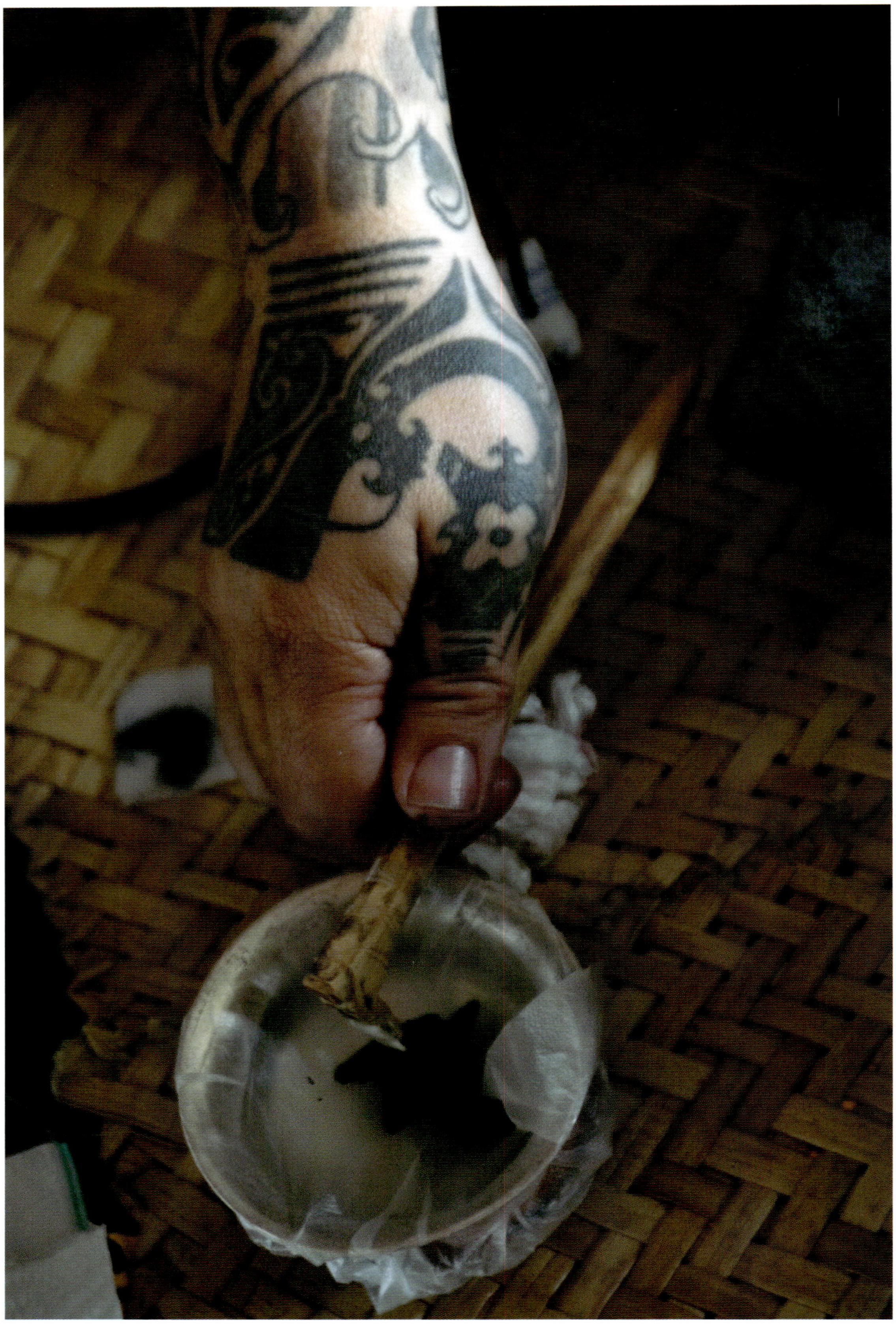

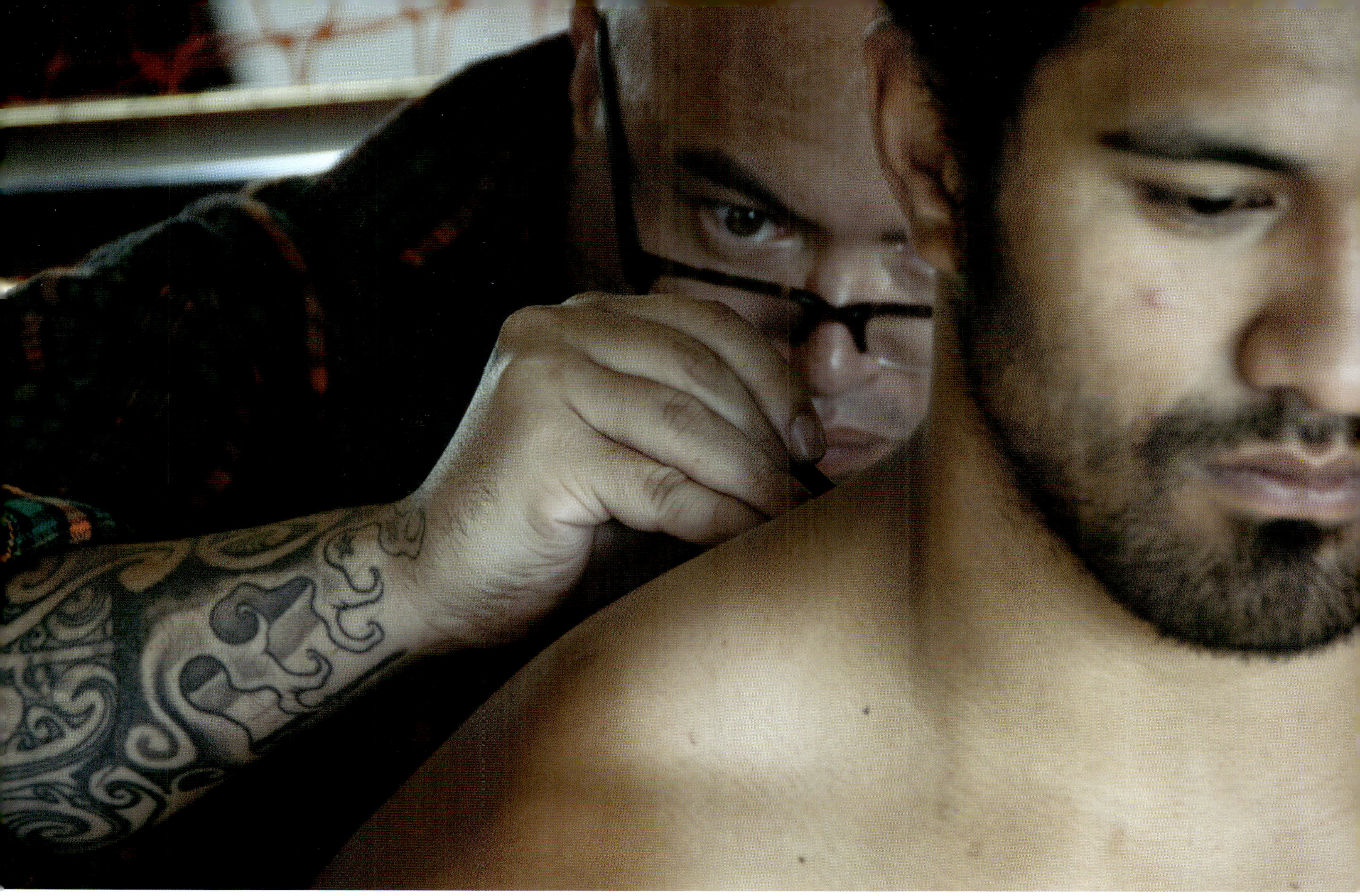

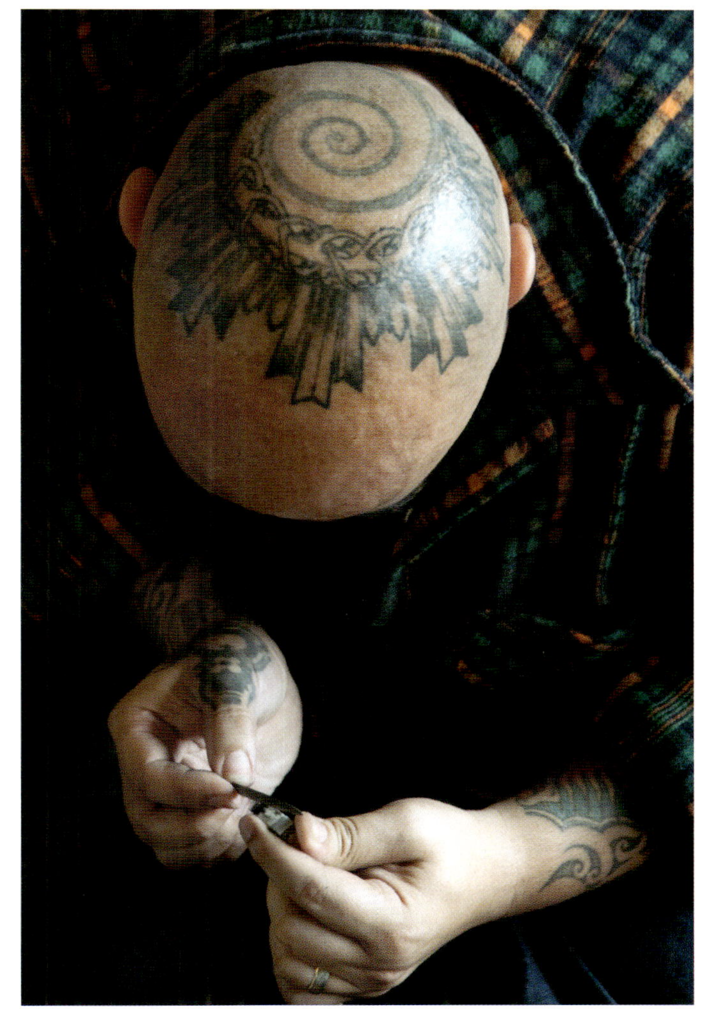

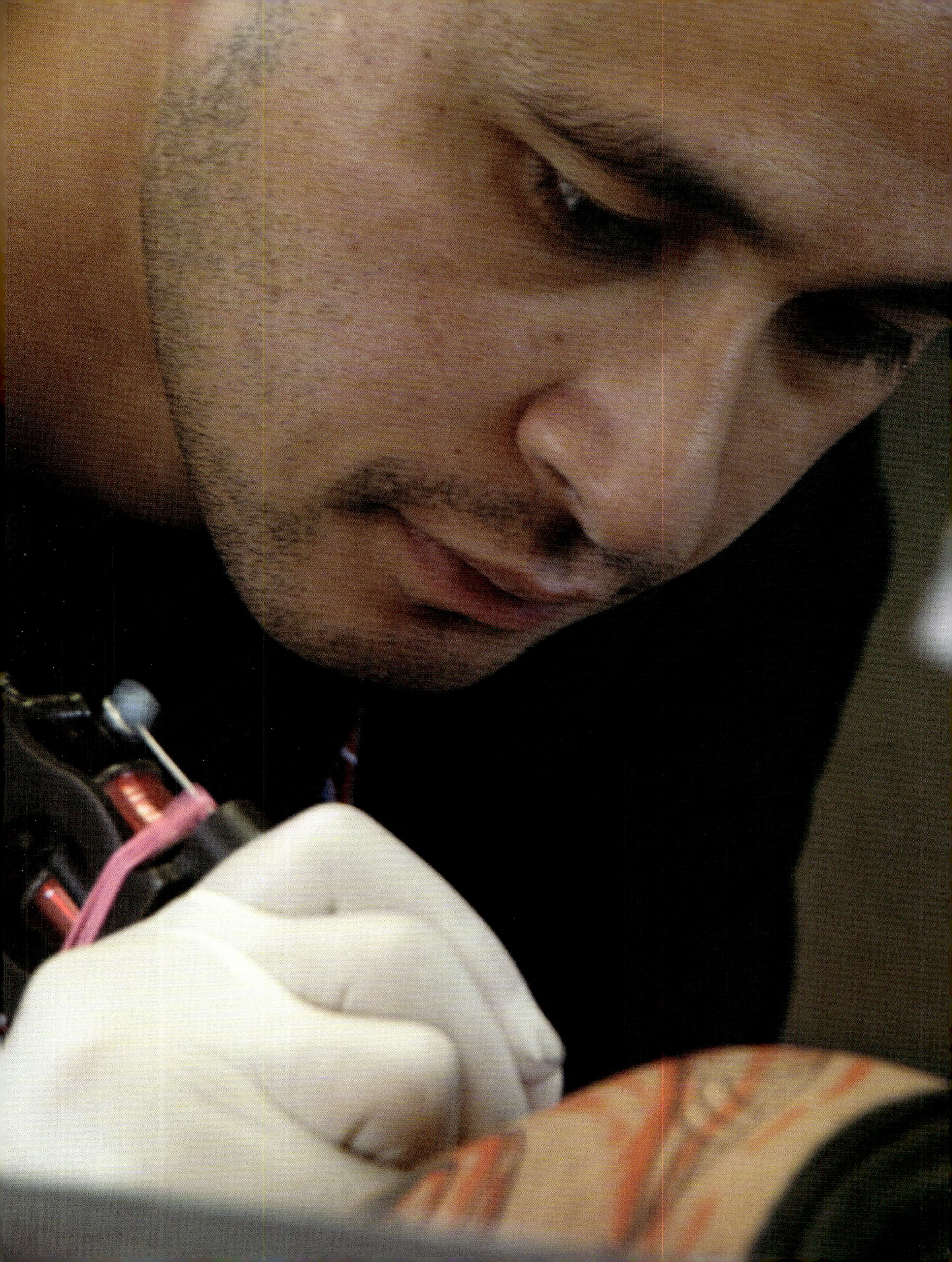

DWAIN **AIONO**

There are not too many tattooists out there whose first customer was one of their parents. But Dwain Aiono's father had always wanted to get a tattoo, and after seeing his son's artistic talents he bought him a machine. It was Dwain's first attempt at a half-sleeve and it took him 16 hours from start to finish. Now, whenever he sees his dad's tattoo, it brings back memories: "It's a good reminder of how I started. When I was little I used to draw on myself and my friends, but I'd never thought about tattooing until my dad asked me."

While living in Auckland, he started doing tattoos for friends and began to gain a reputation for his skills. Then Dwain decided to relocate to Hastings and started Spacifik Ink in 2008. Initially he worked out of a home studio, then in 2011 he opened a new shop in central Napier. Business is good, and he is constantly booked a month in advance.

"Most people come to me for Pacific Maori stuff because I know the patterns. I would like to do more portraiture and Japanese-style work but you've got to do what the customer wants. Most customers want Maori- and Samoan-style stuff. So you've just got to roll with it."

And in most cases, Dwain's work is freehand: "I do stencil if I have to and it's a portrait, but I'd rather do it freehand. The customer is getting a one-off piece, that's what it's about. These days it's about the art, not just the tattoo."

Lately he's been getting a lot of customers from Europe, among them a customer from the Czech Republic who got a three-quarter sleeve from the top of the shoulder to the forearm. Dwain spent three days working on it: six hours on the first day, four hours the next and another two hours to finish. "And I did another guy from Holland. He'd been on a rugby tour, had ended up in Napier and wanted a Pacific-style tattoo."

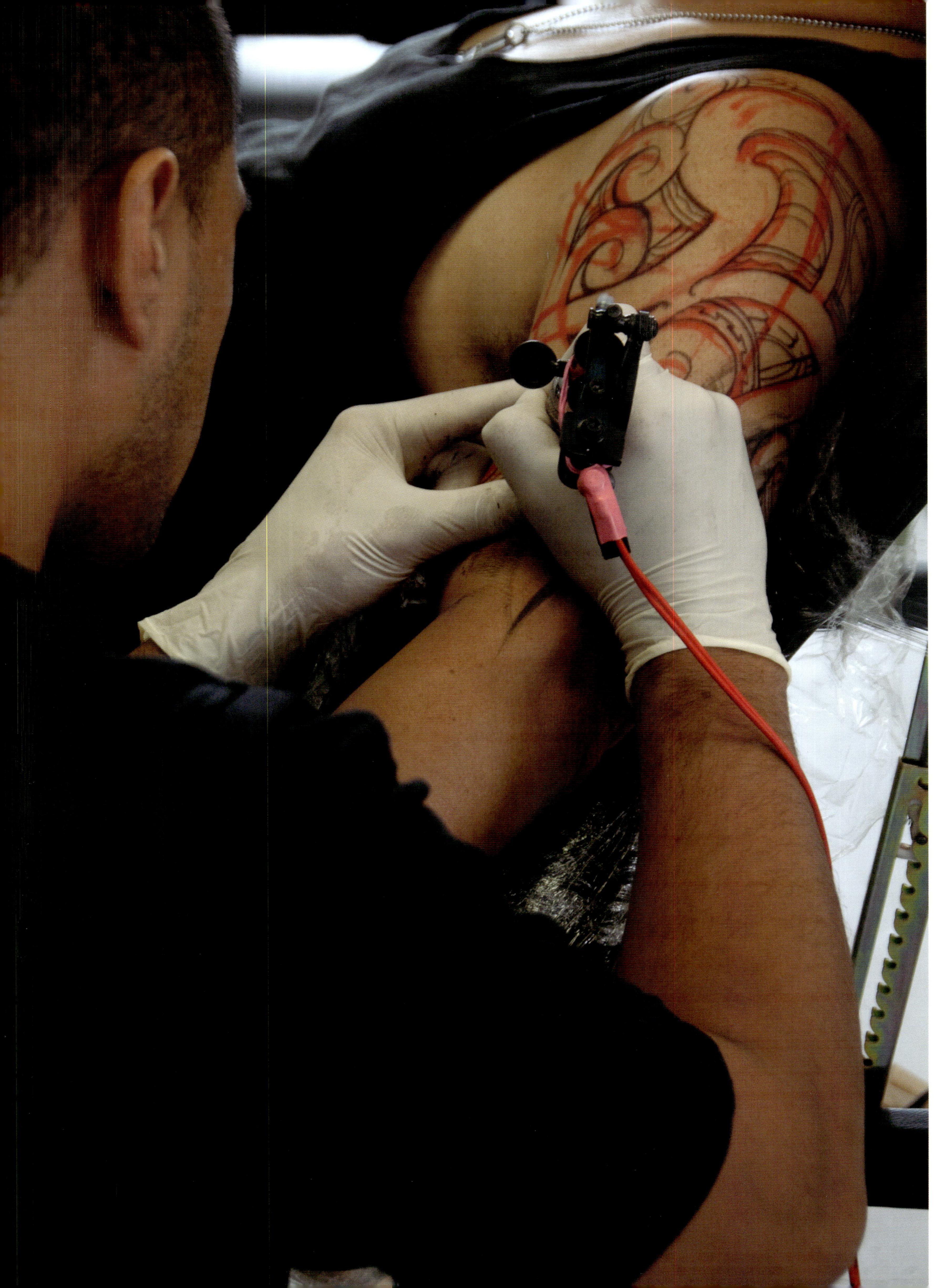

Dwain doesn't stick to one style in a tattoo and likes to blend Samoan, Maori and other Polynesian patterns. "I like to mix them up. You can put a lot more detail and depth into it."

He's used to working by himself, but recently took on an apprentice. "The industry is continuing to grow; there are so many tattooists out there it's crazy. Unfortunately there are still a lot of backyard operators and I spend a lot of time covering that stuff up. Some people think tattooing is a get-rich-quick scheme, but if you don't want to put in the hard yards you shouldn't be a tattooist."

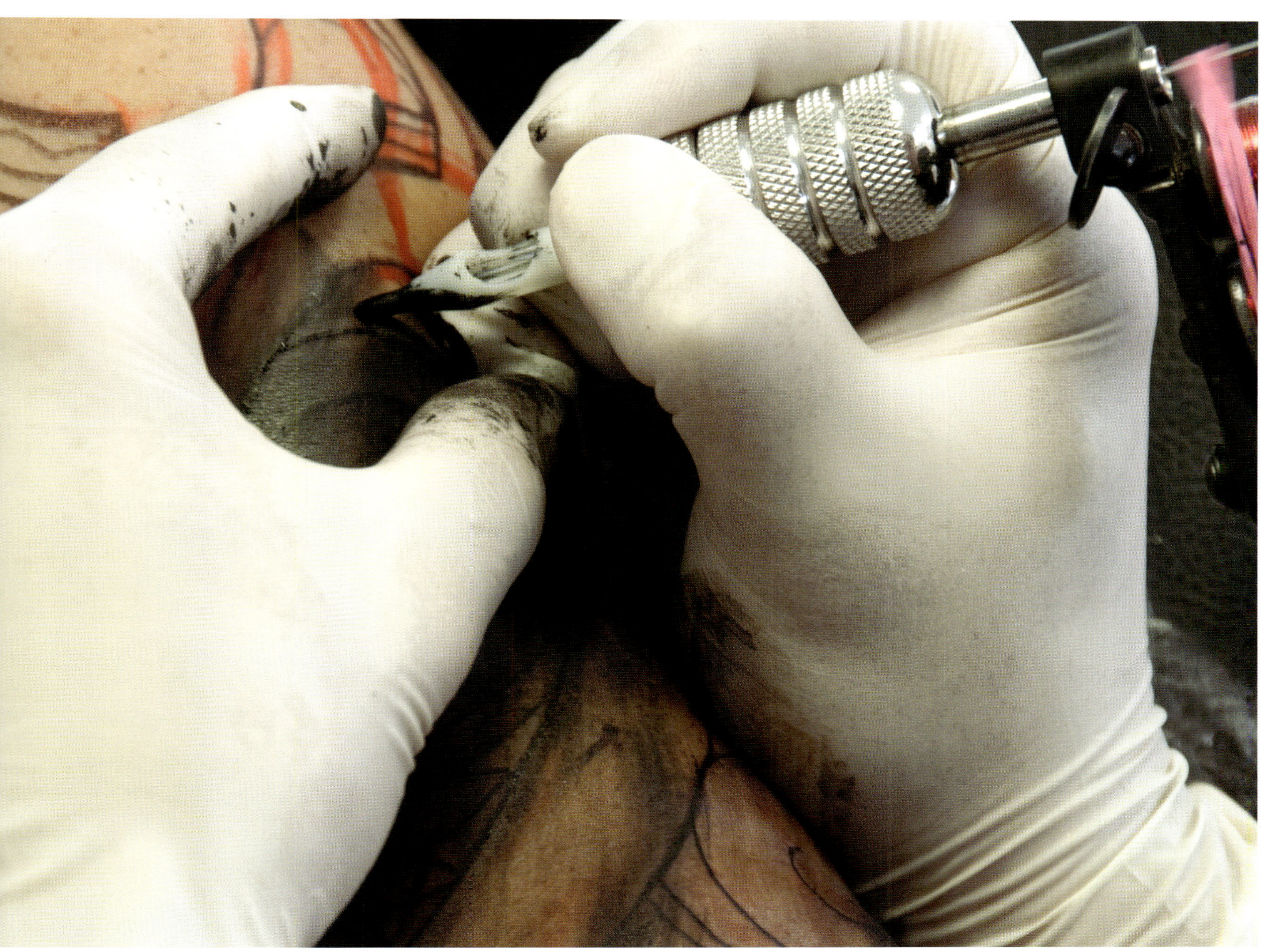

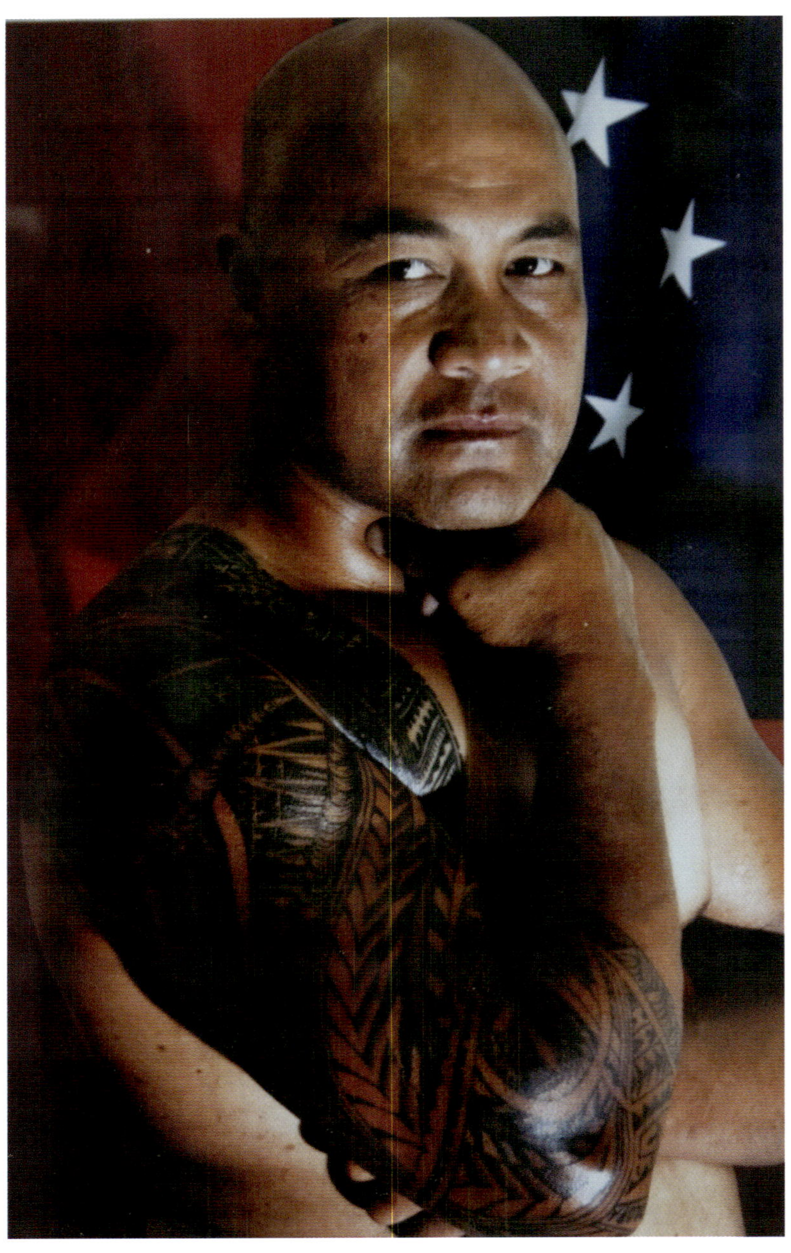

Mike Mu Aiono, Dwain's father.

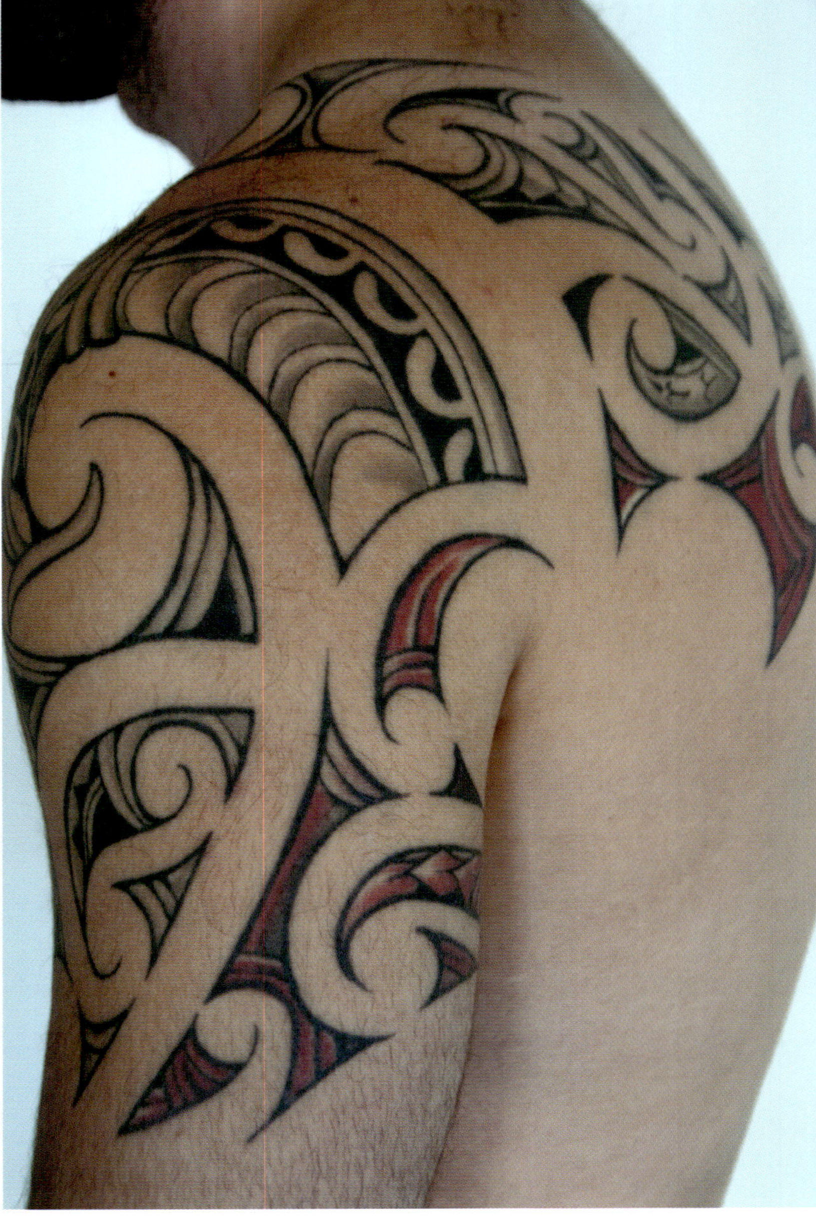

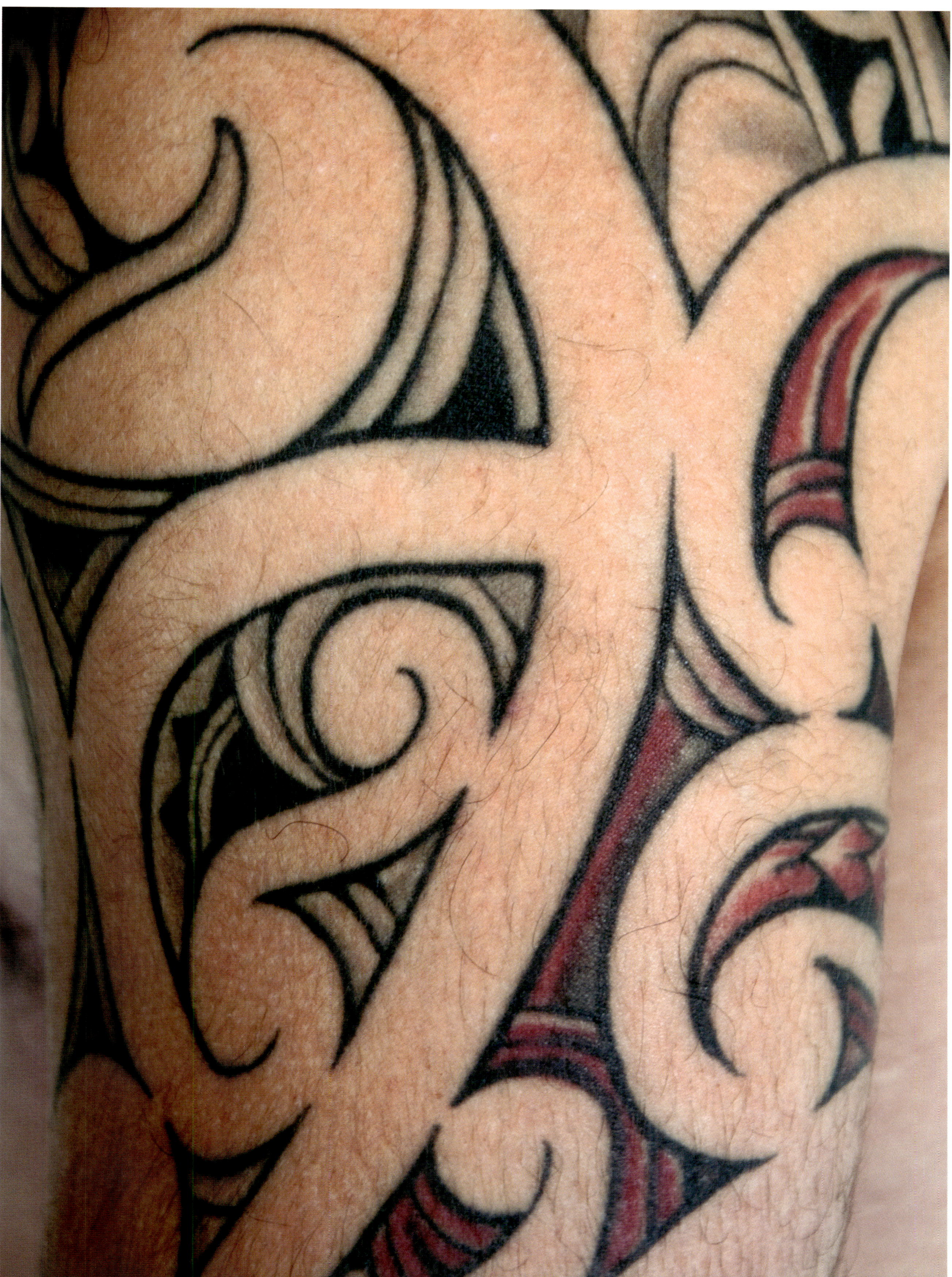

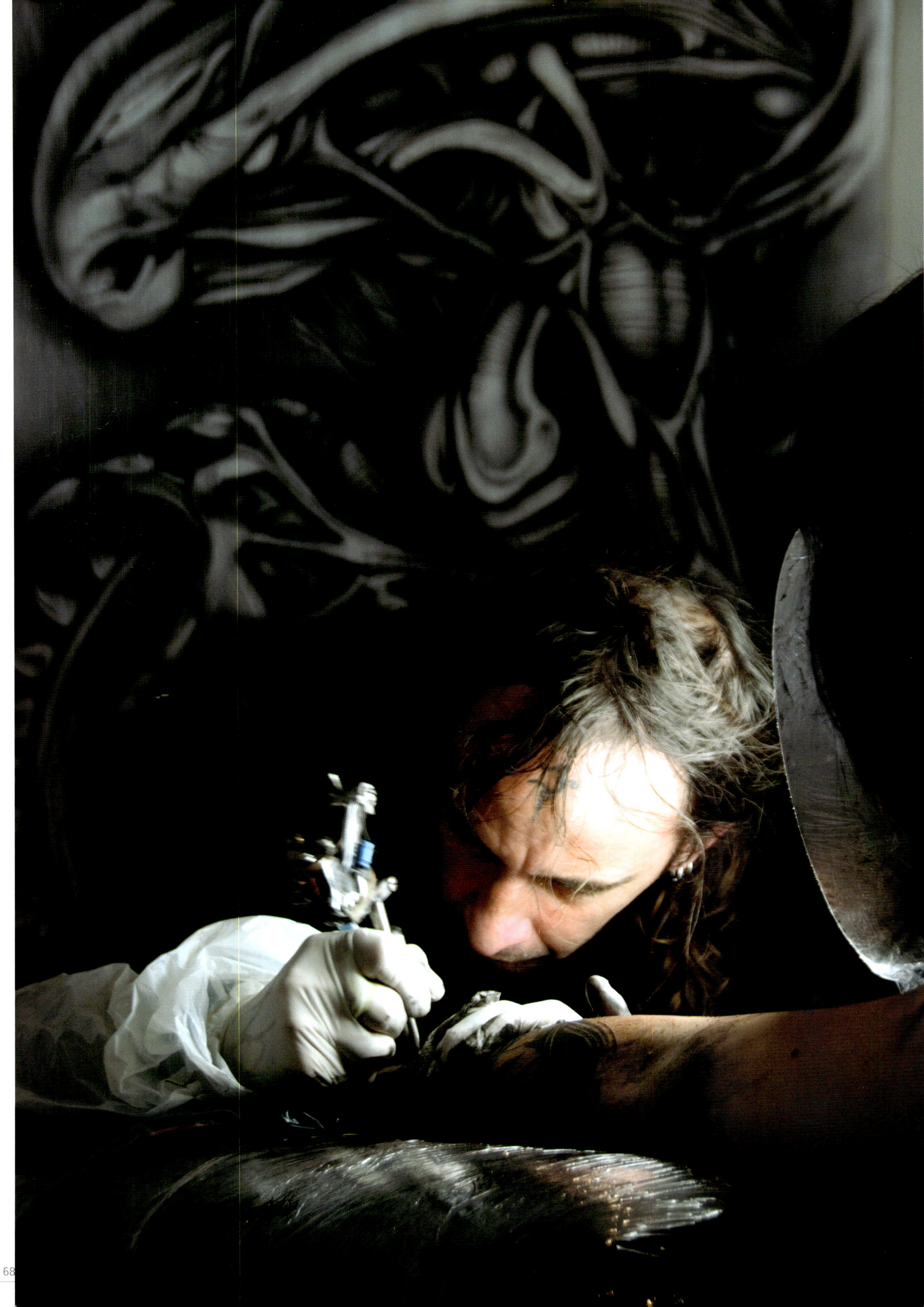

JASON **HARDWICK**

BLACK DAHLIAS TATTOOING

Just five minutes from the west coast and 20 minutes from Mt Taranaki you'll find Jason Hardwick's studio in the small town of Hawera. He's busy working on a new tattoo. It's a dimly lit studio and he's using a converted dentist's light and mirror to get up close for the detail work — a bit of Kiwi DIY at its finest. "It's bloody good, it doesn't mess with your eyes too much," he says.

The walls of his Hawera studio are covered with some of the awards and accolades he's received over the years. He proudly displays his membership certificate from the US-based National Tattoo Association, signed by secretary and legendary tattooist Bill Funk. "There are only a couple of us in New Zealand who are members. I regard that as one of my biggest achievements," he says.

Jason moved to the Taranaki with his family in 1996, as he thought it would be a better place to bring up his children. "And it's a great place to tattoo. Being so close to great surf and the mountains means I'm never short of customers. It's only in recent years that there's been an influx of tattooists into Taranaki. They are popping up everywhere — it's unbelievable."

Originally from Papakura in South Auckland, Jason has been tattooing since he was 19. Largely self-taught, he's picked up tips and been influenced by many other artists over the years. When he first came down to Taranaki he worked at the Tattooing Collective in Fitzroy, but he decided to go it alone and opened Black Dahlias Tattooing in 2002.

He got the name for the studio after watching an unsolved murder show on television about a woman nicknamed Black Dahlia killed in the United States. "I thought that would be a good name for a studio. I do any style of tattooing, from really fine to really bold. I do a lot of freehand. But a lot of people still come to me with their own designs. I probably do 60 to 70 percent freehand and the rest are transfers," he says. He doesn't tattoo ready-made designs "off the wall" but prefers to do one-off creations.

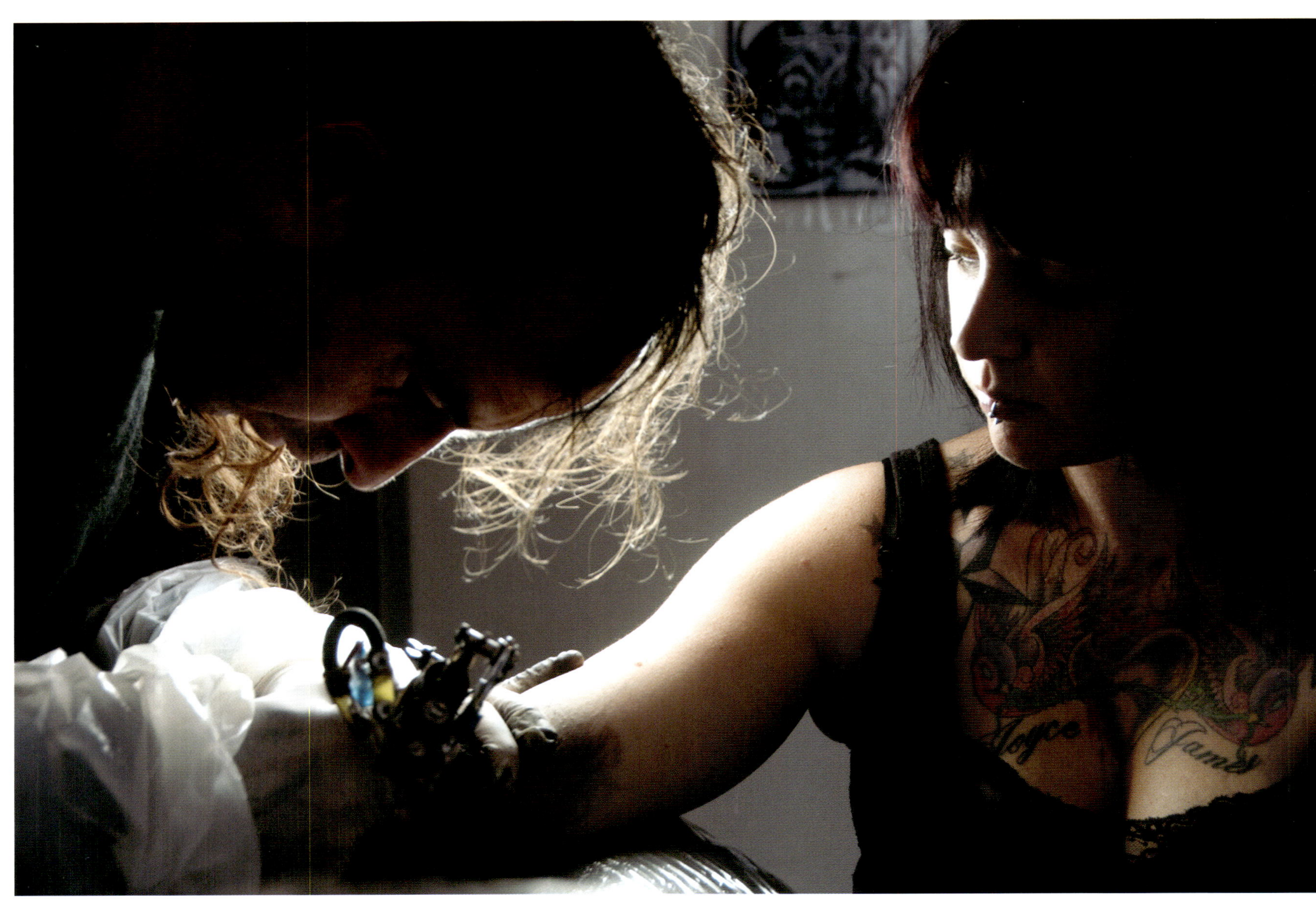

After four and half hours' work, Jason's finishing the tattoo
he started that morning. The piece includes three shades of
black and three shades of grey, and a lot of detailed shading.

Fellow Taranaki tattooist Paul Gledhill speaks highly of
Jason's work: "I can tell if it's Jason's tattooing as soon as
someone walks through the door. He's got a very distinct
style." Paul believes the other thing that makes Jason stand
out is his speed: "He's one of the fastest tattooists I know."

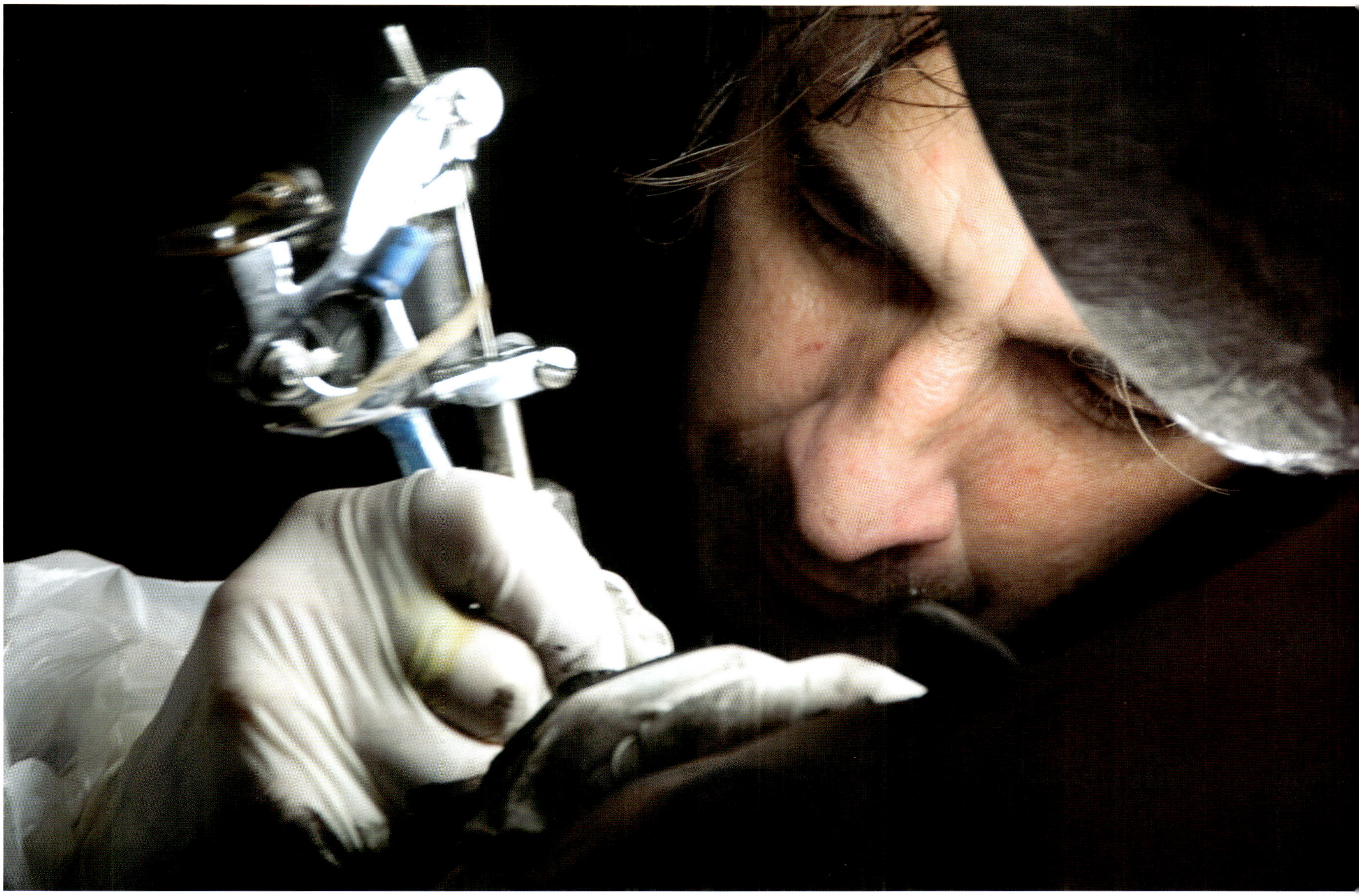

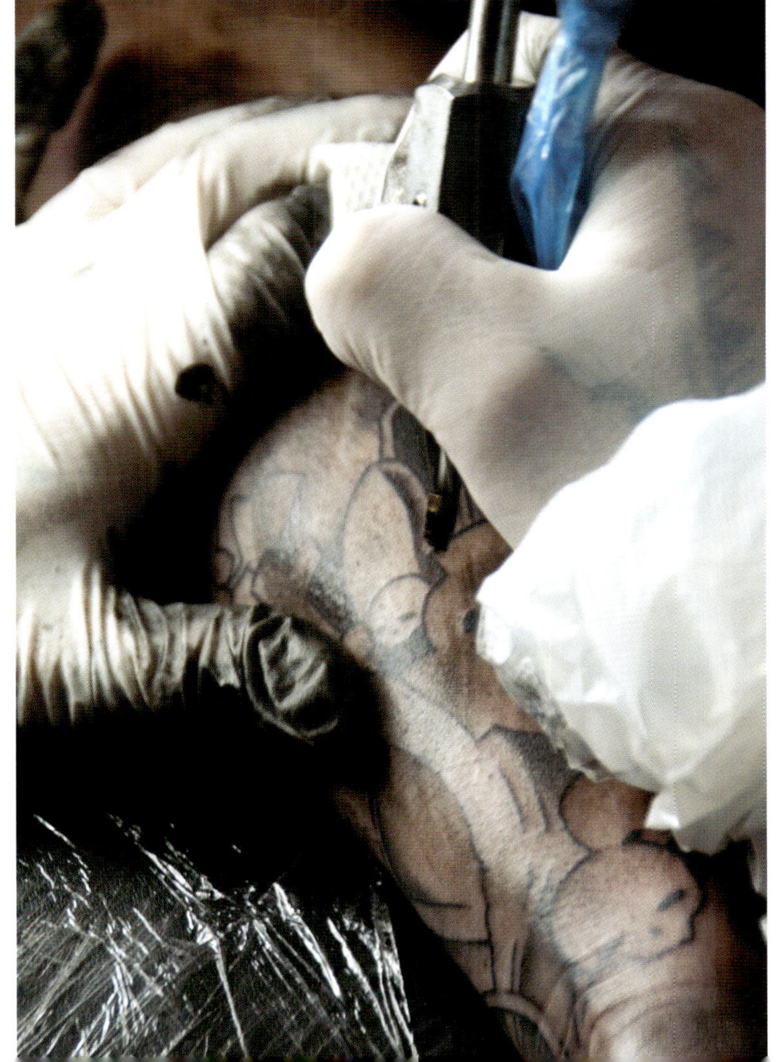

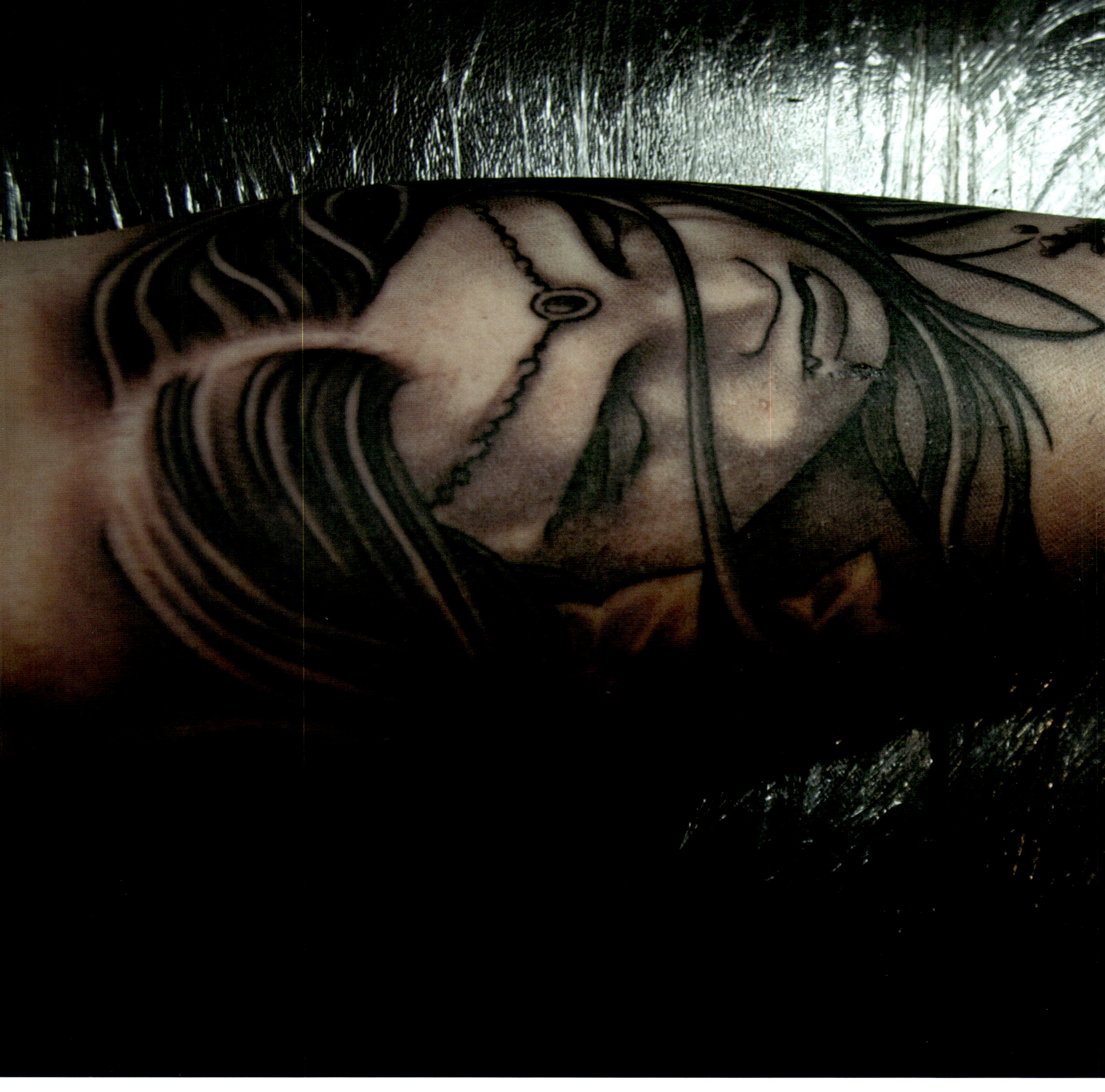

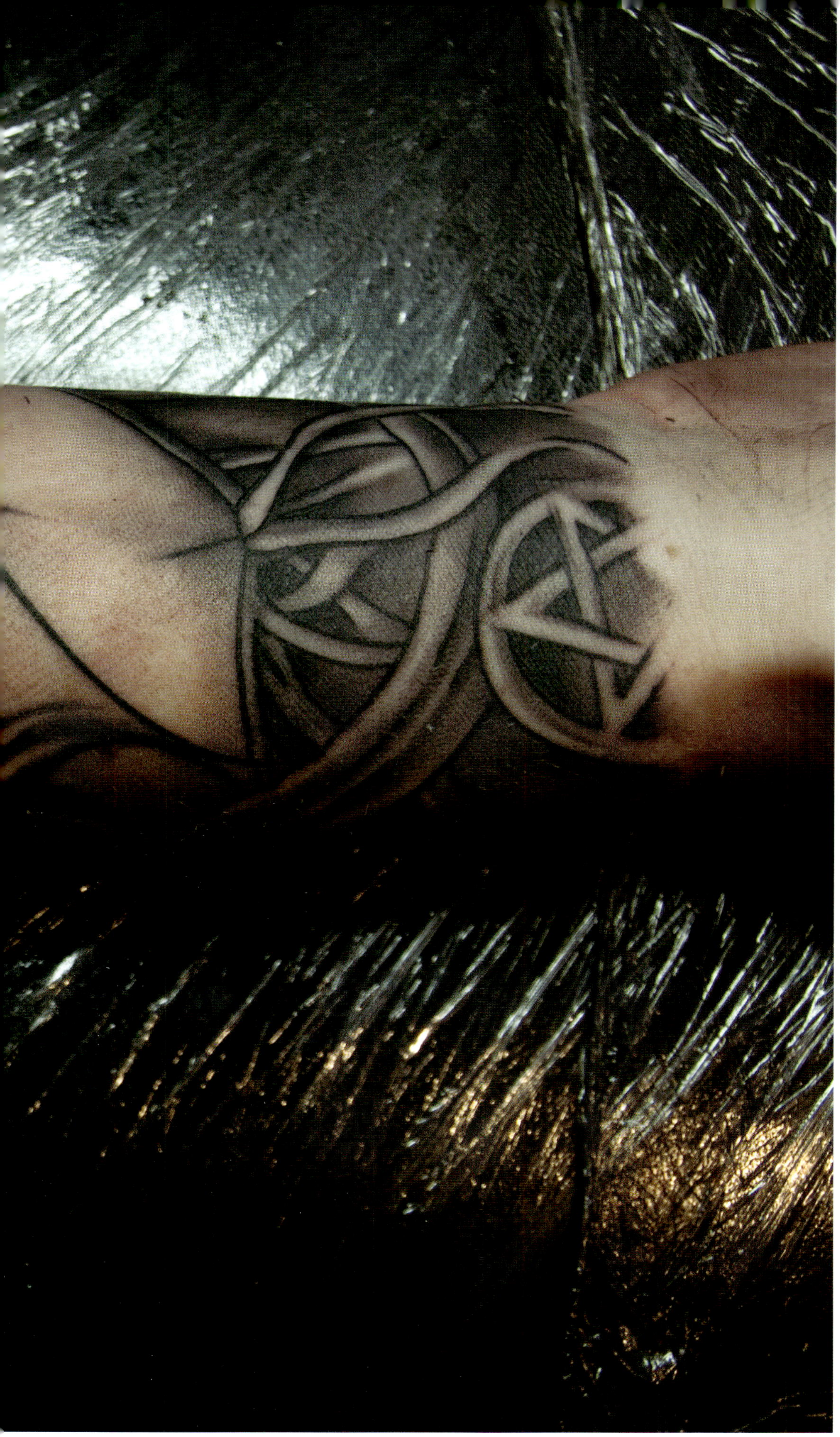

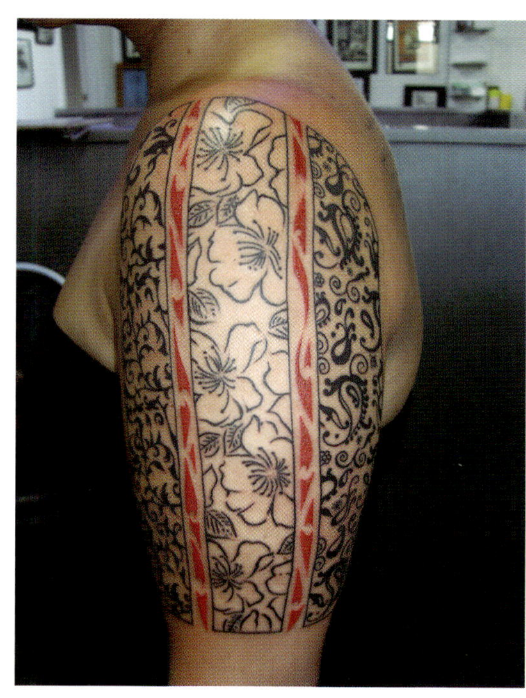

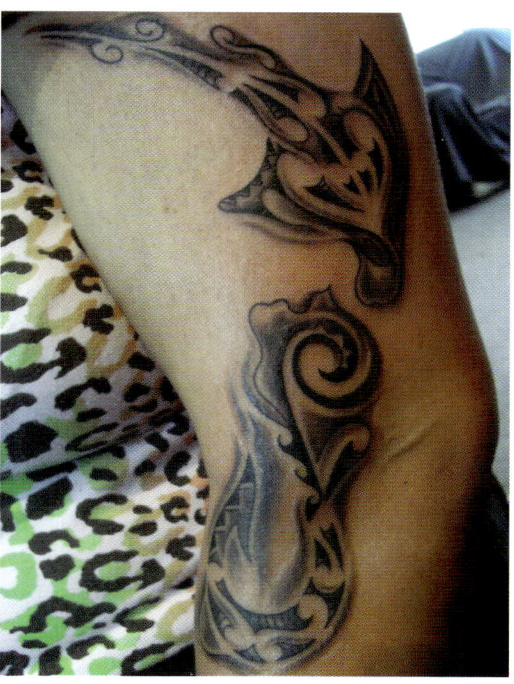

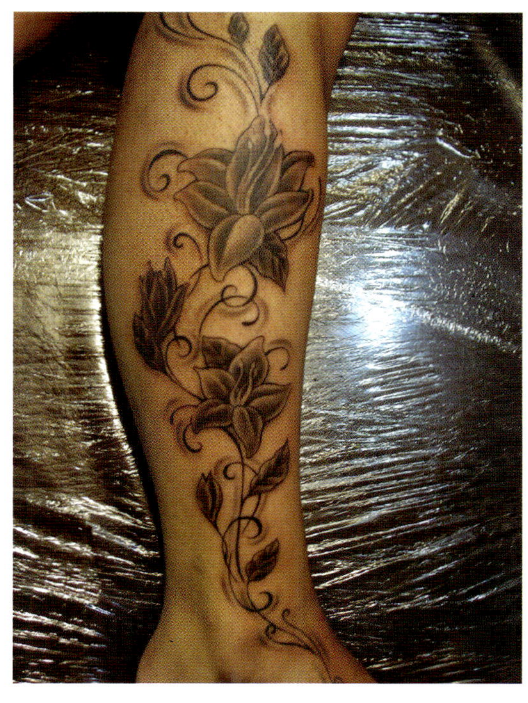

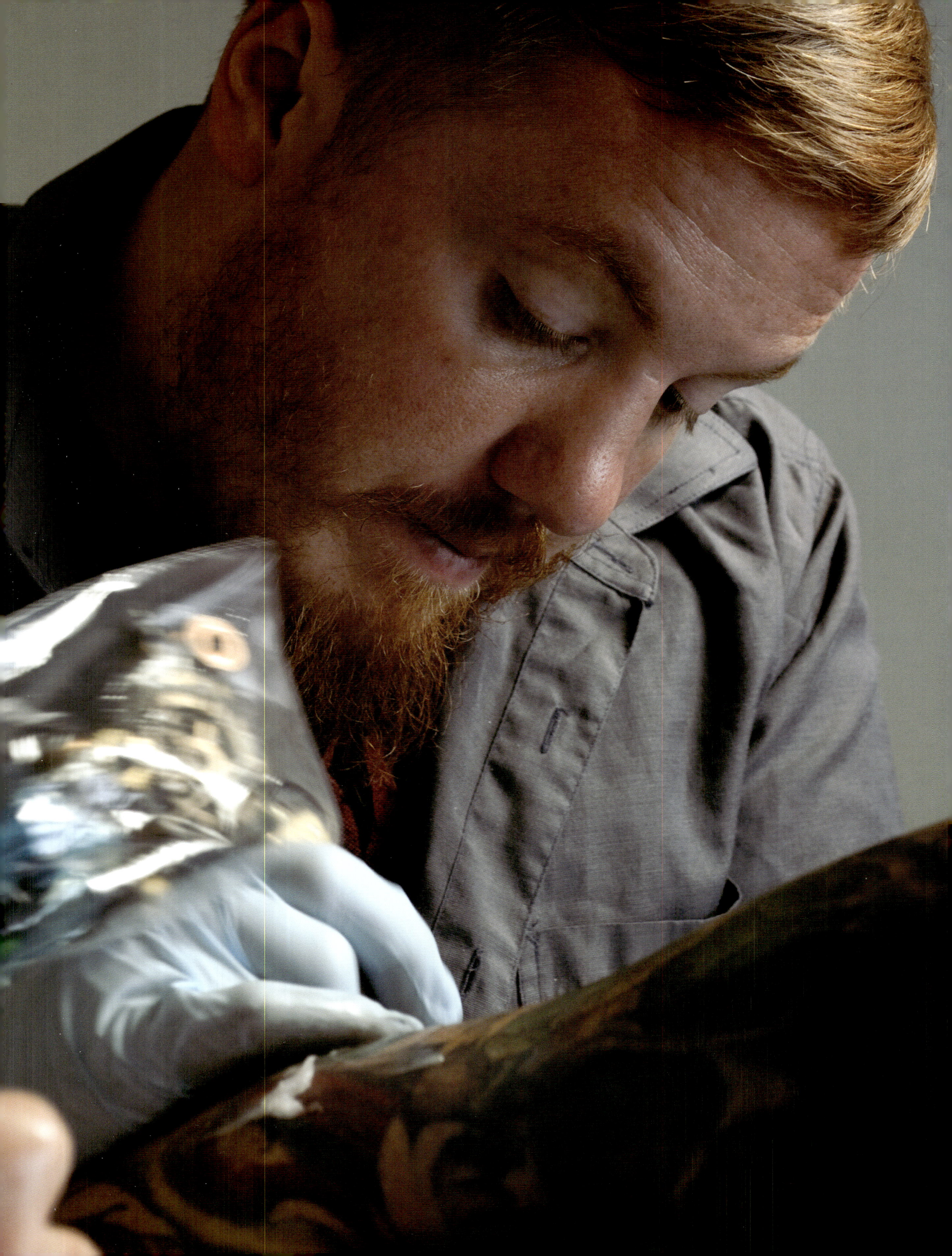

ANDY **SWARBRICK**

THE LEFT HAND PATH

Until 2011 you would have found Andy Swarbrick at The Left Hand Path in a shop at 239A Linwood Avenue, Christchurch. That building is gone now, a casualty of the great earthquake of 22 February.

However, The Left Hand Path has reopened in a former Freemasons' lodge on Dickens Street in the suburb of Addington. The old wooden building was flexible enough to withstand the quake (whereas Dig A Tattoo, just down the road, was built of concrete and collapsed). In the large kauri-lined interior several apprentices are at work drawing and helping out, while tucked away in the back corner Andy Swarbrick is at work on his finely-tuned coil machine — the nerve centre of The Left Hand Path.

Andy learned his craft in the Linwood shop, and has taken up the mantle from founder Holger Mauersberger, an East German artist who had worked with Brad Sims in South Norwood, London, before moving to Christchurch in 2001. Holger, a left-hander, also wanted to set up a studio that provided an alternative to other ways of tattooing and was committed to great graphics.

Andy impressed Holger with his art portfolio, and started an apprenticeship in October 2004 while working in a tannery. Tattooing also had its menial element but it was a path to art. Andy had thought of studying fine art at university and perhaps becoming an illustrator, but through tattoo he learned of artists like Bob Tyrell and Robert Hernandez, and this changed his path. "Holger is a tattooist's tattooist, a great technician with a training in traditional Japanese tattoo," says Andy, who bears a Japanese tebori done by Holger.

Learning about machines was a key part of Andy's early years in the business, and is one reason why he is now a recognised coil tattooist in an era where rotary machines are becoming standard. "I was taught how to build machines as part of my apprenticeship. I can tune my machines to do what rotaries do, so there's no need to change. Plus I like the fact that I can fix my machine."

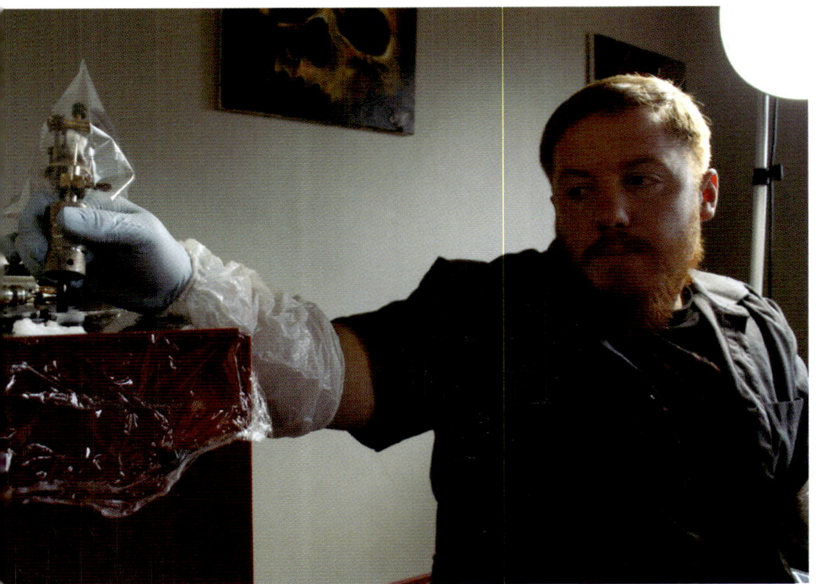
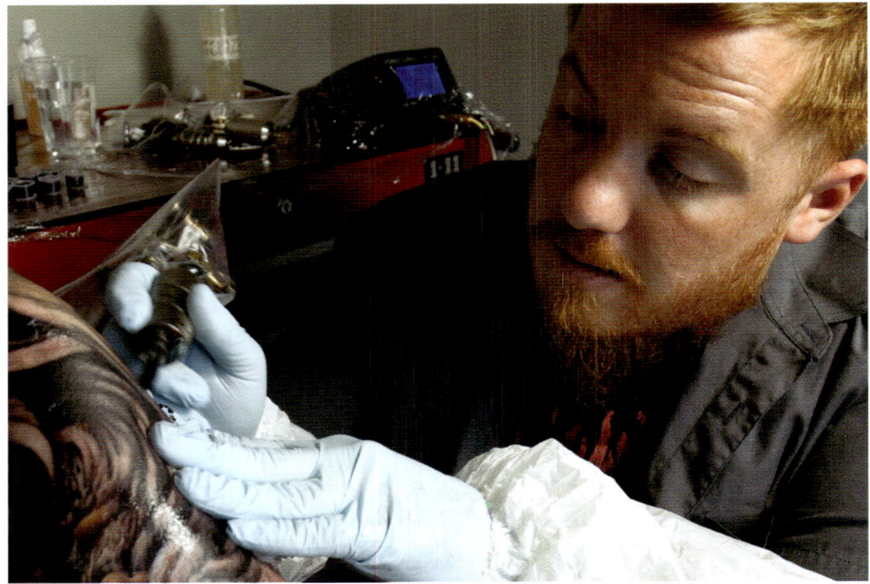

The Left Hand Path lost most of its records and art in the quake, but thanks to support from the tattoo community and loyal clients, the business is back on its feet. Andy is booked six to eight months in advance, a situation that allows him to pick the sort of work he wants to do and bring on apprentices of his own.

Colour is his preference, but with the Japanese influence of balancing out with grey or black. "Traditional Japanese tattooists pick out their colours — an element like a samurai or a koi will be coloured against a black or grey background. It's about knowing when to restrict yourself." At the same time his influences are strongly from off-the-skin artists, and he's inspired by maintaining technical perfection while creating something that hasn't been done before.

Today his style of colour realism work is in high demand throughout Australasia. "There are serious collectors of tattoos from different artists," Andy says. "It's wonderful when you can put your works next to your heroes." About a third of his forward bookings are from the North Island or Australia. Cheap airfares mean travel is just a fraction of the cost of a good tattoo by a favourite artist, and makes it worth getting something good.

"It's only permanent" is Andy's rejoinder to those who want to economise or rush into what they get on their skin. Despite the permanence of tattoo, he still sees older-style tattoos where the emphasis is on coverage rather than quality. "Television exposure and the increased prevalence of tattooing mean that clients of today are better informed," he says.

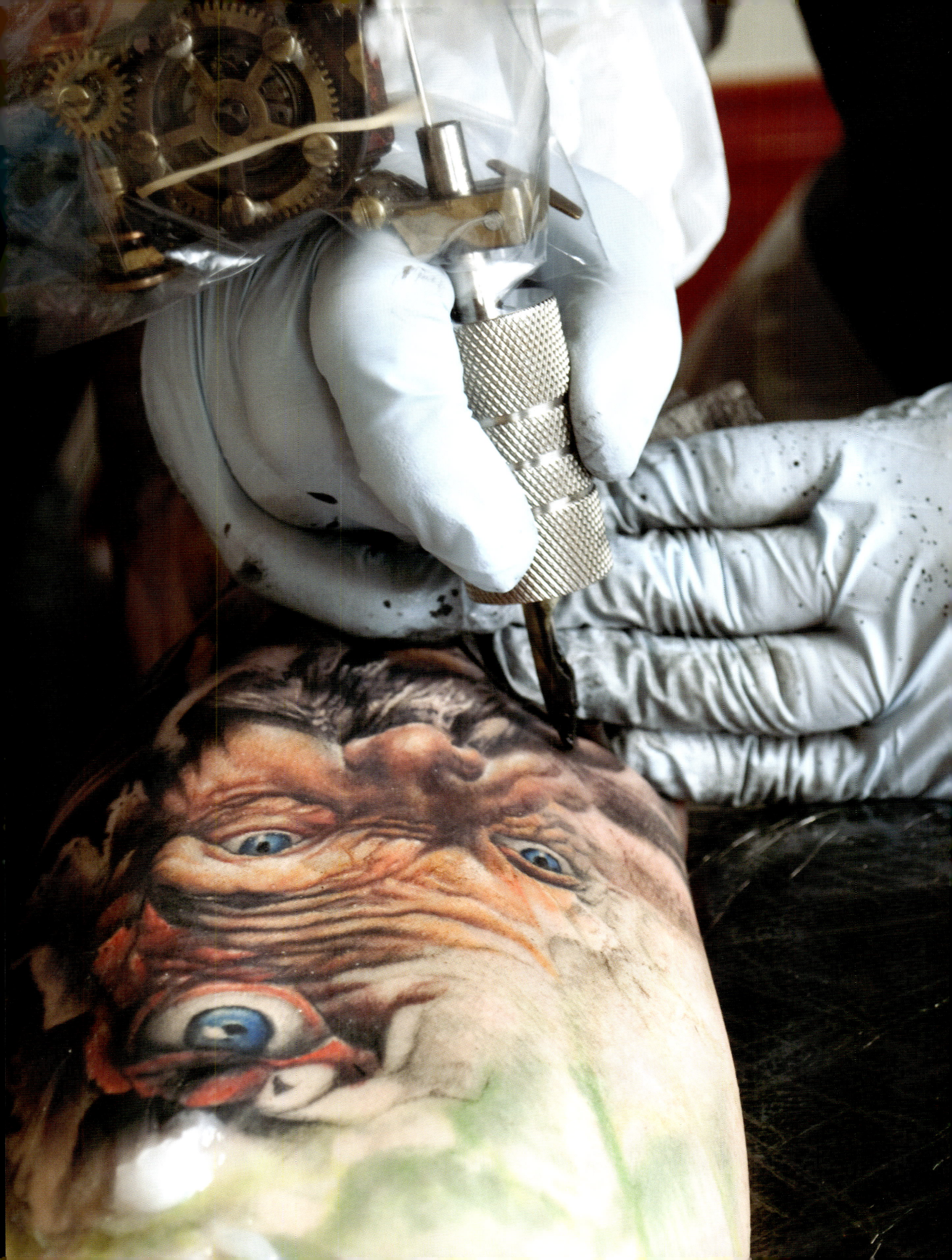

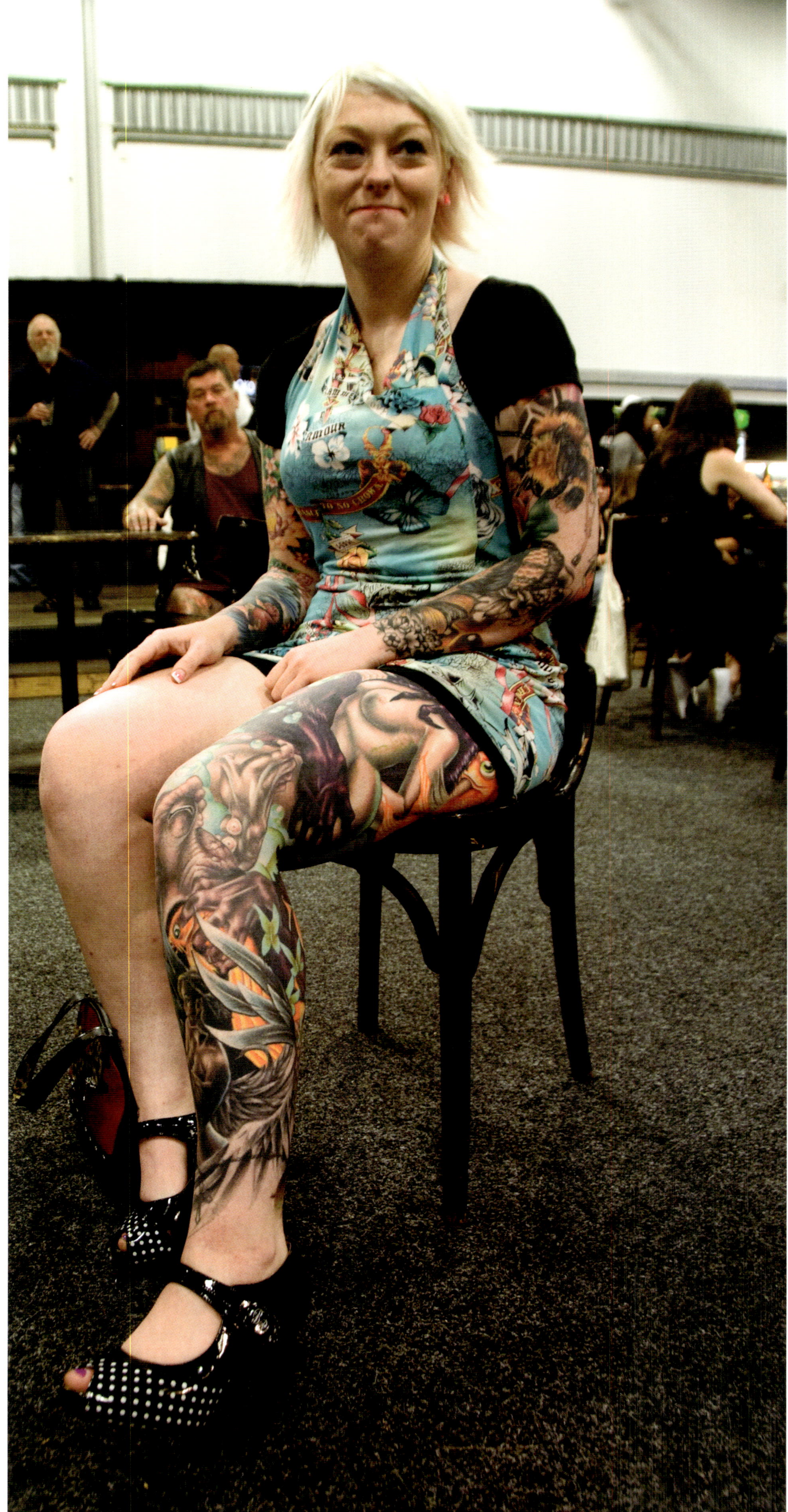

Still, the industry lags in standards and hygiene
requirements. Andy's wall displays the certificates he has
received from attending international courses on managing
hygiene and preventing infection, and he is fanatical about
sterilising his equipment. He shares the concern of many
tattooists at the lack of industry regulation. Aside from cities
like Auckland, Napier and Dunedin where local government
has introduced bylaws, the modification industry (tattoo and
piercing) operates without regulation.

While The Left Hand Path follows strict bagging and hygiene
rules, there is no guarantee that other practitioners comply.
This leaves both public health and the industry's good name
vulnerable to dodgy operators. Andy is emphatic that industry
standards are needed now: "Regulation will come in, and unless
the body modification industry is educated and informed about
it and has a hand in it, we'll have legislation imposed by people
removed from the reality of New Zealand tattooing."

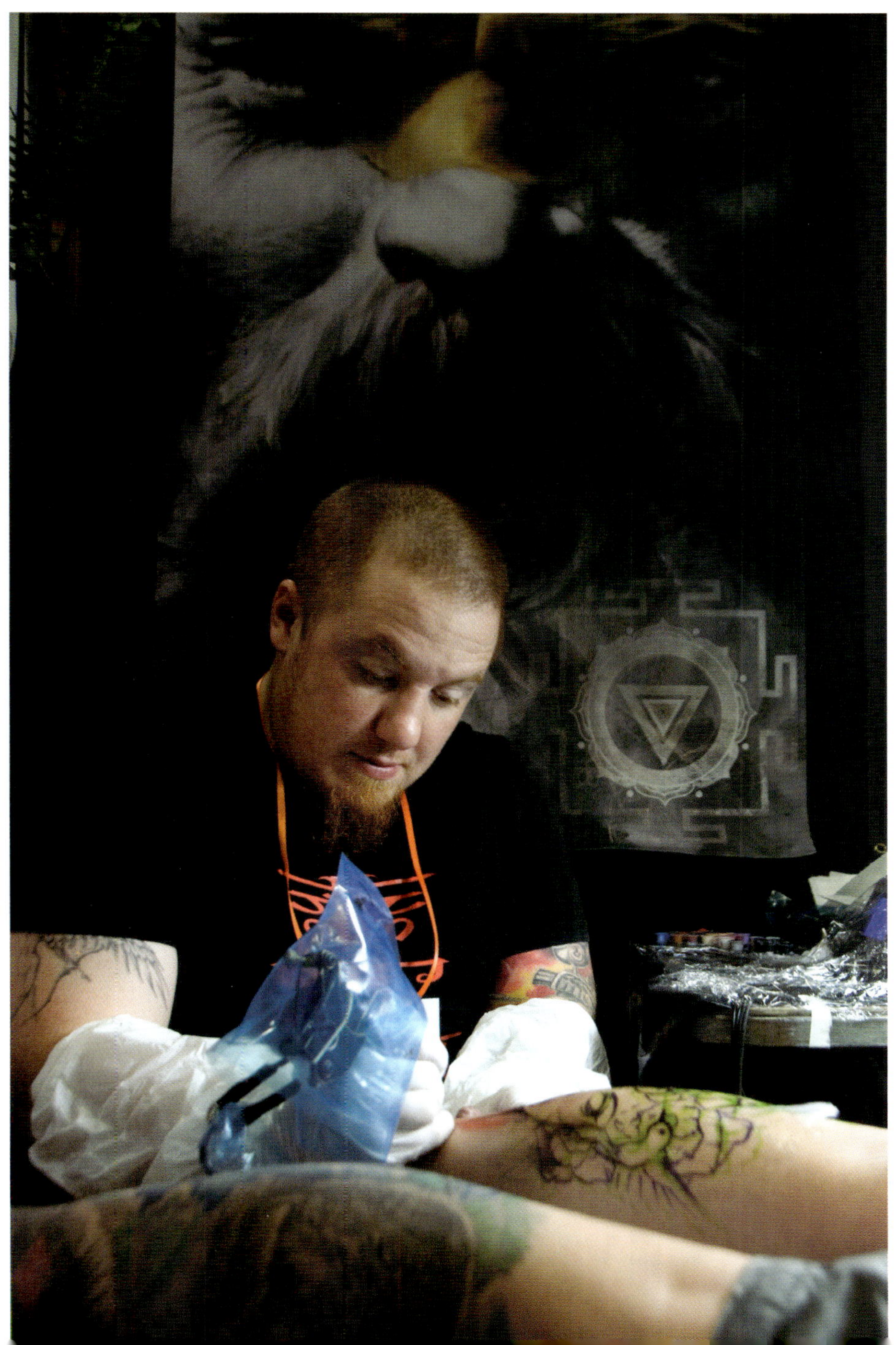

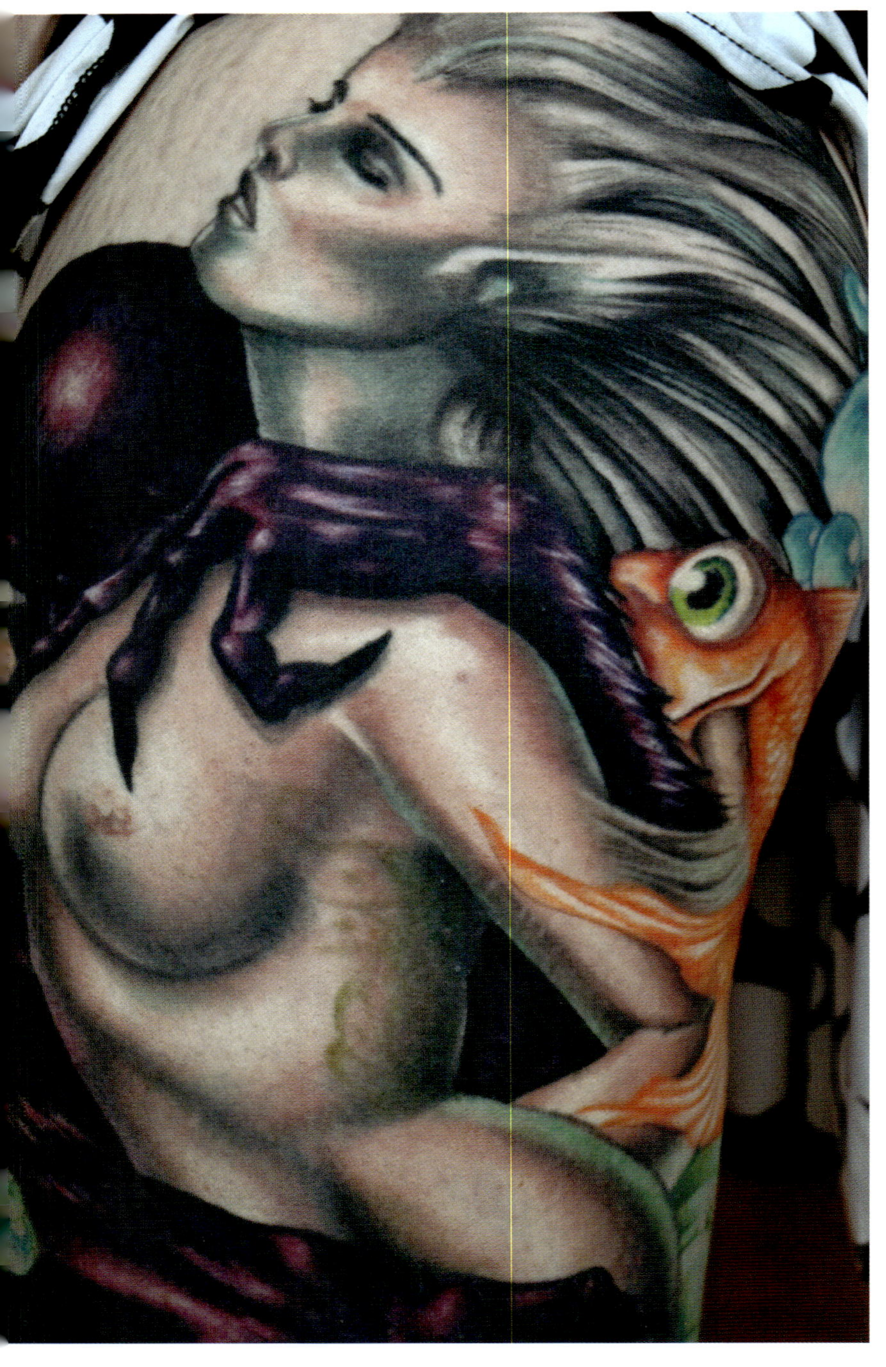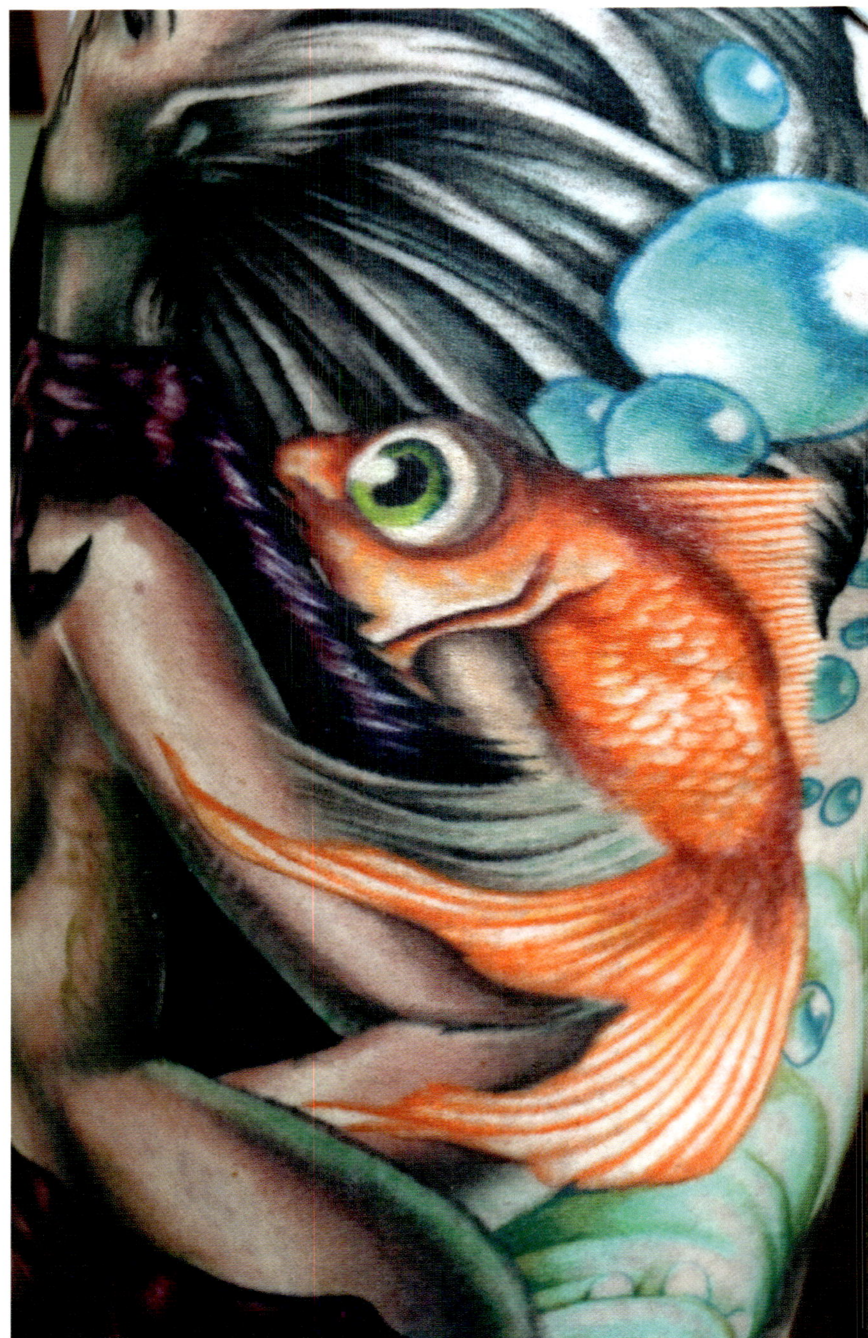

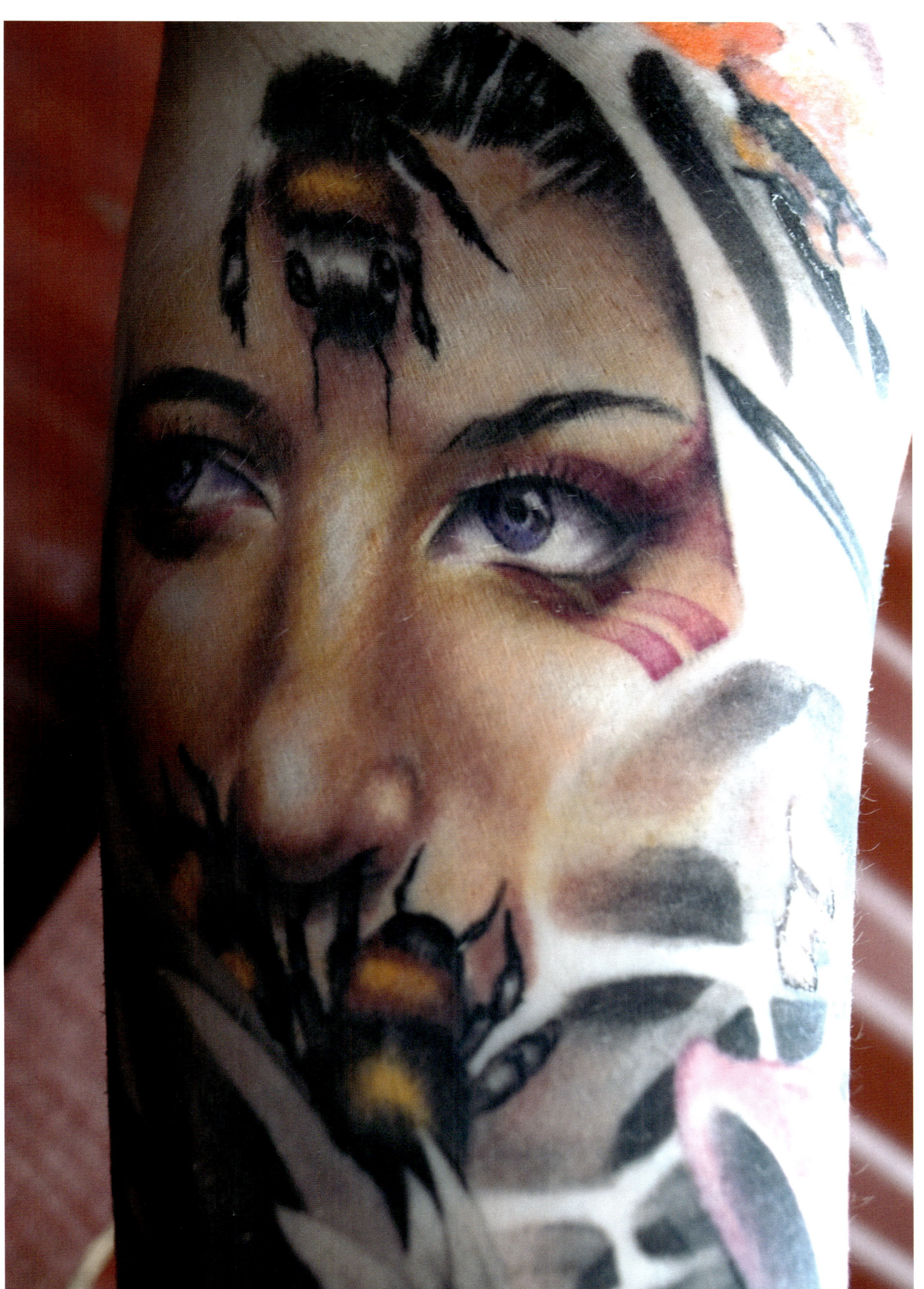

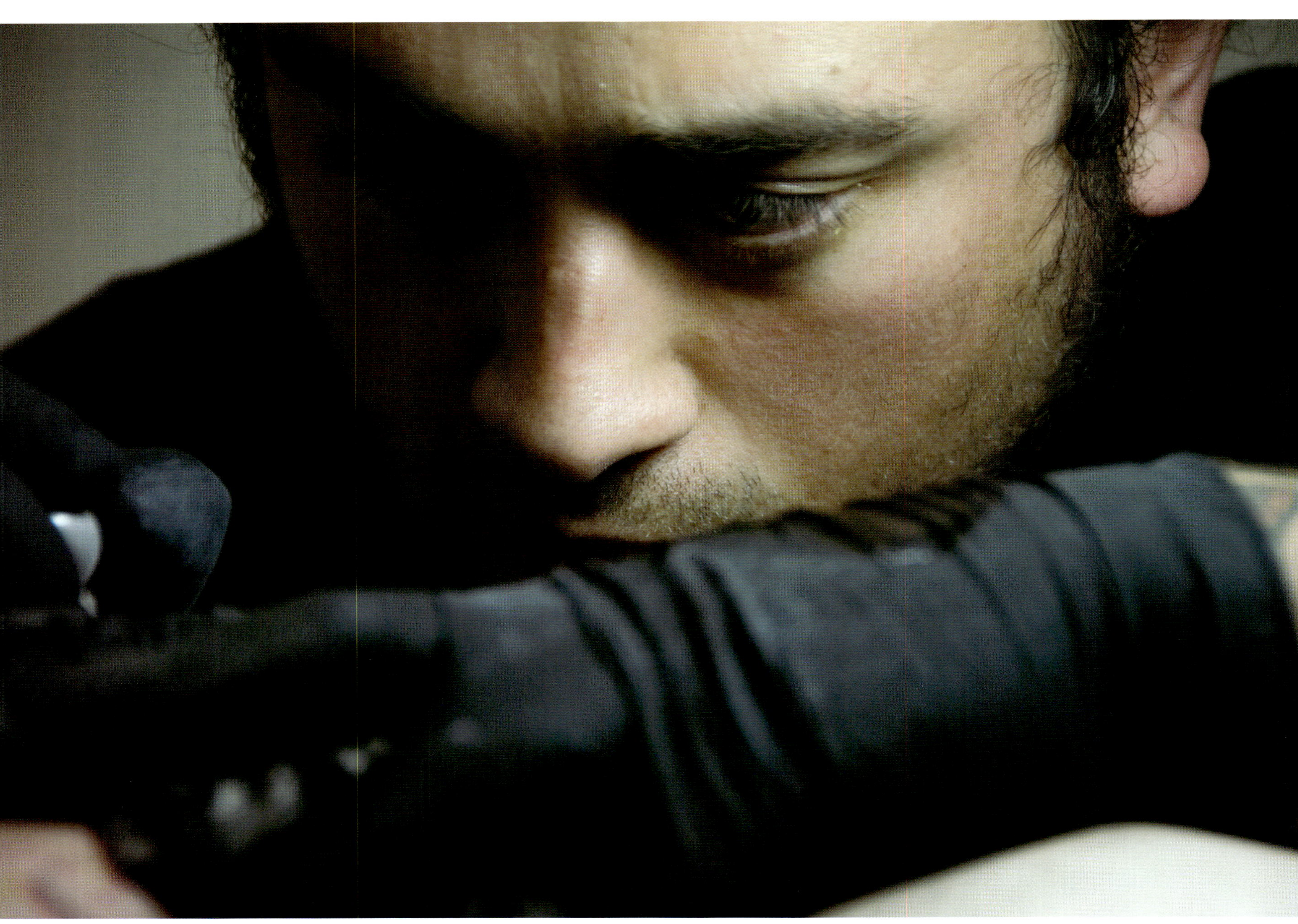

DANIEL (**RANIERA**) McGRATH

Daniel (Raniera) McGrath is part of a new generation of ta moko artists. An art school graduate with a keen interest in research, he didn't start out working in tattoo studios as part of an apprenticeship. Instead he studied arts at Waikato before following it up with further studies in Maori art and design in Gisborne. These days he is the owner of Moko Kauri in Kaitaia, the last stop before Cape Reinga at the top of the North Island. He's currently working out of his own studio alongside Graham Tipene: "In our studio here we try to be more than just a tattoo parlour. Every design is a one-off."

After living in the Chatham Islands until he was ten, Raniera moved back to the mainland with his family. "But I'm from Kaitaia; this is where my people are from. That's why I've got this studio here," he says.

It's a Wednesday and he's tattooing Pouri Thomas, who's just flown into the country from Sydney and wants to get his shoulder and arm tattooed. Raniera has a regular clientele from across the Tasman, largely expat Kiwis coming back to get work done. He also goes to Australia fairly regularly to work. "It's easier for me to go over there sometimes."

Before tattooing, Raniera did carving and made traditional Maori musical instruments. But he was always drawn to the ancient art of ta moko: "Even when I was growing up, the people with ta moko always caught my attention. You could look at them and you could see their mana." He was captivated by the works of Goldie and Lindauer, and still is: "My influence comes from those Goldie and Lindauer paintings — they set the standard."

He studied ta moko at the Tairāwhiti Polytechnic School of Maori Visual Art & Design in Gisborne, under the tutelage of Derek Lardelli. Derek is the school's principal tutor and is renowned for his designs, not to mention his work in carving, kapa haka, composition and graphic design.

Raniera is studying for his master's degree at Te Whare Wānanga o Awanuiārangi in Whakatane. He's researching the history and designs of ta moko in Northland. "To do that I'm speaking to all the elders up this way and getting their stories." He's hoping to complete the degree in 2013 and is relishing the chance to learn more about the art form: "I've always been doing research; that's one of my passions."

Raniera met Te Rangitu Netana in 2010. He admires his work, especially his skills with the uhi, or chisel, and would like to learn to use the traditional tools. But he recognises that ta moko has evolved, and has no problem with using modern tattoo equipment for his work: "If they'd had the machines we have now, they would have used them too."

Moko Kauri had its own stall at the 2011 Auckland International Tattoo Convention and Raniera was busy on the machine all weekend. "That was my first-ever convention," he says. The fact that the two-day event included ta moko, tattoo and tatau meant there was a lot to take in. "I appreciate other traditional styles of tattooing. I like the Japanese tattooing and the Pacific Island tatau," he says. "But I don't know much about the mainstream tattoo industry."

The next day Allen Duzevich arrives at Moko Kauri. He is back home for a visit from Perth, where he lives with his family. He was keen to get a moko done in New Zealand and because his family is from the Far North, decided Raniera was the man to see. Allen pulls out a book of his family's genealogy and discusses potential designs with Raniera. "A lot of the guys I've worked with over there have flown back to New Zealand to get their moko done," he says.

Raniera sketches a design and puts it on Allen's arm. He explains the meaning behind the northern scroll patterns he's using. A hammerhead shark's head is used to symbolise strength of character, while a kaka bird's beak represents knowledge. "Everything has a meaning — even the colours." Unlike some ta moko artists who use only black, Raniera does use other colours. "But it depends on the person getting it done."

While Raniera is hard at work tattooing Allen's arm, Te Uri Reihana walks into Moko Kauri. Te Uri works as a police iwi liaison officer in Kaitaia and has had extensive work done by Raniera. "I've got to be honest, for years I hated tattooing," he admits. "It didn't matter if it was ta moko. But then I just had an urge to get something done. It was just to recognise who I am."

The design starts on Te Uri's right shoulder and upper back and runs down his back to cover both buttocks, thighs and hamstrings and his calves. It was done in a series of five-hour sessions spread over two years and took a total of 60 hours' work.

Raniera's goal is to reflect who a person is and where they are from in every piece he does. With his ongoing research into the history of the art form, his future as an artist looks strong.

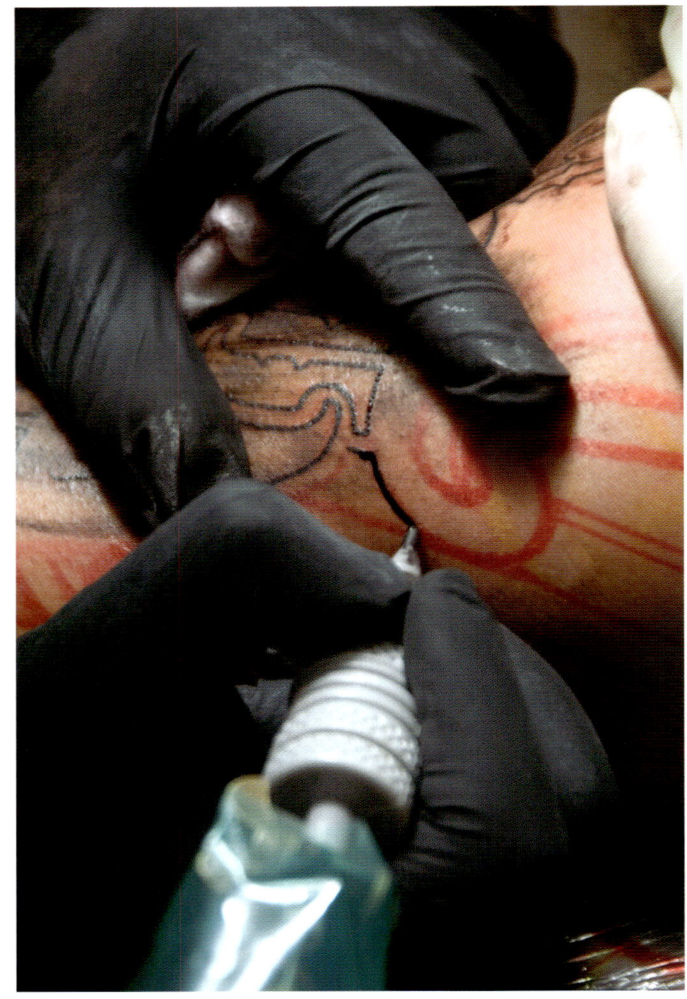

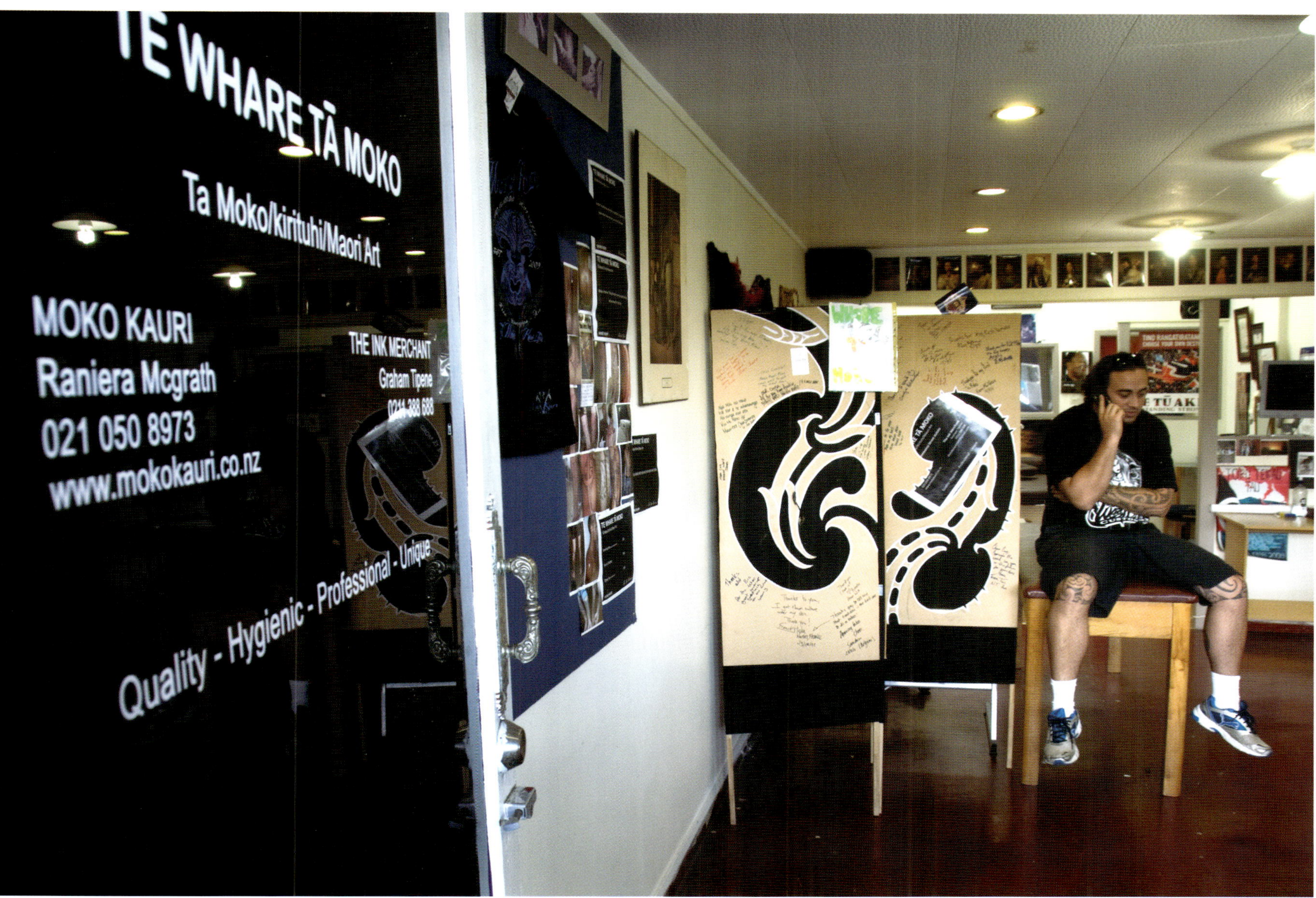

TE WHARE TĀ MOKO
Ta Moko/kirituhi/Maori Art

MOKO KAURI
Raniera Mcgrath
021 050 8973
www.mokokauri.co.nz

THE INK MERCHANT
Graham Tipene

Quality - Hygienic - Professional - Unique

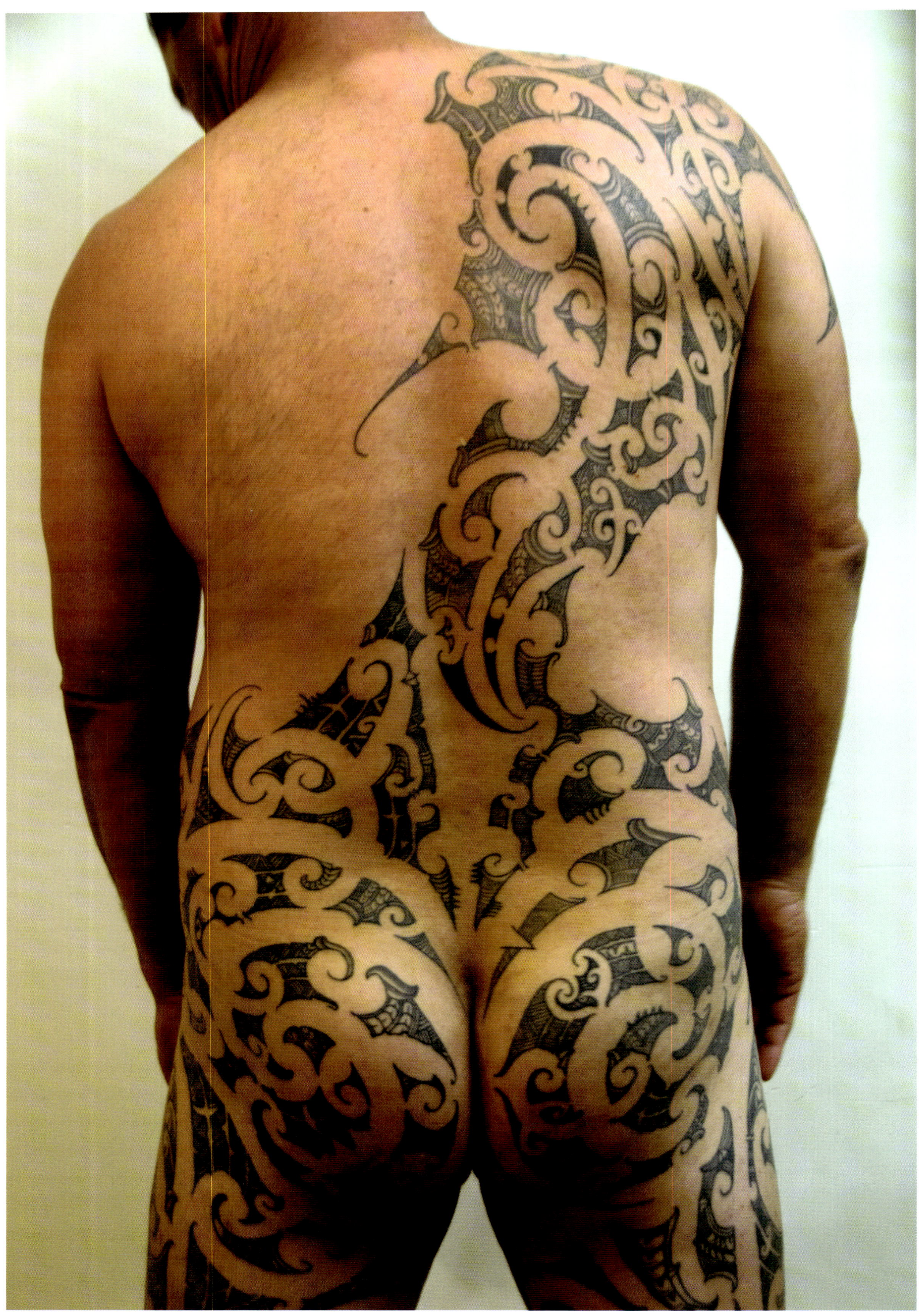

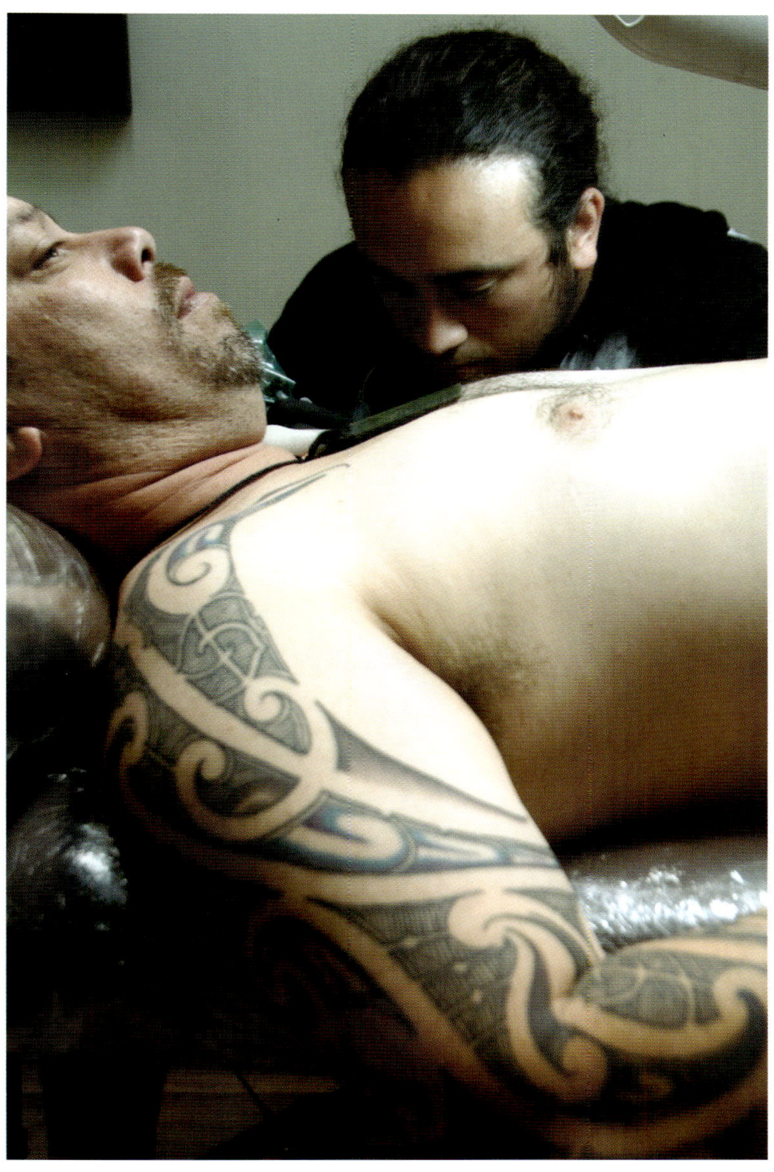

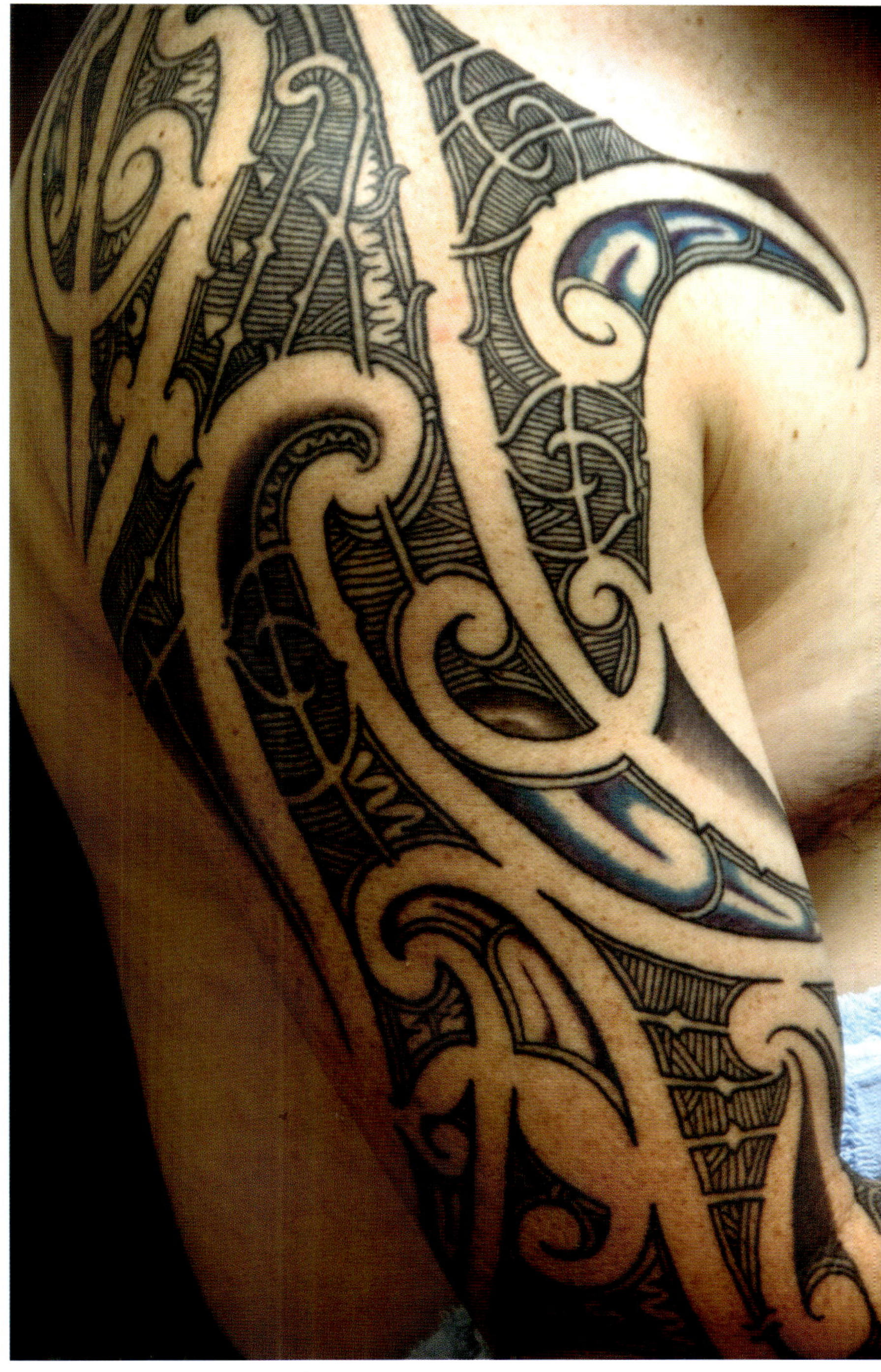

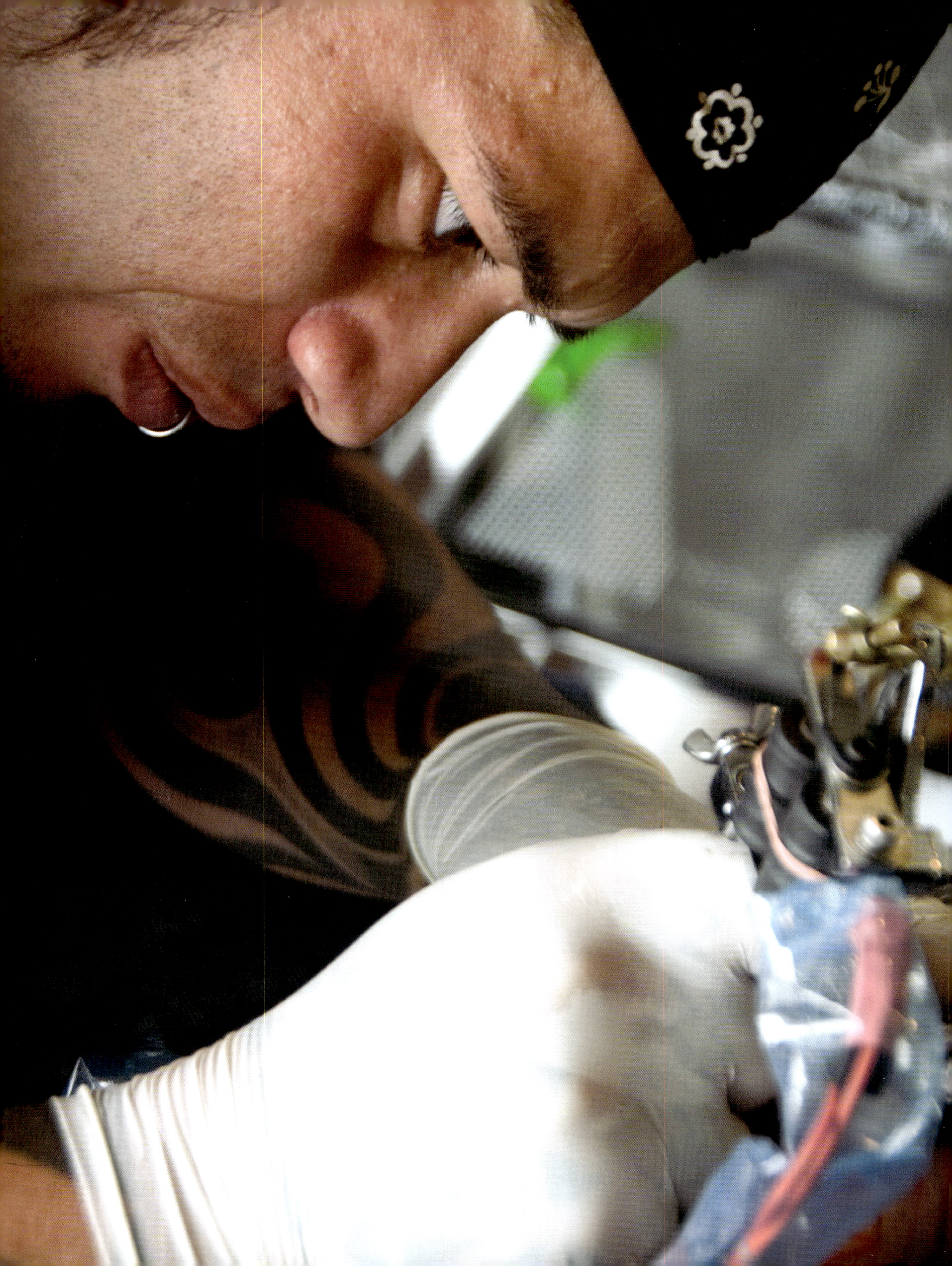

COREY **WEIR**

"Tribal" is how Corey Weir describes his designs. He sees them as a fusion of Pacific styles and Maori moko, with a strong Japanese influence. Corey, who is part-Samoan, has been interested in tattoo since childhood and got his first one at the age of 15.

The late Paulo Suluape created Corey's traditional Samoan sleeve design using traditional tools, including a needle crafted from a pig's tooth. "My father and I got tattooed together. I was told in Samoa they get it done in pairs so there are only two people with the same design; if one person dies, there's still another person with the same tattoo."

But it wasn't until he lived in Japan that he decided to try his hand at the art form. After leaving school he had studied Japanese language and business, and when he turned 20 he left New Zealand for the Land of the Rising Sun. He was to call Japan home for the next 16 years.

Corey had thought that to become a tattooist he would have to master all different styles of the art, but when he realised he could specialise, he decided to try his hand at it.

"I had a studio, Life Under Zen, with another guy in Tokyo, the Japanese/Brazilian tattooist Jun Matsui. We based it on these tribal designs." The pair worked together for about ten years and had a lot of demand. Corey was also exposed to traditional Japanese tattooing. "I was definitely influenced by it," he says, "and I worked with a lot of Japanese artists."

However, Corey never attempted the designs himself: "That's their style," he says. "To the Japanese what we did was quite exotic and they were really into what we were doing.

"My strongest influences are Samoan and Maori tattooing. I love the bold, geometric lines of the Samoan style. And with the Maori I like the elegance of it — the flowing curved lines. So I've developed a fusion of those approaches. I would say it's more of a Pacific style."

He thinks it's important as an artist to focus on what they are good at. "And I would rather do something that I know I can do well."

Corey came back to New Zealand to live in 2008. In 2009 he opened the Monk3ys Tattoo and Design studio in the West Auckland suburb of Te Atatu. Creating unique tattoos is the vision, rather than churning out "cookie-cutter" designs: "If you do that I don't think there's any consistency. It's important that it goes in a more specialised direction, instead of trying to say 'we can do anything'. Most of the tattoos I do, I design specifically for that person."

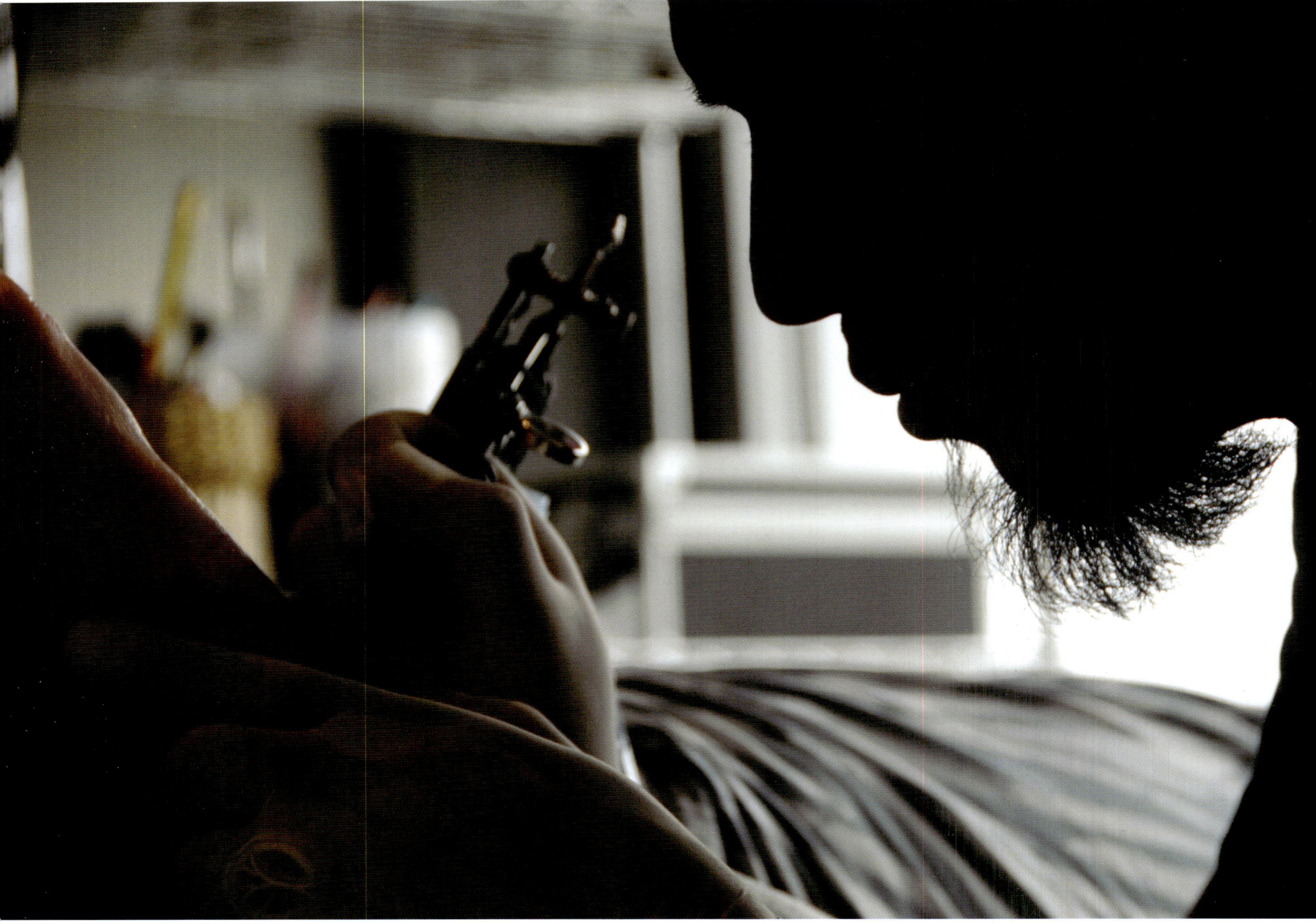

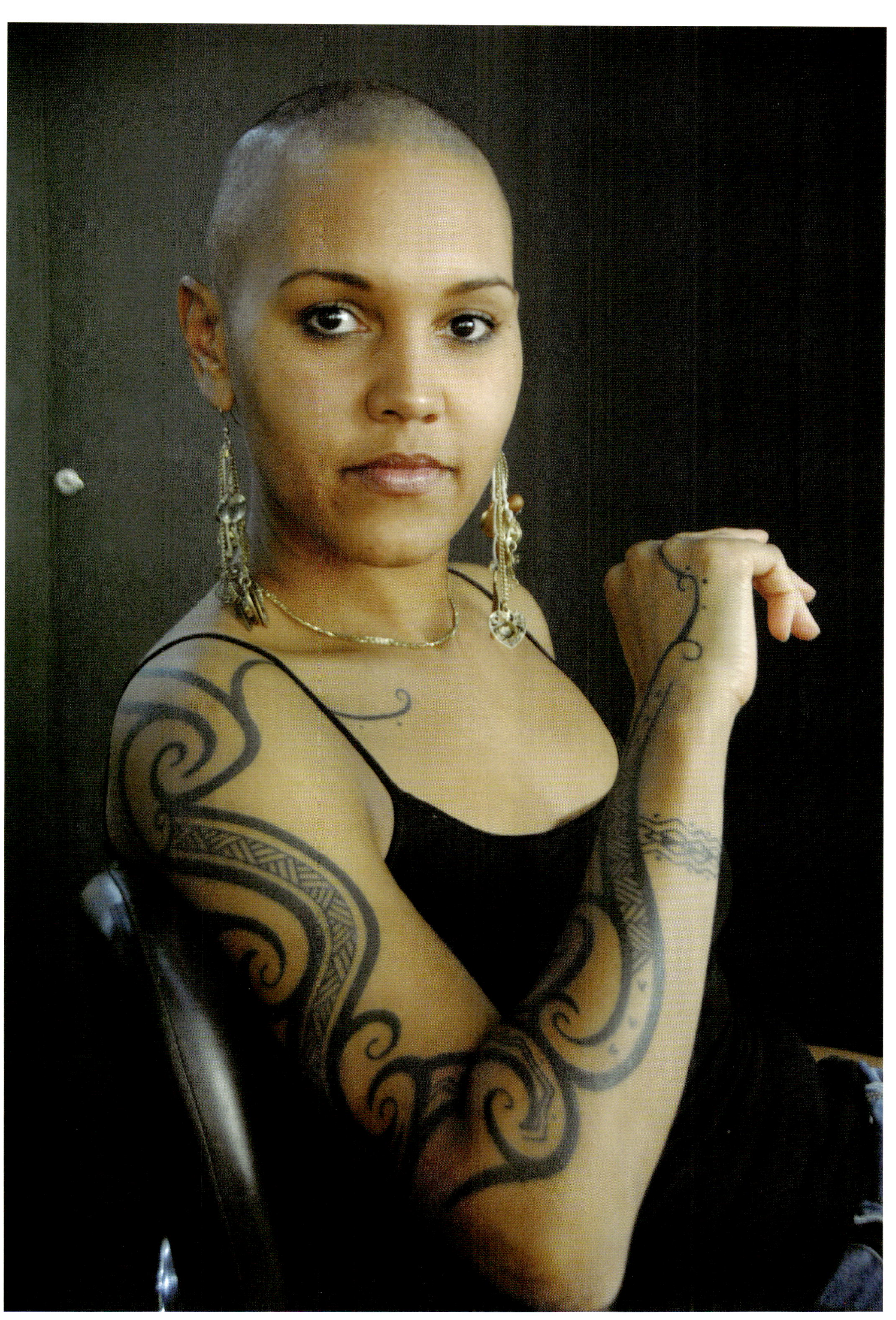

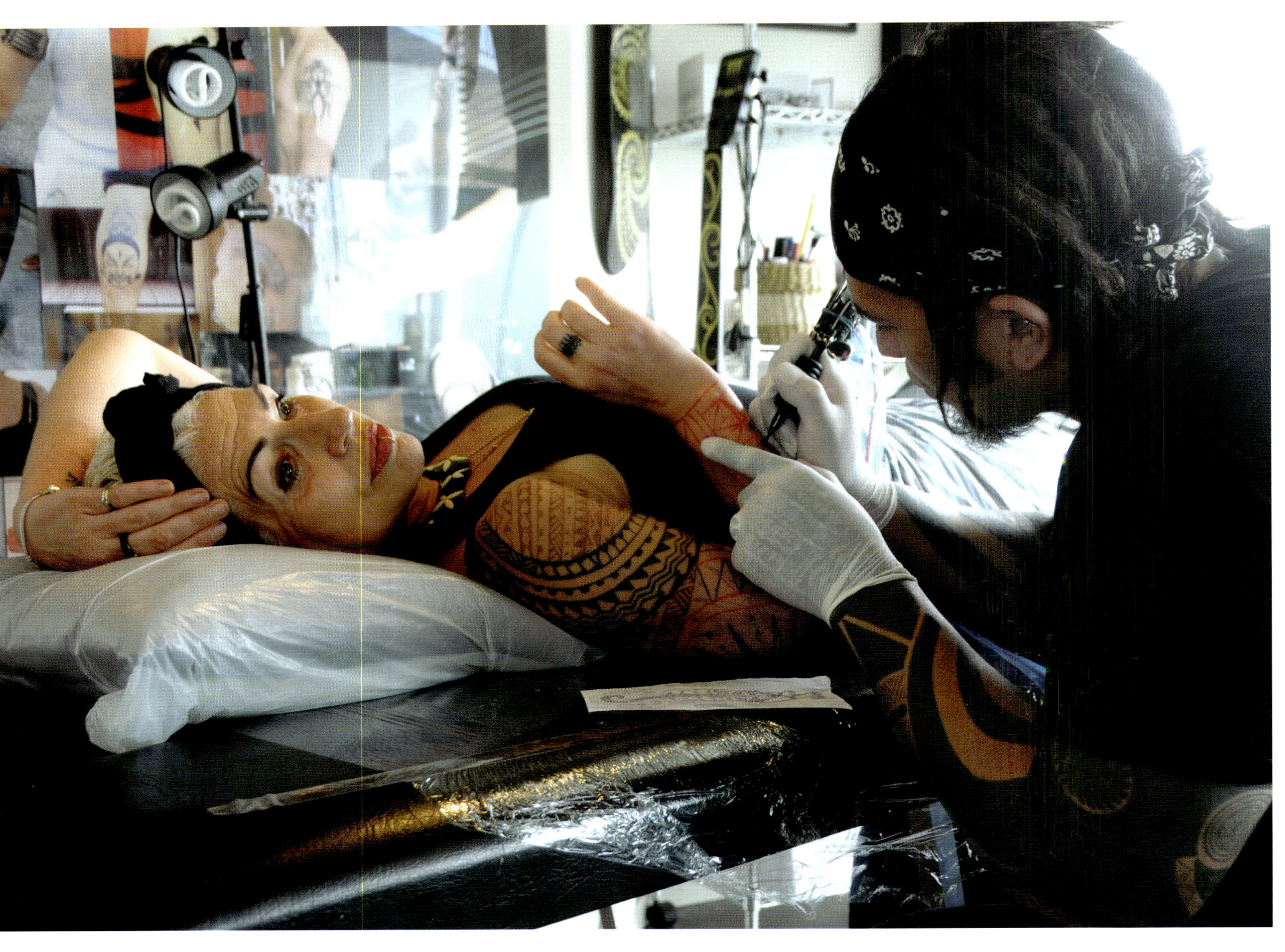

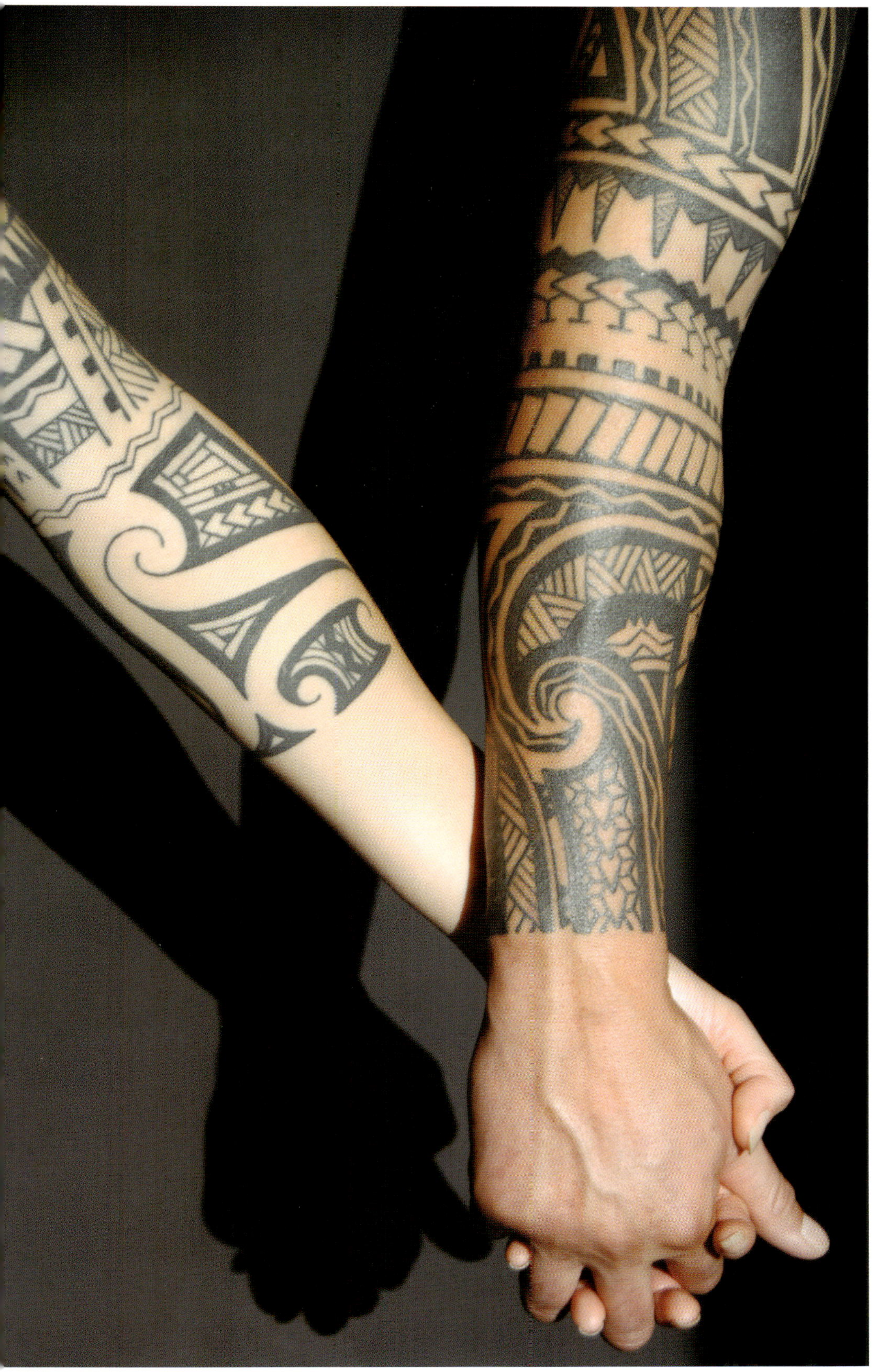

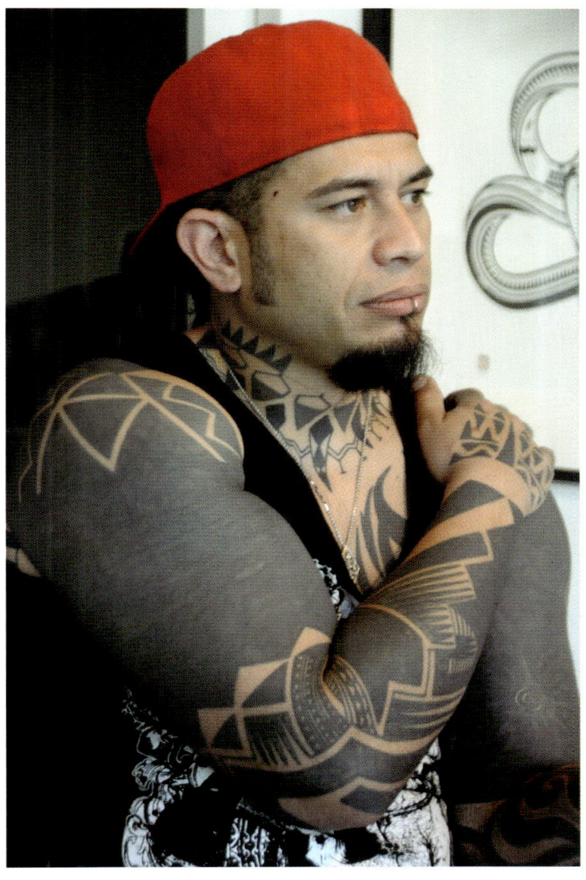

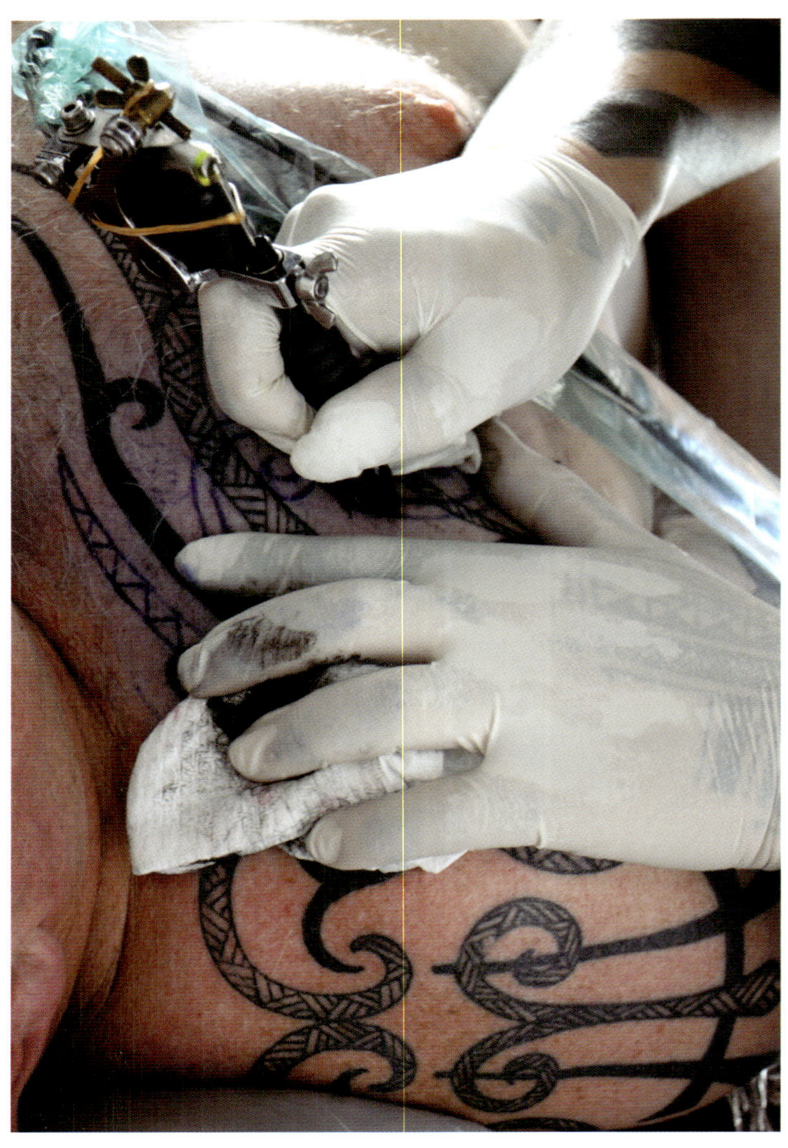

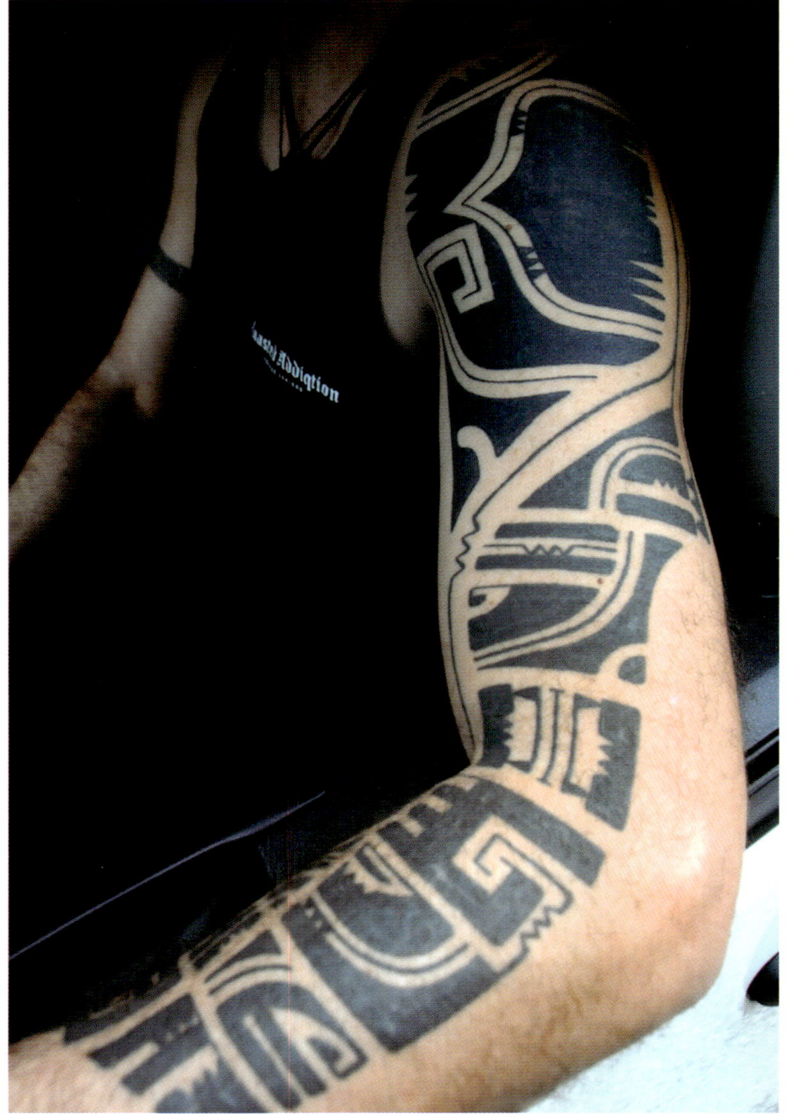

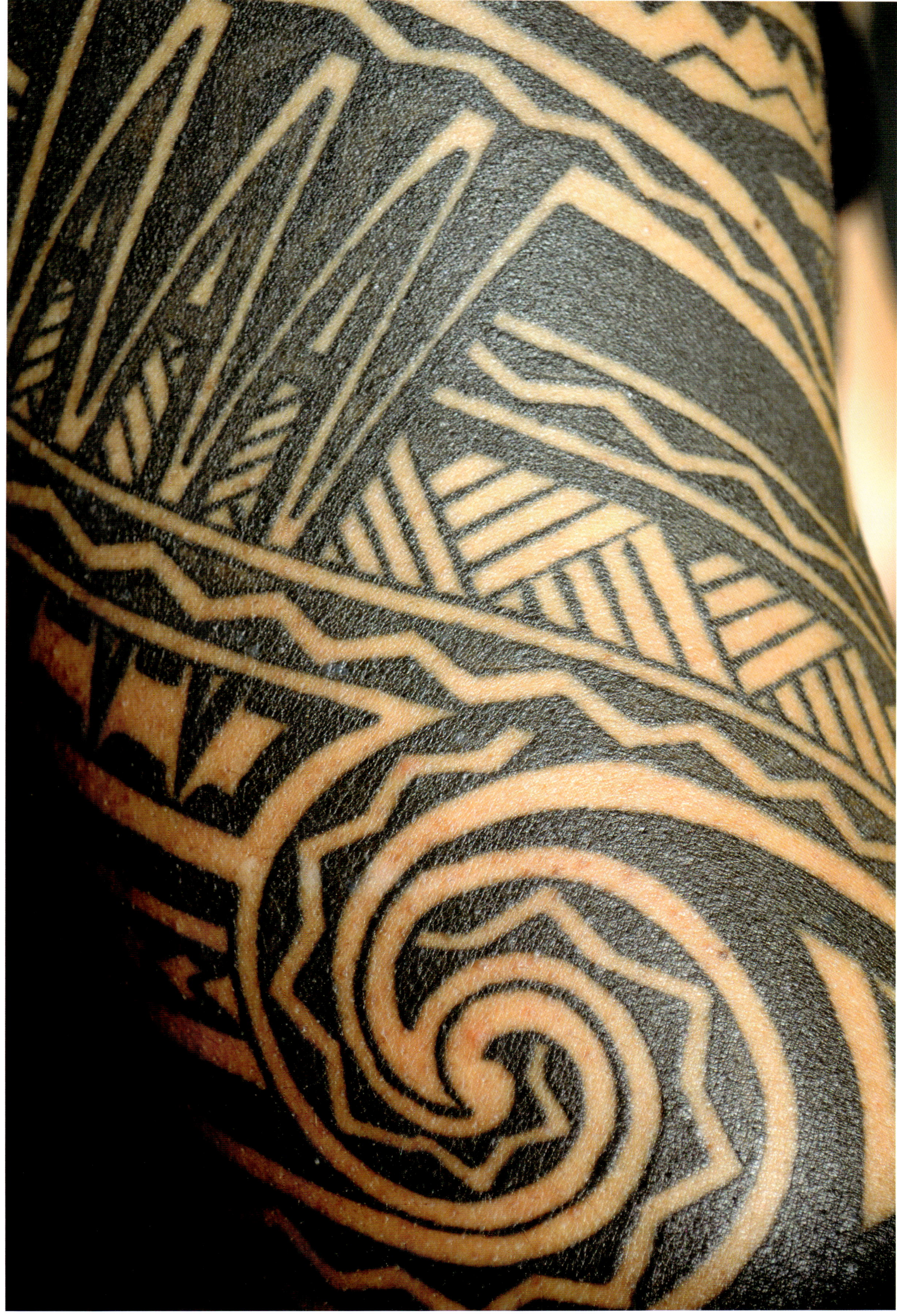

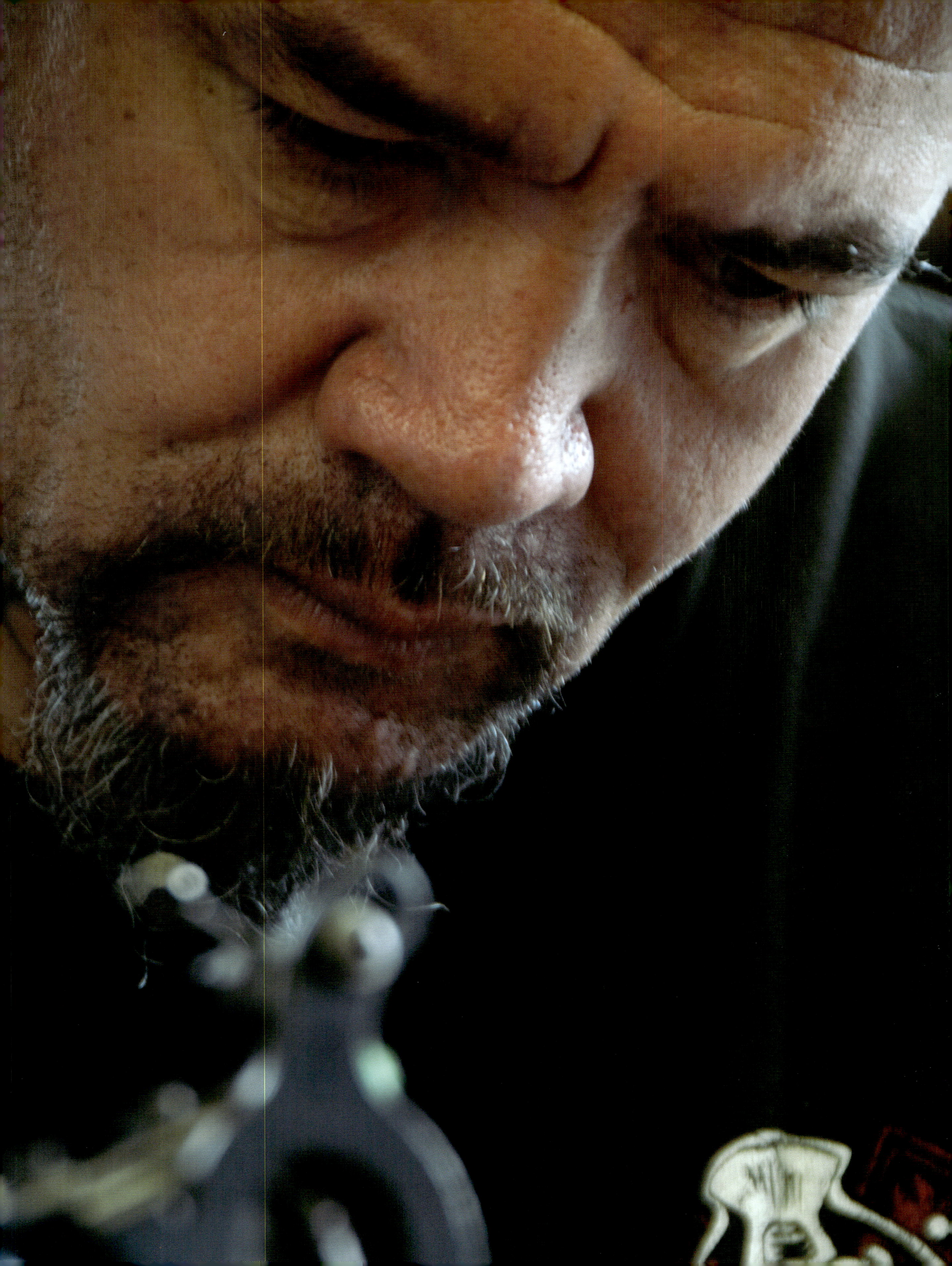

GORDON **TOI**
(aka GORDON HATFIELD)

It was from his work as a carver that Gordon Toi learned the bold moko patterns and designs that are now his stock in trade. His story reflects the important role that Maori carving has played in the rebirth of ta moko.

Gordon is one of a number of contemporary ta moko artists, such as Mark Kopua, Riki Manuel and Laurie Nicholas, who come from a background in traditional Maori carving. He learned to carve at the New Zealand Māori Arts and Crafts Institute in Rotorua in the early 1980s. It was during a period of Maori cultural renaissance that coincided with the birth of kohanga reo and the growth of kapa haka.

"Modern ta moko was still in its infancy at the time, but people wanted to reconnect with moko and the obvious place to look was the carvers," he says. With the decline of ta moko in the 19th century some of the only people who maintained the ancient patterns were carvers, who continued to use the traditional designs on wood, stone and bone. Impressive examples of such carving can still be found on marae around the country.

His tattoo career started in the mid-1990s when he began working with ta moko artists Laurie Nicholas and Te Rangitu Netana. While he had a knowledge of the moko patterns and knew their history, this was a different realm. Also, instead of working with bone, wood or stone, he was now using skin. "Technically it was a whole different ball game."

He learnt a lot from the two artists: "We were travelling around the country and we were tattooing around the clock. We'd tattoo at different marae around the country. It was an interesting period because some of our own people weren't sure if it was the right thing to do, to bring back this art form.

"We used to have some heavy conversations. The elders would discuss with us their family members who wore moko. It was really interesting. But the real learning curve for me was going overseas and working with other tattoo artists." In 1999, during his time in Europe, he did a guest spot at Hanky Panky's Amsterdam Tattoo Museum. "It was a great experience for me. That place really started my journey in the tattoo world.

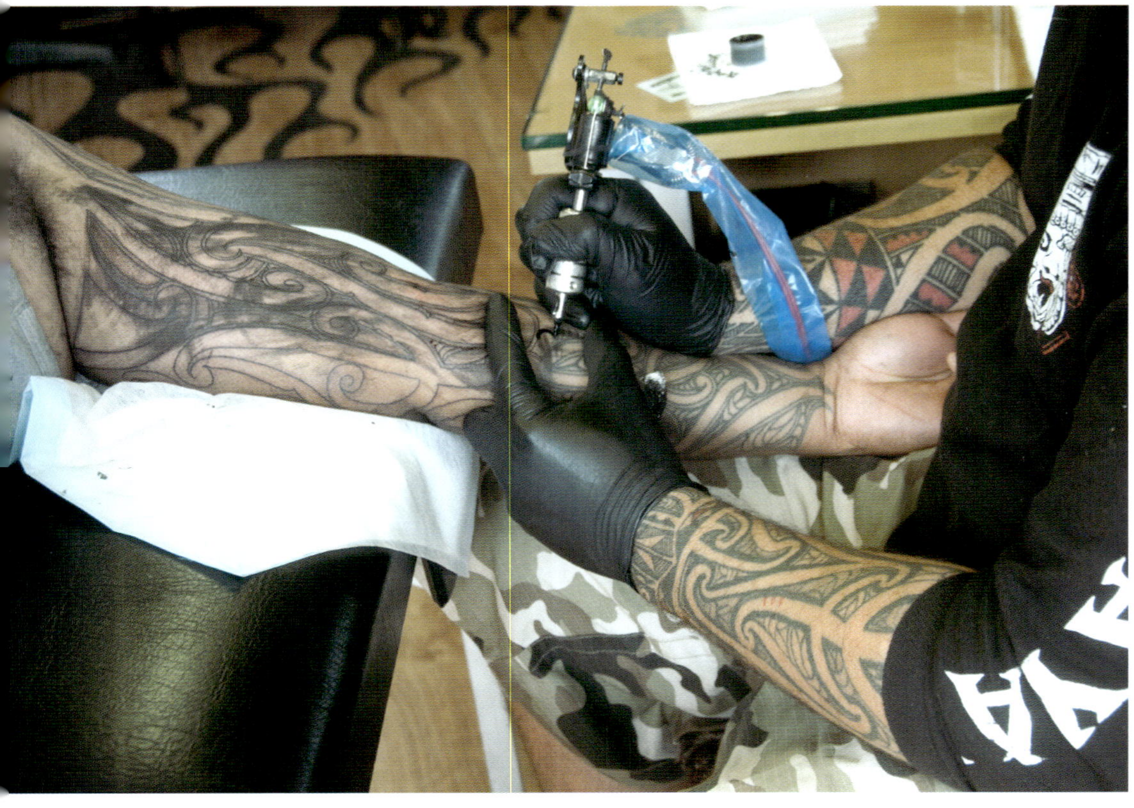

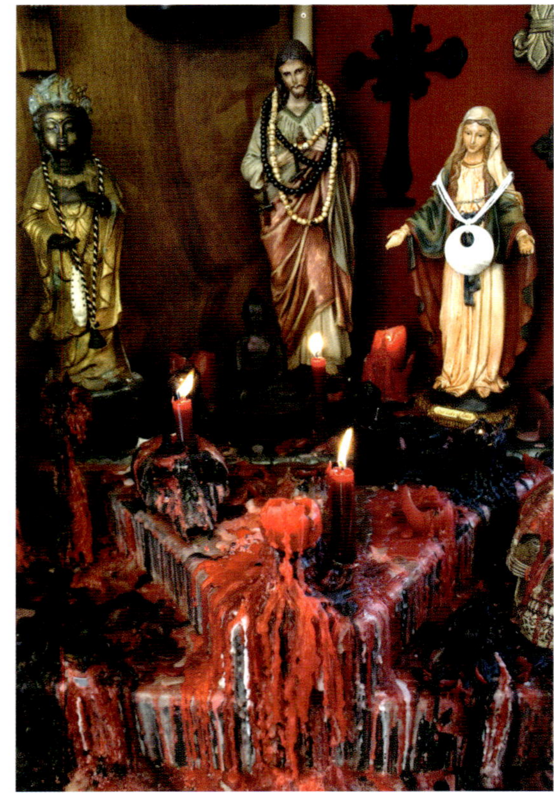

"I found it very hard to make any gains here in New Zealand in terms of learning the craft because I didn't go through a normal apprenticeship in a tattoo shop. And at that time it was quite clear that what the tattooists were doing wasn't what we were trying to achieve. They had the technical side of it, no doubt about that. But it was different because there is a difference between ta moko and tattooing. What makes ta moko different is the genealogy and the philosophy behind it."

These days he works from his studio, He Tohu O Te Wa, at his Mangere Bridge home. He works with both a modern machine and traditional tattooing equipment, depending on whom he's tattooing: "A lot of people want to have work done with the traditional tools, the uhi, but it's the last thing we can call our own. So I won't tattoo a non-Maori with the tools. I only use the traditional tools on my own people. And I wouldn't do a full body suit or facial moko on a non-Maori."

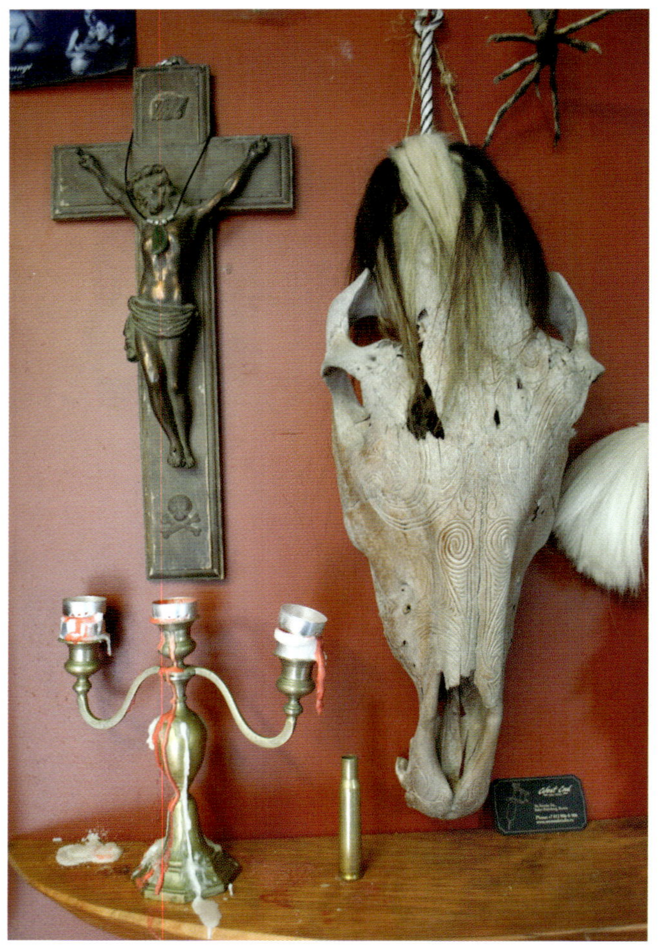

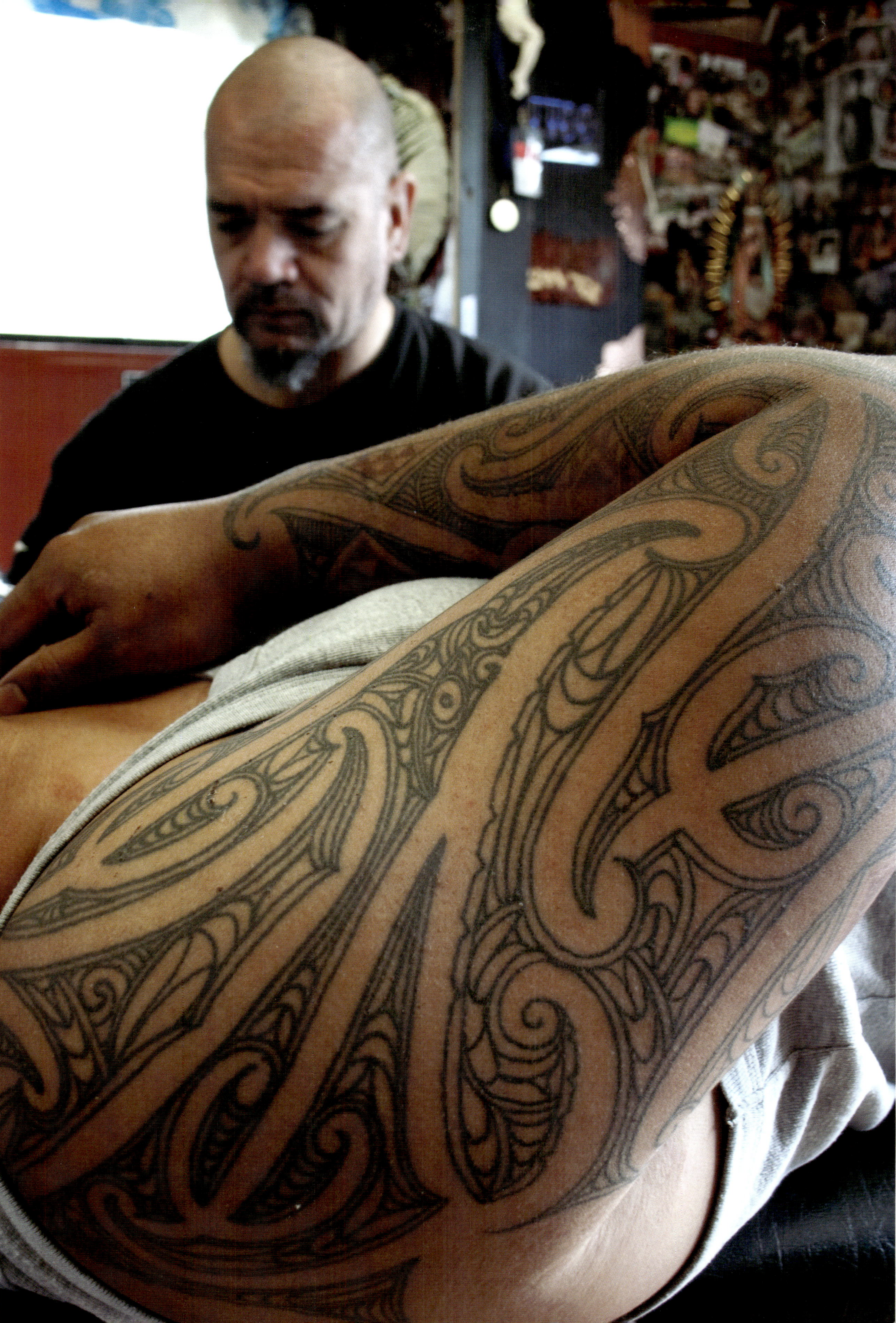

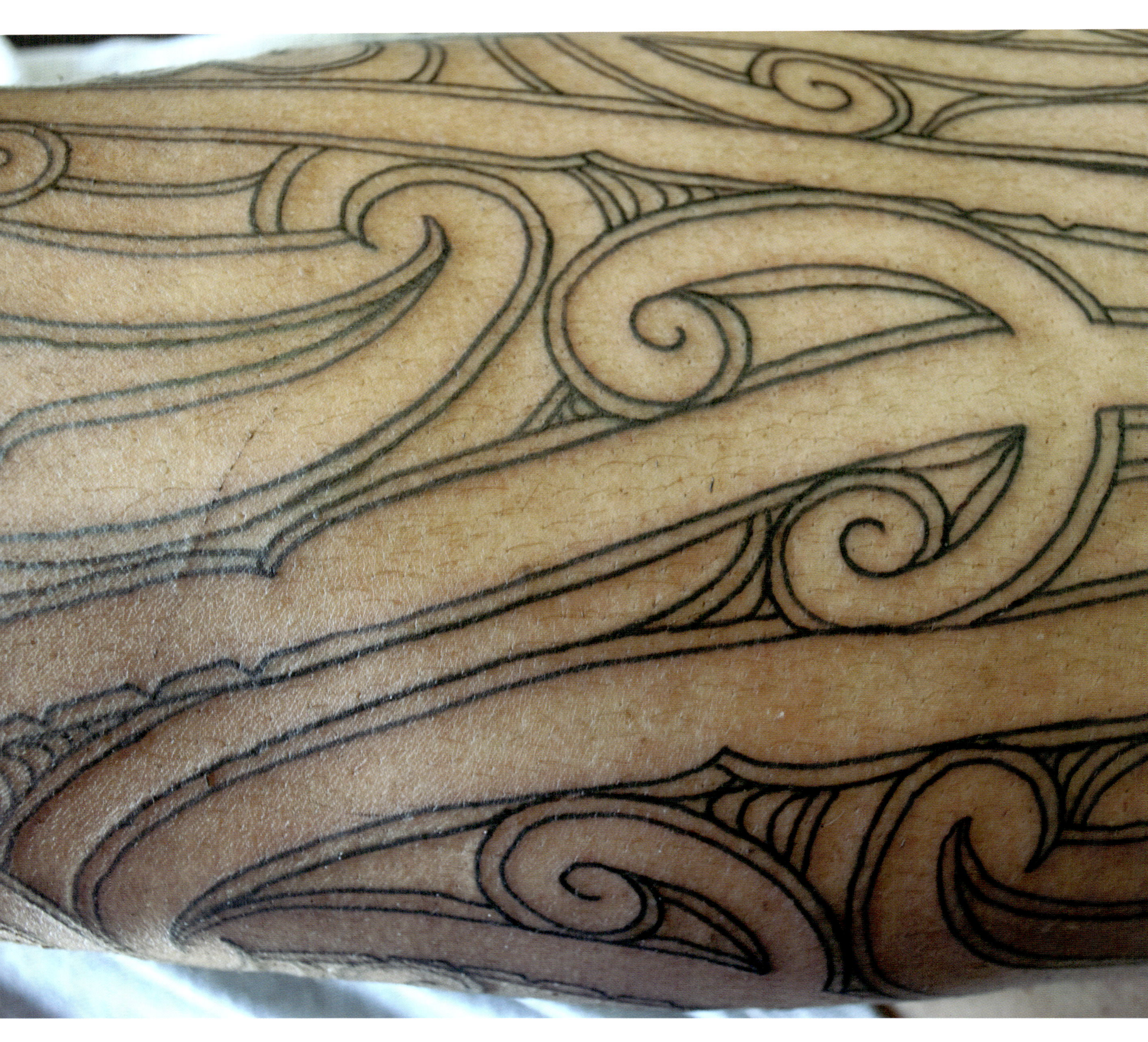

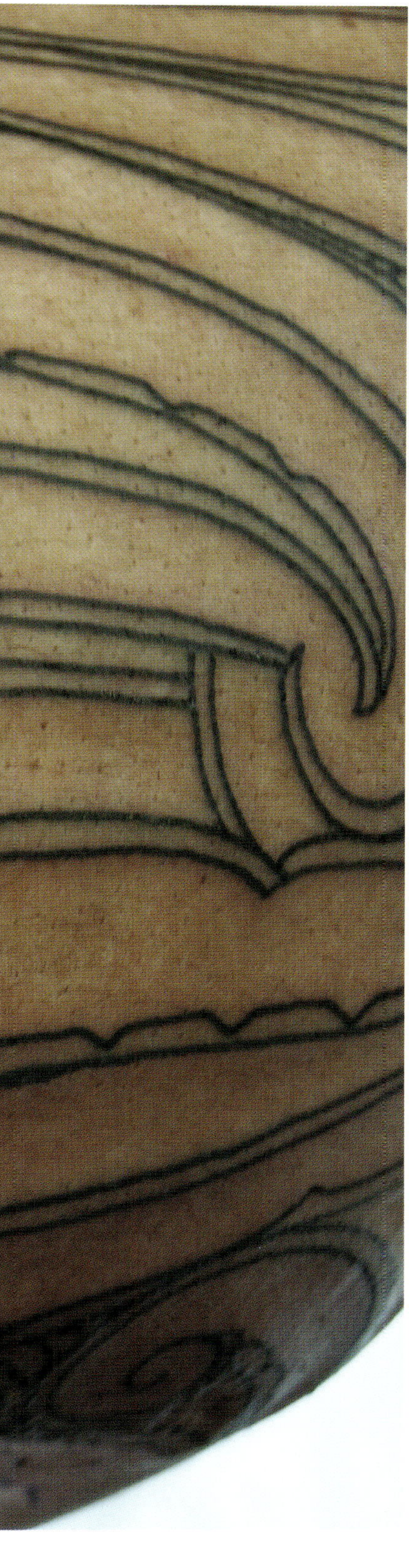

Gordon has observed a growing social acceptance of ta moko in recent years. A contributing factor is that more and more well-known sportspeople are wearing tattoos, he believes. "When we were starting out, if you saw someone with a facial moko you thought they were a gang member, but now the whole social acceptance of moko has changed. You still get cases of people being refused entry into bars and nightclubs, but those cases are few and far between."

Being able to spend a couple of months a year working overseas, with his own client base in the US and Europe, helps to keep him exposed to new influences. He values seeing what other artists around the world are doing, and he's always keen to learn from other tattooists: "I'm always learning. When you start out you think you know everything but you soon realise you don't."

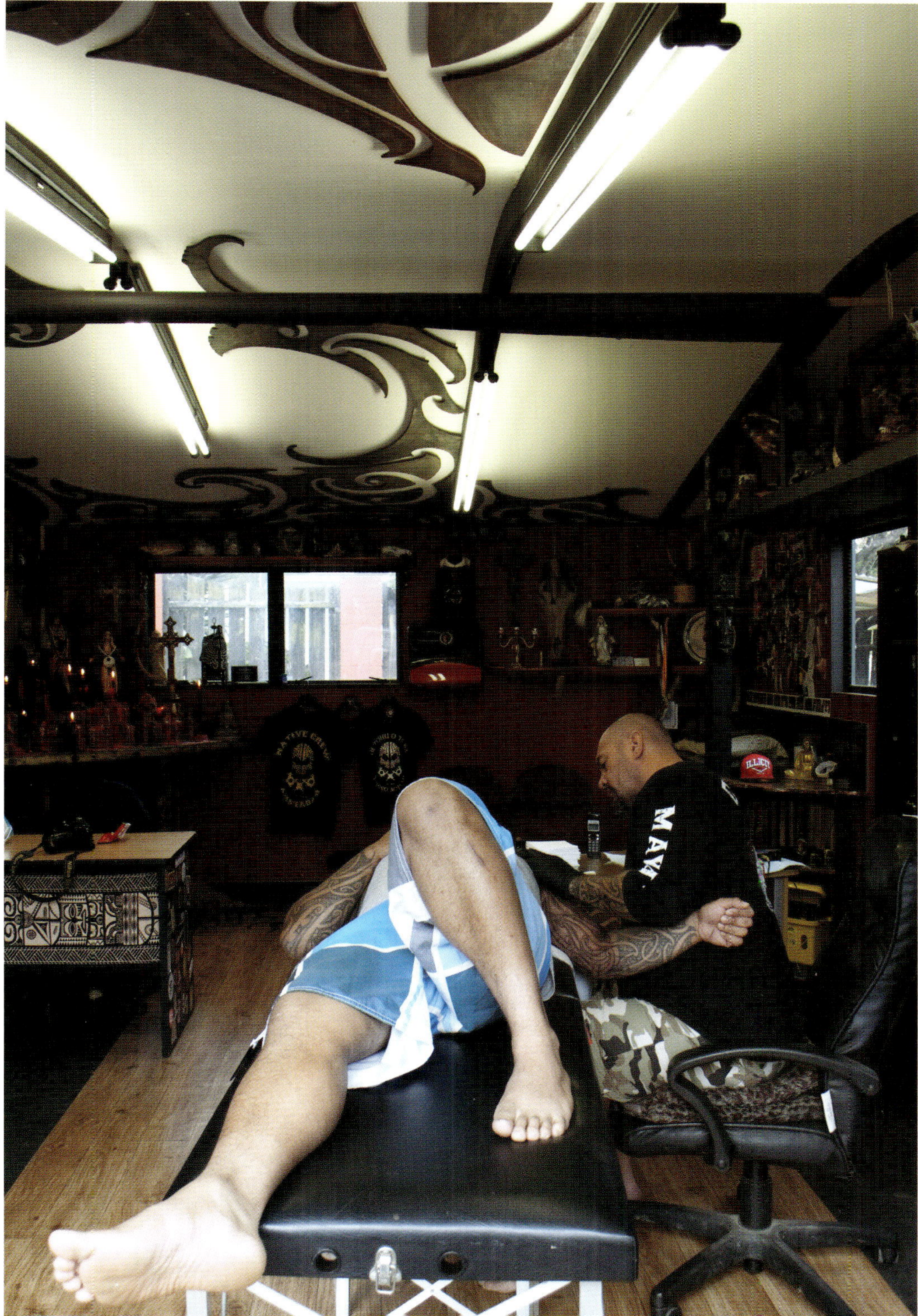

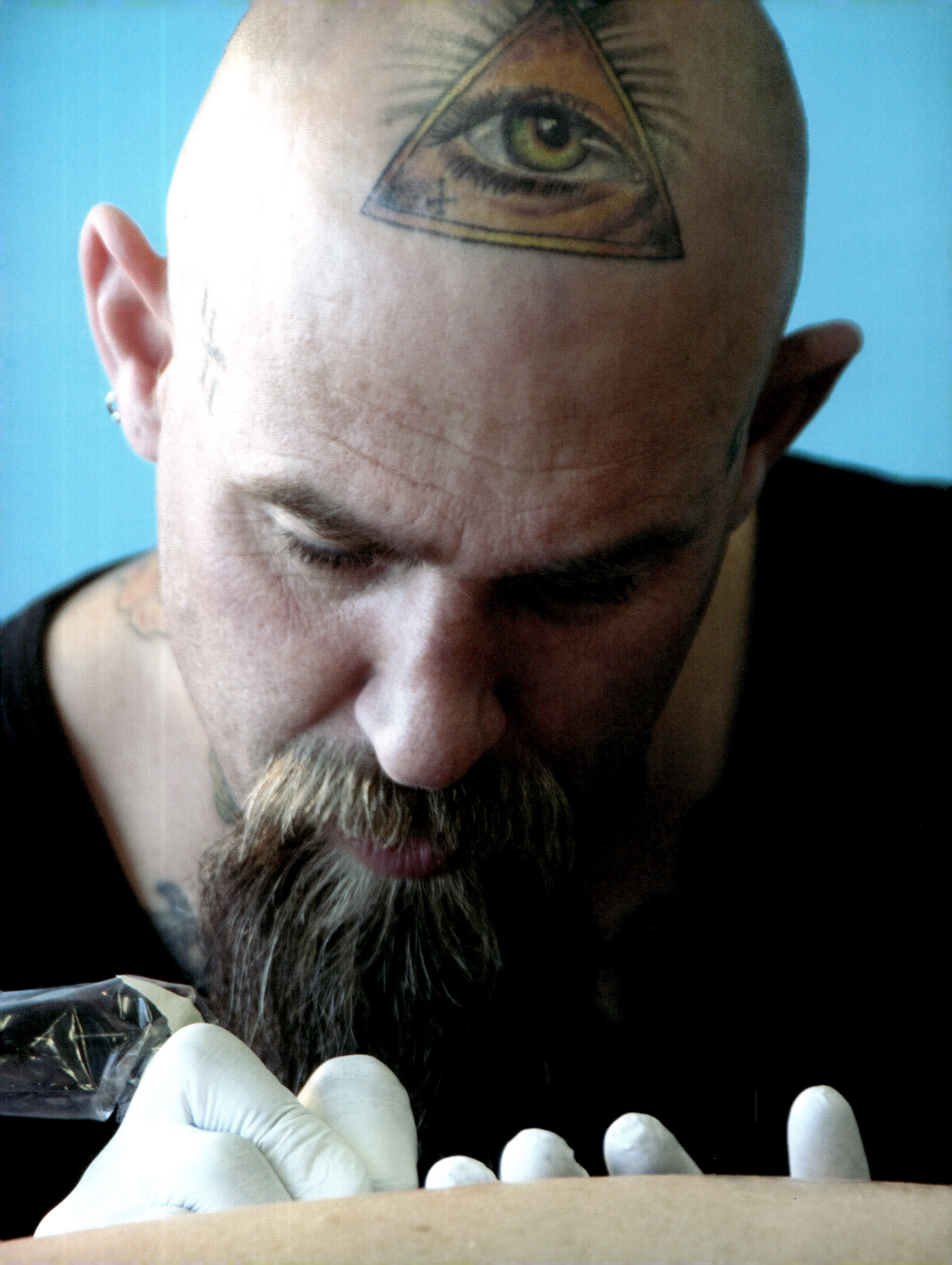

JASON **PARKINSON**

Epic Ink nestles in a row of suburban shops on the flat streets of Papanui in northern Christchurch. For Jason Parkinson and wife Tina, who commute there daily from rural Hororata, the studio they opened in April 2010 fulfils their vision to put some realism into tattooing and give their customers an honest deal.

"Life's too short to worry about offending people," is how Jason describes his approach to people and art. Tina coined his nickname, The Mad Tatter, to capture the spirit of this one-time builder and painter who has now dedicated his career entirely to tattooing. "Jason's well known for being straight up," Tina says.

That career commitment freed him to get his own neck and head tattooed, a decision not to be taken lightly. "Hands and necks are sacred when you have full sleeves and your top half done and nowhere left to go. When someone asks me to tattoo their face or hands, I ask them, 'Do you want a job that isn't a labour job digging a hole somewhere?'" Consent forms and parental involvement for teenagers is another line he draws.

Realism is key: "It influences everything I do, even if it's not direct," he says. "I'm trying to get as close to drawing what it would be if it was a real object." Colour work and portraits are favourites, but he's happy to handle black and white or themes that interest the client: "We want the customer to get exactly what's right for them with the right artist.

"For me it's about putting the reality into tattooing and making it available to everyday people," Jason reflects. The realist approach has a raw edge in the wake of the Christchurch earthquakes, with a surge in demand for tattoos of the city's ruined cathedral, names of lost loved ones, and clocks reading 12:51 (the time of the 22 February 2011 quake). For a woman who lost a leg in the quake, Jason created a tattoo saying "Breathe", the word her husband comforted her with by cellphone as she lay pinned in rubble.

Epic Ink swung into action in the quake's aftermath, hosting the Get Inked for Christchurch event of 6 March 2011. It was an epic event with nine tattooists volunteering their work from 9.30 that morning until after 1 a.m. the following day, while street performers and bands outside kept the queues of customers entertained. Jason and Tina also welcomed Mike Slade permanently to Epic (Mike had lost studios in both the September 2010 and February 2011 disasters).

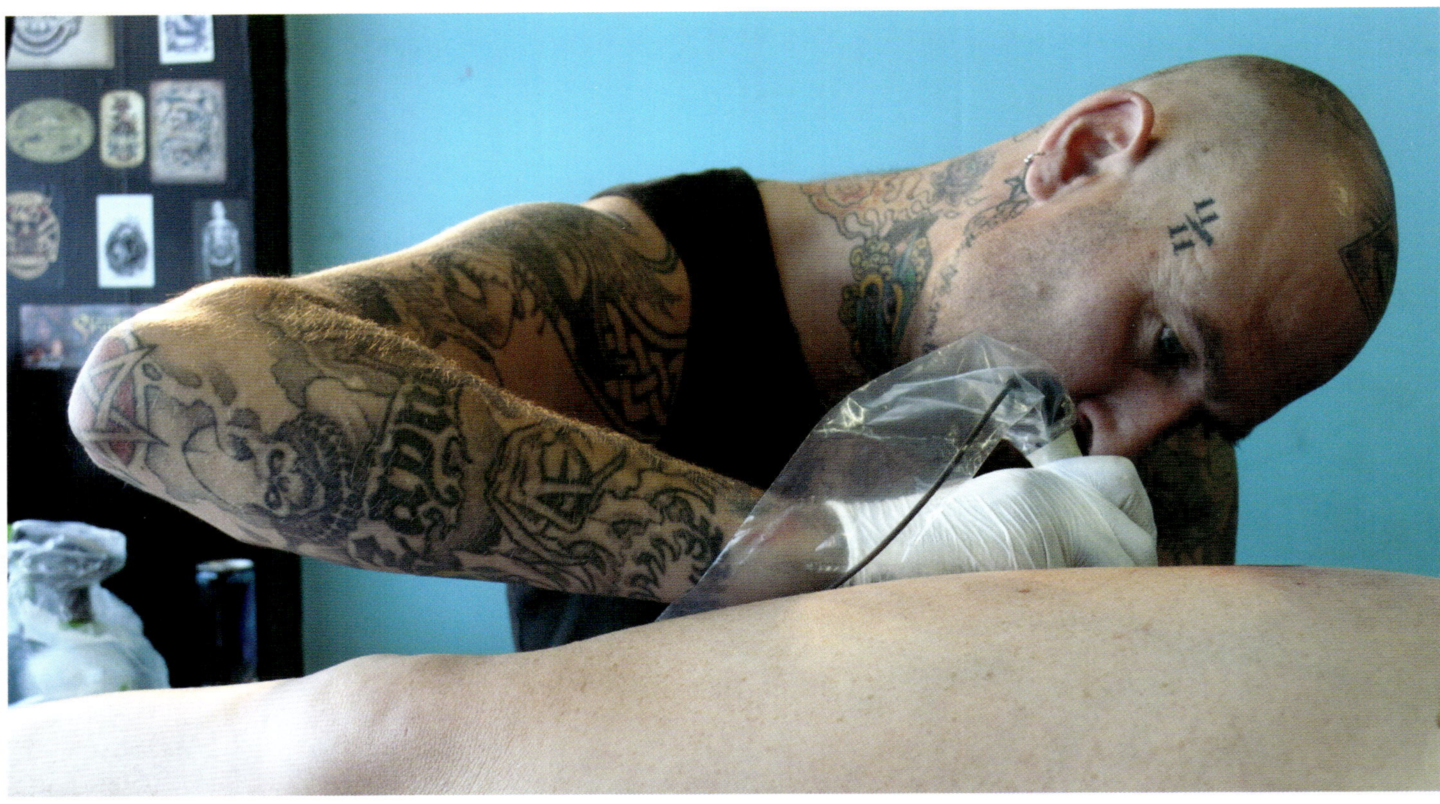

Jason learned his craft on the Kapiti Coast after being drawn to the skin artistry. "I got tattooed by Roger Ingerton in Wellington in 1991 and decided I could do it too." Back then apprenticeships were hard to find and with no internet, getting equipment was a waiting game. Jason sent a bank cheque to an American supplier for a kit, learned to make his own needles, and got started with friends.

After moving back to Tina's home ground in inland Canterbury in 2004 with their three kids, Jason tattooed in Christchurch studios before the couple set up Epic, with Tina managing the studio. Epic is in a big, open-plan store with space and freedom to employ tattooists with different styles — Frankie Jay is another regular in the shop alongside Mike — and to host visiting artists. International visitors keep coming as a result of the Parkinsons' faithful attendance at all the major conventions in Australia and New Zealand.

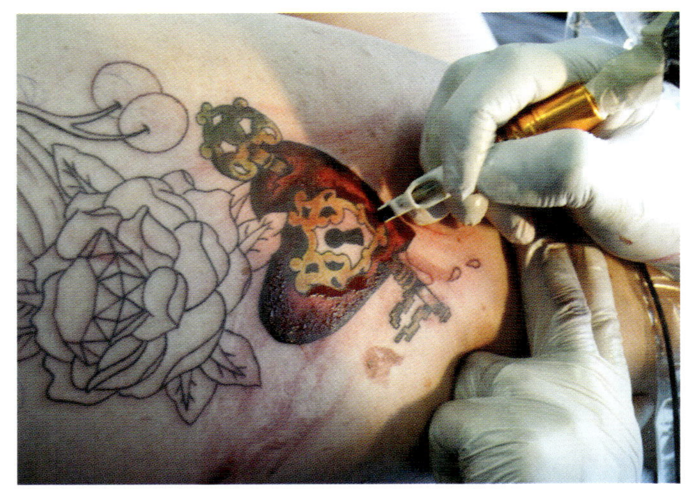

Jason and Tina like the increasingly open environment at tattoo expos, and the high calibre of work on show. "We're spoilt for the talent that's out there, and there are a lot of people that I can learn from," enthuses Jason. At the shows, Epic booths host artists from around the world — they had 13 different artists working at the International Tattoo and Art Expo in Hamilton in February 2012. "Nowadays people are more willing to socialise and learn from others. The more we share the better we can get."

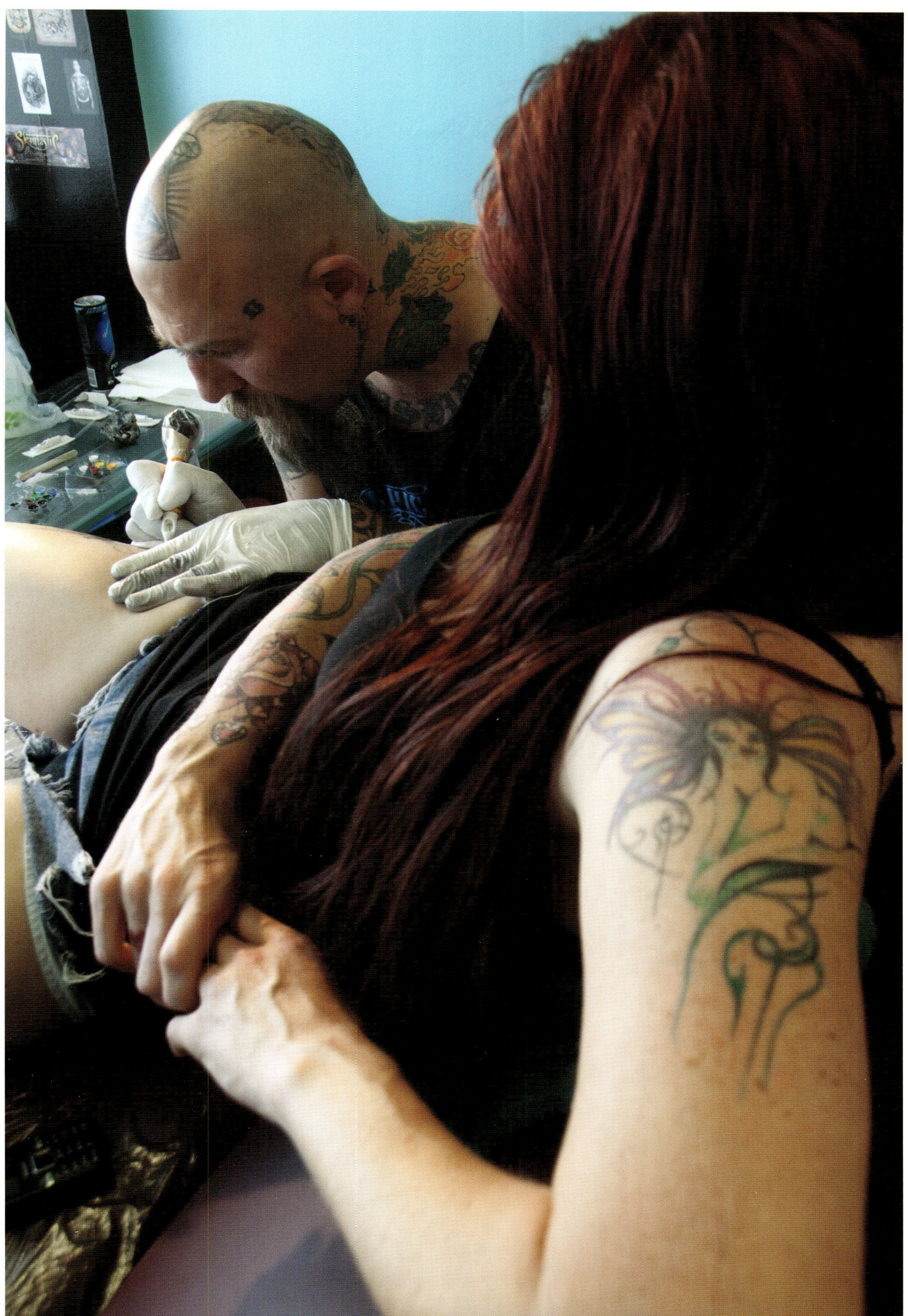

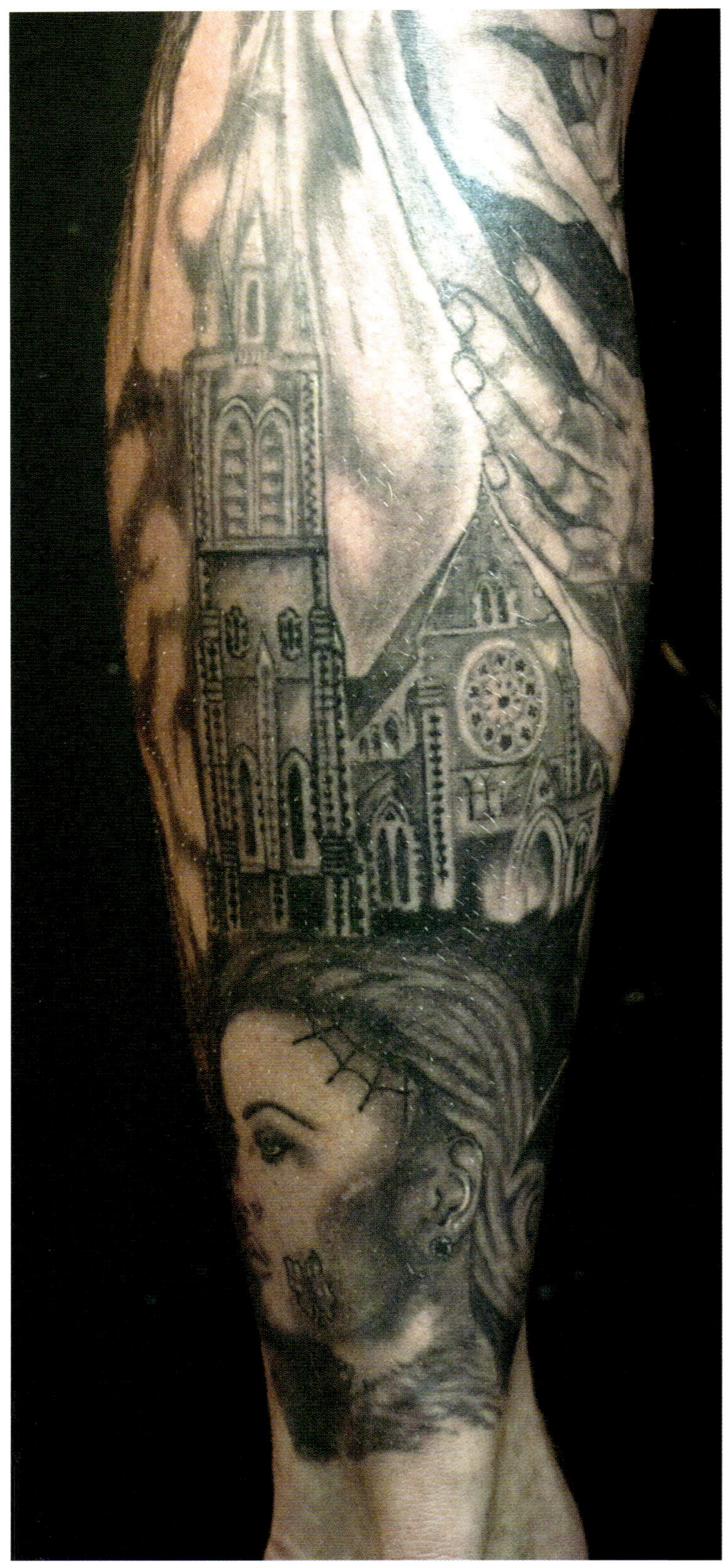

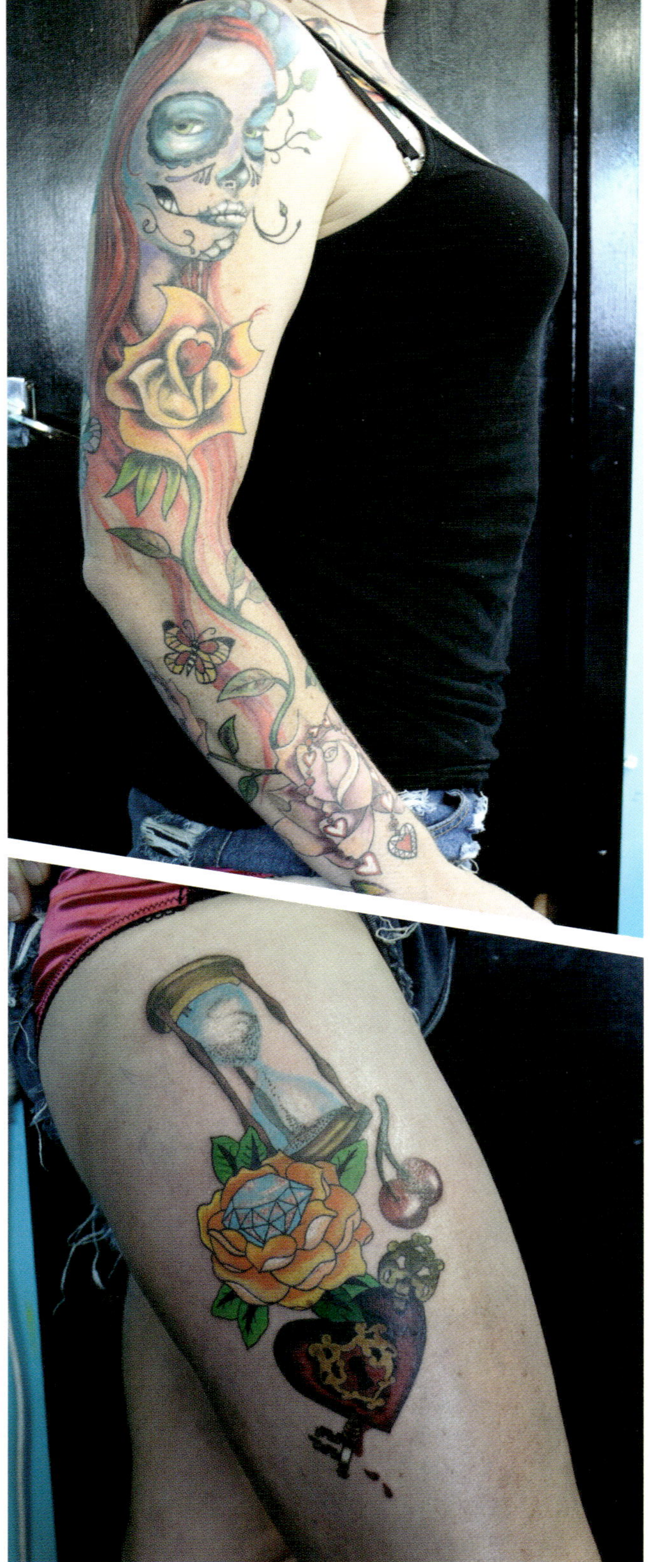

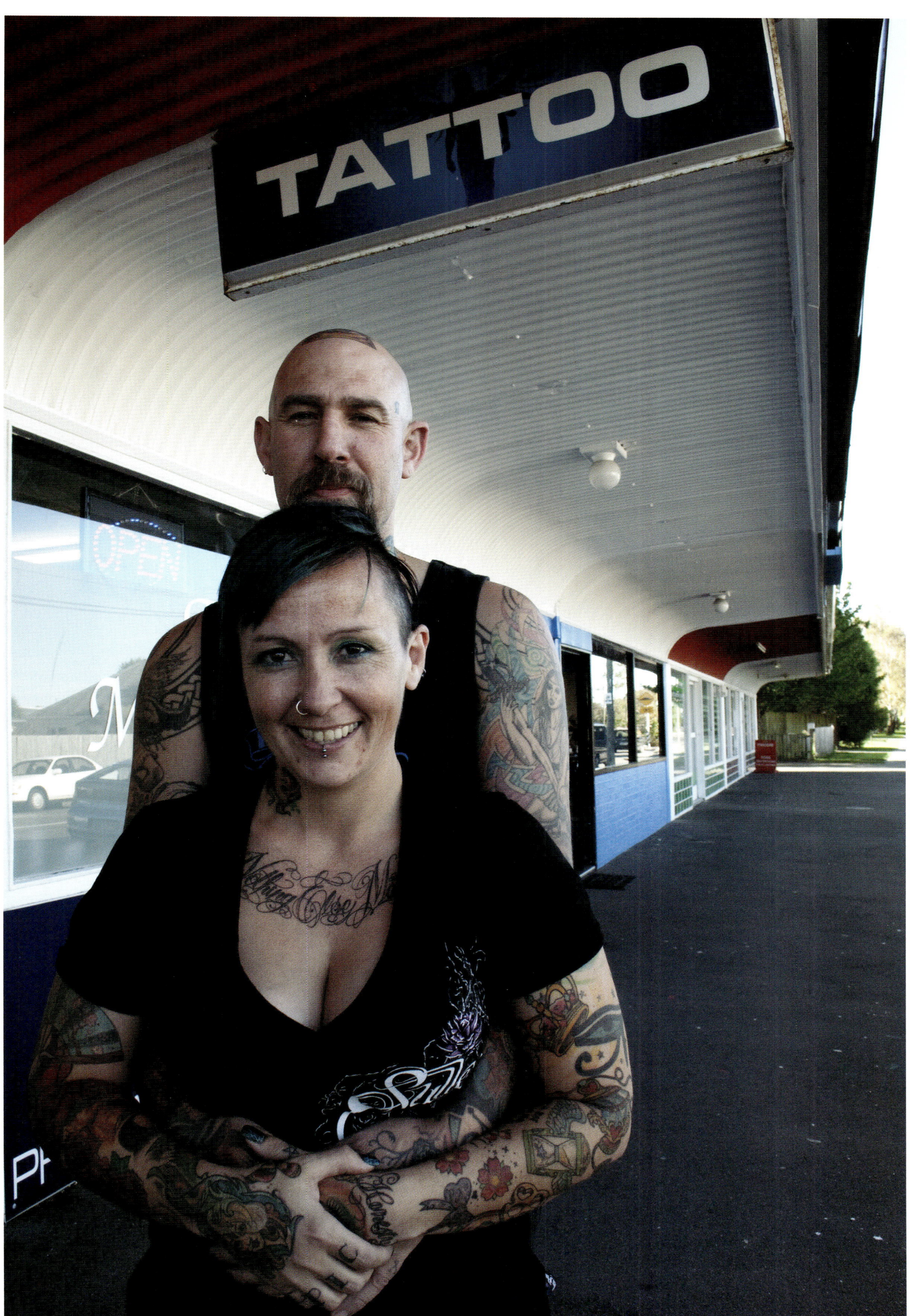
TATTOO
OPEN

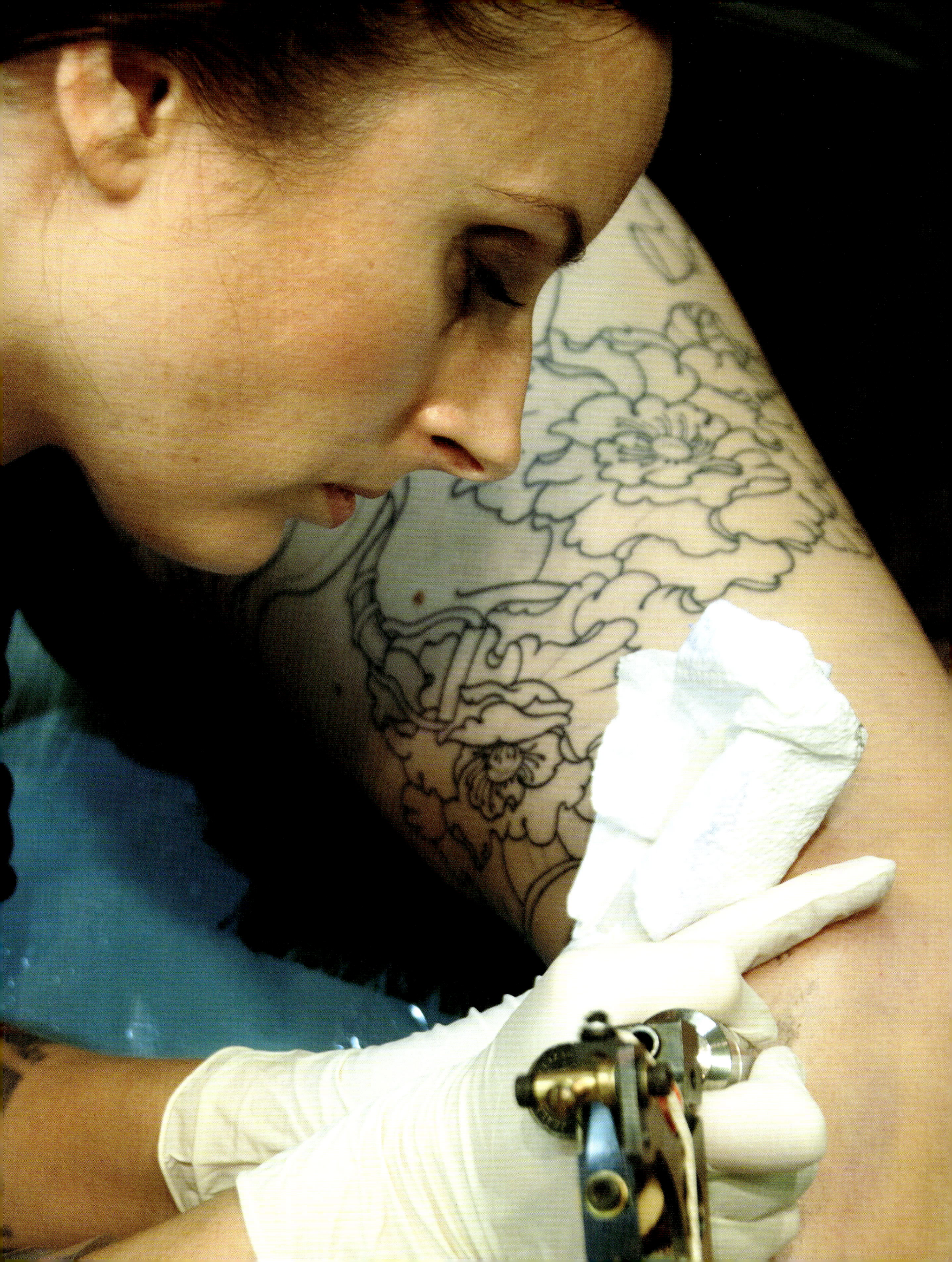

LIESJE

Liesje is one of five tattooists that make up the team at The Tattooed Heart on Auckland's Karangahape Road. The studio was opened in 2009 by artists from Illicit Tattoo.

Since cutting her teeth she's developed a name for doing everything from detailed old-school designs to Japanese-style work. "These days I do a lot of illustrative poster art."

She describes a piece she's been working on that is based on a Russian Communist-era propaganda poster: "I had to measure his arm as though I was making a clothes pattern. Then I had to match the colours from the book to the tattoo. These things take hours and hours of planning before you even start tattooing. It's quite complicated and time-consuming.

"With a big piece on someone's back you've got a flat surface, but arms and legs are a different challenge. I like doing really large pieces that fit a person's body — things that have a certain amount of flow and fit with the place they are in." She also likes doing Japanese-style tattooing: "There are a lot of rules with it in regard to what goes together. If you aren't brought up with it you've got to be aware of those things."

Liesje first tried her hand at tattooing when she was living with her boyfriend in Los Angeles about ten years ago. They were both trying to learn: "We'd go down to see this Japanese guy, Jiro, who had a small studio in a skate shop." He was really helpful to the young couple and provided them with some much-needed advice. "We also knew some guys who had a studio called Devil Doll Tattoo and Body Piercing Studio, in the Valley. We swapped some artwork with them for some machines." But they were still finding their feet. "We had the equipment but we were mucking around and didn't know what we were doing."

She returned to New Zealand in 2003 and it wasn't long until she met Adam Craft, who offered her an apprenticeship at Illicit Tattoo. "I started the traditional way — making needles, drawing all the time, breaking down the equipment, sterilising the equipment. The stencils would be made by hand." Since then she has developed a reputation for her work and regularly features at the country's top tattoo conventions.

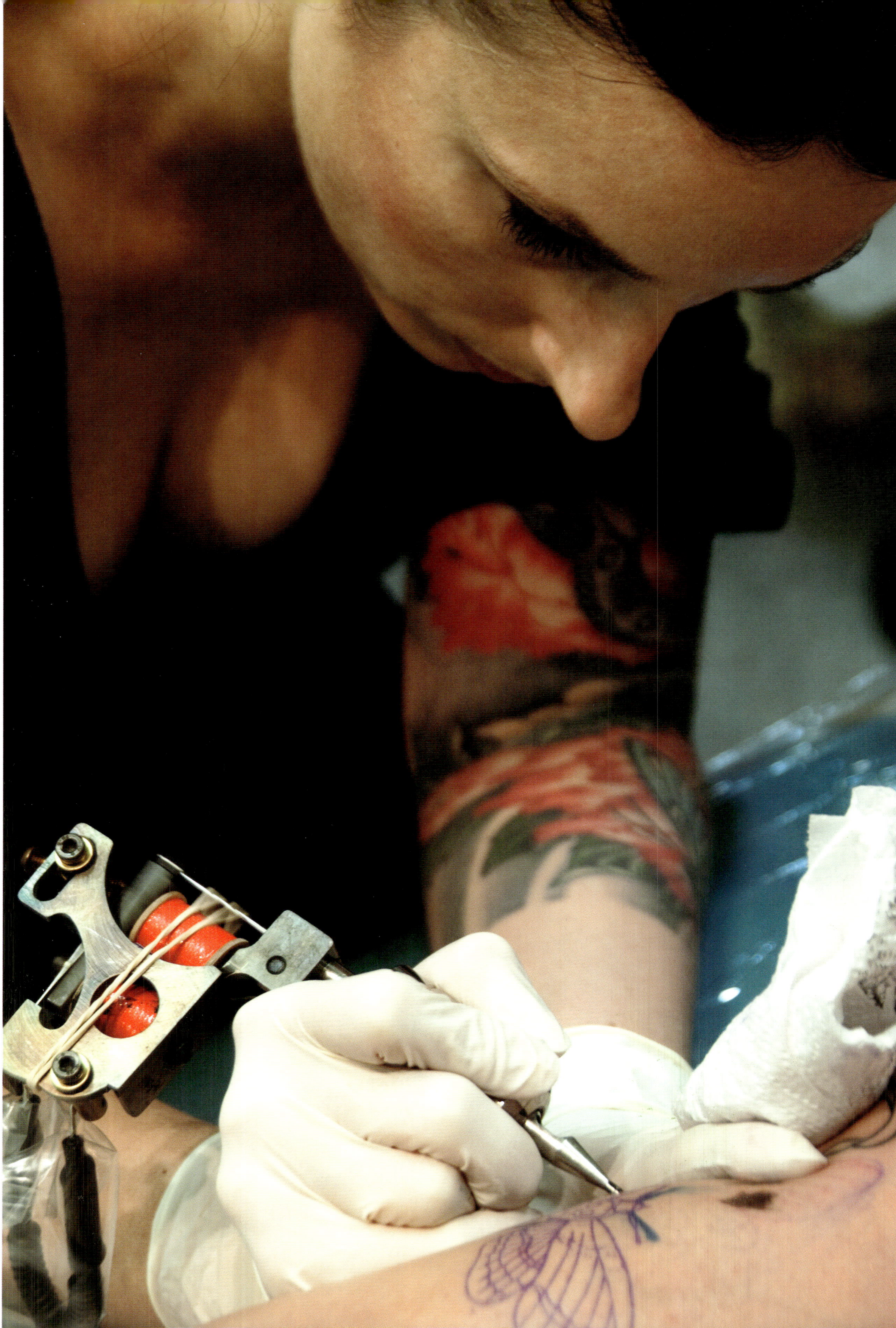

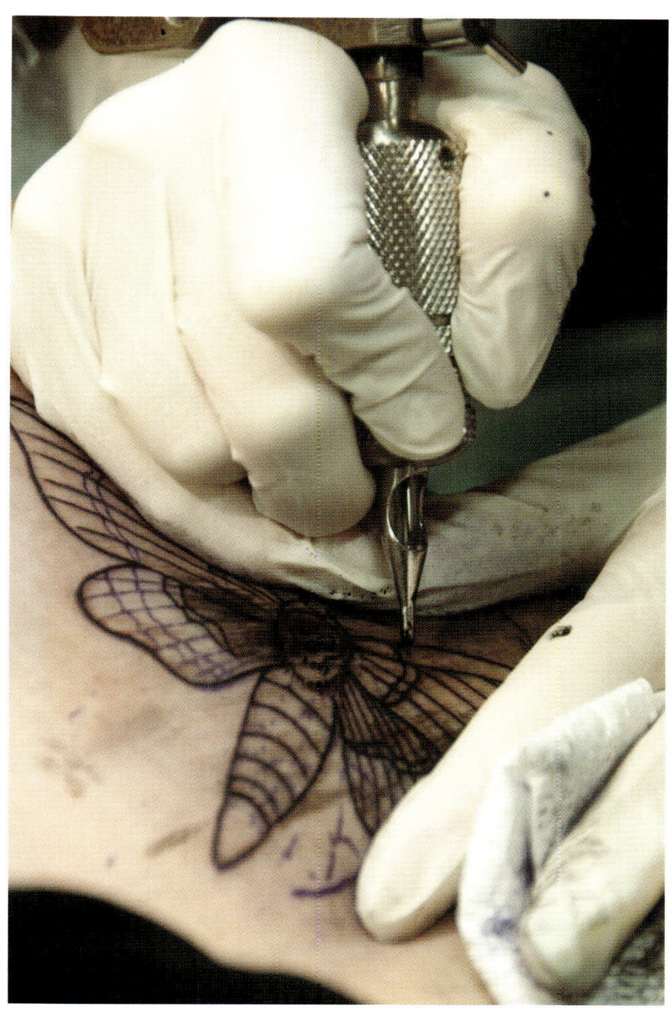

New Zealand tattooing is in a strong position, Liesje believes: "I think it's pretty healthy, even if it's a bit crowded and there are a lot of new shops opening up. Someone told me there are now 30 studios in Wellington alone. Whenever any profession becomes popular everyone starts doing it. You would hope it would lead to higher standards."

Despite the popularity of her own work and the money tattooists can make, she is adamant that the art should come first: "None of the people I consider to be at the top of the profession are concerned with the financial side of it. Their only consideration is their own thoughts and those of clients and peers."

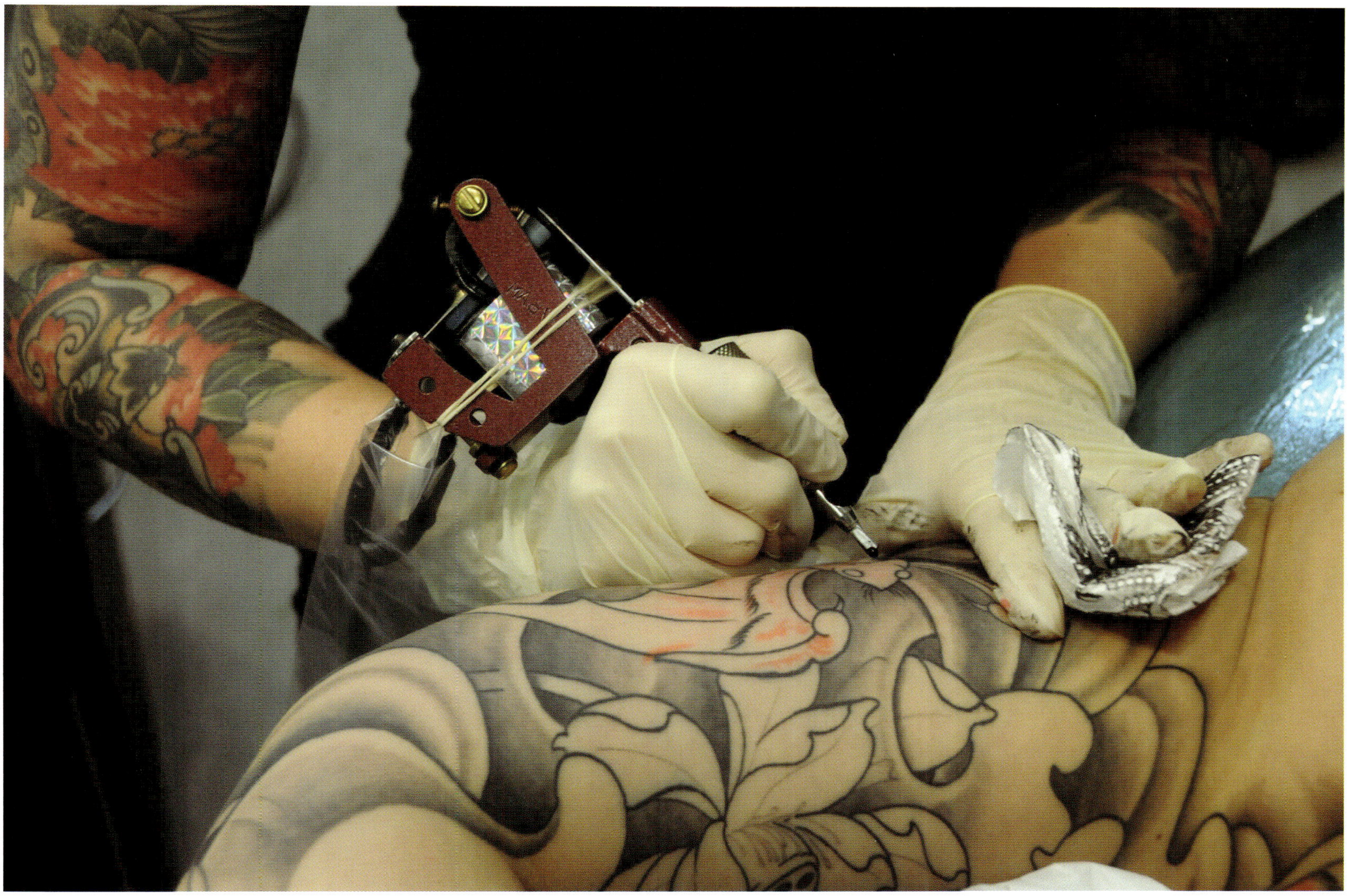

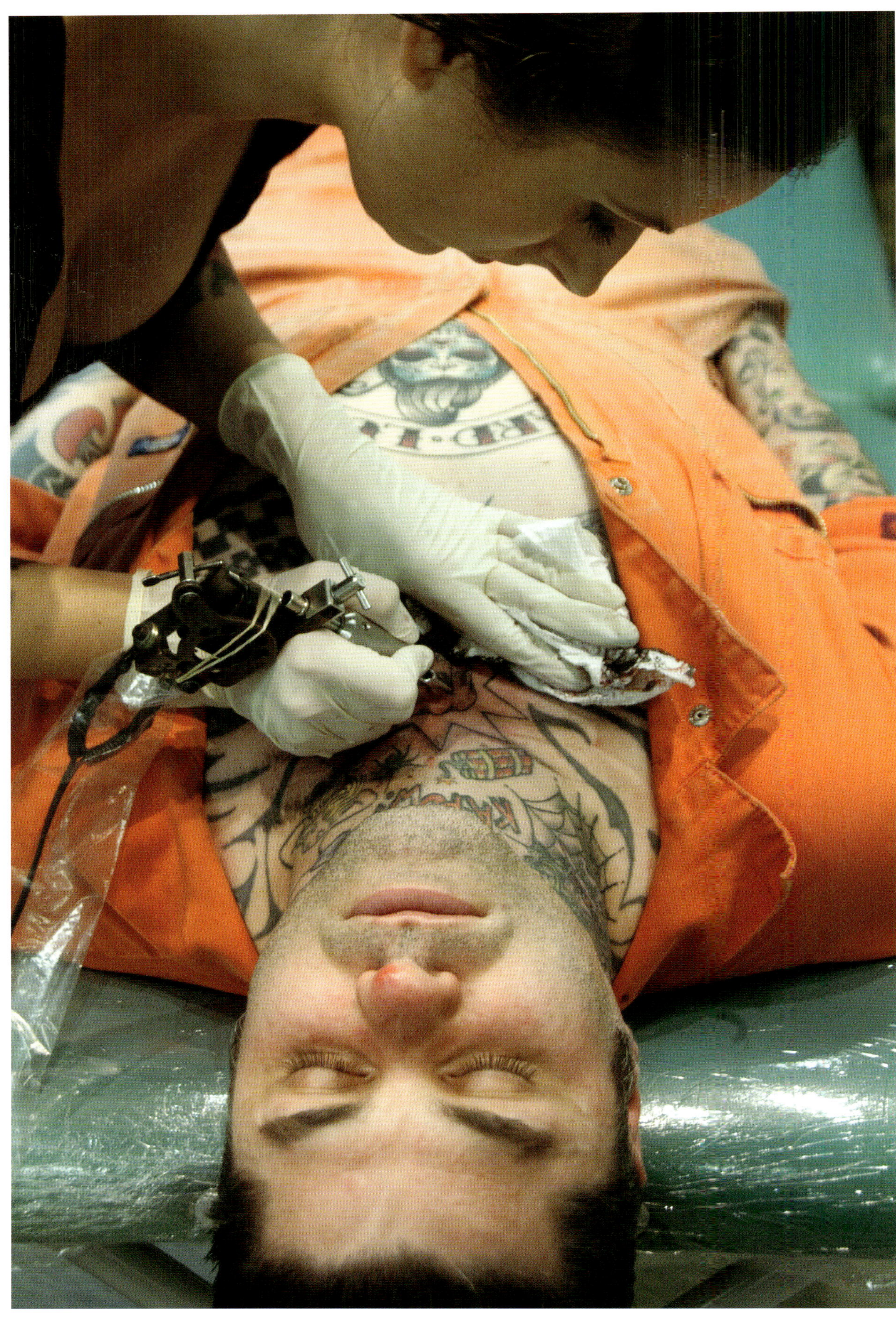

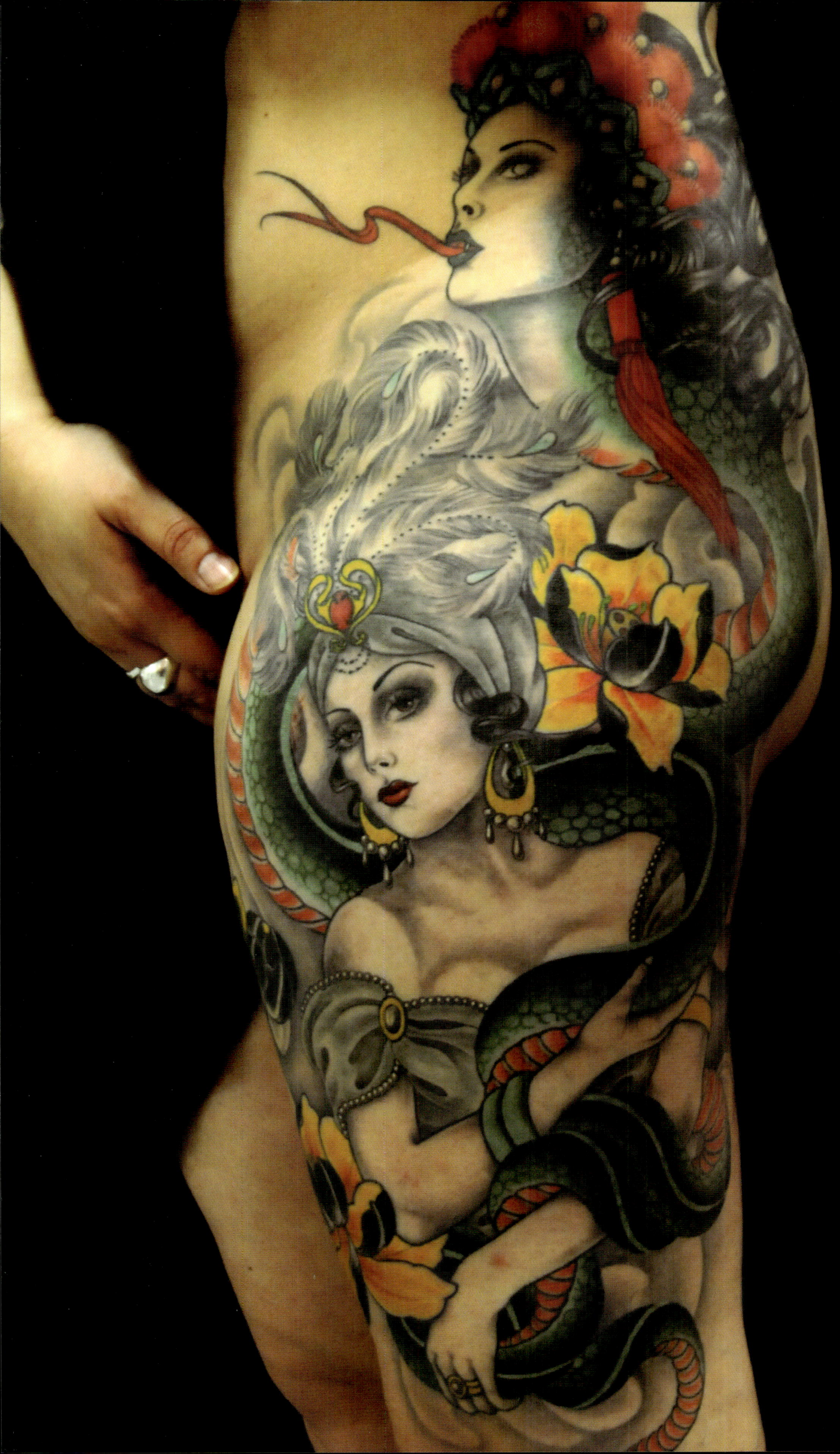

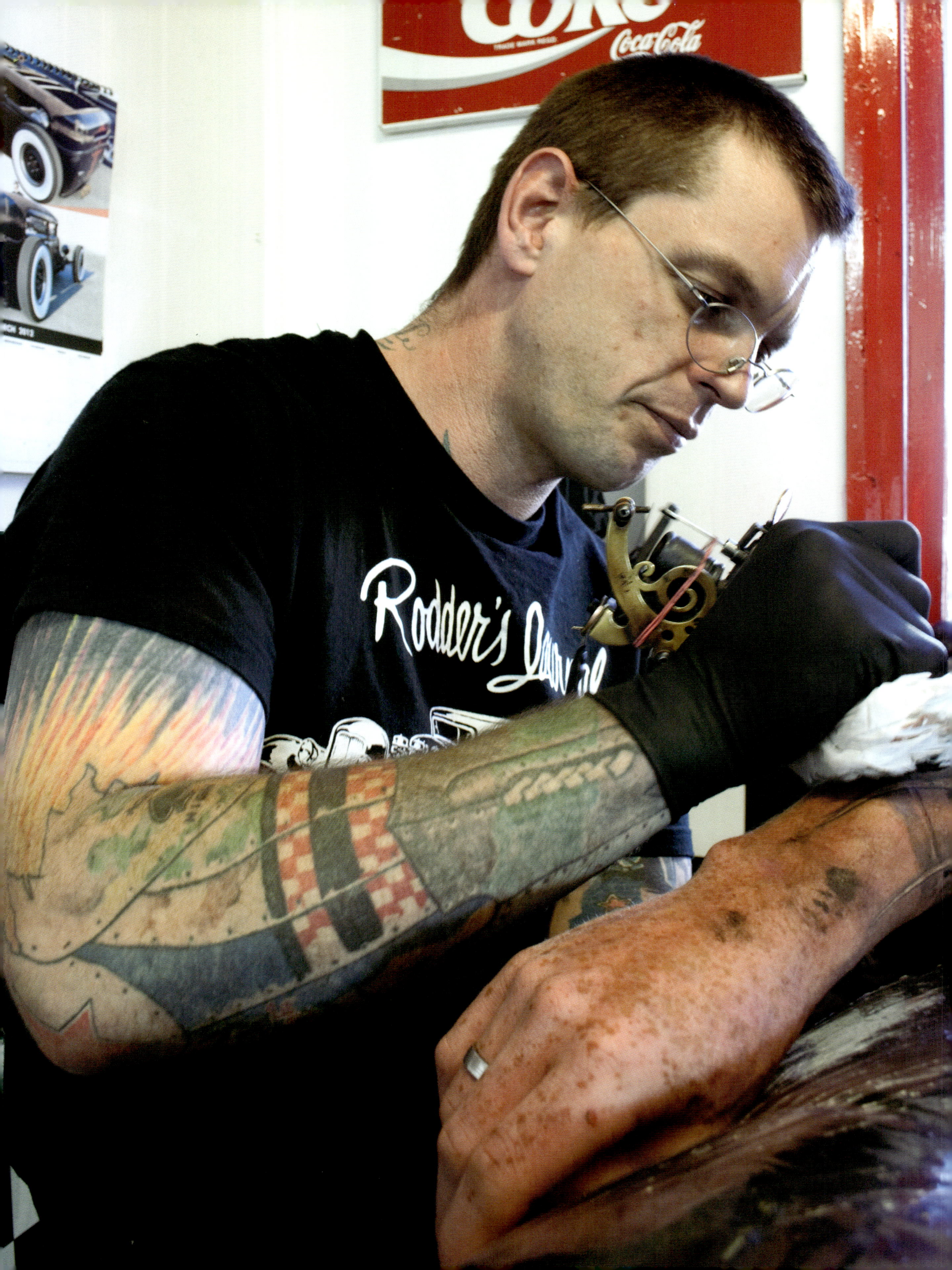
Coke
Coca-Cola
Rodder's

NICK **REEDY**

DIG A TATTOO

Dig A Tattoo is a name synonymous with tattooing in the South Island. John 'Digs' Diggle founded the studio in the old inner-city suburb of Addington, Christchurch, in 1986. Over the years Dig A Tattoo expanded to include a mobile truck-and-trailer unit that travelled the island (John now works only from this) and a shop on Princes Street in Dunedin (run by a former Christchurch employee, Brendan Smith, now trading as Agency Ink). The original studio on Lincoln Road in Addington was destroyed in the earthquake of February 2011.

But Dig A Tattoo lives on in Greymouth, under the direction of Nick Reedy. Brought up on the West Coast, Nick spent over 17 years in Christchurch, almost all of it working with John. He came back to Greymouth in late 2009 to set up studio with local tattooist Ange Woods in a space they renovated with the same red-and-white branding as the Lincoln Road studio. Happily settled back with his family, Nick imagines he'll always stay tattooing under the Dig A Tattoo flag.

In 1991 Nick had been studying for a Diploma in Visual Communications at Christchurch Polytech and immersing himself in the local music scene. Then he met John and decided he liked tattooing. John invited Nick to become his apprentice and he took up the challenge in 1993. "I learned everything from Digs: I didn't really mix with other tattooists, and stayed in Addington. At the end I couldn't believe I'd stayed there for that long," says Nick as he works on Tainui Street in Greymouth.

Steve Johnson gave him his first tat (a Batman head) in 1991. Nick still has a fascination with Marvel comics and science fiction that led to the "dark Gotham" flavour of that tattoo. "I do a lot of biomechanical and sci-fi stuff, more modern than steampunk. My style is black and white pencil for my own drawing, then the art I do is whatever people want."

Auto car art is another string to his bow, and car drawings adorn the studio walls. "First I was right into tattooing — I was a tattooist. Then I was a tattooist because that was my job; and then I became interested in muscle cars, then home-made hot-rods and rat-rods, or jalopies." But working six days a week in the Lincoln Road nerve centre didn't leave much time for his two sons, let alone the Scavengers car club.

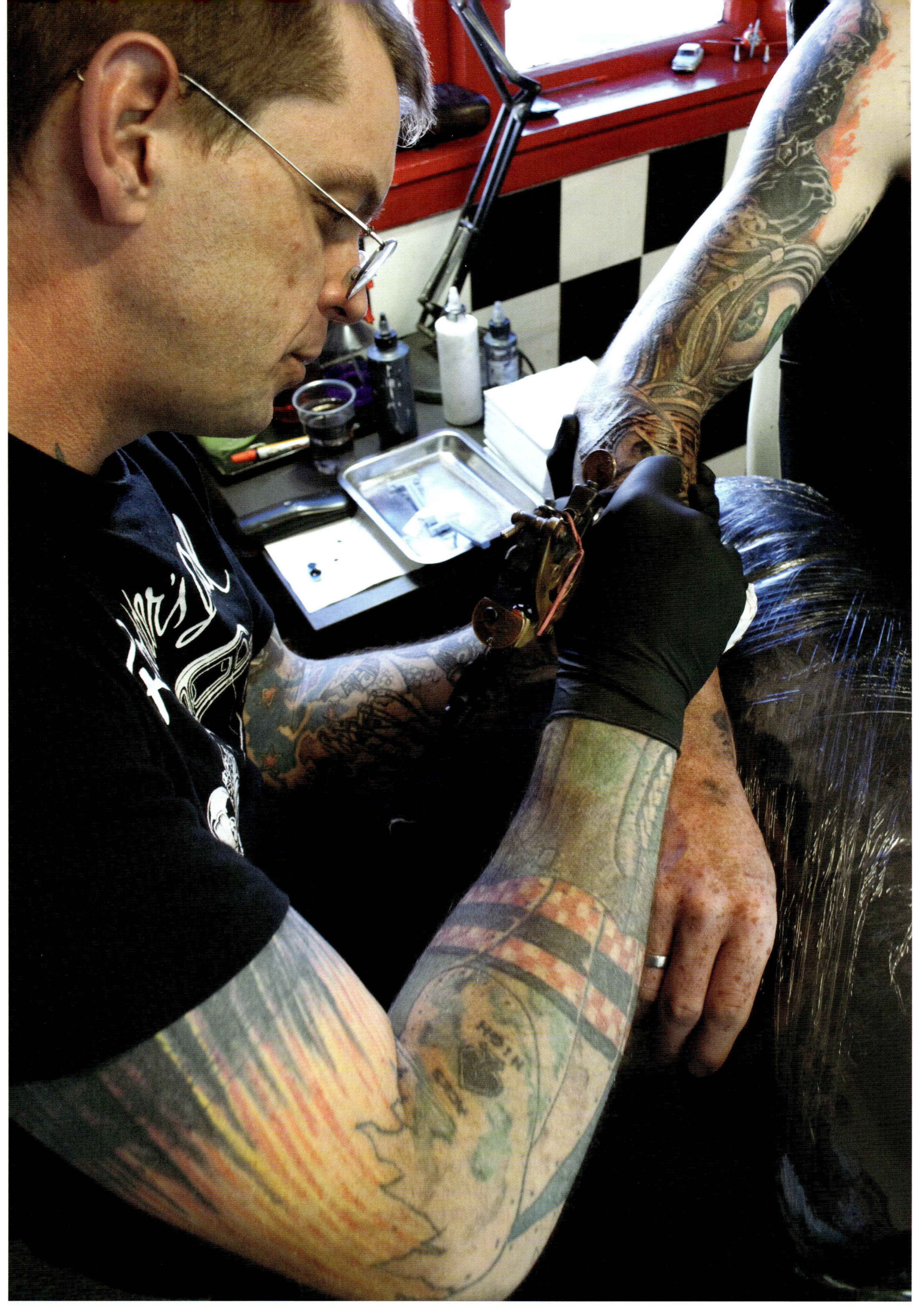

In Greymouth he's working five days a week and reconnecting with the local community (wife Deb is also a Coaster). Coal mining has rejuvenated the town since he was a boy here, Nick says, and he tattoos a lot of coal miners now. "They're a tight crew, really a good bunch, very compassionate and switched on."

After the Pike River mining disaster on 19 November 2010, Dig A Tattoo gave free tattoos to families of the miners. Nick created a schema of Gothic roses to commemorate those who died, with the size of the flowers indicating their ages. What struck him was how few of the miners were represented by full blooms, since most of those who died were in their teens or twenties.

Nick ended up tattooing at least 200 people, but is modest about the exhausting effort he put in: "We were all in it together and they were upset. Everyone had to be involved in the helping and moving on."

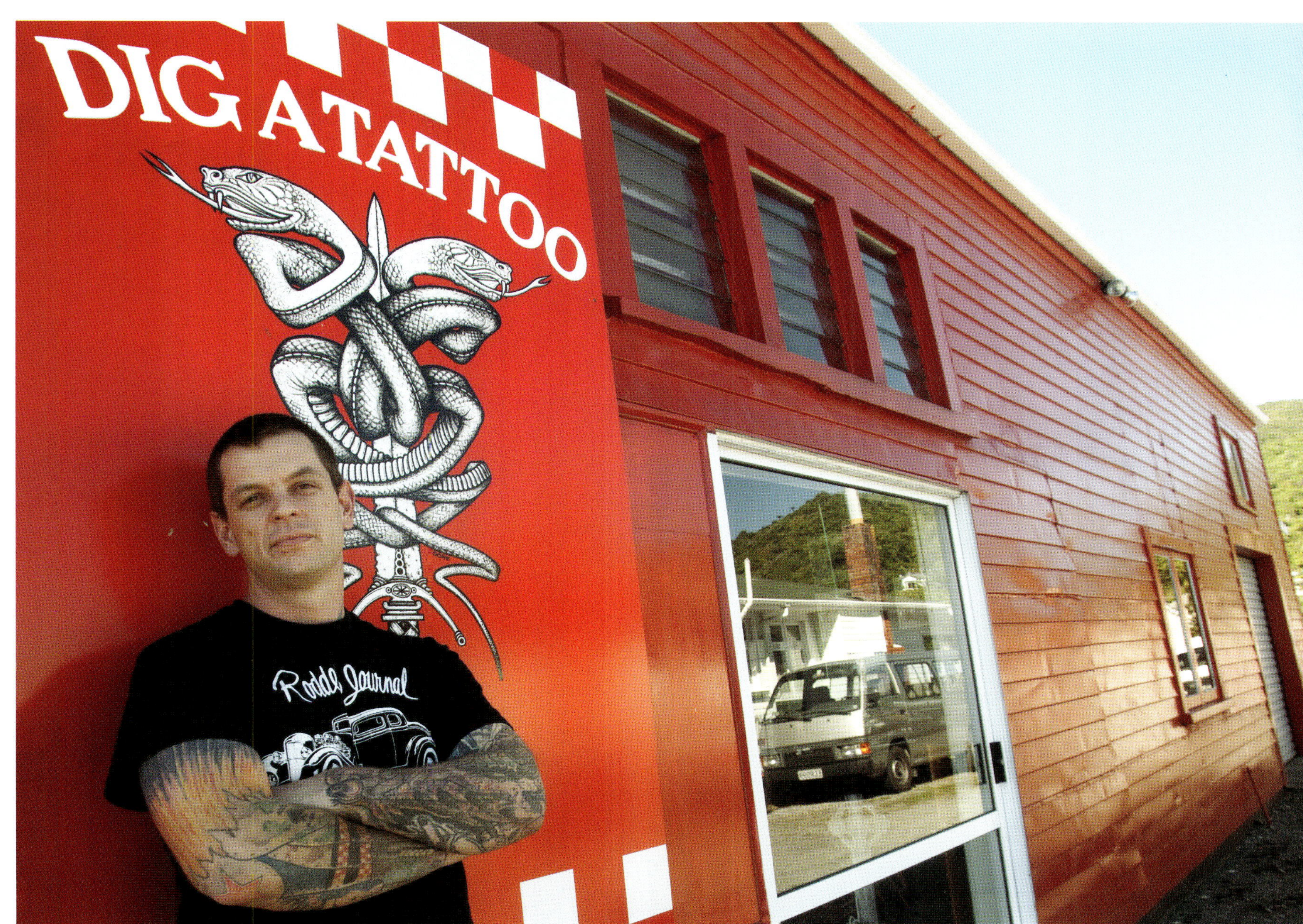

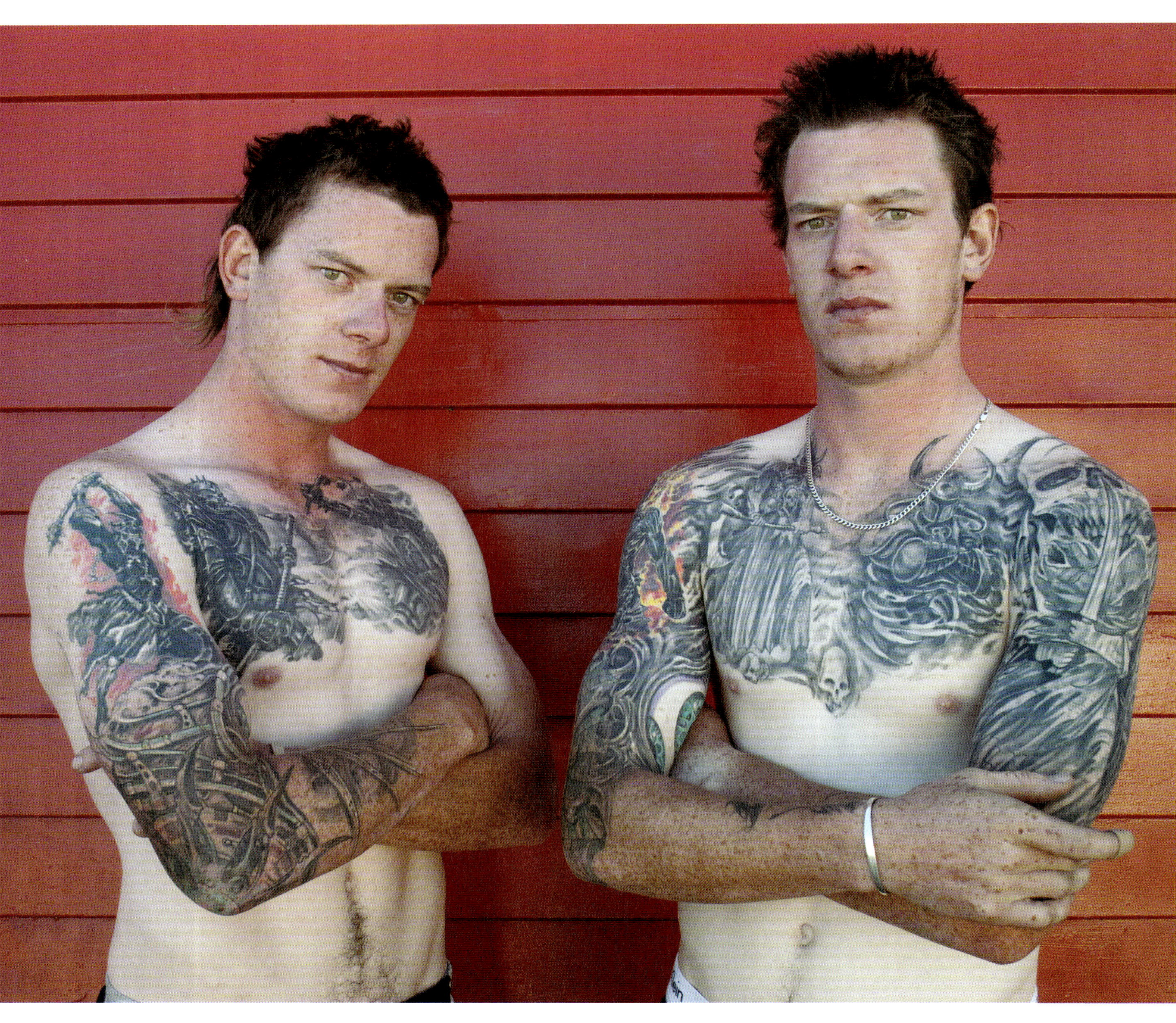

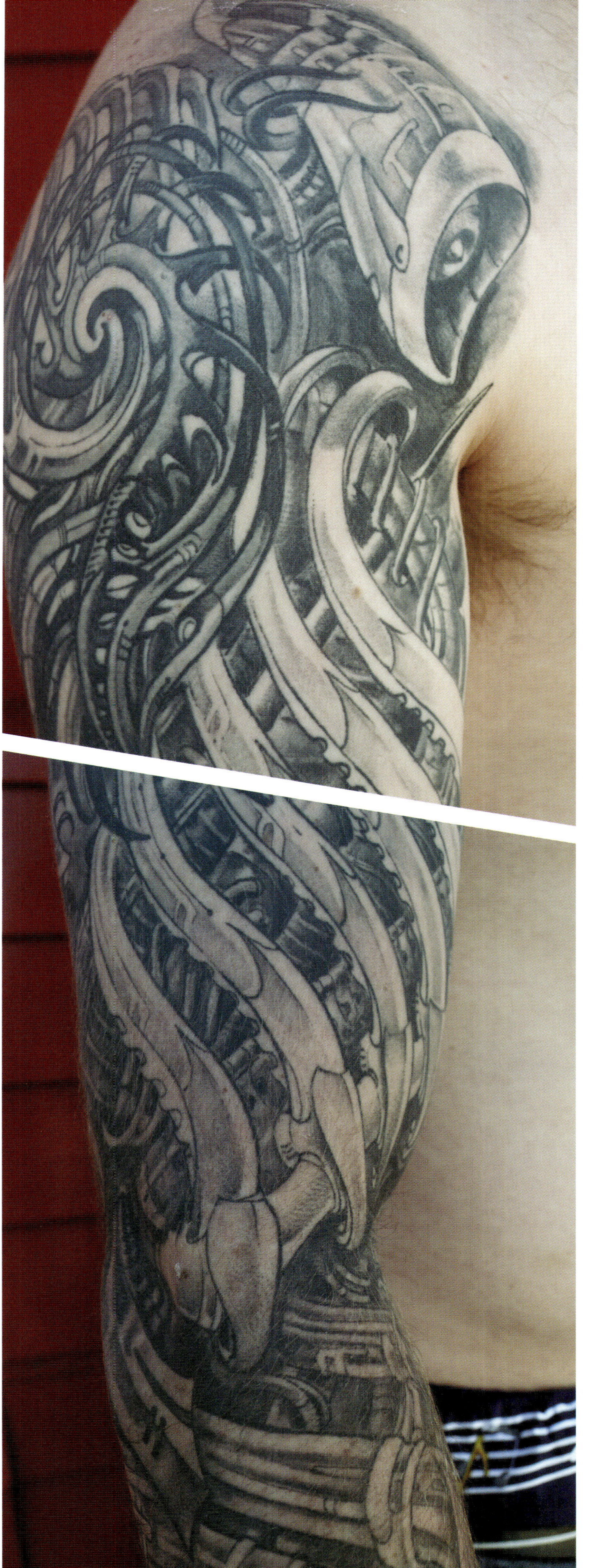

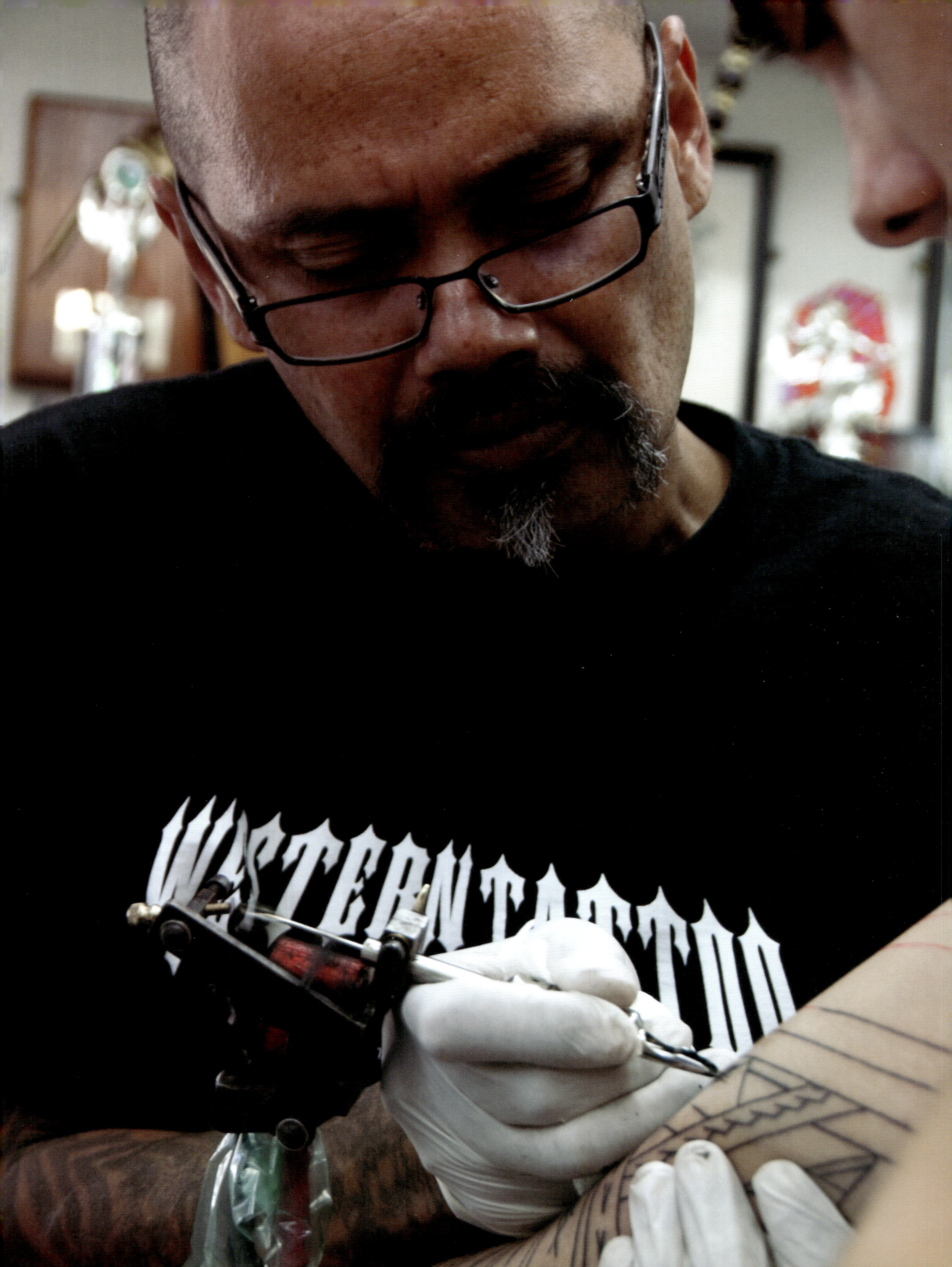

WESTERN TATTOO

STEVE **MA** CHING

Over the past 30 years Steve Ma Ching has developed an international reputation for his tattooing. Nowadays most of his clients at Western Tattoo, the West Auckland studio he started in 1994, come from overseas. "They'll fly in the night before and I'll do a full sleeve in a day. Then they fly out the next day," he says.

Steve started tattooing when he was still a teenager. He'd tried getting work from Auckland tattooist Merv O'Connor, to no avail. But he wasn't deterred, and when Sailor Geoff Kelly opened Mt Albert Tattoo he started hanging out at the new studio. "One night when he was really busy I said I'd draw up the transfers to help him out." Steve went back the next day and was told he had a job. "I was only 16 and he gave me an apprenticeship."

It was a big step up for him: "I was working in a shoe factory at the time, punching the sizes on shoes." Within three years he owned Mt Albert Tattoo. In 1986 he decided it was time to move on and opened a new shop in a market on Queen Street. But after two years the owner of the market went bust and Steve moved out and took a break from the industry.

"Then one day I caught up with Merv O'Connor and he asked me if I wanted to work with him in his shop in Richmond Road. I thought I'd work with him for six months, but ended up staying for five and half years. I owe a lot to Merv: he taught me the business side of things.

"And he changed my outlook on life. When I first started most tattooists were drunks and party animals. Drugs were rife in the industry, but Merv was always level headed. I never really got into that, and that's why I'm still a tattooist after 31 years. I've seen a lot of guys drop out of the industry through drugs and misadventure."

Around the same time he met Paulo Suluape, who offered to teach him and encouraged him to use traditional tools. But Steve decided to stick with the machine. "Then I ended up opening Western Tattoo in New Lynn. I had the first permanent tattoo shop out here."

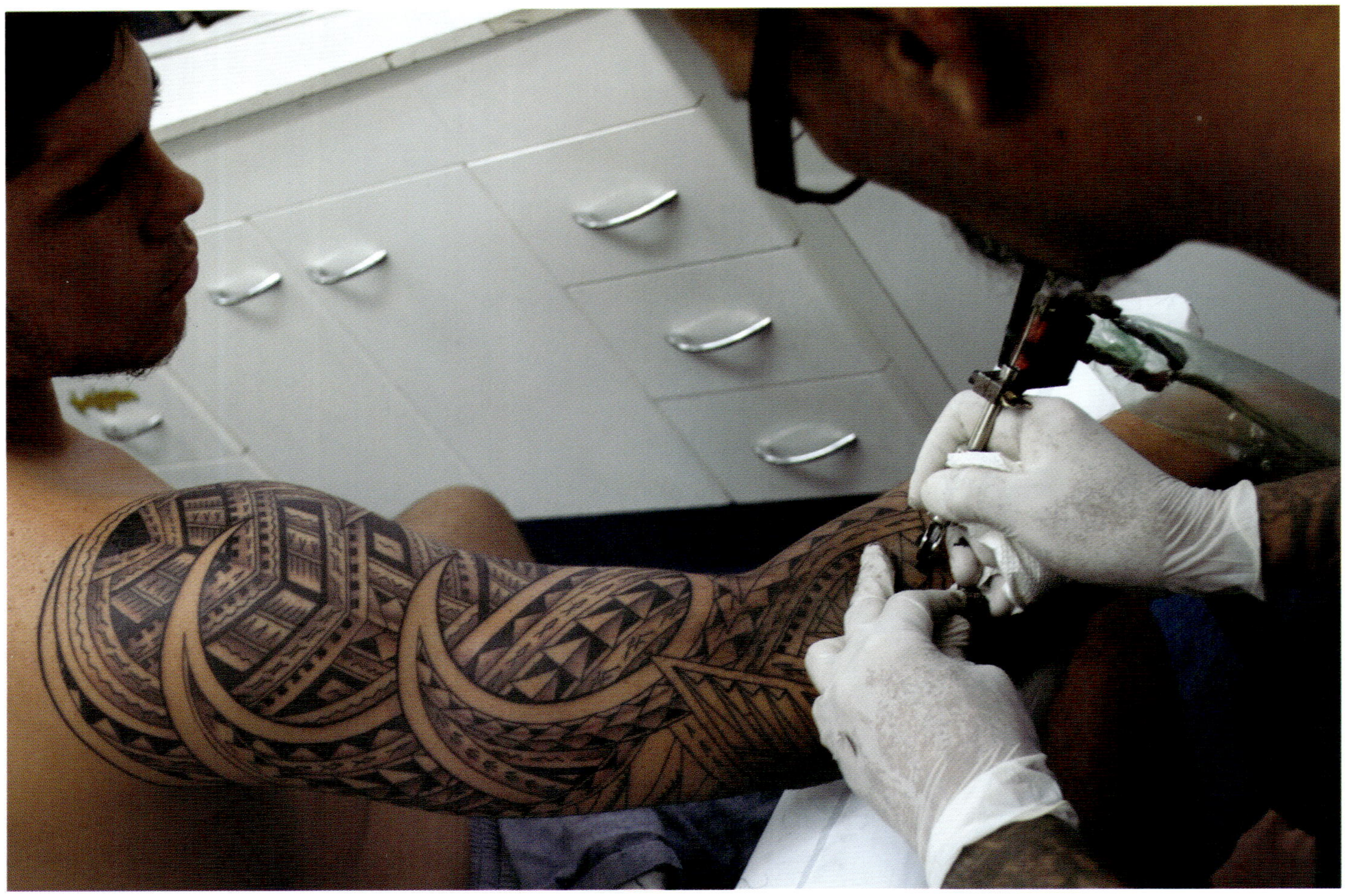

Steve says New Zealand tattooing is better than ever. "There are some guys doing unreal work. It's funny to see the revival of old-school tattooing, but some of these young guys have turned it into an art form. I'm lucky that I changed my style and I'm doing more tribal and cultural stuff.

"When we started we were limited because a person would say they wanted design X off the wall. It would only be occasionally that you could do something different. But nowadays you get art school graduates working as tattooists. My mum used to be embarrassed to tell people that I was a tattooist. It used to be the seedy side of society, but not any more."

Steve has been heading offshore as well: "In the last few years I've been working overseas, off and on, in Hawaii and the States." This has included guest spots at Steve Suluape's Pacific Soul Tattoo in Honolulu and Wu's Humble Beginnings Tattoo Studio in San José, California. "But the main guy I've worked with is Bong Padilla at Tattoos by Bong in Honolulu."

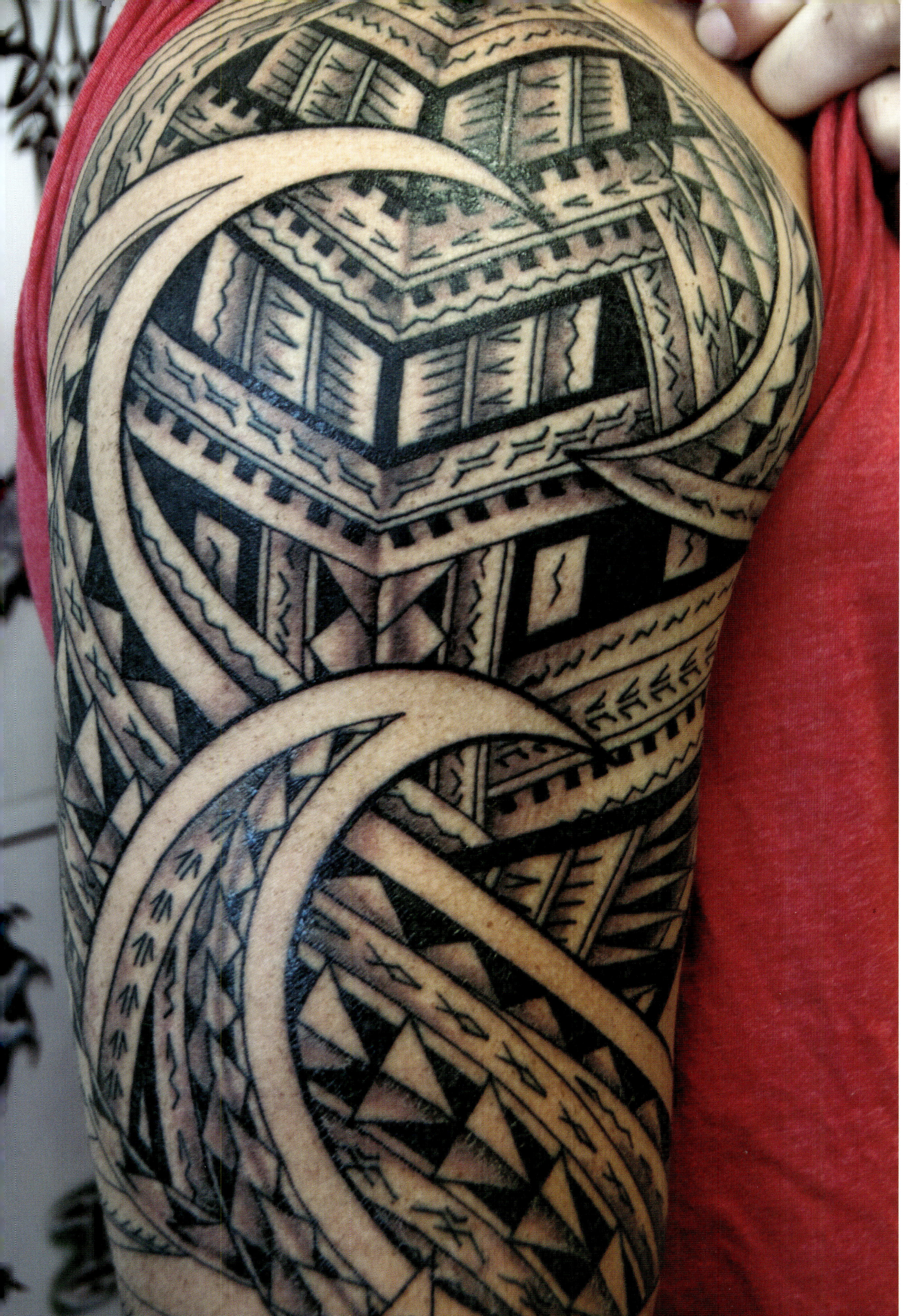

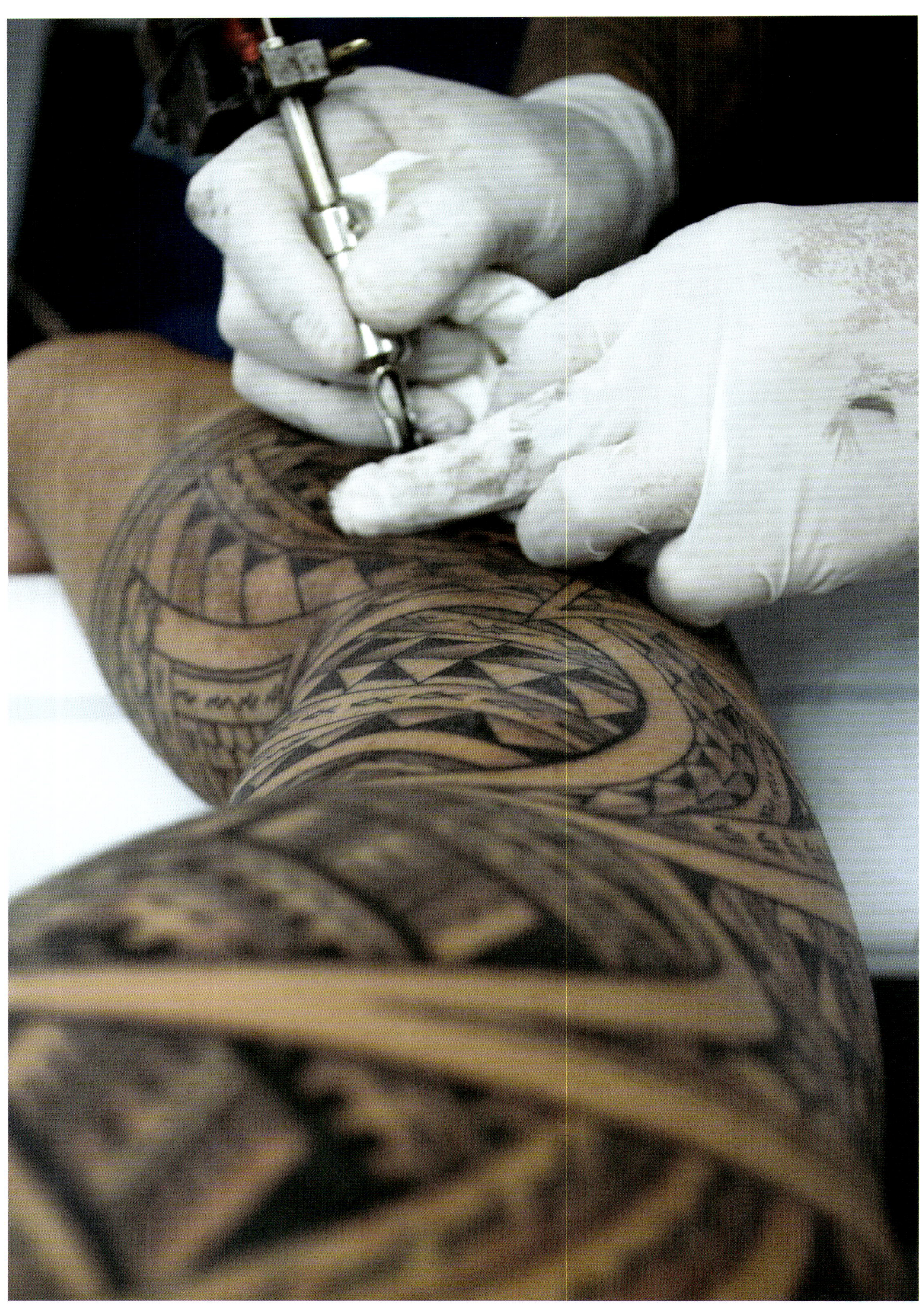

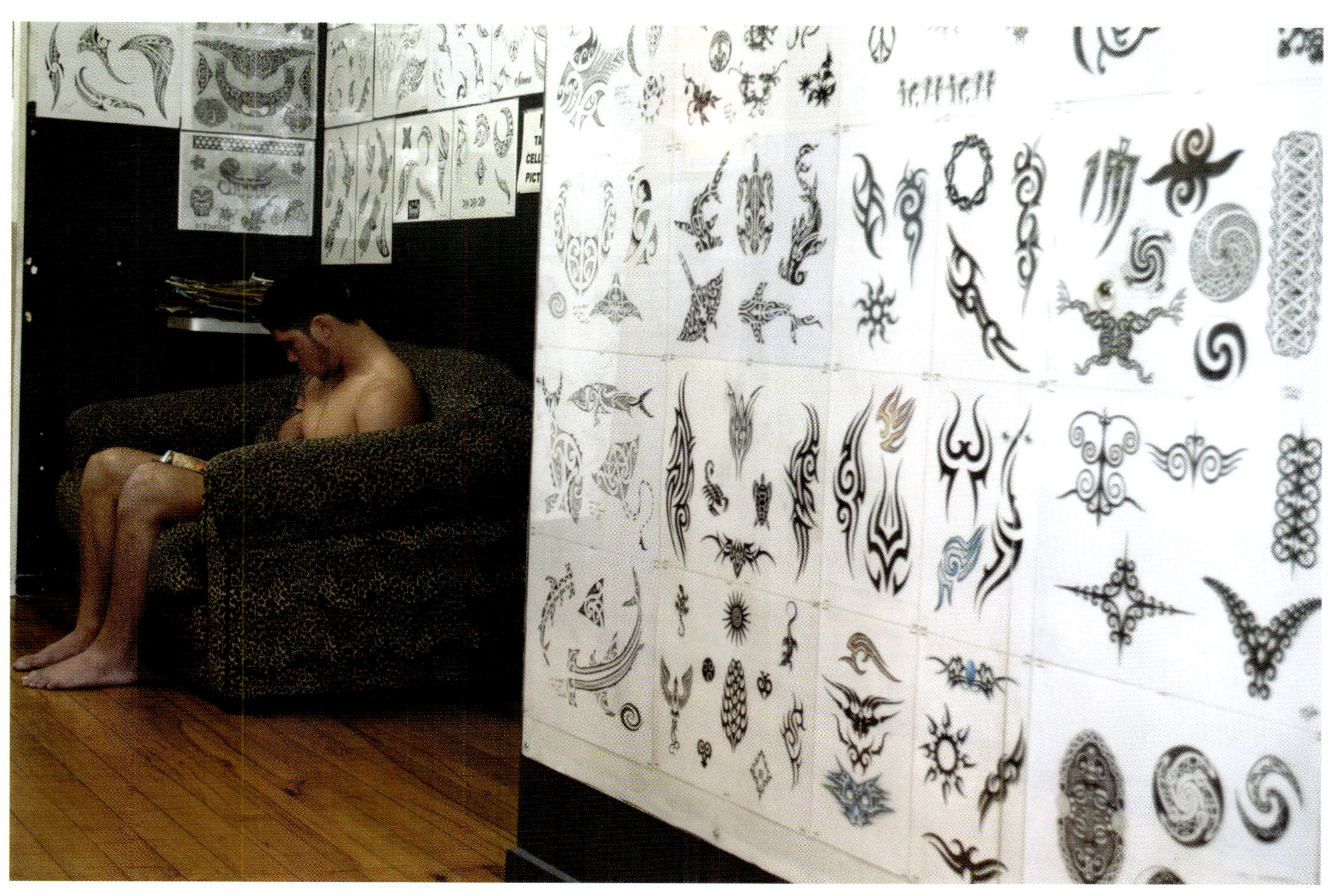

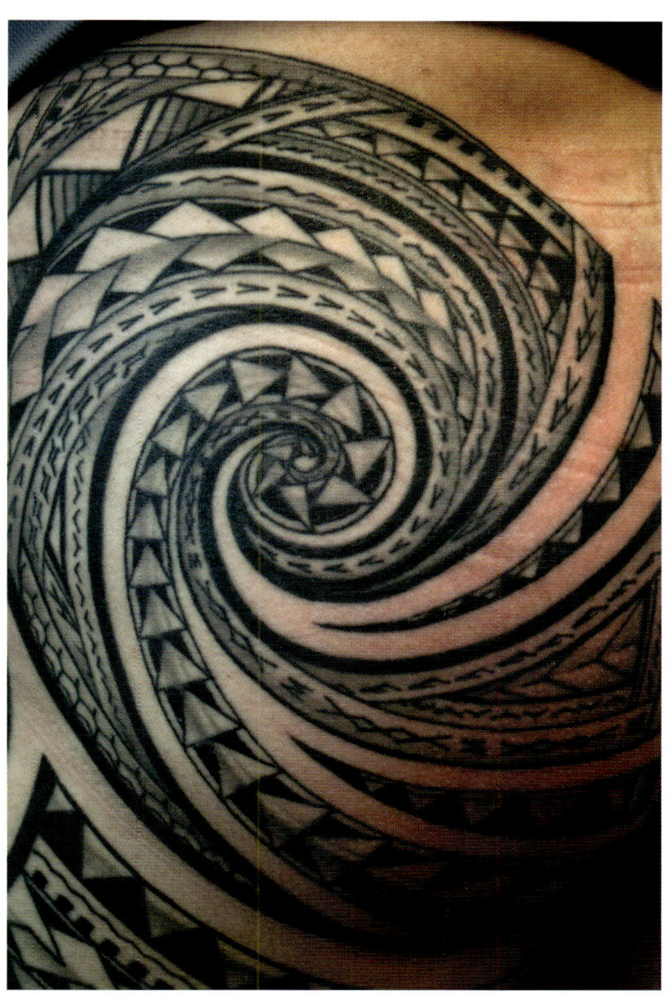

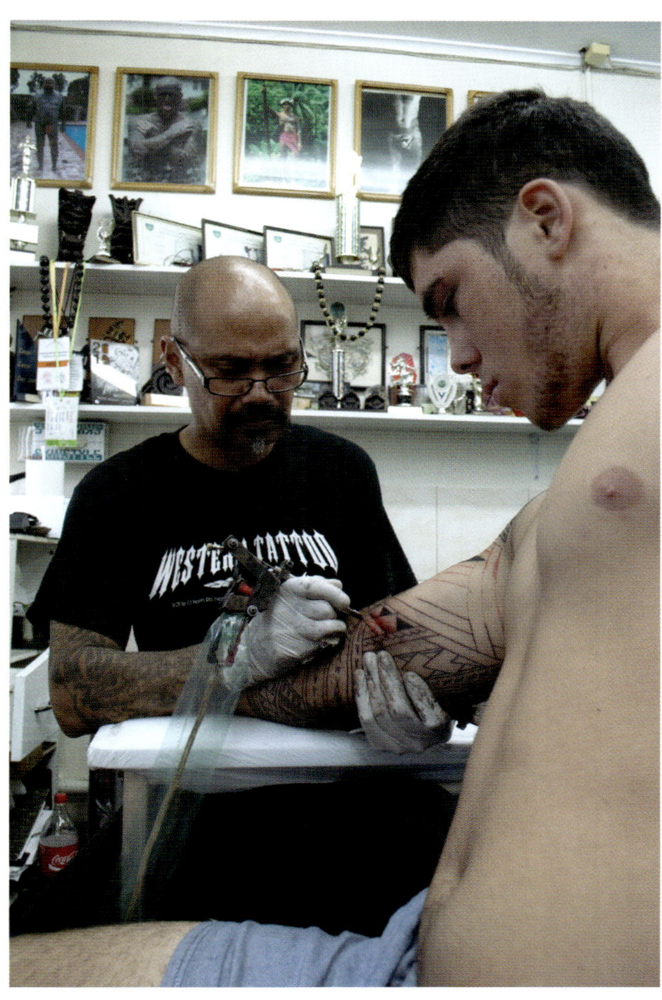

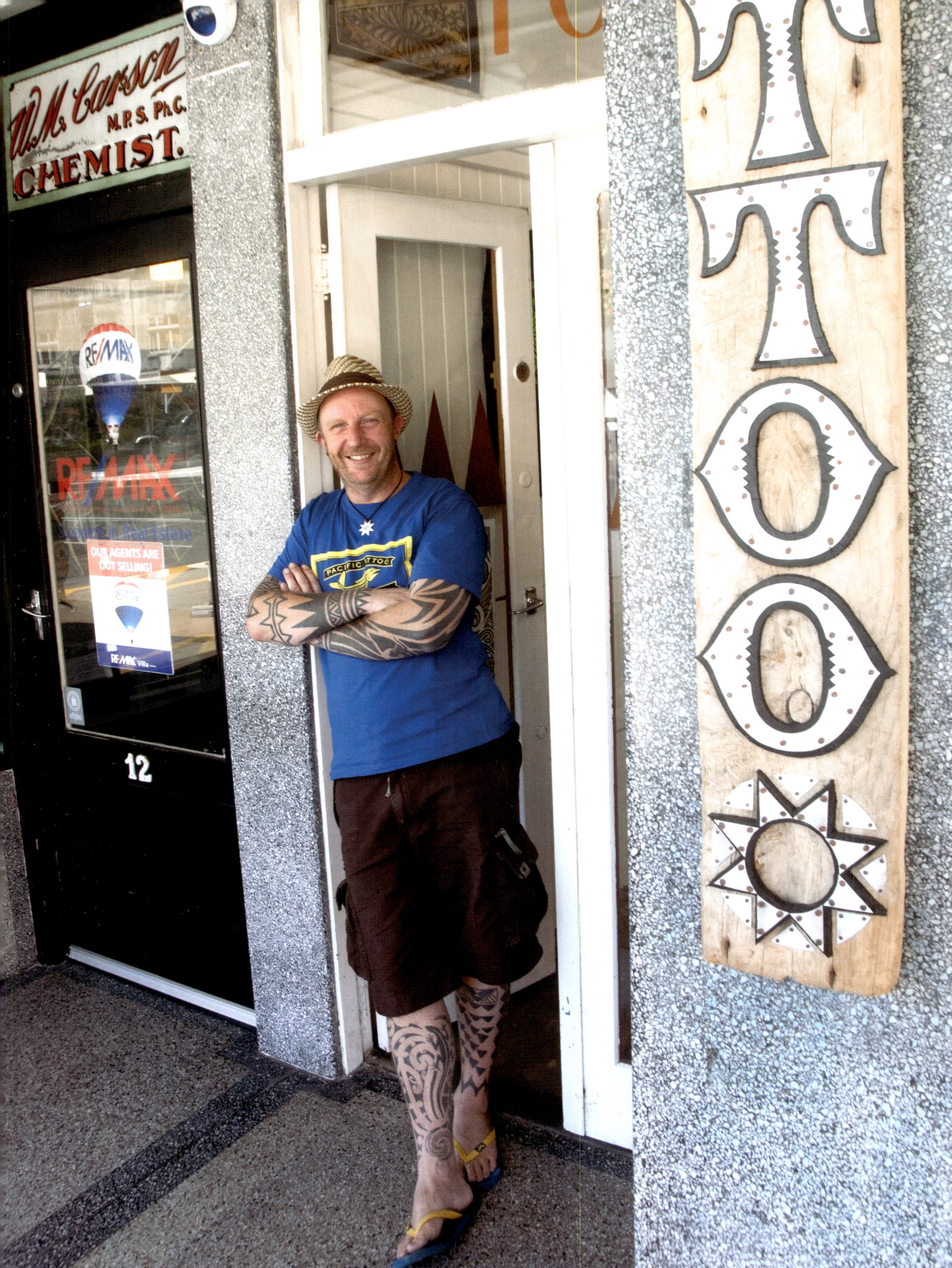
W.M. Carson
M.P.S. Ph.C.
CHEMIST.
RE/MAX
RE/MAX
Leaders in Real Estate
OUR AGENTS ARE
OUT SELLING!
RE/MAX Villa
12
PACIFIC TATTOO
TATTOO

TIM **HUNT**

Pacific Tattoo is located 30 minutes north of Wellington in the small Kapiti Coast town of Paekakariki. Tim Hunt opened the studio in 2008 and has established a reputation for his contemporary Polynesian work. He was first introduced to tattooing by Inia Taylor, who opened Auckland's Moko Ink in 1998. When Inia first opened the shop he needed someone to handle client bookings and help around the studio. Tim was keen to learn more about tattooing so he jumped at the chance.

In 1999 Tim attended a convention in Samoa that was organised by the late master tatau artist Paulo Suluape. There he met US-based tattooist Leo Zulueta, who invited him to work at his Los Angeles studio. Zulueta is seen as one of the pioneers of the tribal tattoo style and Tim seized the opportunity: "I stayed at Leo's place for three months and he taught me to tattoo. He got me behind the machine and gave me free rein to tattoo the customers that came in.

"Leo taught me a lot about the ethics of tattooing. He would always say the priority is not how fancy your tattoos are but how you look after your customers. Respect them. That doesn't mean you do only what they say, but you work with their ideas."

Tim returned to New Zealand in 2000 and worked at a couple of Auckland studios, then worked briefly with ta moko artist Gordon Hatfield doing stone carving. But he wanted a change: "I had a great time but I was missing tattooing and wanted to make that my priority. So I moved back to Wellington in 2001."

Tim joined the crew at Ken Miller's Tattoo City in 2003. He says it was an interesting insight into mainstream tattooing. "I was getting used to doing different types of tattoos, but people started asking me to do that Polynesian style. Over the next five years I built up a reputation for doing that almost exclusively. At that stage there were no specialist shops doing those Maori or Polynesian styles in Wellington." He continued to work at Tattoo City until he left to open Pacific Tattoo in 2008. "I'd decided it was time to move on. A shop became available and I thought, why not give it a shot? It was about making my work fit my lifestyle."

The decision to move to Paekakariki has proved to
be the right one. "It's close to Wellington, the Hutt and
Porirua. People like coming out here; it's got a great holiday
atmosphere. It makes the tattoo a bit more of an experience.
I walk along the beach on my way to work every day. I tell
people it's a million-dollar lifestyle without the million dollars."

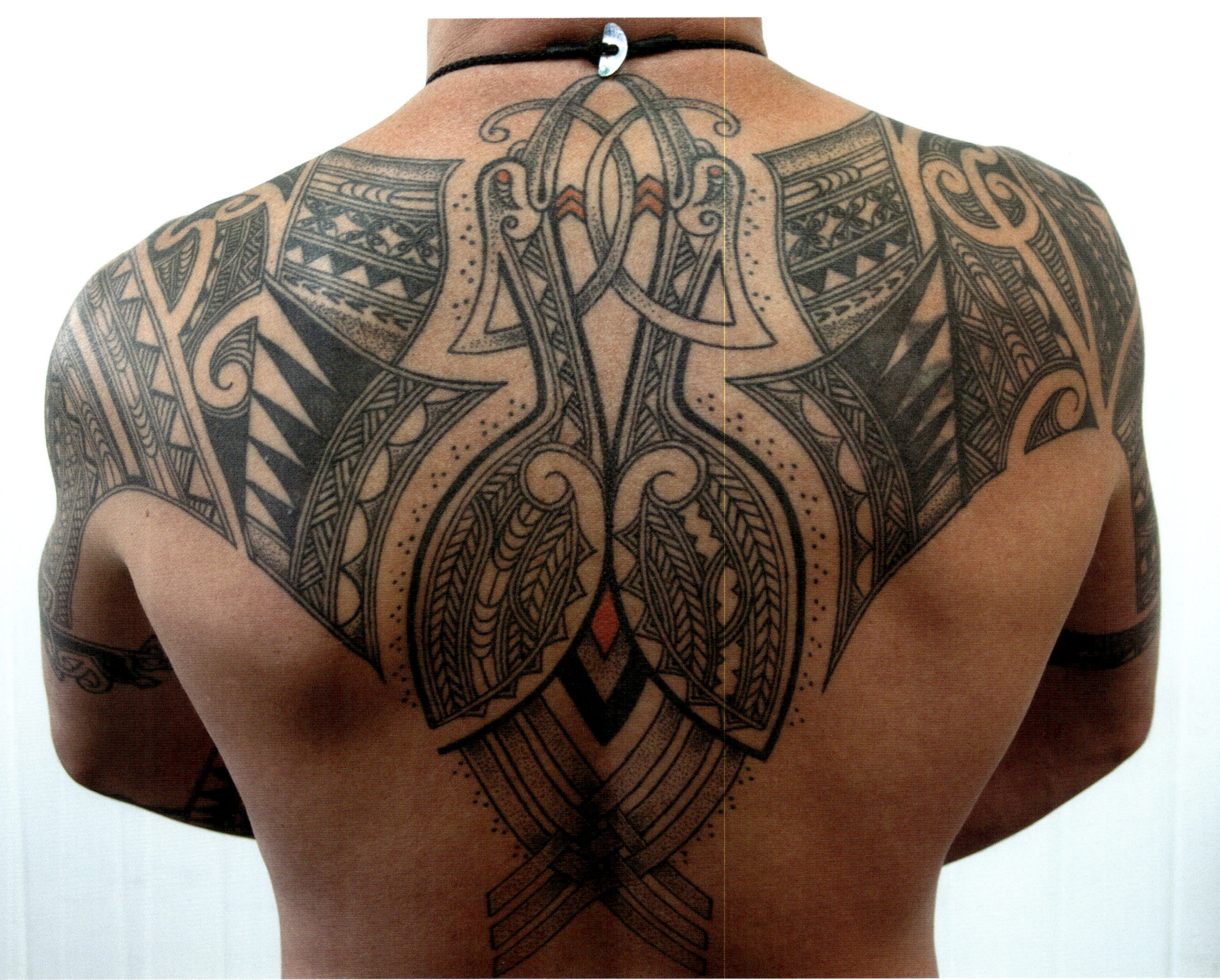

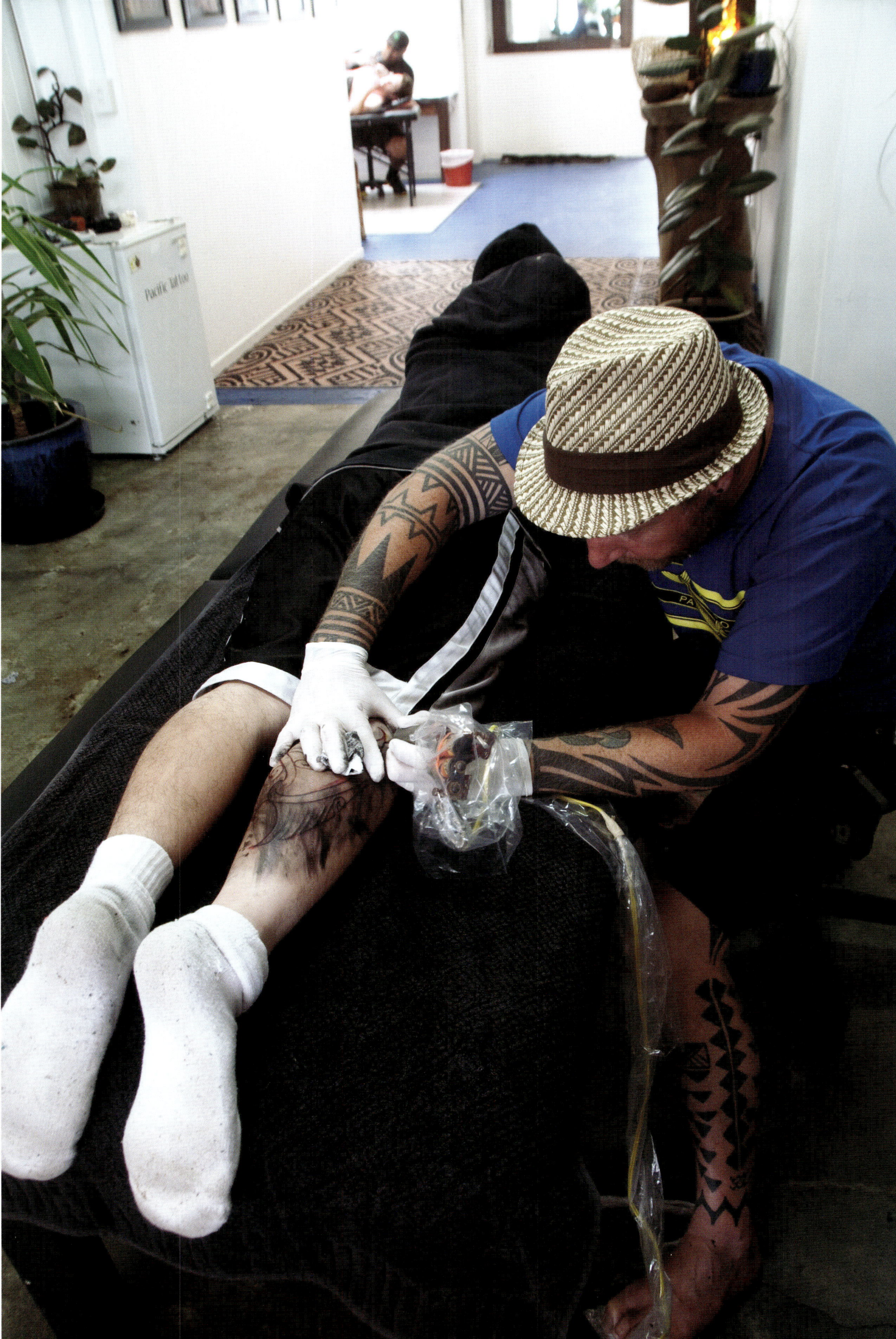

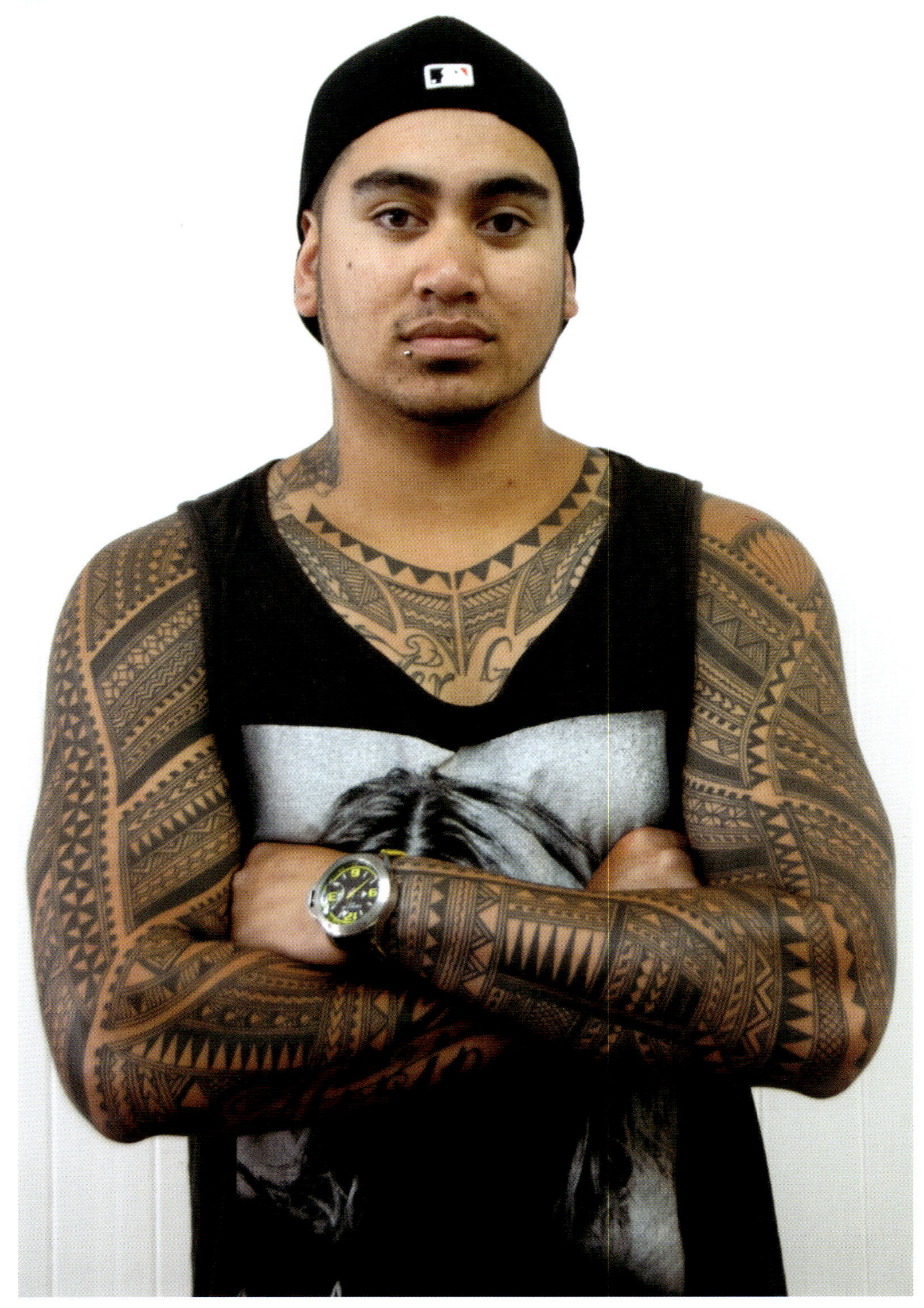

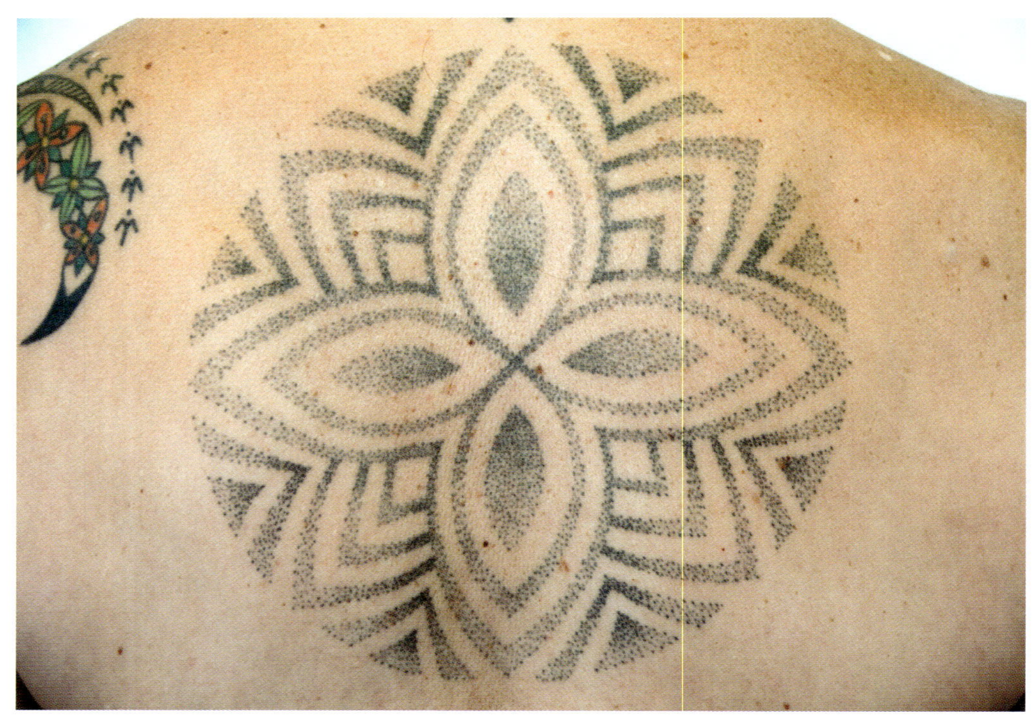

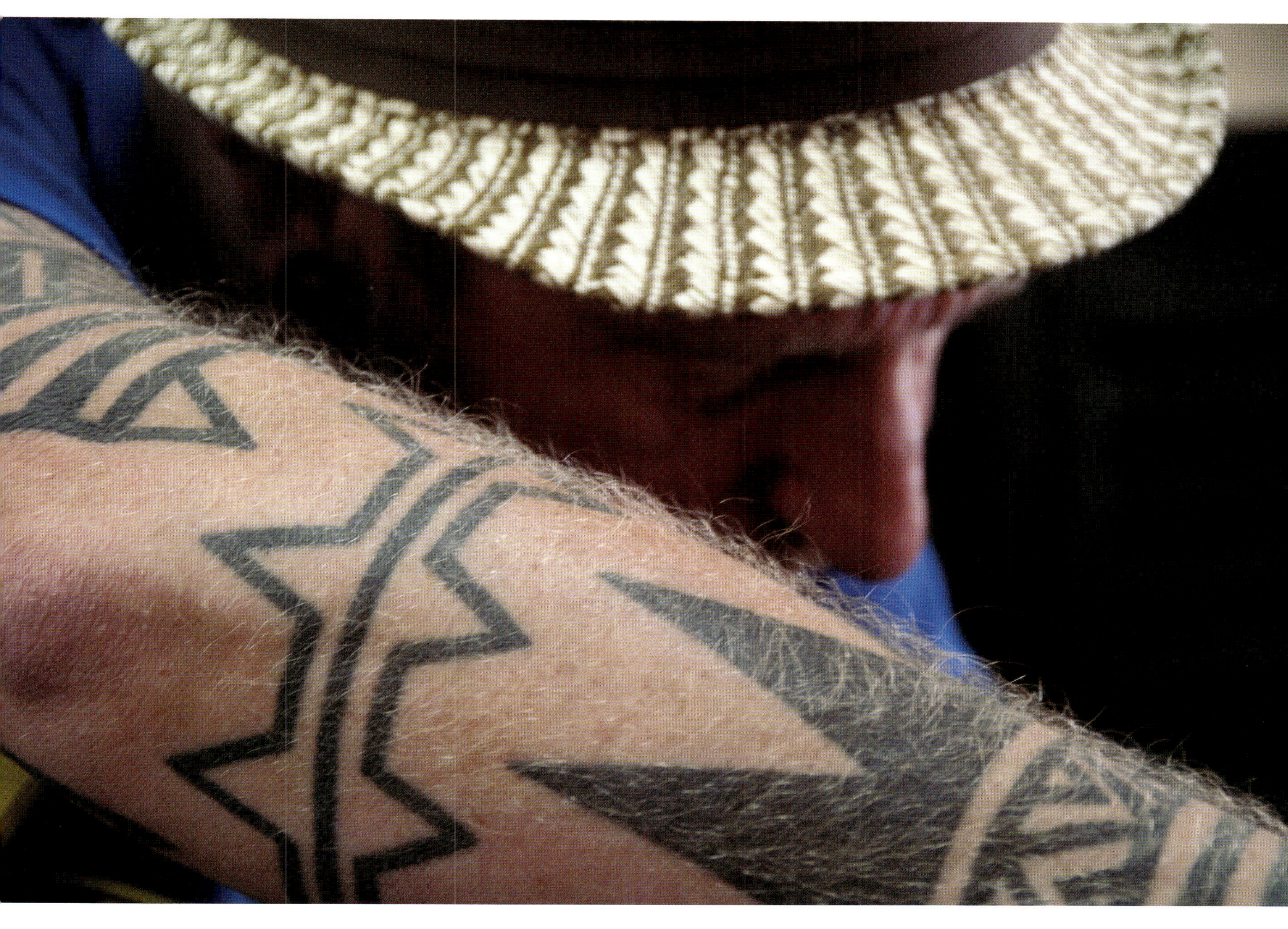

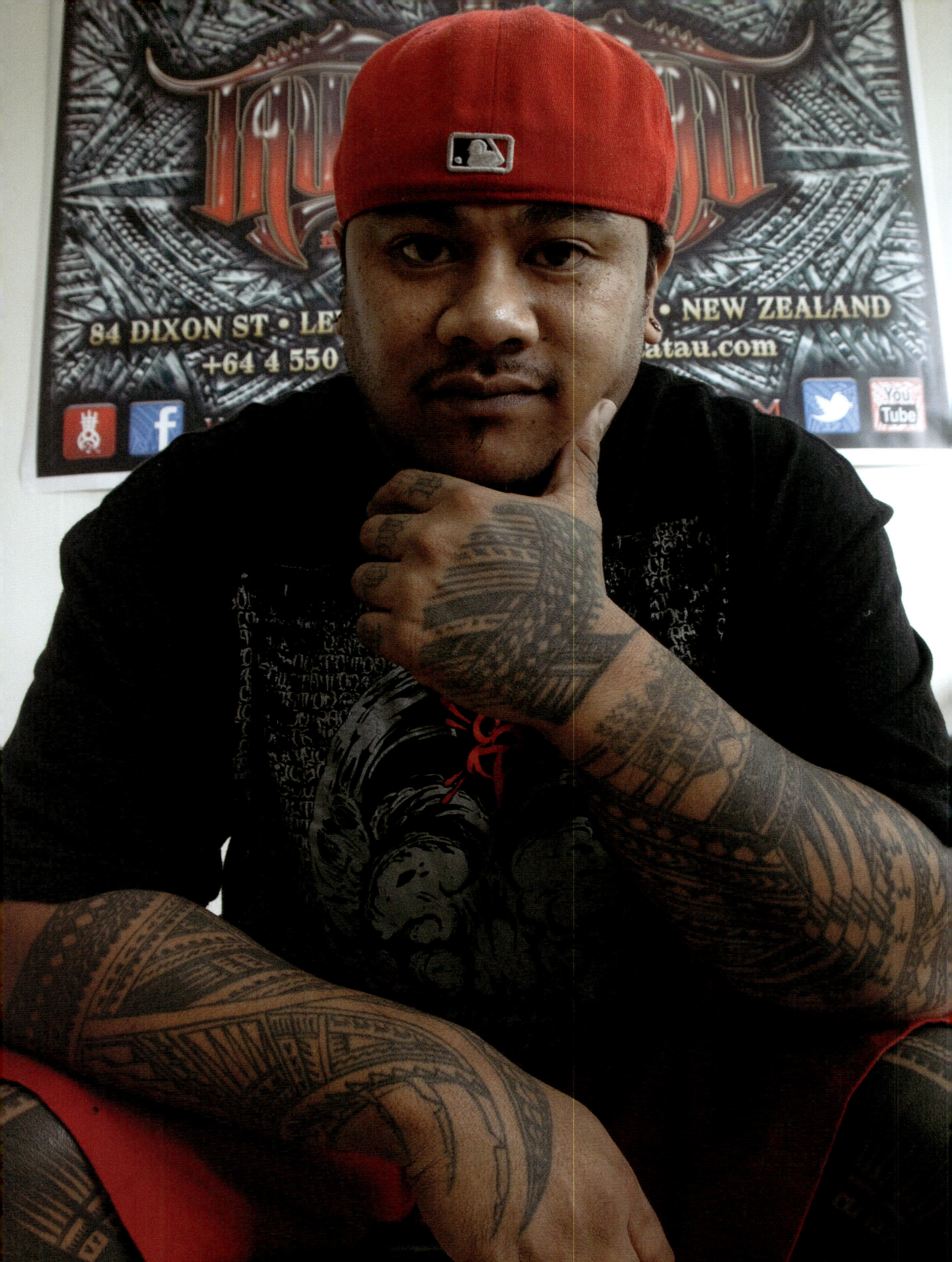
84 DIXON ST • LE
+64 4 550
NEW ZEALAND
atau.com

ANDY **TAUAFIAFI**

Instead of starting out as an apprentice and working his way up through the ranks, Andy Tauafiafi chose a different path to become a tattooist. He entered the profession after completing a fine arts degree at the University of Auckland and had been looking at going further with his studies. "I'd started the first year of my master's degree, but I had a family and had to get a real job."

He'd moved up to Auckland to study, and had become friends with Western Tattoo owner Steve Ma Ching. "One day when I was getting one of my sleeves done he asked me if I'd ever thought of becoming a tattooist." Despite the fact he had never worked in the industry, Andy decided to give it a go. "So I started tattooing my cousins and friends to experiment. I wasn't like other people who got an apprenticeship; I just started tattooing from home."

After Andy had spent the best part of a year learning the new art form Steve offered him a job. He spent the next five years working at Western Tattoo before heading overseas, where he did guest spots in Australia and Hawaii. This included stints at Tattoos by Bong, Tattoo Rich and Pacific Soul Tattoo in Honolulu before he returned to Wellington in mid-2010.

It made sense to him to return to his home town, where there was a gap in the market for Polynesian-style tattooing: "Steve [Ma Ching] is really established in Auckland and it wouldn't have mattered if I moved out east or south, there was no point trying to compete with him."

Andy opened Taupou Tatau in June last year and has been giving it all his time and effort. He has a team of two working with him, plus he's looking at taking on another tattooist who will do tatau with both traditional tools and a machine.

He describes his style of tattooing as custom Pacific freestyle: "We don't use any stencils here. Everything is custom." Andy's proud of his Samoan heritage and wants to see the tradition of tatau continue. He says in New Zealand there has been a renaissance in Polynesian-style tattooing, which he attributes to sportspeople like Sonny Bill Williams wearing them. "Ten years ago a lot of New Zealand-born Samoans would be scared to get a traditional tattoo if they weren't fluent in the language."

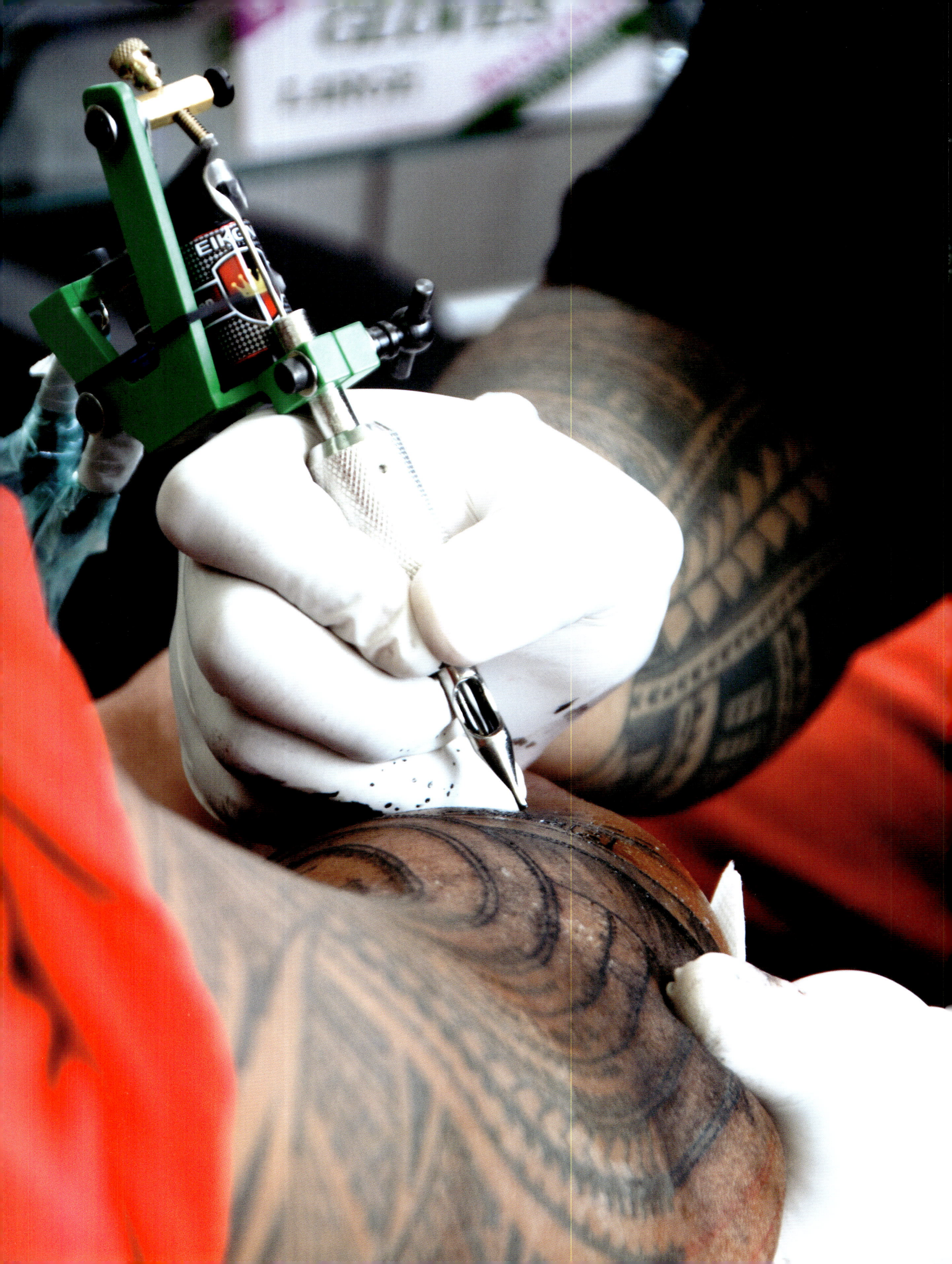

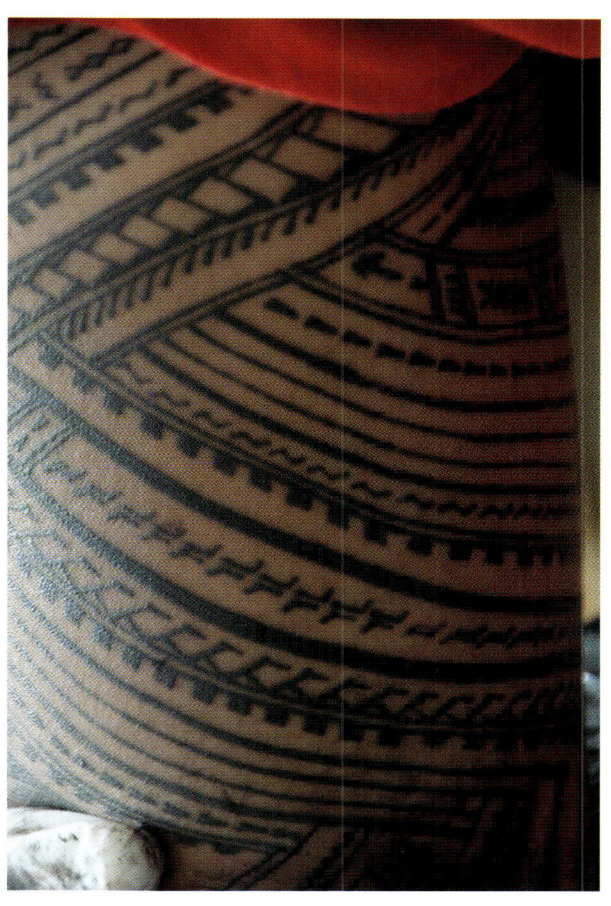

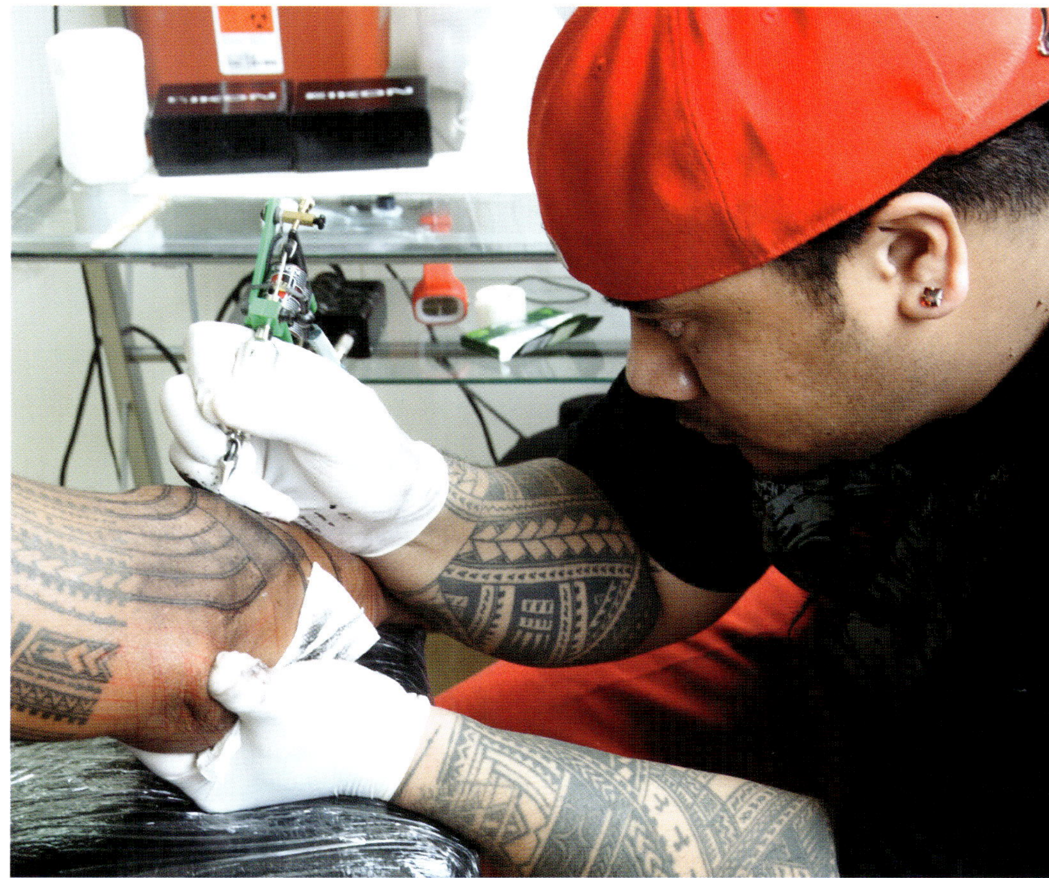

But things have changed. Andy feels that tattooing in New Zealand has gone from strength to strength in recent years: "Ten years ago if you had a full sleeve people would look at you as if you were a criminal. But now, especially in New Zealand, it's so accepted. You've got people from all walks of life getting tattoos."

Despite the number of tattooists now in the industry he's not worried about the increased competition. "With all the new tattoo shops opening up there's more room for people like me to specialise."

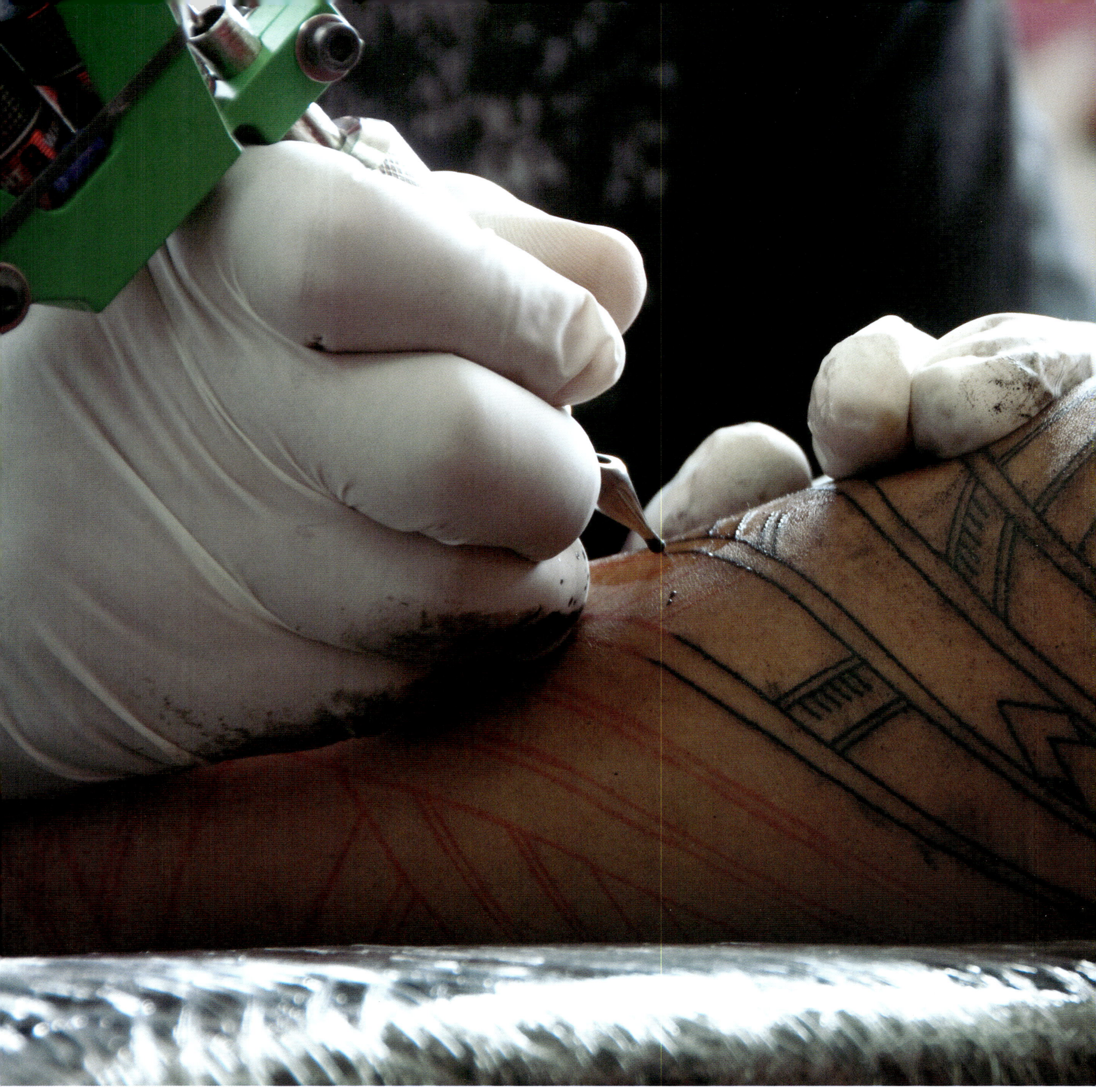

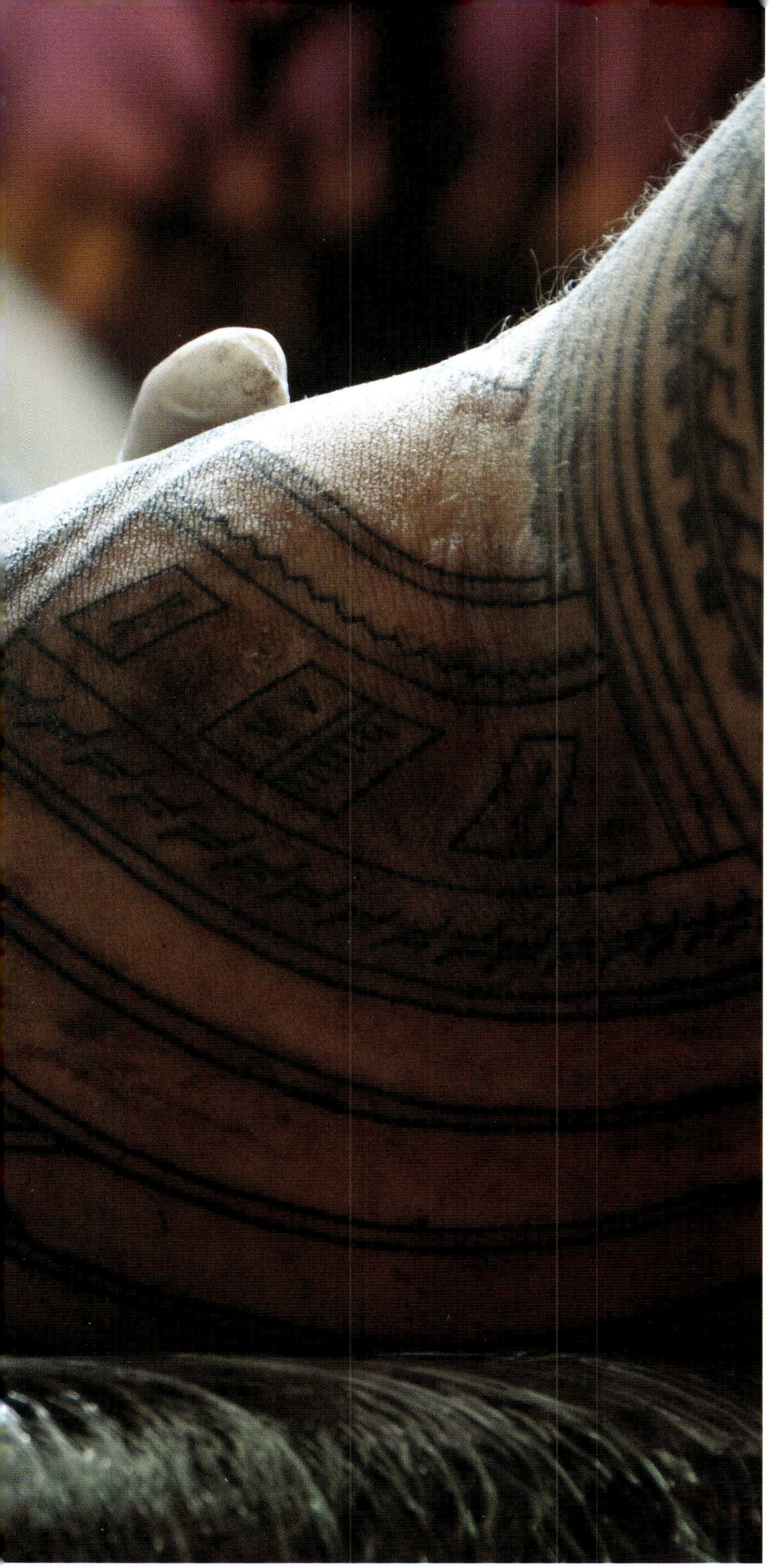

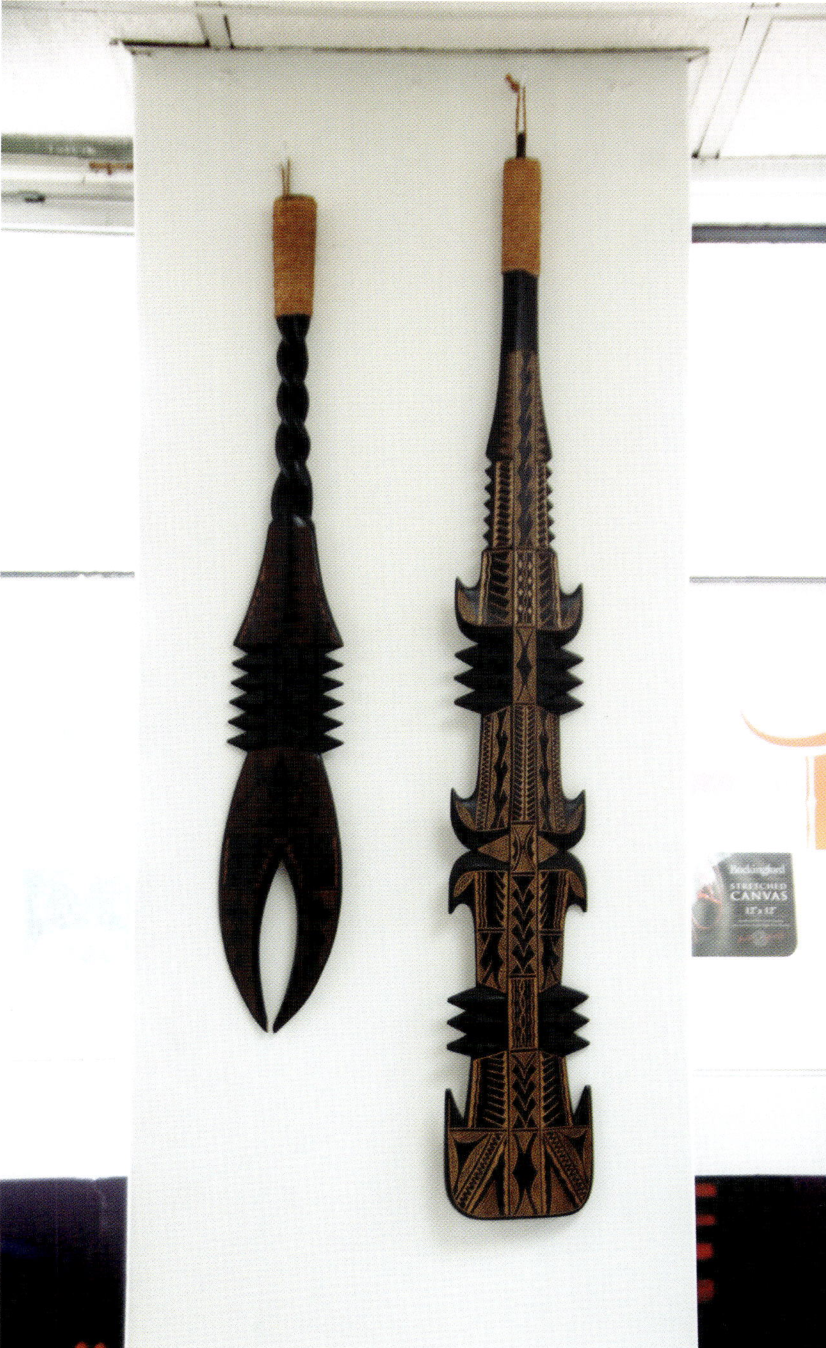

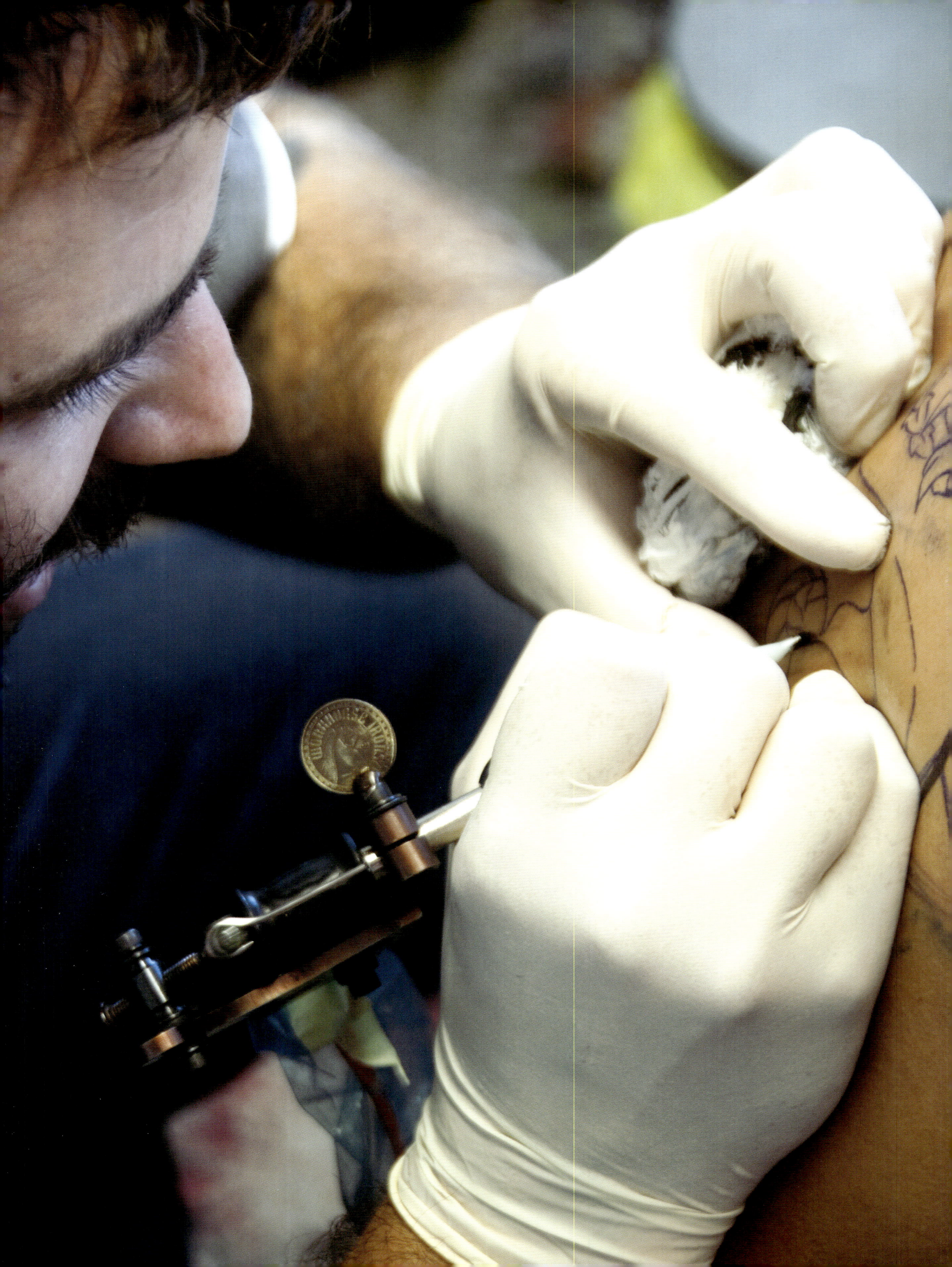

GLEN **SCHOLLUM**

He's only been in the industry for six years but Napier tattooist Glen Schollum is already looking at bigger and better things.

Glen opened his home studio in 2008 and now wants to open a new shop so he can expand. He's already spoken to a couple of other tattooists who are keen to join him. And he knows what he's looking for: "I want to have two or three tattooists so we can cover all the styles. But I want to make sure we maintain the quality." Glen says there are only a handful of tattoo studios in Hawke's Bay, but there are lots of backyard operators.

When he was growing up Glen had a keen interest in art, and spent hours drawing sketches in his spare time. He worked as a graphic designer in Auckland for a couple of years and did a lot of commercial work and children's book illustrations.

But he wasn't cut out for the corporate world and got bored with it, so he moved back to Hawke's Bay in 2005 and was offered an apprenticeship at Monsta Truck Tattoo in Napier. He'd already designed tattoos for friends, so getting into the industry seemed like the logical next step. "I just wish I'd got into it years ago."

Glen took on his apprentice Sam Van Zoomeren in late 2011. "It's good working with someone else because it pushes you a bit and you get some honest feedback." He doesn't specialise in only one style of tattooing. "You have to be versatile if you want to get a wide range of customers; and with all the different styles out there now it's no good trying to tweak the customer's idea to fit what you do. Switching from realism to solid black line work is quite cool and at least you don't get bored."

He makes sure to keep a close eye on what other artists are doing. Seth Wood from Saved Tattoo in New York, and George Campise from Seventh Son Tattoo in San Francisco, are a couple of his favourites. Glen's started to get clients from Australia: "They plan a trip around getting a tattoo over here. It's a different experience for them."

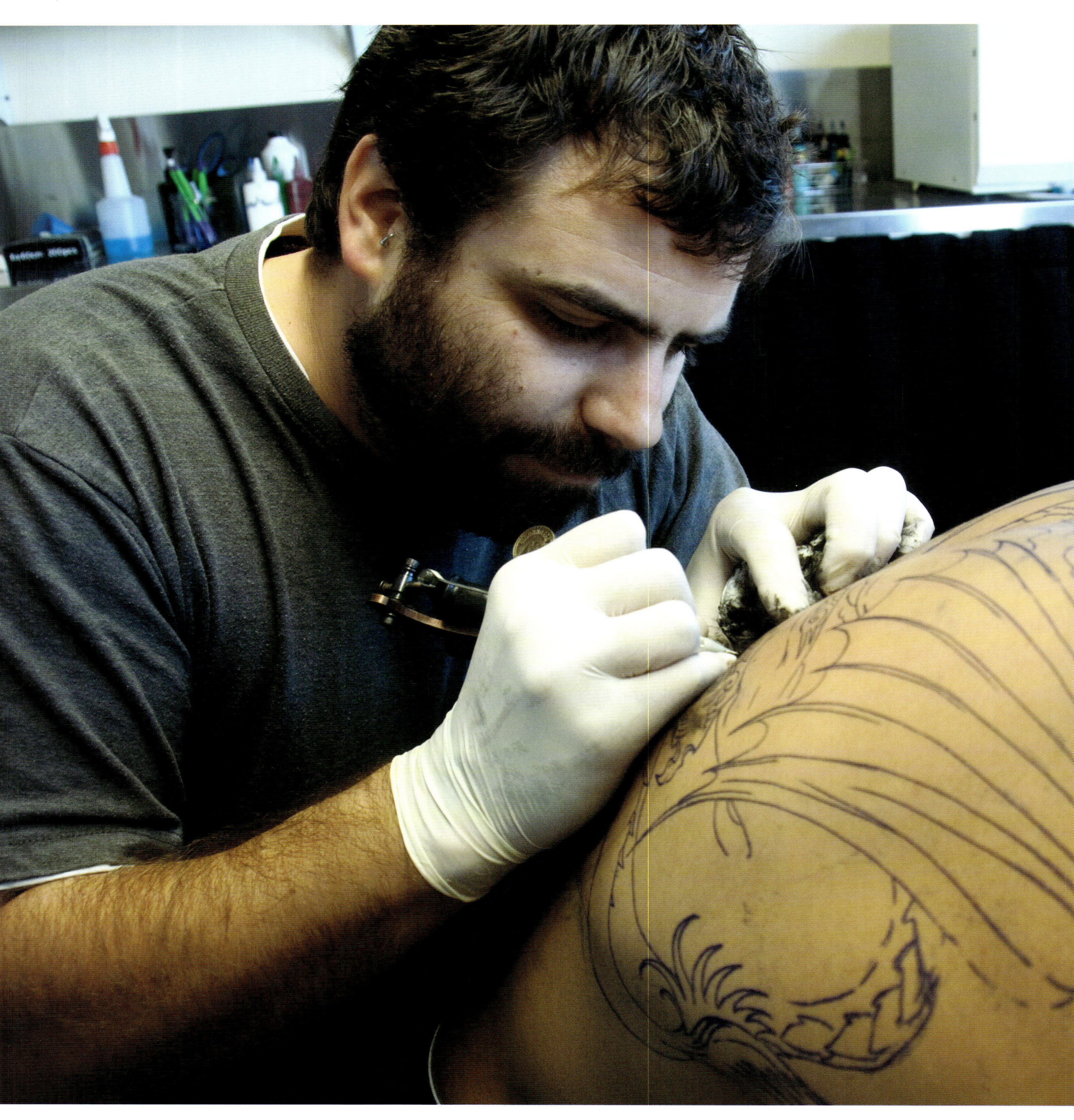

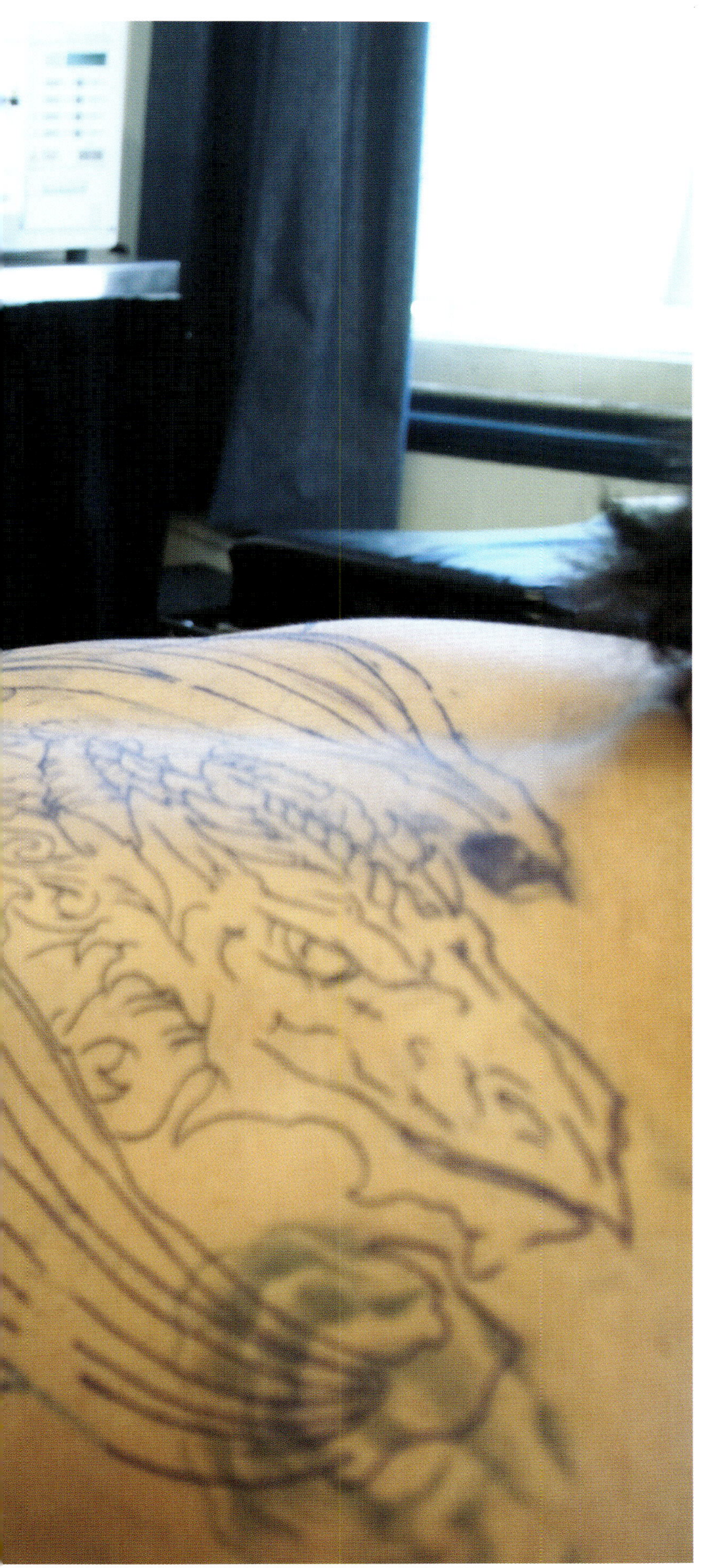

The social acceptance of tattooing in New Zealand has changed a lot over the last decade: "Many people in New Zealand have a tattoo now and that's what the foreigners comment on. When I was growing up you only saw tattoos on the hard bastards. But now it's more of a fashion statement than a form of rebellion." And the industry's different, too. "Twenty years ago you had to be a hard customer just to be a tattooist. But now it's more in the hands of the artists and they are taking it to the next level. Nothing is impossible now."

Glen would like eventually to work overseas, considering the international demand for New Zealand tattoo artists. But working he wants to develop his skills first. "I'm still developing as an artist," he says. "The priority is to get the new studio up and running first; then I can travel."

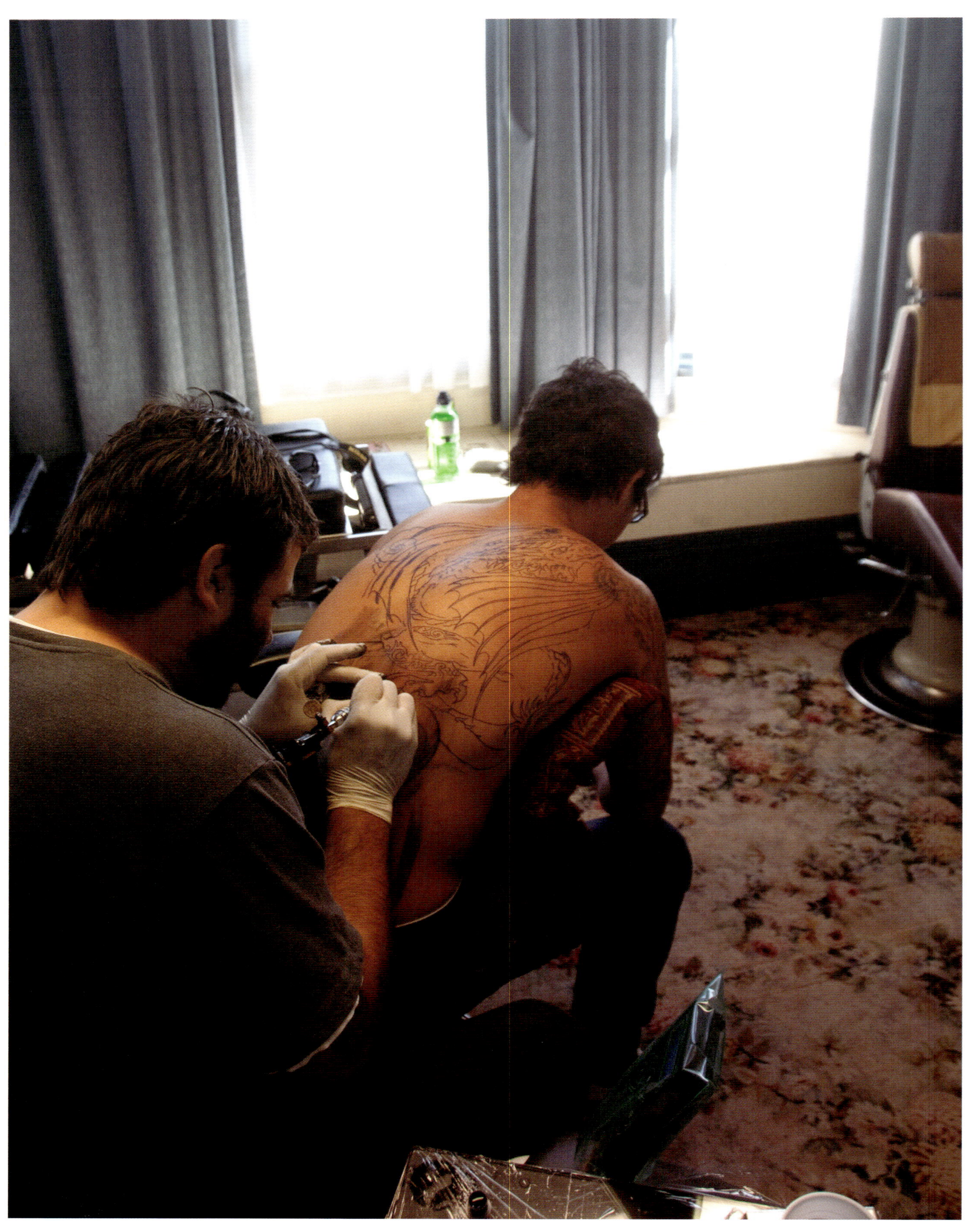

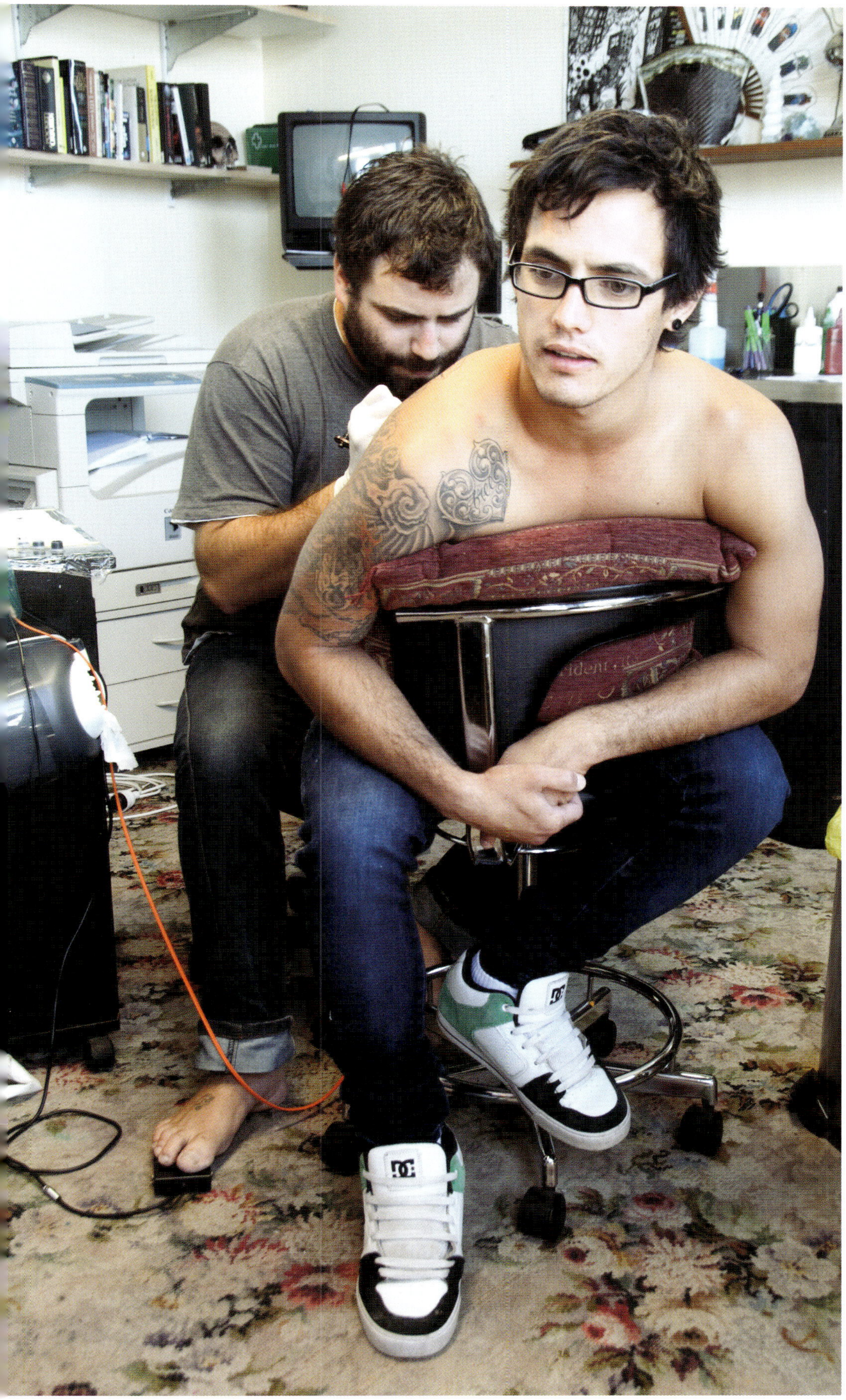

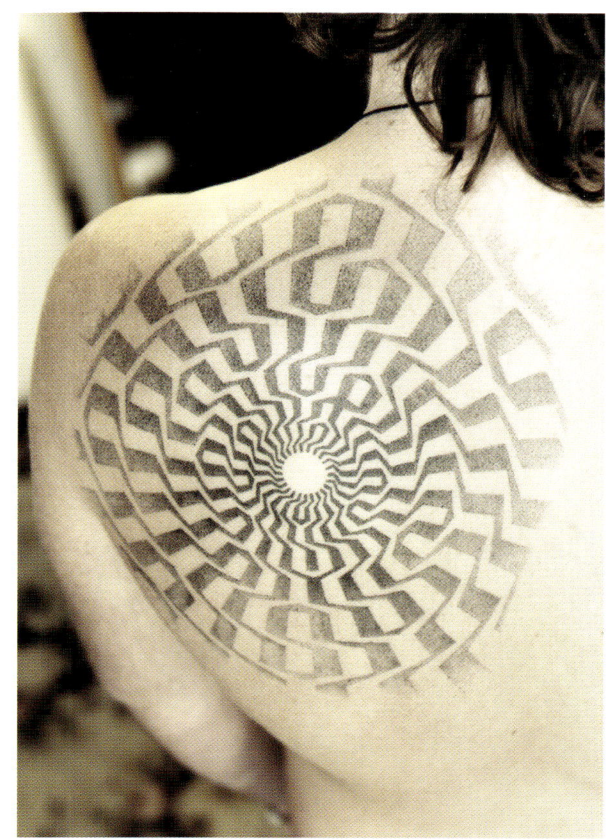

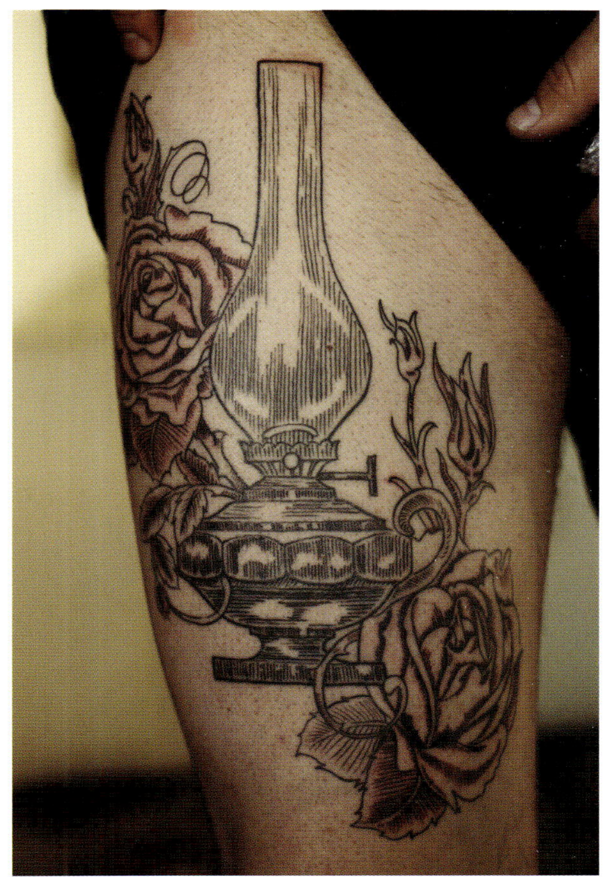

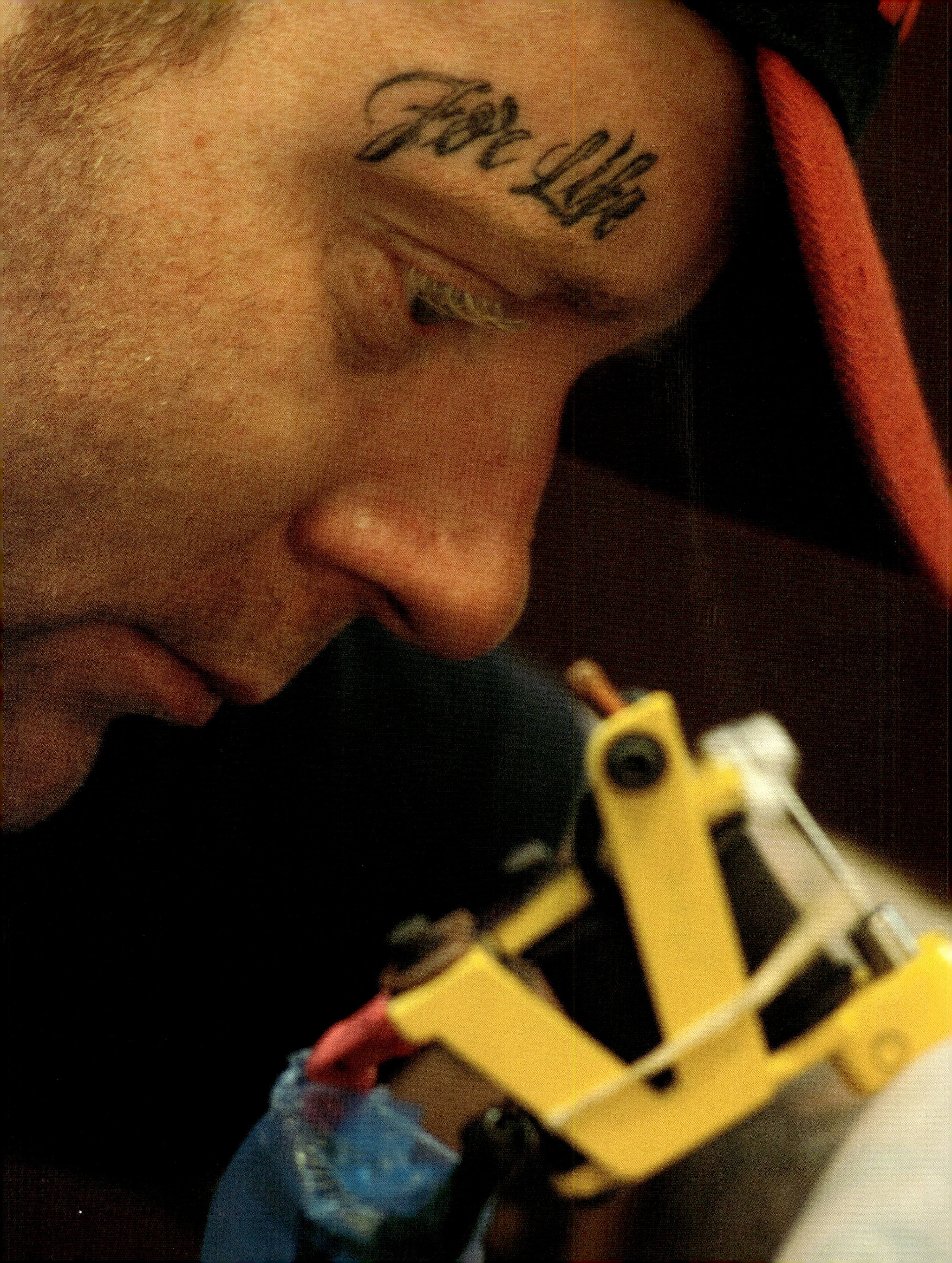
For Life

BRAD **CONE**

O T A U T A H I   T A T T O O

When the city of Christchurch was hit by a 6.3 magnitude earthquake on 22 February 2011, Brad Cone's life was turned upside down. The city had already been hit by a major quake in September the previous year. "But we'd worked through that and had opened again in January. We were humming along and the bookings were rolling in. And then 22 February happened."

The Hereford Street building where the Otautahi Tattoo Studio was located was severely damaged. "We were right in the red zone. The whole street was a wreck," Brad says.

He had to choose between running his business out of a garage or leaving Christchurch, and he chose the latter. It would prove to be a pivotal moment in his life.

Brad moved to Auckland where he opened the new Otautahi Tattoo studio in Karangahape Road in April 2011, and he hasn't looked back. "People up here have been really supportive. Once you get your head around it, it's just another city. And we've had a lot of support from our clients in Christchurch since we moved up here."

He thinks the location of the studio couldn't be better. Unlike other people who might be threatened by all the competition on Karangahape Road, he's inspired by it: "Already I've met people up here I know I will be involved with for the rest of my life."

Despite the massive upheaval his life's taken in the last year he's not planning to rest on his laurels. He's already opened a new studio in West Auckland, where he now lives. "I love it out there, it's just like home. It's just like Christchurch." Brad has plans to open studios in Christchurch, Wellington and Queenstown. "It's just a matter of finding the tattoo artists that are good enough."

But it's not as though he's struggling to find them. Three tattooists working in his Auckland studio were taught by legendary ta moko artist Derek Lardelli. Brad believes the future of New Zealand tattooing is looking stronger than ever: "It's going off the hook."

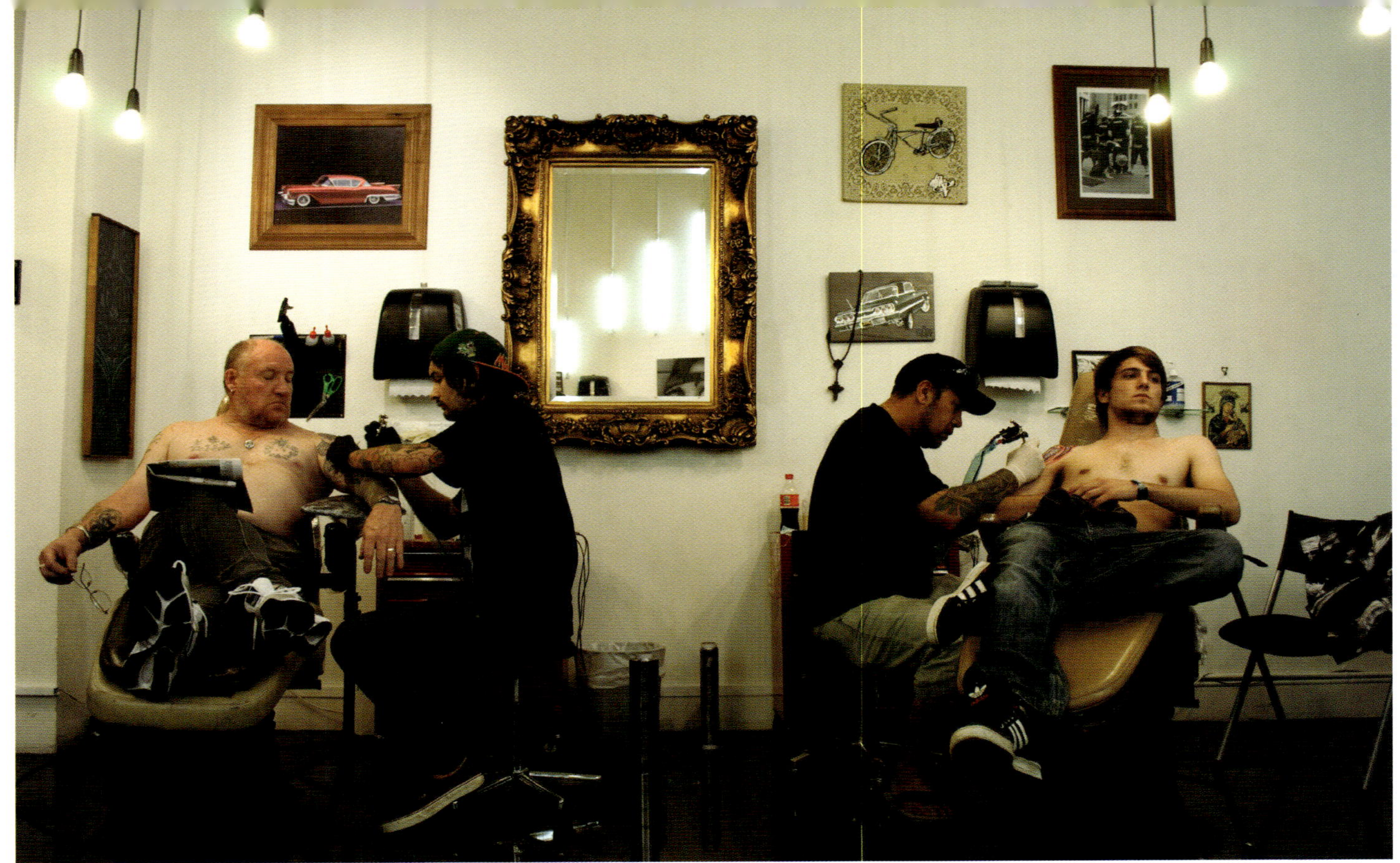

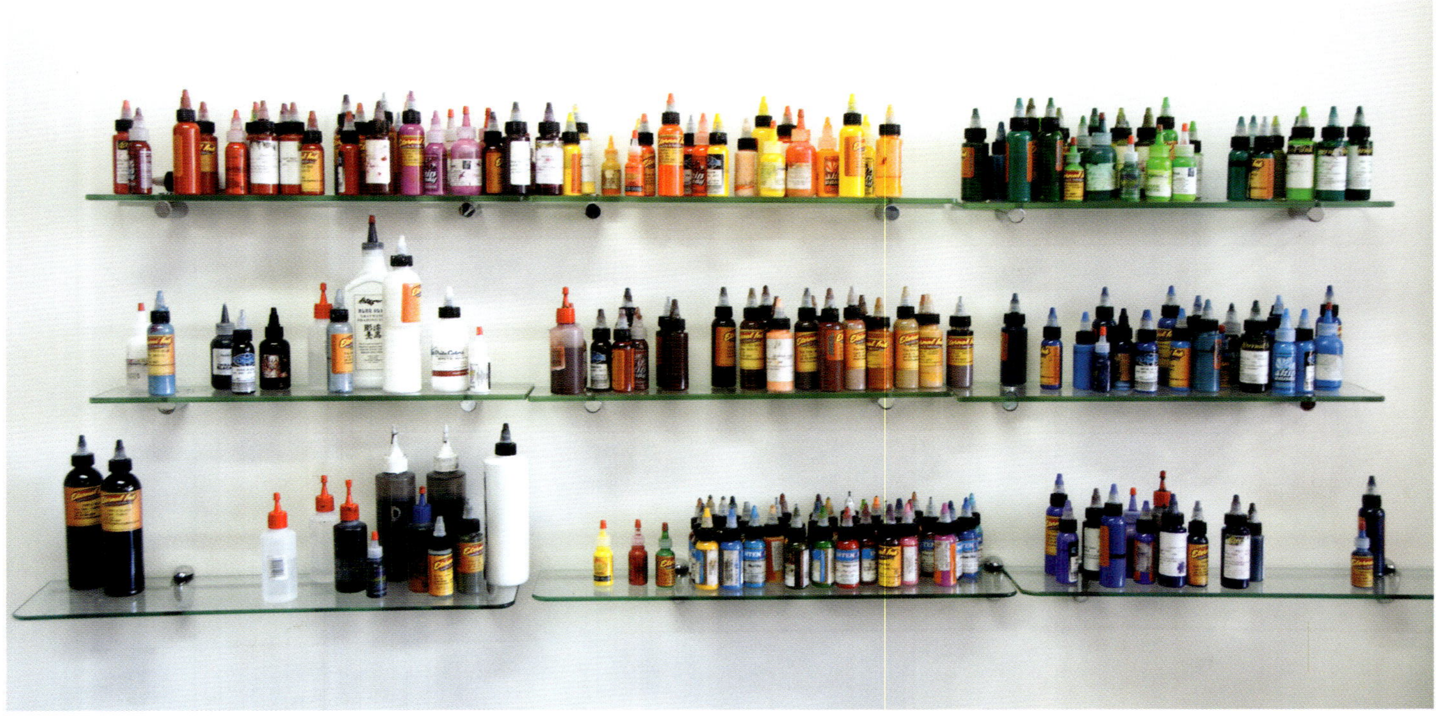

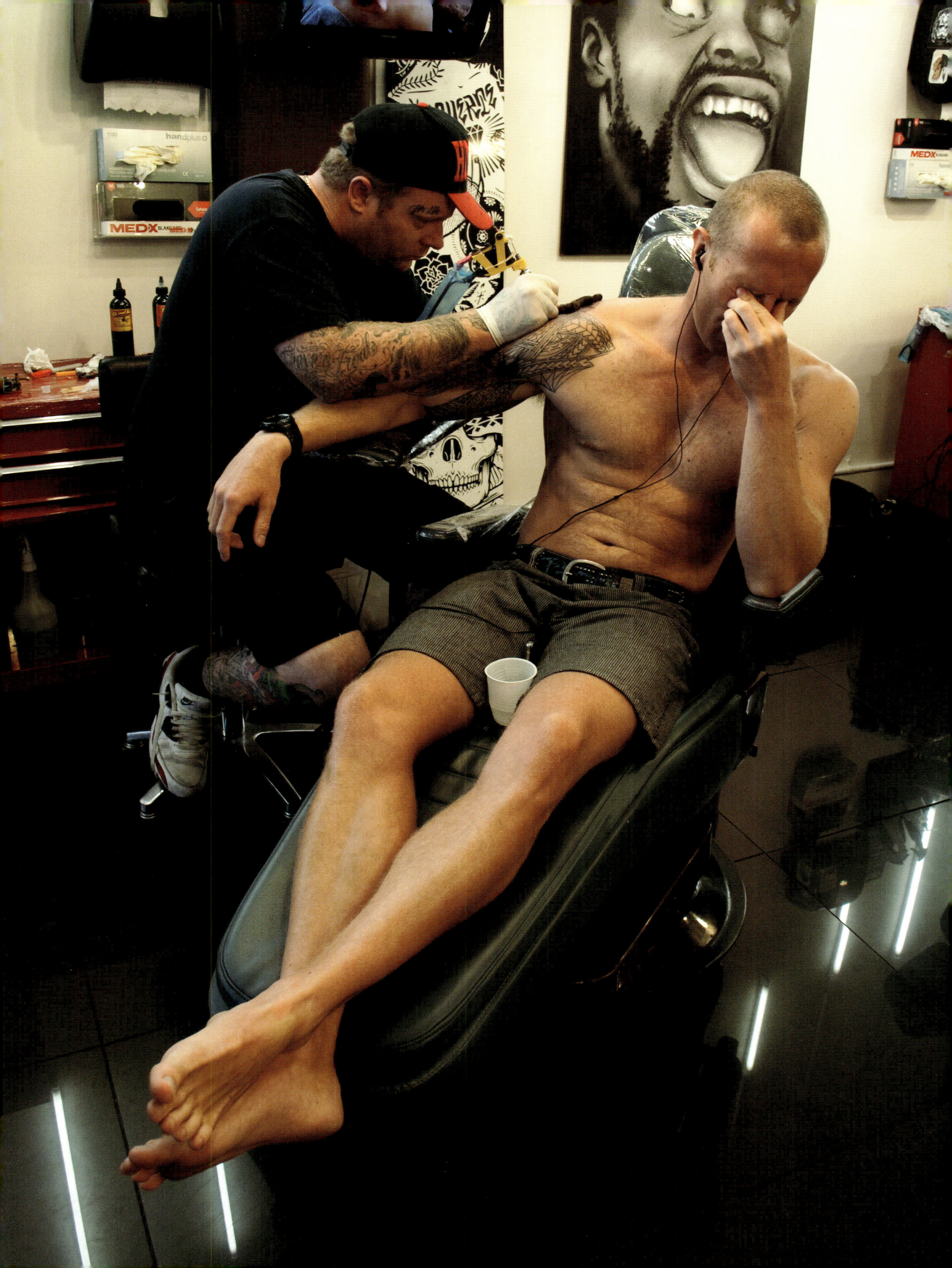

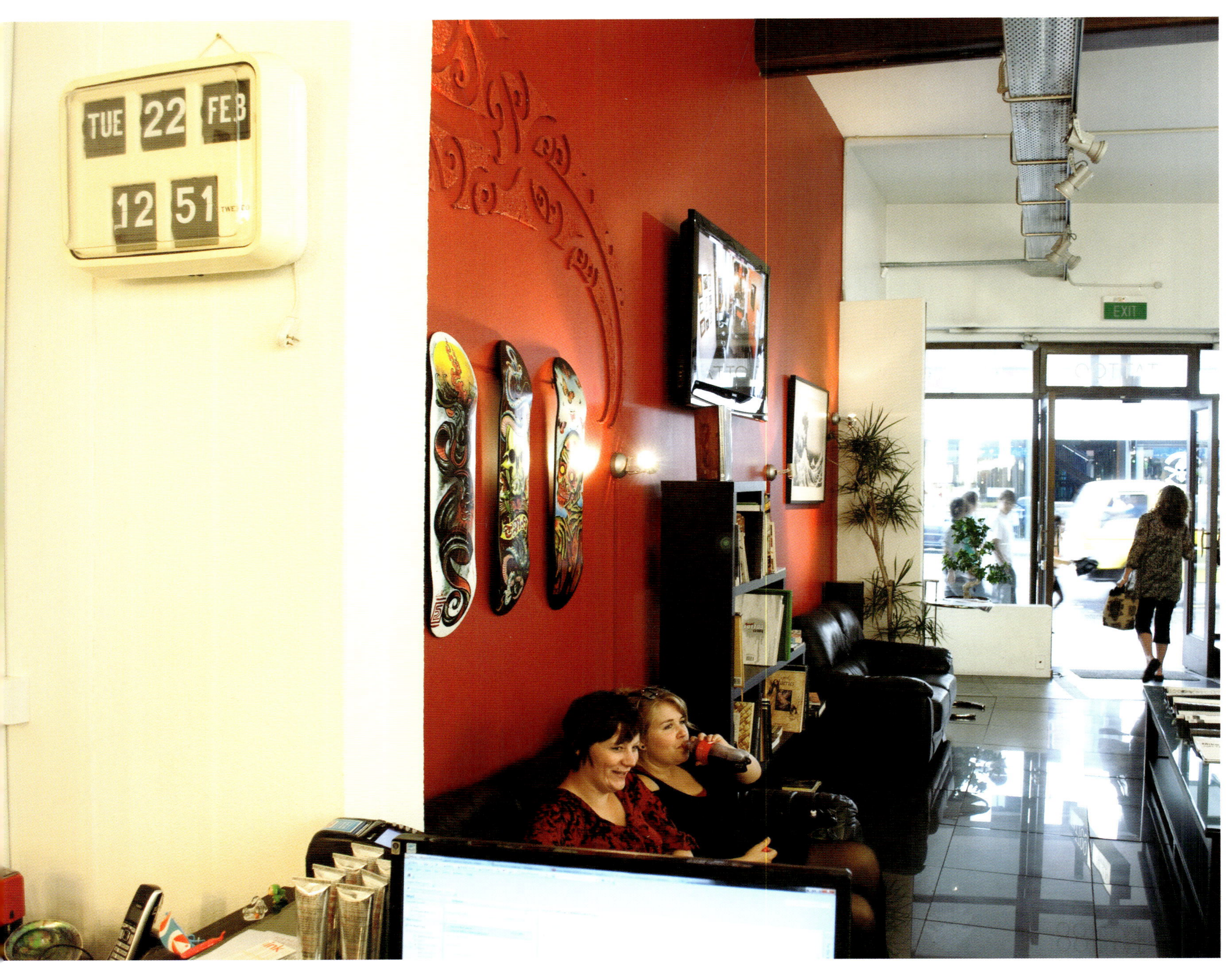

The clock in Otatauhi Tattoo s Karangahape Road studio reminds all of the date and time of the earthquake that wrecked their Christchurch premises.

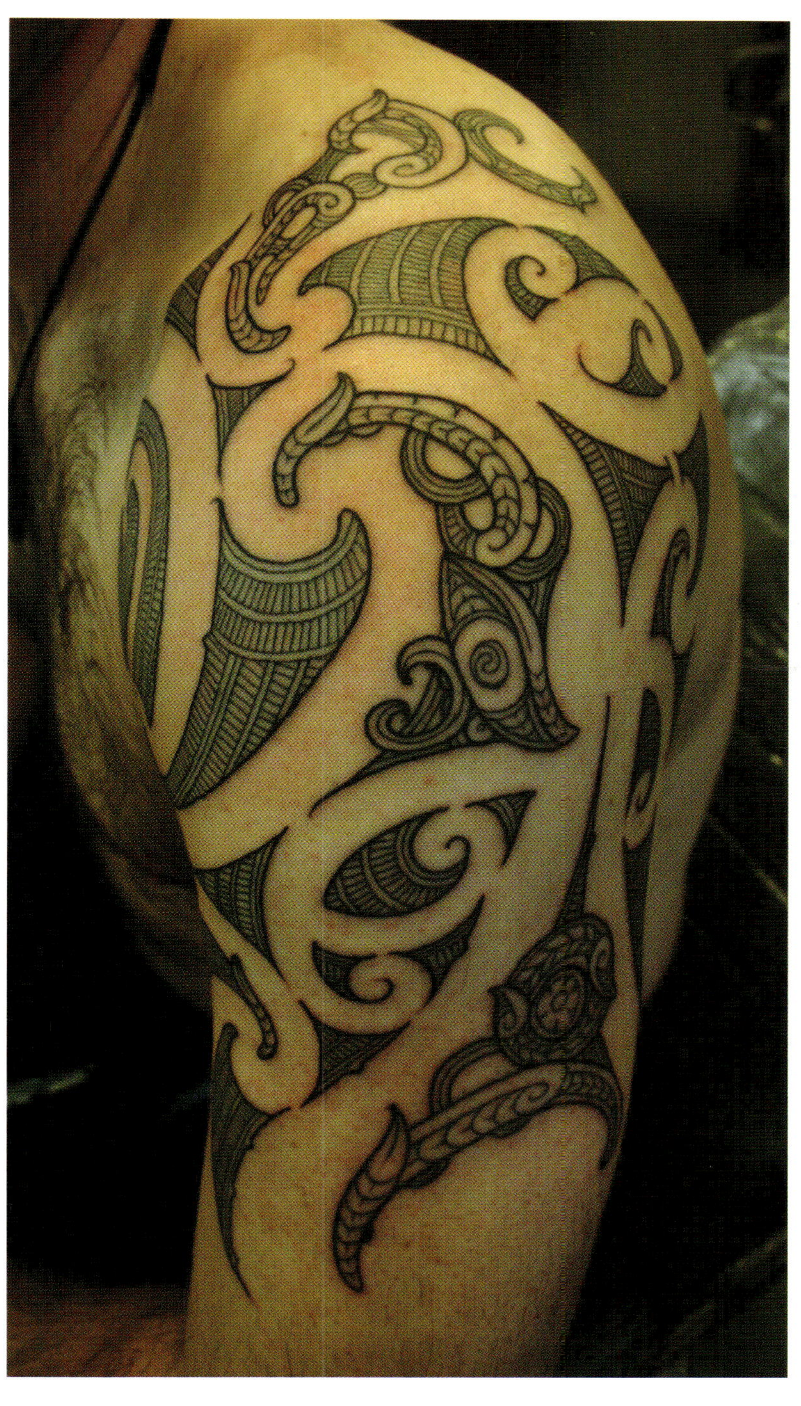
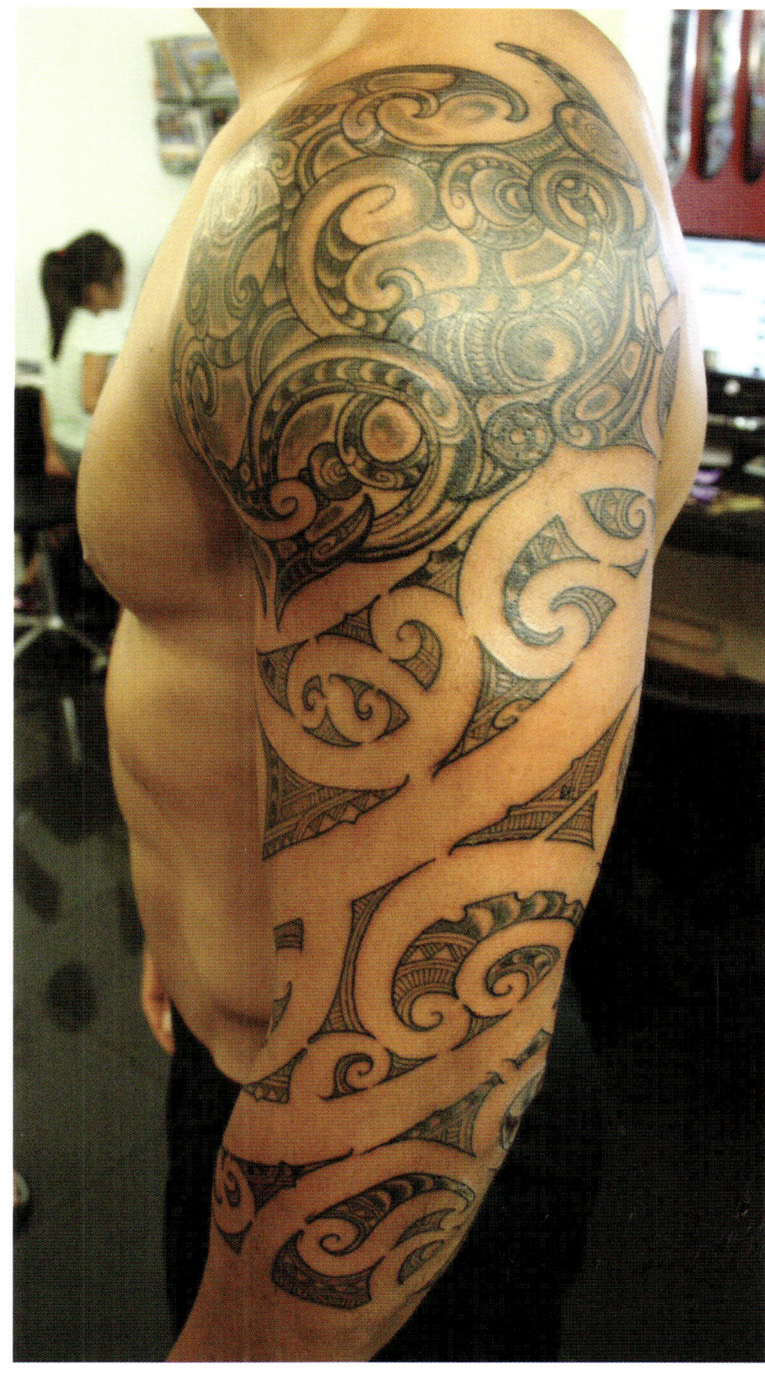

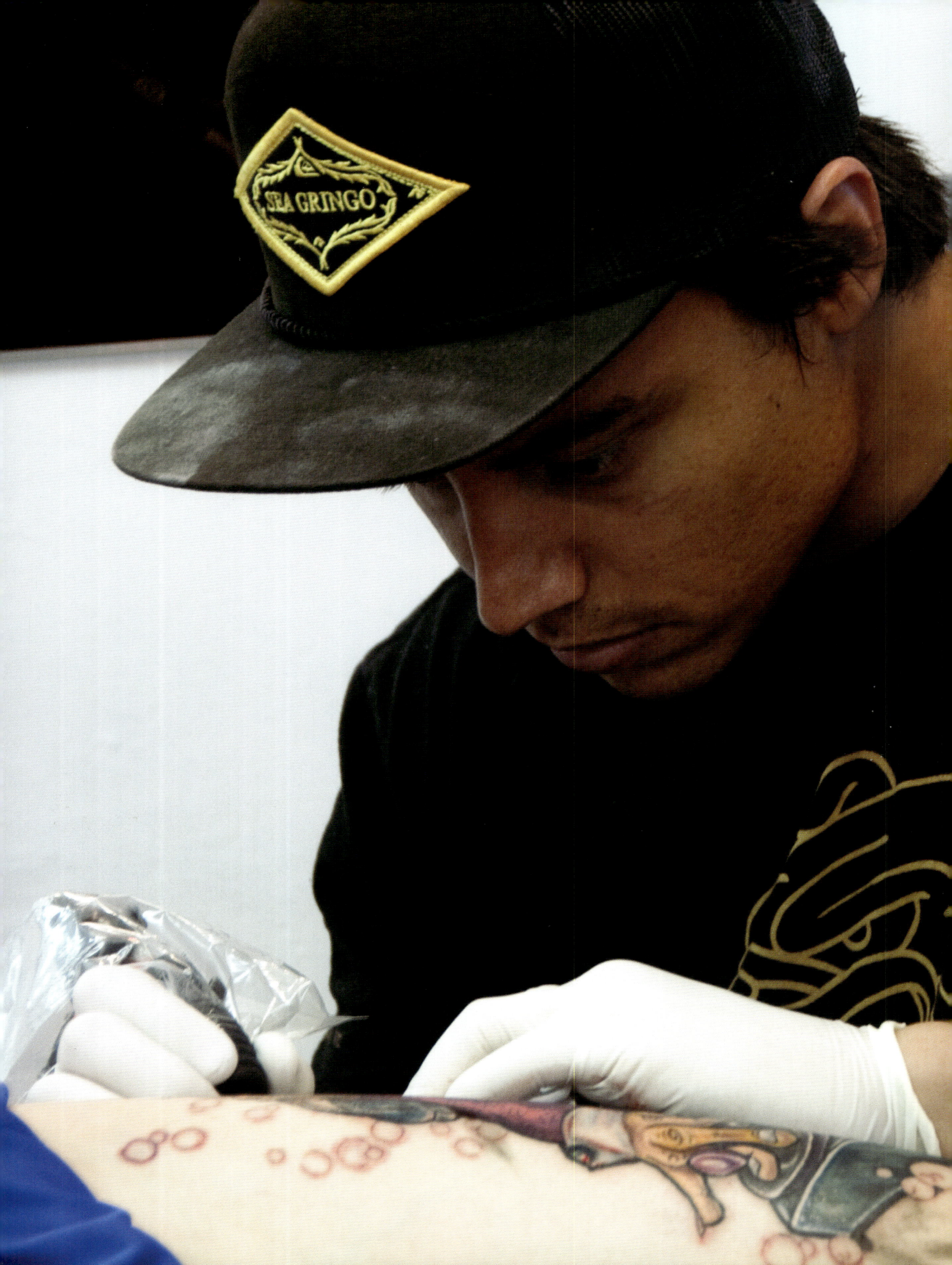

PAUL **GLEDHILL**

Paul Gledhill's forté is colour cartoon tattoos. "That's what a lot of people come to me for," he says. "Not many tattooists are doing stuff like this, so it makes me a little bit different from the rest." His studio, Ink and Anchor, is located on the outskirts of New Plymouth on State Highway 45 — the Surf Highway. "I've been tattooing now for three years and I was an apprentice for a year before that."

He learnt to tattoo in Perth, Western Australia. "I was training to be a rigger on an oil rig and one of the guys on the course told me about his mate who was a tattooist, who was looking for an apprentice." He'd worked as a commercial illustrator and a graphic designer, and it seemed like an obvious path to take. But learning tattooing in Australia was pretty tough: "I had a very old-school apprenticeship, working 60 hours a week for no money, doing the cleaning. It was an honour to just change the rubbish bins when I started."

He came back to New Zealand in April 2009 although not with the intention of opening a studio. But the owner of the shop Paul was working in wanted to get out of the industry. He sold Paul what was left of the business in 2009.

Paul changed the name to Ink and Anchor and since then the studio has gone from strength to strength: "I've got a six month waiting list," he says. "I was hoping I could find a market back here." Paul always had a waiting list in Australia, and when he moved to New Zealand he was pleasantly surprised that New Zealanders were seeking high quality work and were willing to pay good prices.

"It's been good that I've been able to build up a clientele in a small town like this so quickly. There's been a lot of talk about New Zealand being one of the most tattooed countries in the world; and New Plymouth has really embraced that culture." He views the biennial NZ Tattoo and Art Festival, held in New Plymouth, as one of the best in Australasia.

While he's quickly developed a reputation for his cartoon style, he's always willing to meet the customer's demands: "I come from a street shop background and I can handle any style that's asked of me. New Plymouth is a small town so if you can't do a bit of everything you will struggle." He's been looking further afield as well. "I do a bit of work in the US each year. Last year I went to the Ink-N-Iron Festival in Long Beach, California." The event was held aboard the old ocean liner *Queen Mary*.

"But this year when I go I'm just doing guest spots. It's a working holiday. It's about making connections, but it's also about having fun. Most tattooists who love their job will say it's fun work. You pick something up every time you go to a new place." But he's not looking at leaving his home town just yet.

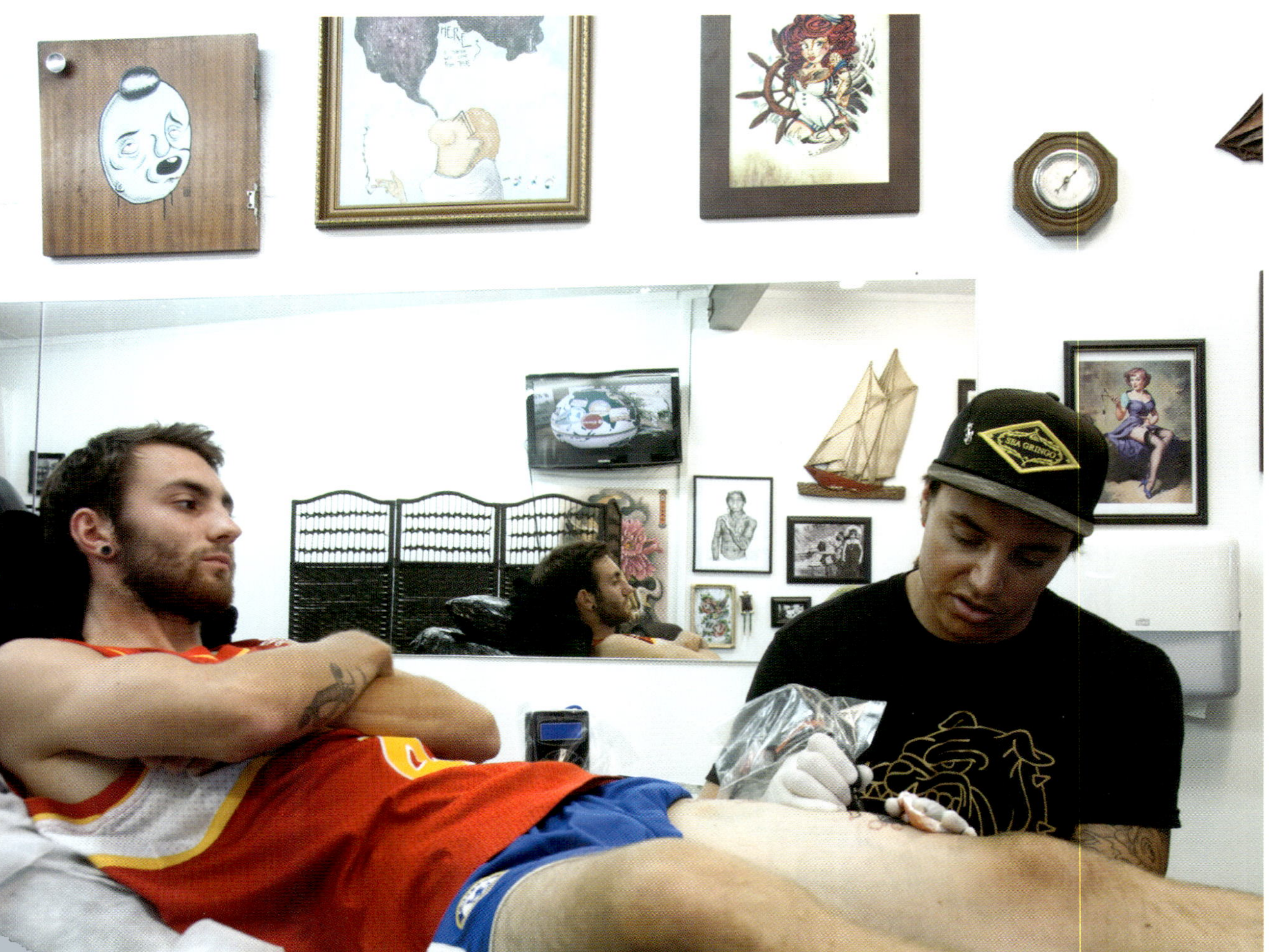

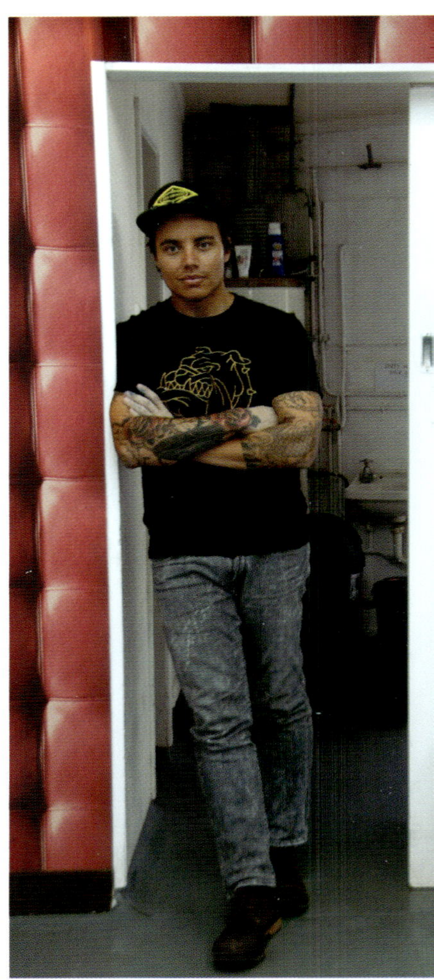

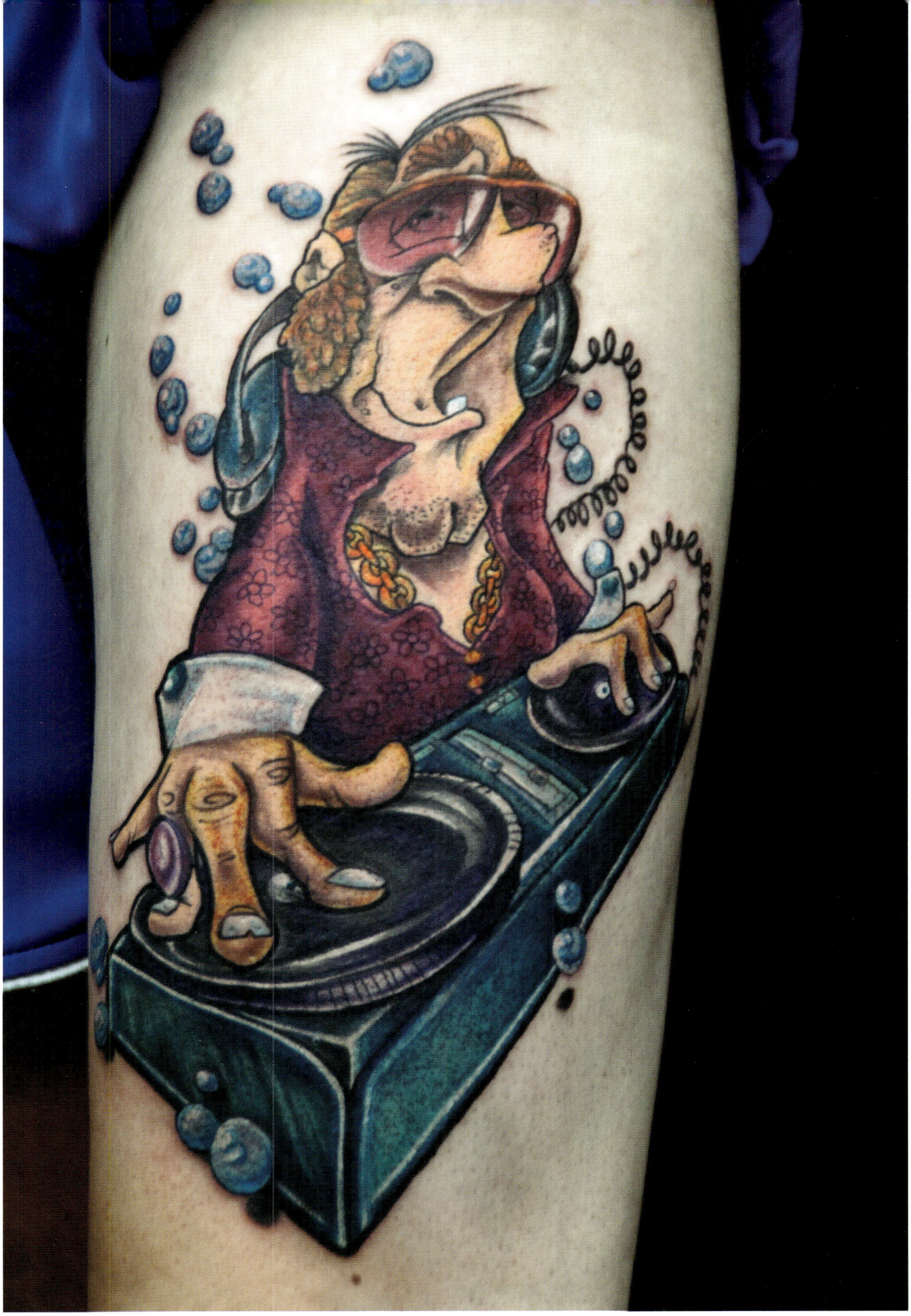

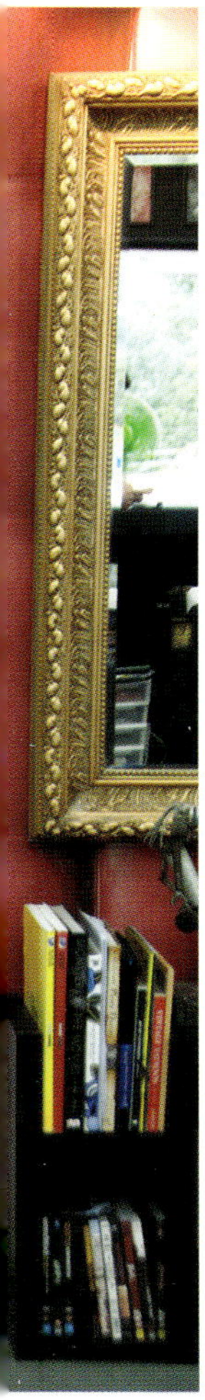

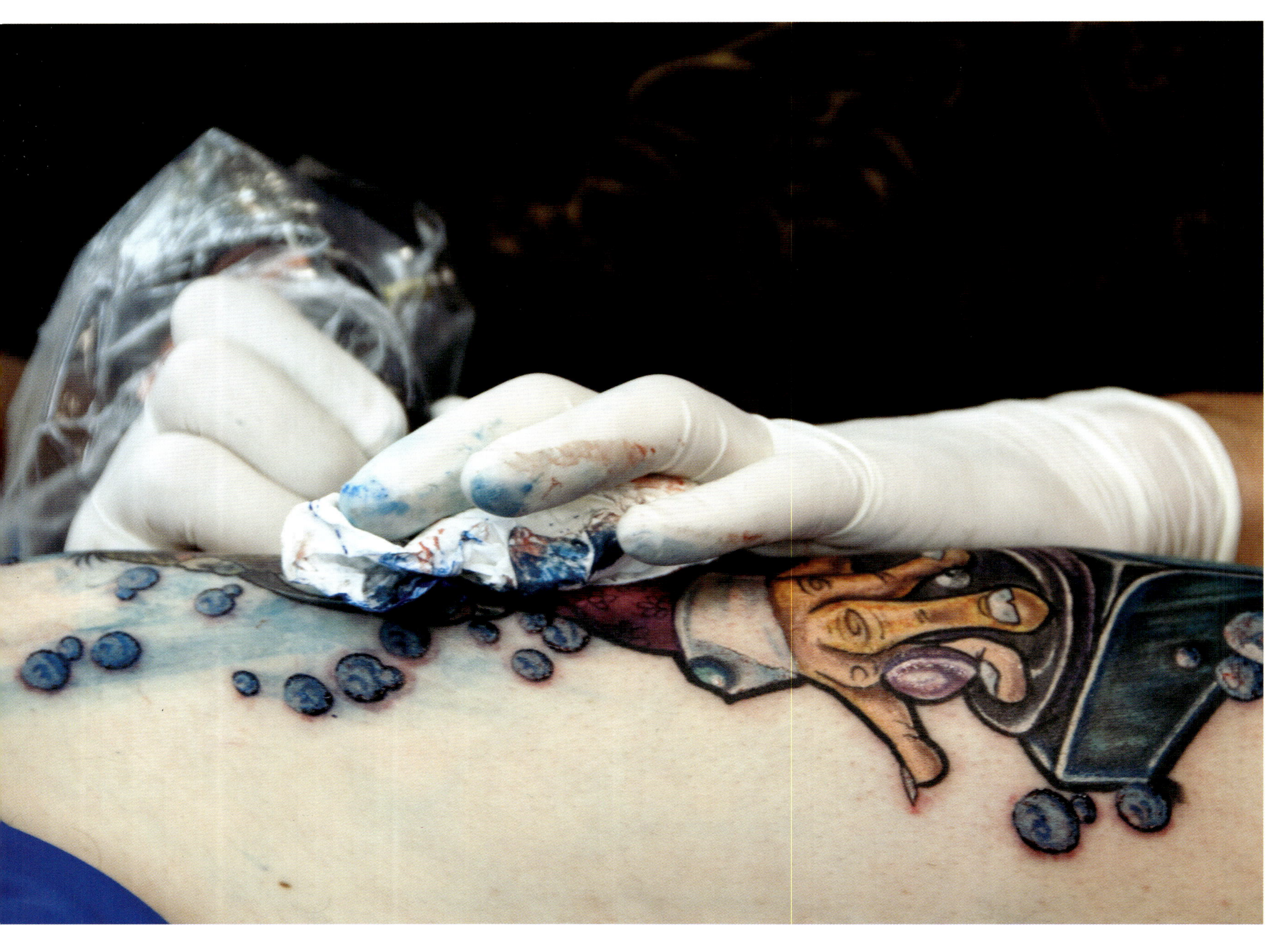

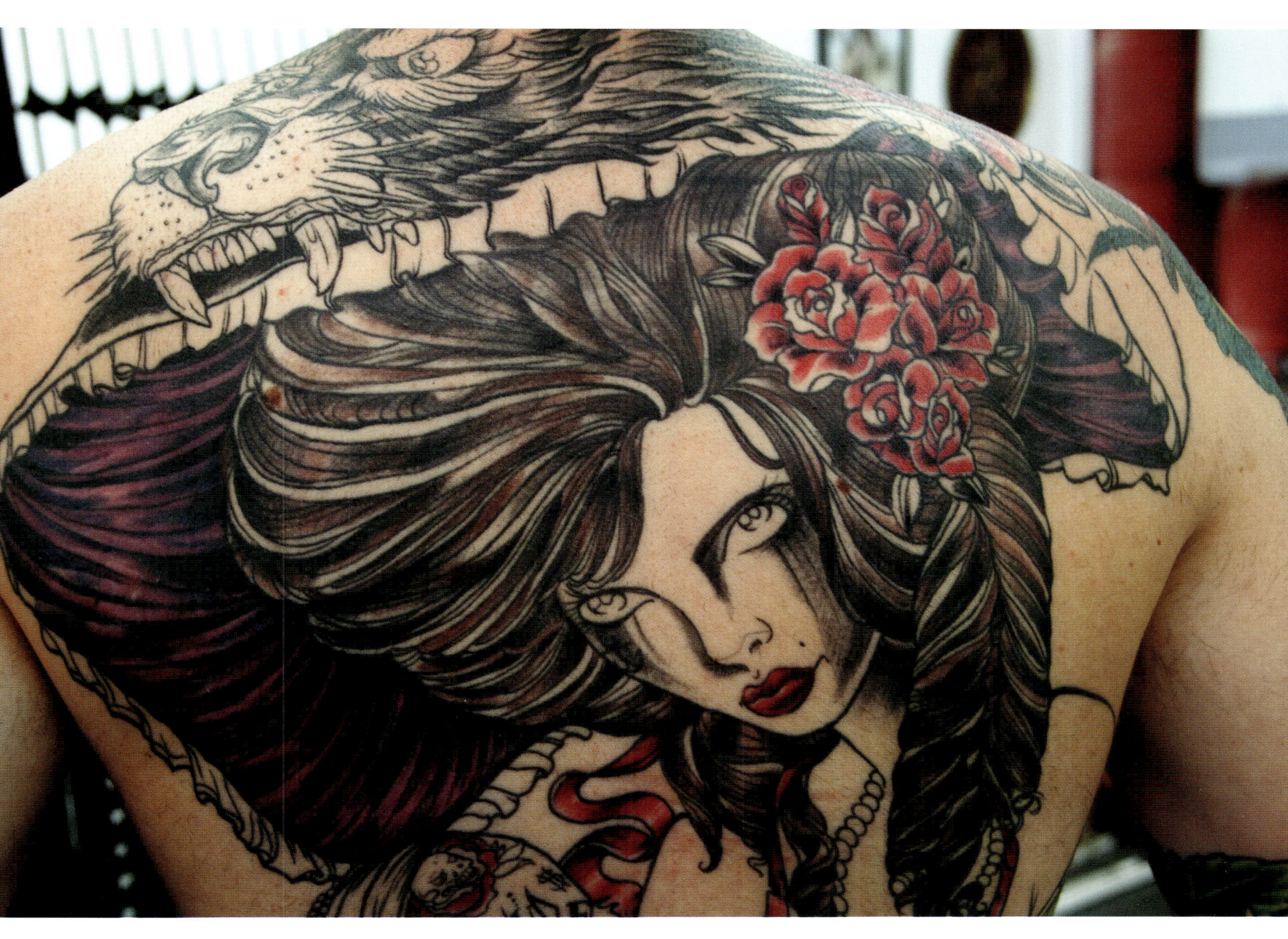

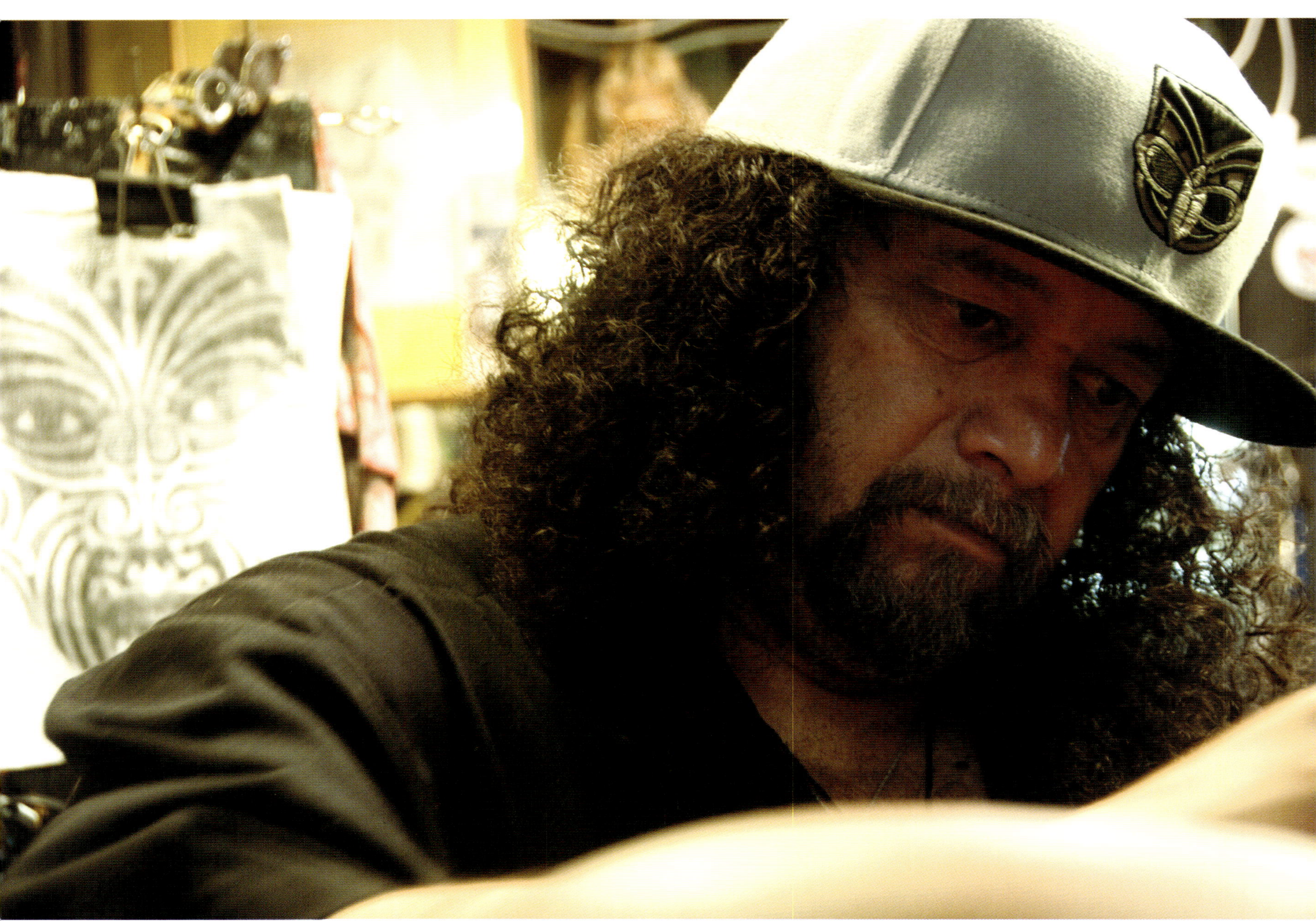

TOMMY **DOWNS**

For the past 20 years Tommy Downs' name has been synonymous with Wellington tattooing. Ever since his early work at the Lower Hutt Tattoo Studio, he's been at the heart of the city's tattoo industry.

These days he runs Roger's Tattoo Art, the Wellington studio started by Roger Ingerton in 1977. Roger retired in 2010 after four decades in the industry and left the studio to his long-time friend. "He gave it to me for Christmas," Tommy says. "It was a real honour."

The studio is decorated with mementoes of Roger's career, from paintings and photos to awards and artwork. "I haven't changed a thing," he says.

Tommy first started working with Roger about ten years ago. "I was at Tattoo City at the time and it wasn't working out, and Roger called me and offered me a job." Tommy was delighted to be able to work with someone he'd always respected. He remembers visiting Roger's studio as a school kid: "I used to skip class to hang out there. I always liked tattoos and knew it was what I wanted to do."

Before long he started getting tips from Roger, and then began tattooing himself in 1986. Tommy started out working from home, but it wasn't until he was laid off work in 1990 that he decided to go professional and open the Lower Hutt Tattoo Studio. "I had that shop for ten years," he says.

There are few styles to which Tommy won't turn his hand. "I'm here to provide a service so there's not much I'll turn away. I do a lot of Maori and Polynesian work now. But whatever someone wants, I'll do it. New Zealand is too small to specialise. You could specialise in ta moko or Island-style work, but with stuff like portraiture you aren't going to get as much business. Not if you want to make a living."

Tommy generally works by himself but has a spare chair for guest artists. "If I know them and they are travelling through I'll let them work with me." These days Tommy's also a keen photographer, something that Roger encouraged him to take up: "He told me if you get into tattooing get a good camera and take photos of everything you do." Tommy followed his advice and it's not uncommon to see him at conventions with camera in hand, firing off shots. "Roger's been a big influence on what I do."

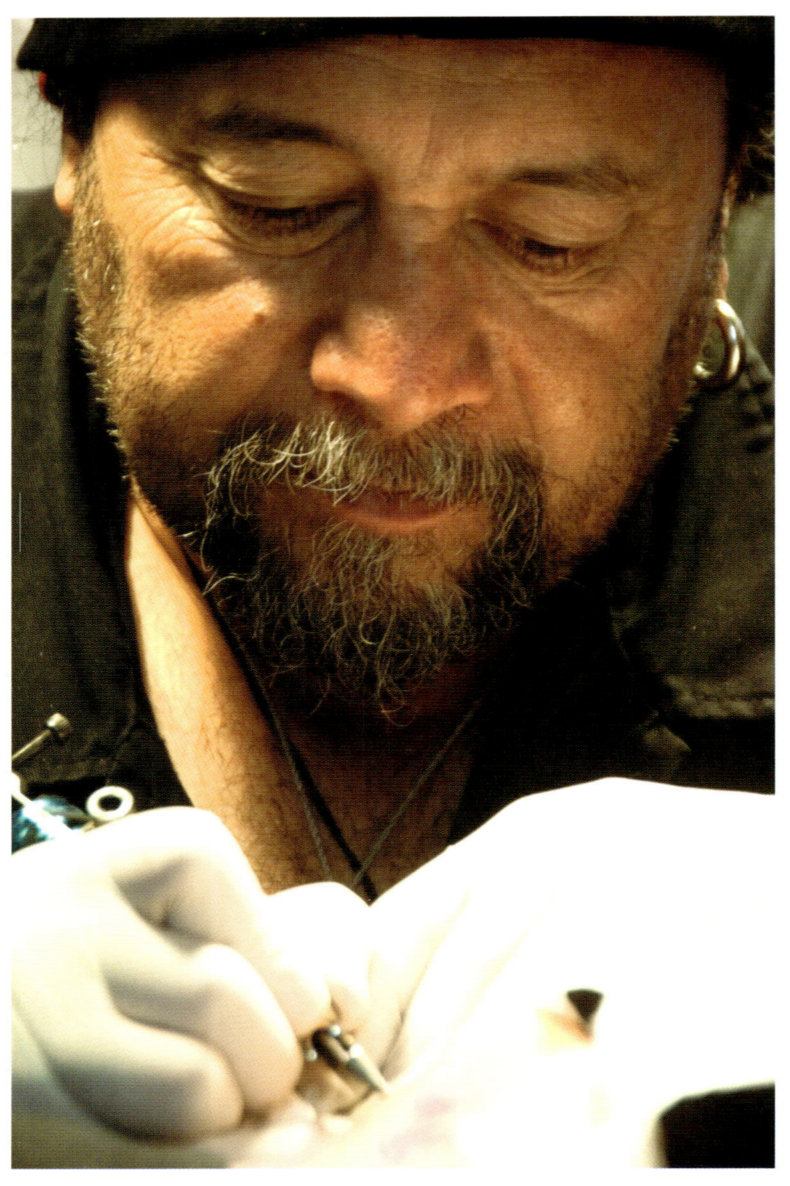

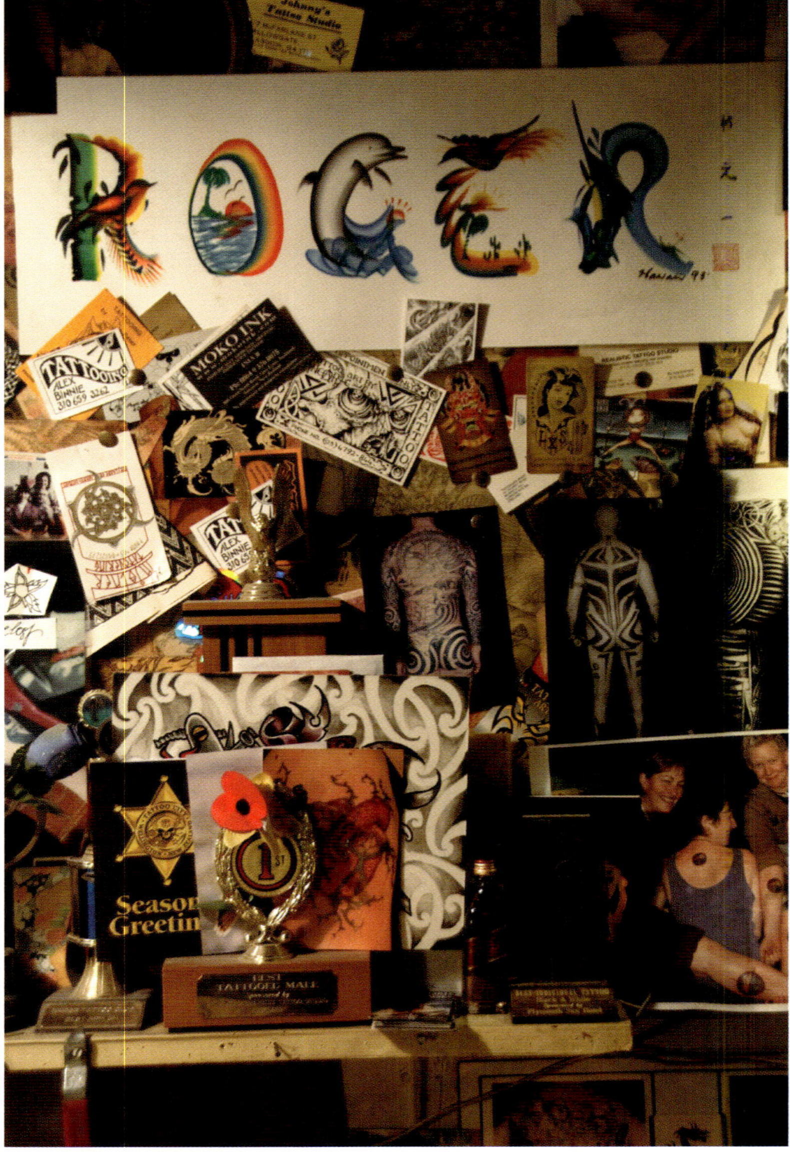

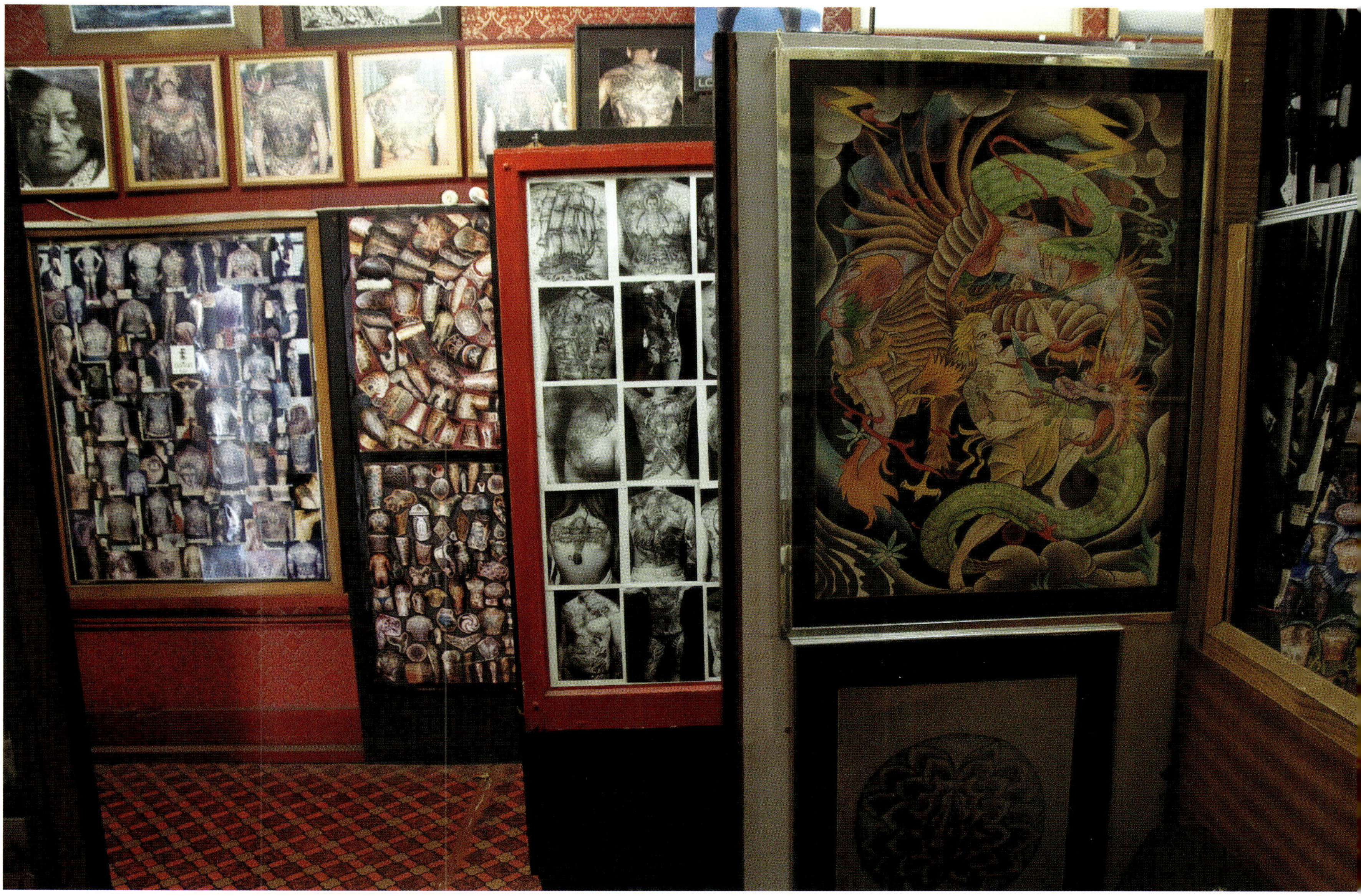

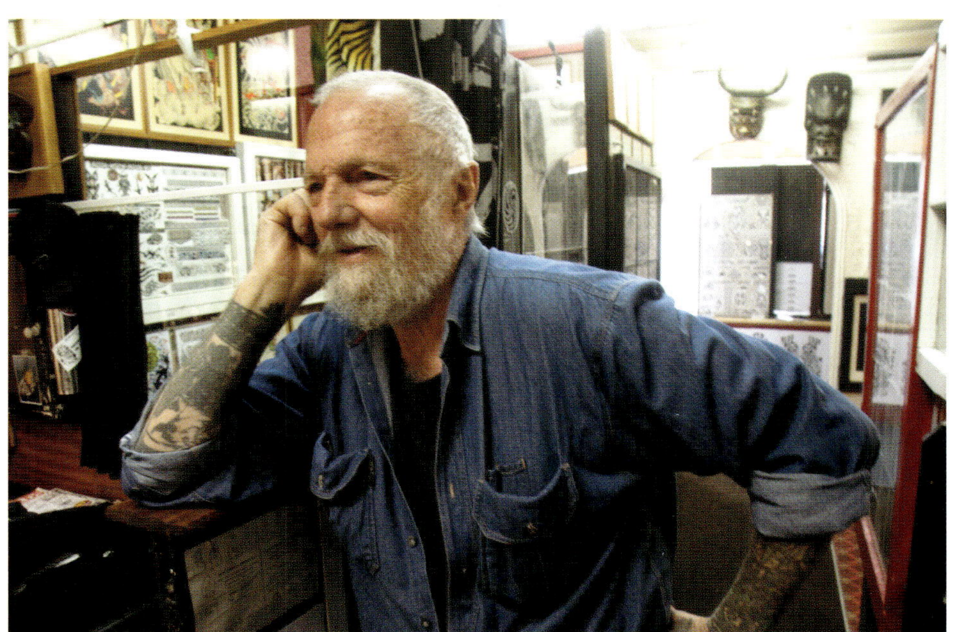

Iconic New Zealand tattooist Roger Ingerton.

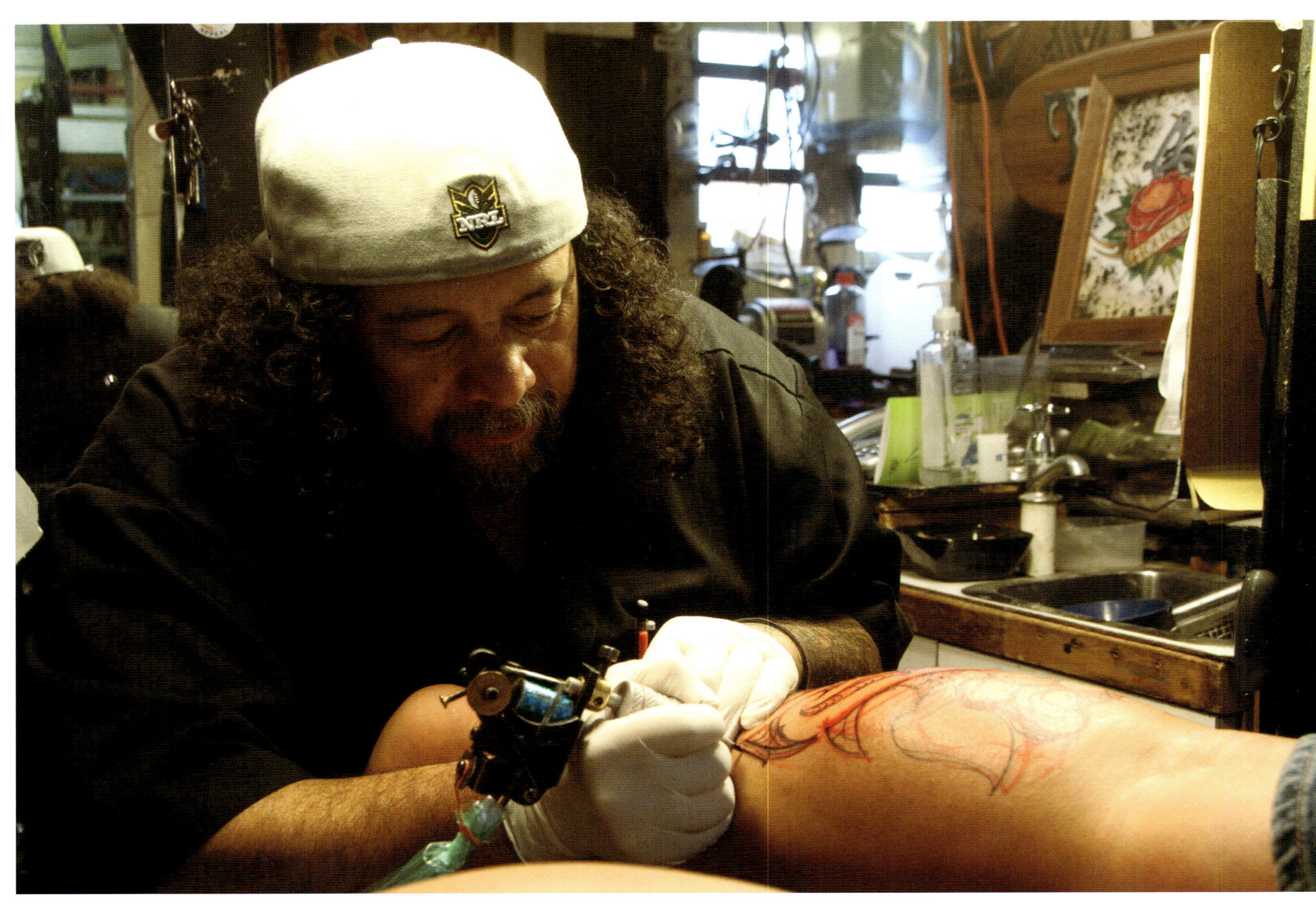

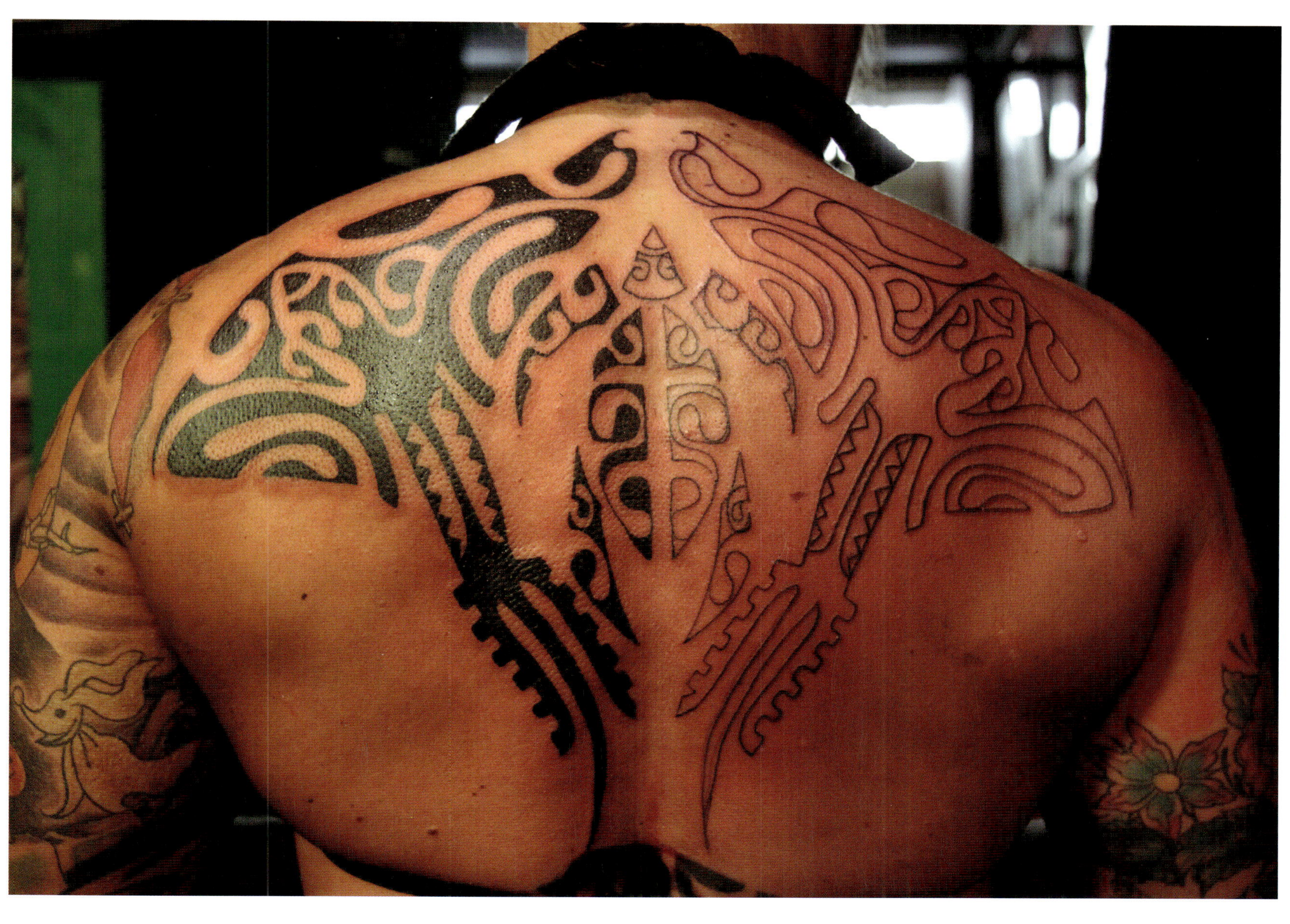

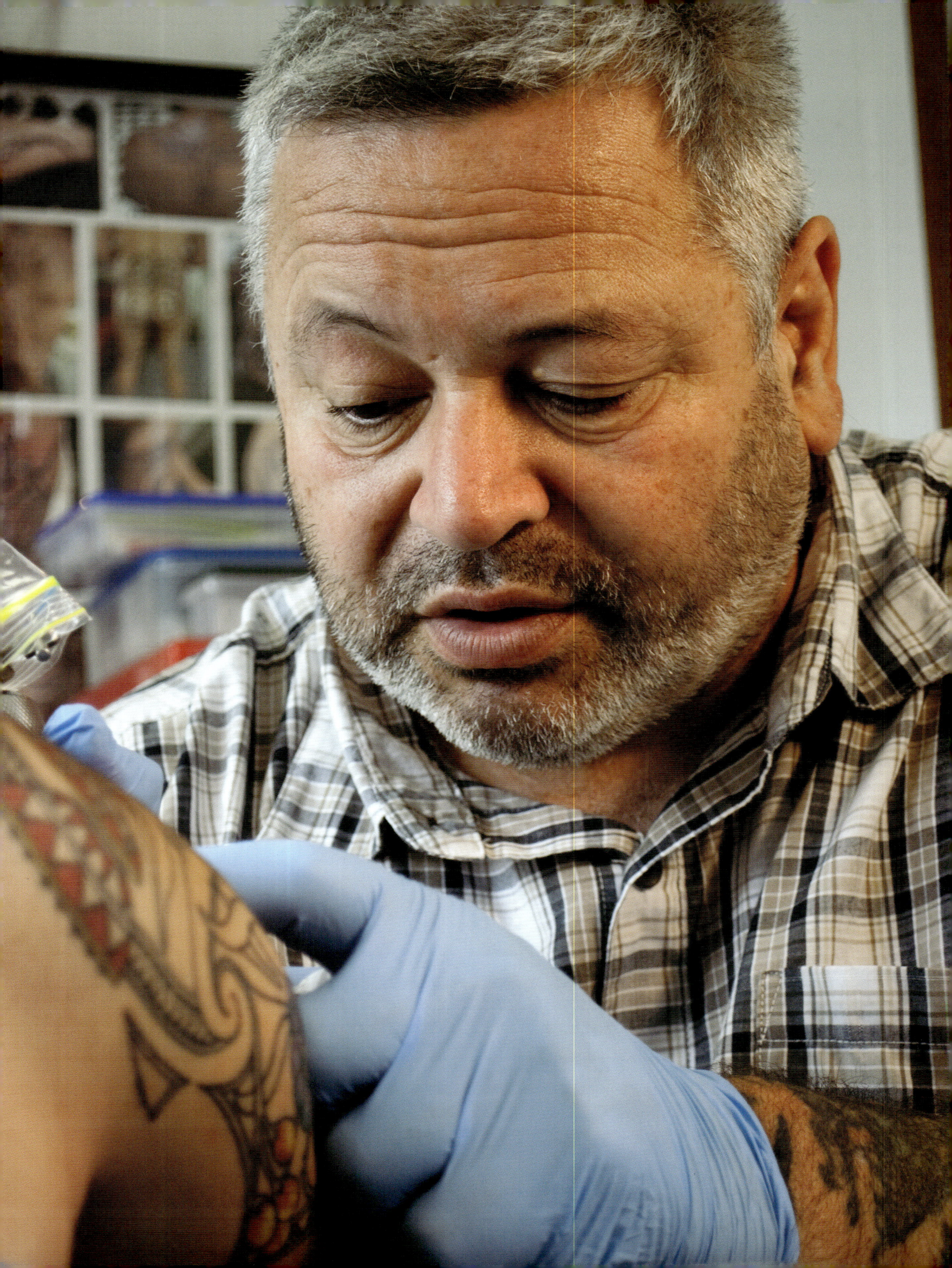

RIKI **MANUEL**

Originally trained as a wood carver, Riki Manuel is also well known as a bone carver — and also a fine exponent of ta moko. There's a lot of intersection with weaving and wood carving, he says, and drawing upon expertise in raranga whakairo and toi whakairo, an artist can move from one to another as creativity and demand dictate.

His whakapapa is Ngāti Porou from his father's side and English and German from his mother's side. Growing up in Greymouth has also cemented strong links to Te Tai Poutini (the West Coast). It was here that Riki acquired his first tattoo — a self-drawn koru etched on his left ankle when he was about 12. But it was in Rotorua that he would complete a three-year apprenticeship at the Māori Arts and Crafts Institute, under the leadership of John Taiapa (who passed away during Riki's final year of study). Adopting carving and weaving patterns comes naturally to Riki, thanks to his carving training: "All these forms borrow from each other."

Some of the names of patterns cross over — like kaokao, which features in taniko, tukutuku panels, carving and ta moko. He still sometimes works in pounamu (nephrite jade or "greenstone"). Riki has recently spent several years overseeing the carving and kowhaiwhai at Rapaki, Ngai Tahu's marae on Banks Peninsula, where he also gave architectural input. He loves traditional chisel work, but for commercial reasons accepts he must use the tattoo machine — after all, it takes a day of highly skilled labour to make up a set of albatross-bone chisels for one person.

Most of Riki's works start with the client's whakapapa, but with half of his client base being Pakeha he is flexible about cultural crossover: "All that I ask from each of the clients, no matter where they're from, is that they articulate my work correctly." He has a strong connection with the Netherlands (he's been there four times doing ta moko), and also feels more influenced by other Polynesian tattooists than by his Maori counterparts.

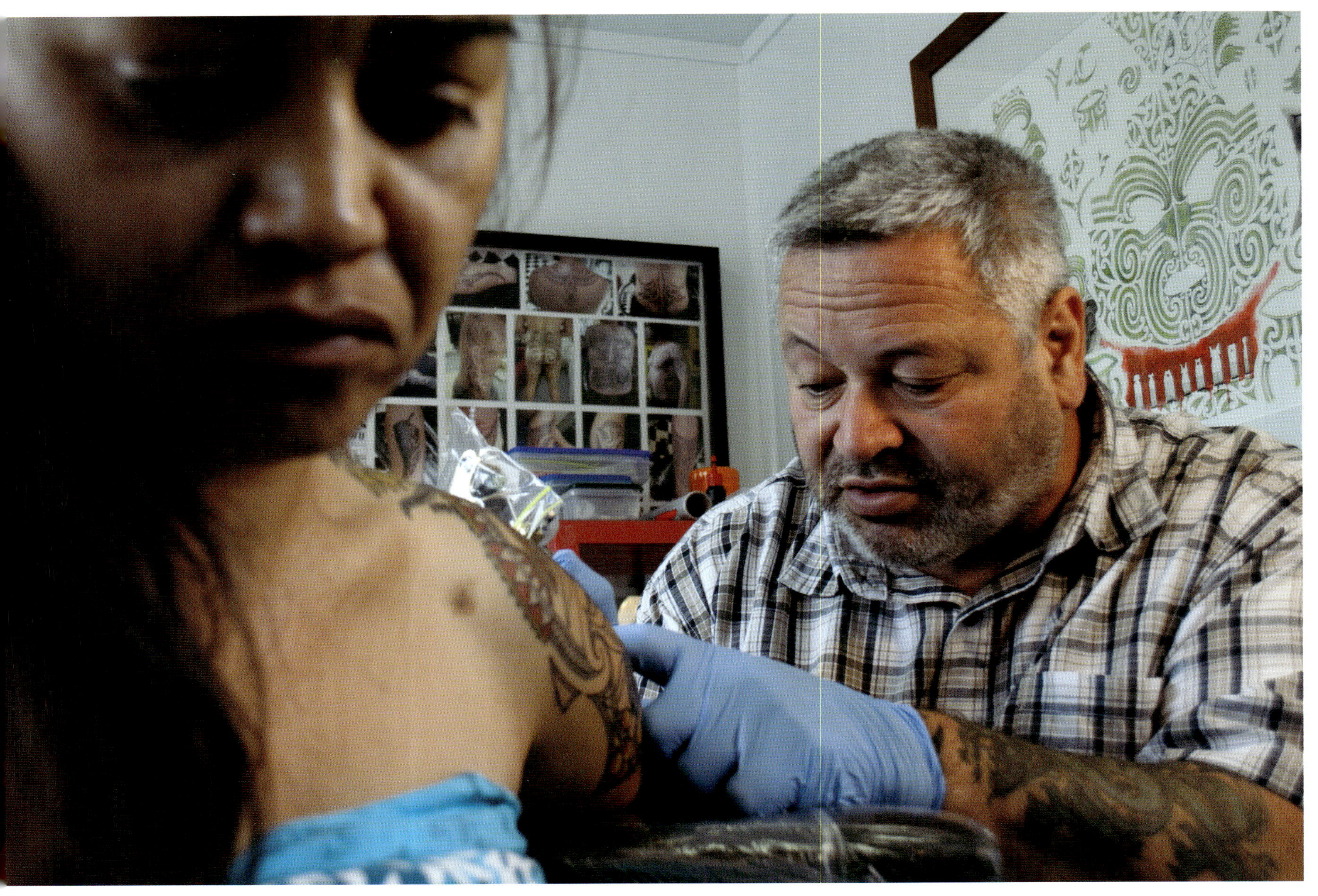

Jim Keenan, a Maori trade trainer who Riki recently tattooed, displays his arm tattoo that bears personal ancestry with special symbols for his children and new mokopuna (grandchildren). For Riki, the design blends traditional symbols of Jim's iwi, Te Ati Awa and Ngai Tahu, with "my own way of doing things." Jim is clear about his take on the tattoo: "I love it. It's almost completed me."

Through his carving education Riki learned the appropriate symbolism in what he describes as "the last of the old schools." Much of that knowledge has been lost today, but those who know can read the tattoo like a book, following the stories of past and present. "As wood carvers we carve moko all the time on ancestral faces or tekoteko patterns," he says. On his own leg are tattoos based on a tekoteko of his ancestor Iwirakau that is now in the Otago Museum, derived from his ancestral marae of Hinepare in Rangitukia.

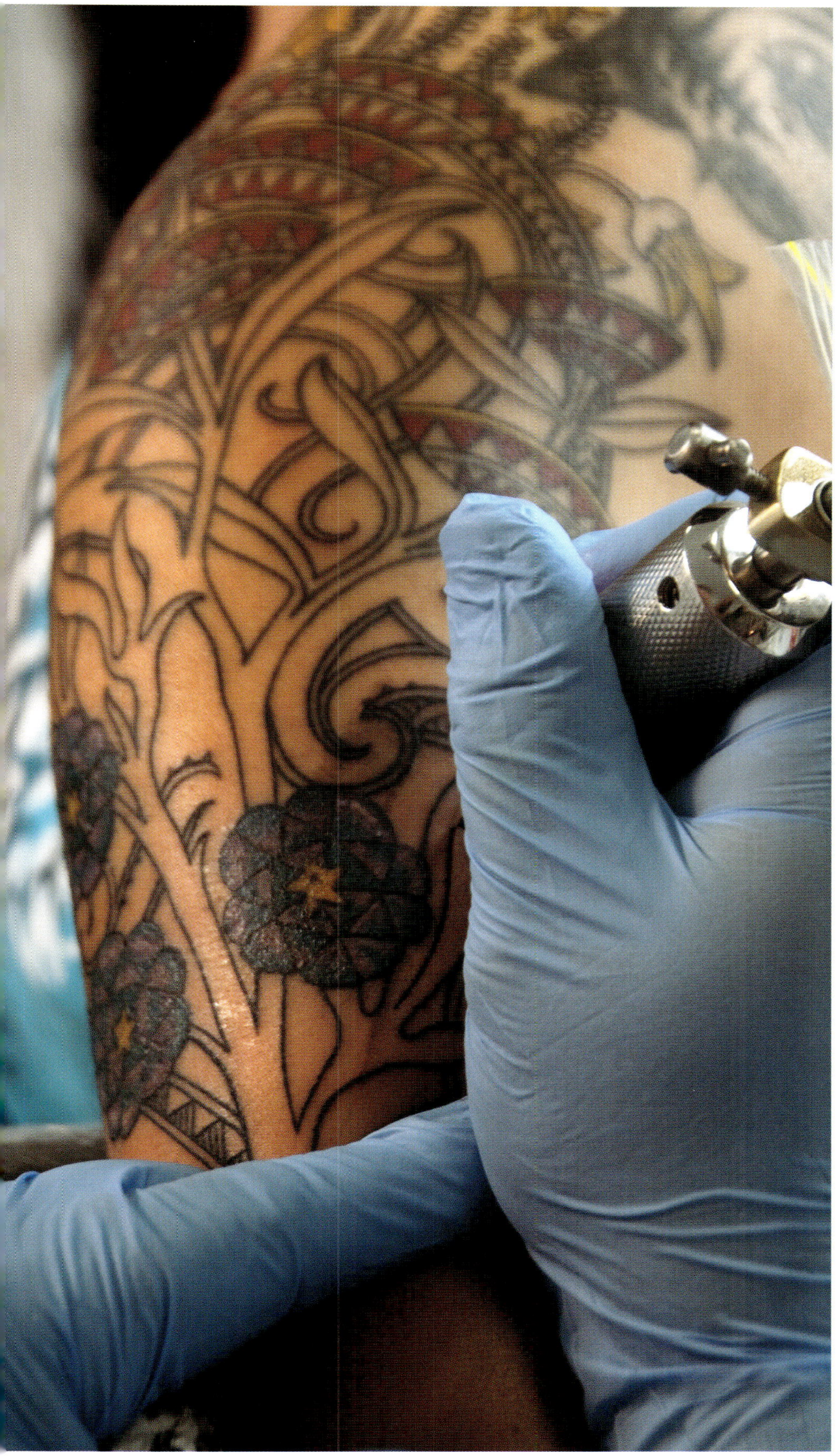

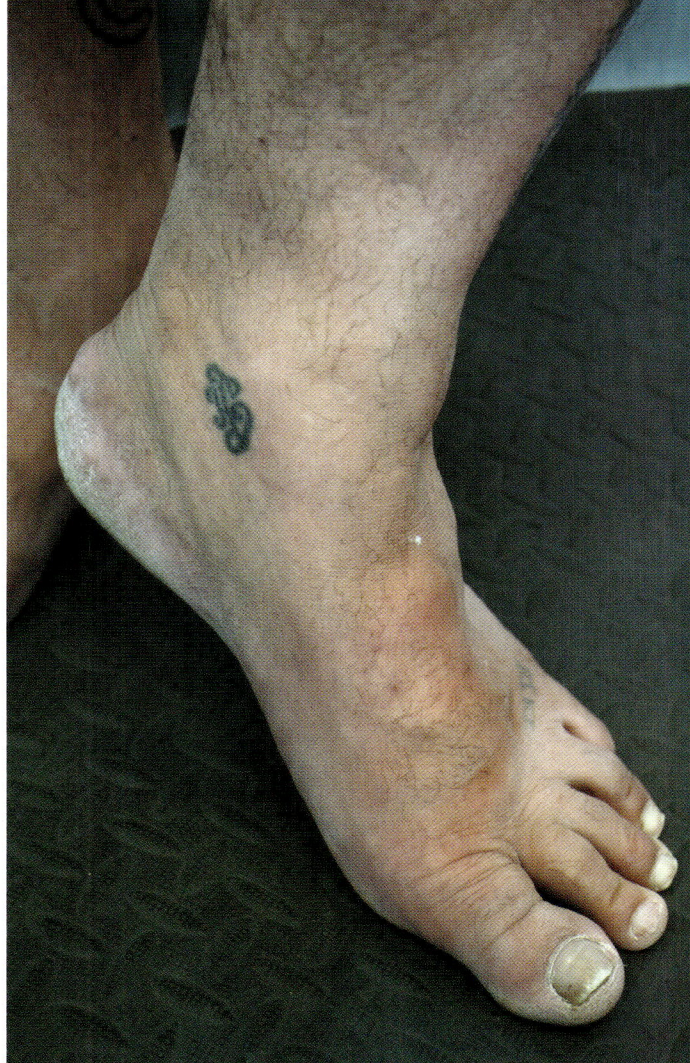

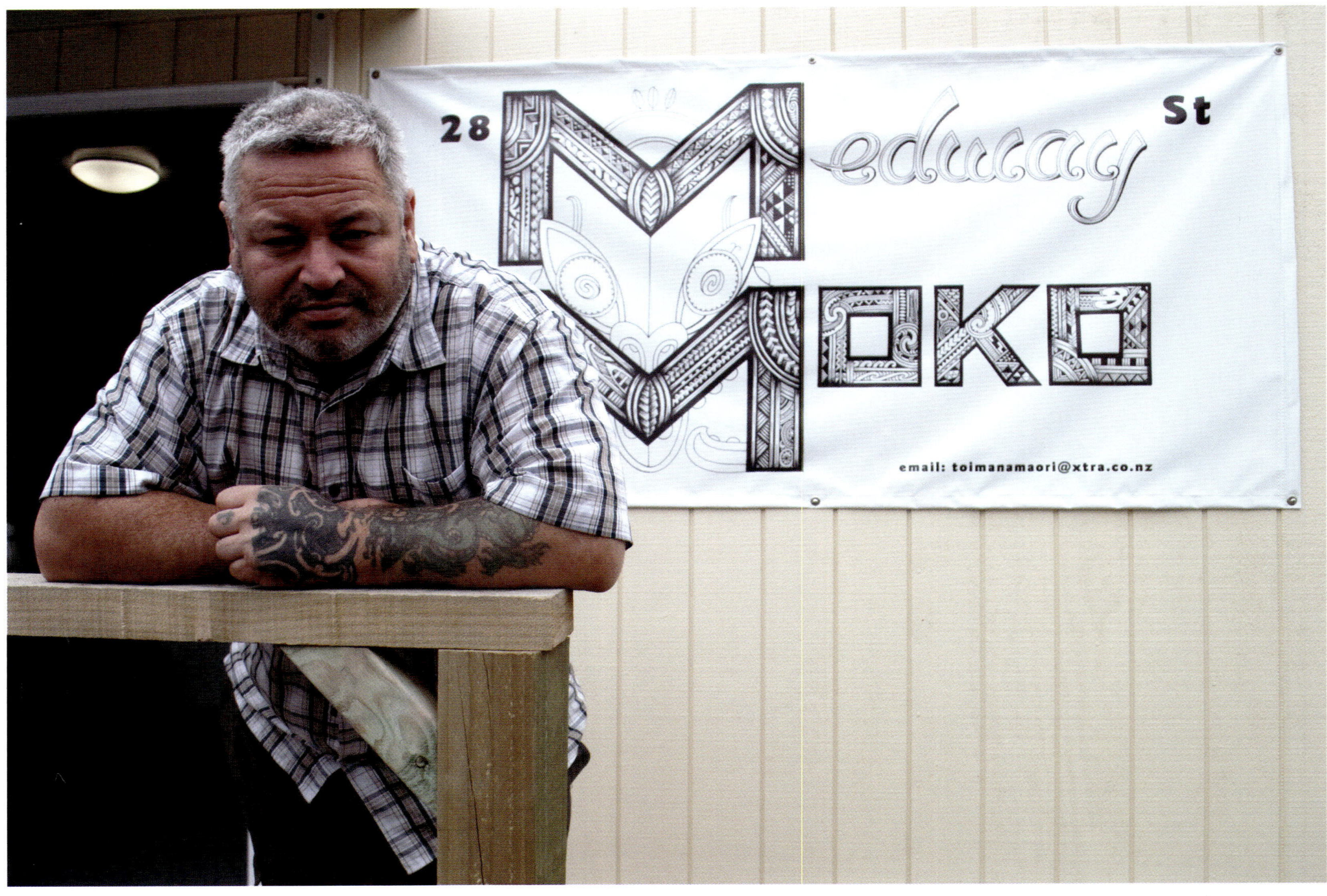

Life for Riki and his wife Viv changed completely with the February 2011 Christchurch earthquake. Chris Doig had invited them to set up Te Toi Mana Maori Art Gallery in the city's Arts Centre in 1984, binding them to earning a living for their six children, but also a demanding retail and production schedule. Now the old studio is facing demolition.

The quake gave birth to Medway Moko, named for the Avonside street where the couple now live in Riki's old workshop, with their children sleeping in a whare he built in the back yard. Their house is a write-off and will need to be rebuilt, but Riki considers himself lucky: from about three houses closer to the Avon River a red zone is in place, meaning all buildings are to be demolished and the land abandoned.

Medway Moko operates from a mobile studio out front, built in six weeks and shipped from Auckland so they could get back to work. "Now I'm picking the work I want to do so I'm lucky, considering we've got no house." His 25-year-old son Waiora is working as one of his apprentices, so the knowledge Riki has built up is going forth. "I've always had young fellas whom I've mentored over the years. Most of them are doing it full-time now, all over the country."

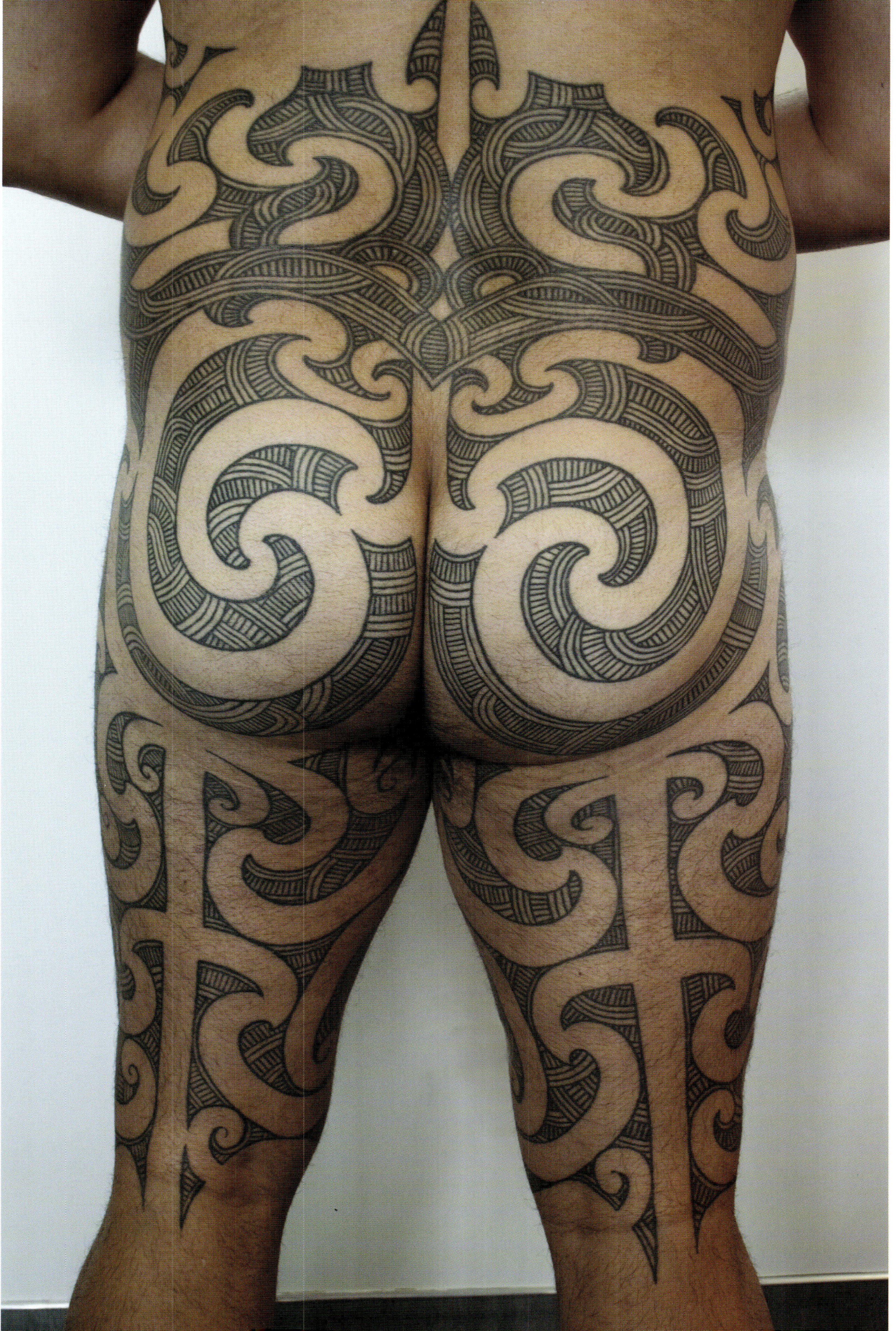

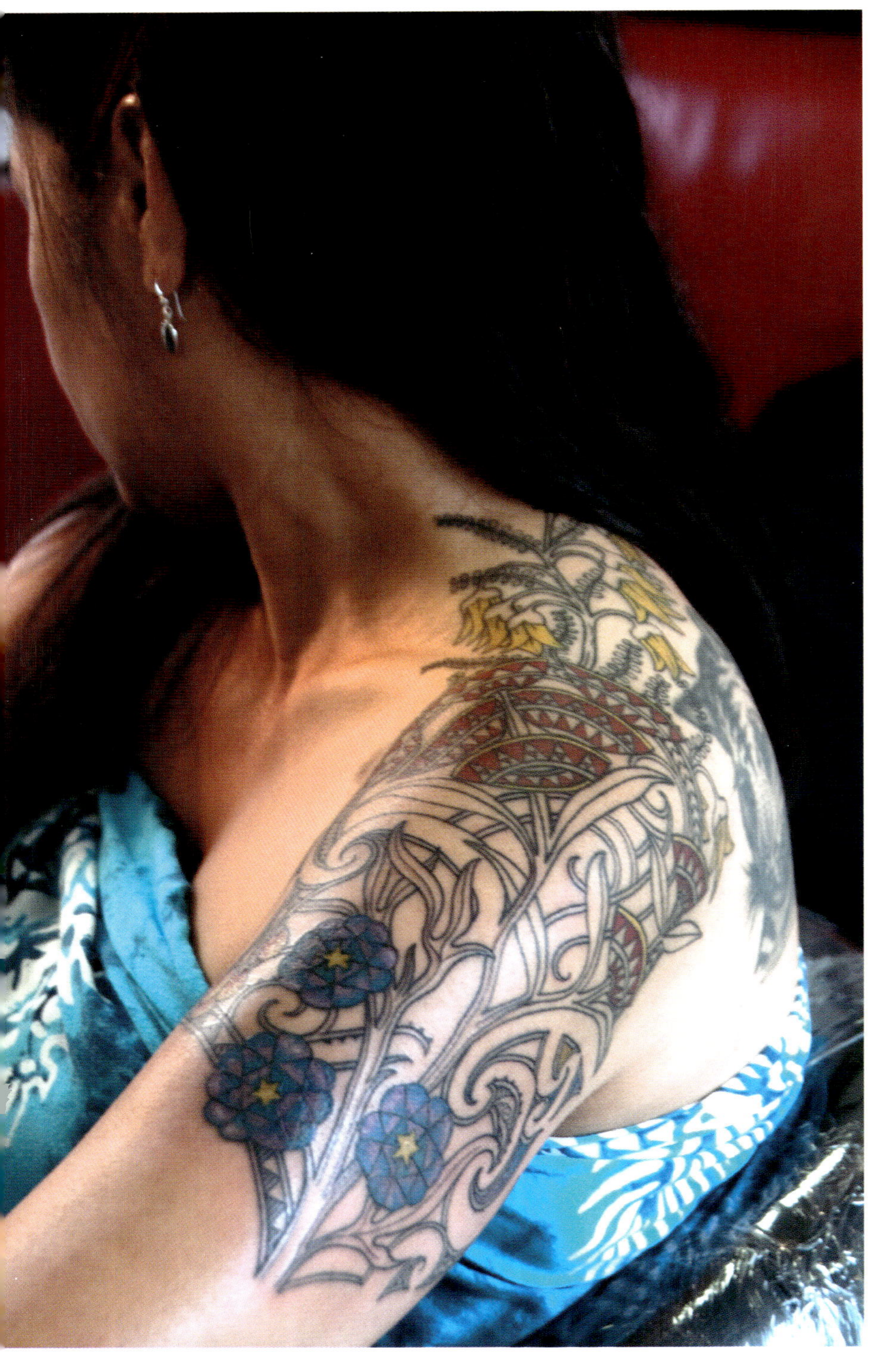

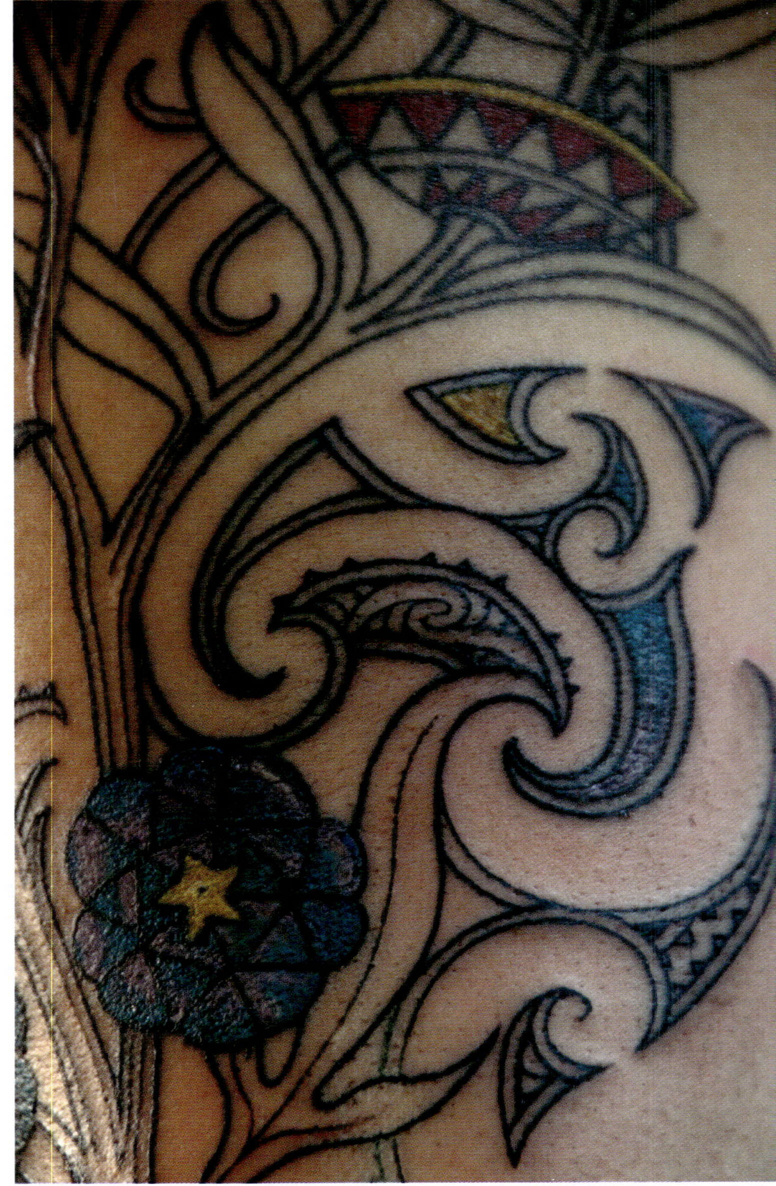

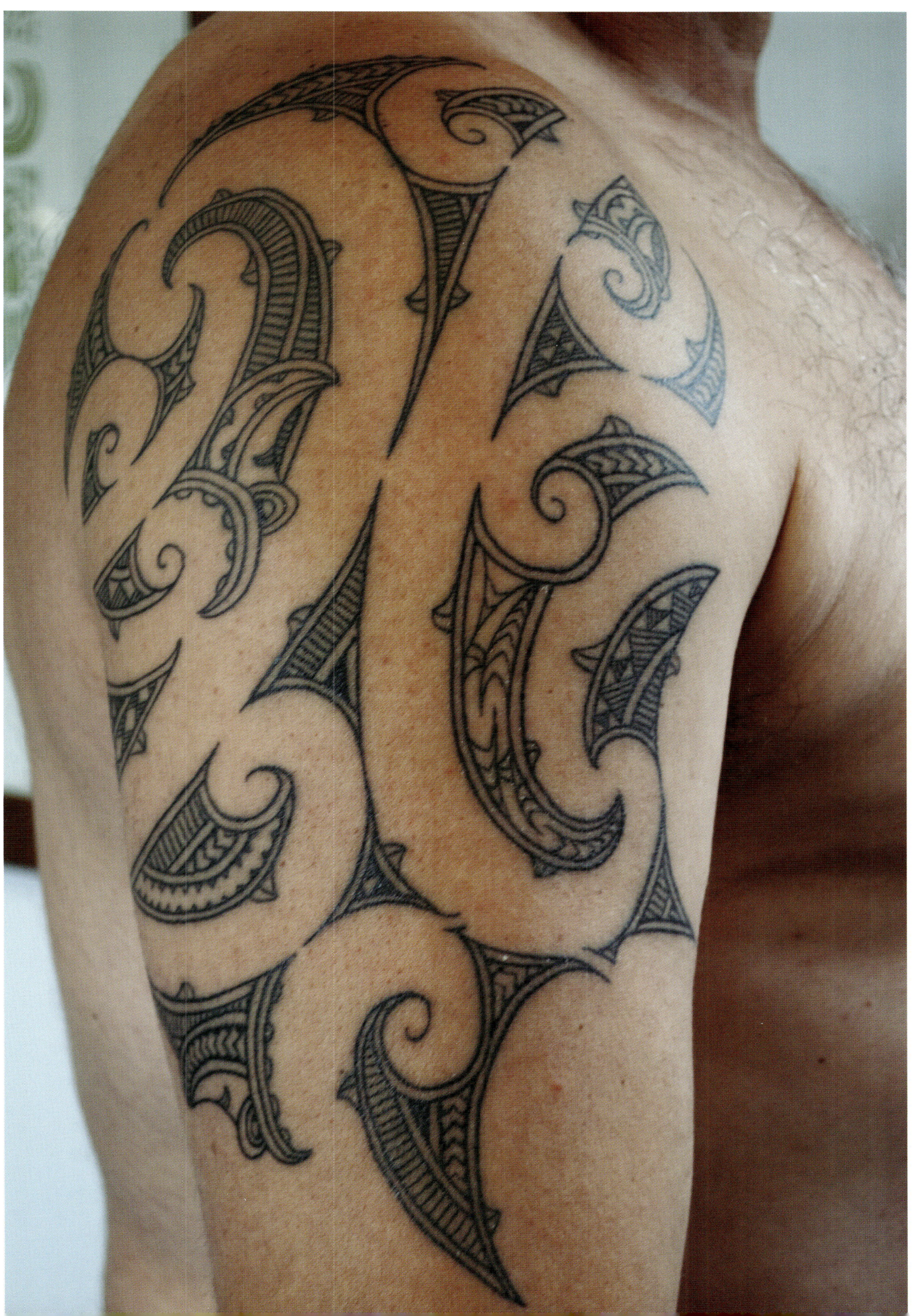

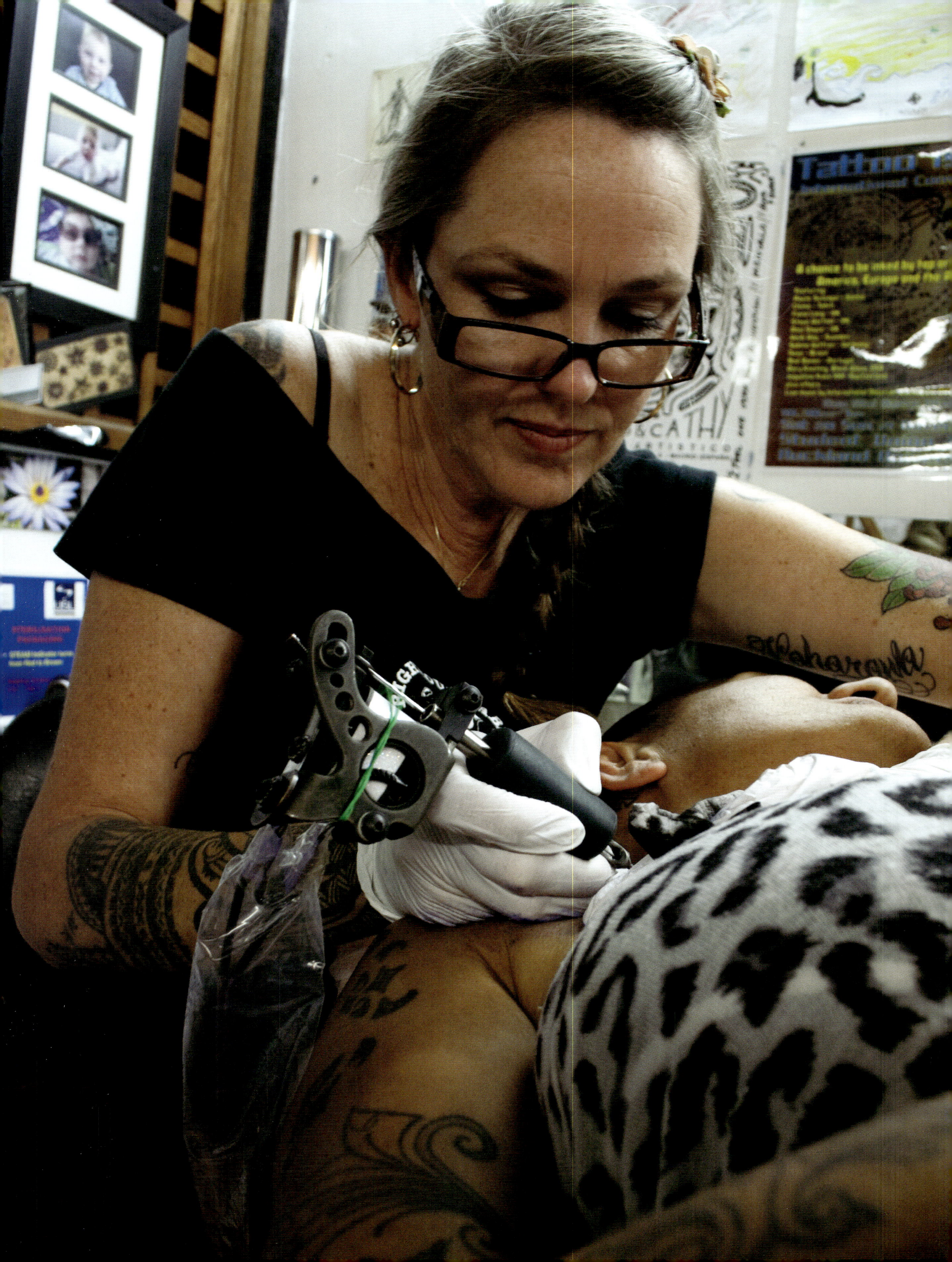

PIP **RUSSELL**

Indigenous patterns are a common feature of Pip Russell's work. From Maori and Pacific style designs to bold tribal motifs, the themes run throughout her work.

These days she runs the Artrageous Tattoo Studio in Auckland, out of the Dominion Road shop started by Paul Peachey in 1997. The studio's website gallery is decked out with images of her handiwork. Pip also turns her hand to other styles. "Because we're a street shop, if someone wants me to tattoo an orange koi carp or some flowers, I'll do it."

Pip started tattooing in 2000 as part of an apprenticeship with Inia Taylor at Moko Ink in Auckland. "Inia had done a lot of sculpture and artwork and I learnt a lot from him. At the time there weren't many studios doing ta moko but Inia got on the international stage quite quickly and through him and Paulo Suluape I got to meet a lot of different artists from around the world."

Pip helped to organise the first Auckland International Tattoo Convention in 1999 and has been one of the key figures behind the event ever since (see page 17). The convention attracts artists from around the world and is a major event on the New Zealand tattooing calendar.

She finished working at Moko Ink in 2001. "I rented a room with the guys from Sacred Tattoo for a while and then I had a baby." She and her partner, ta moko artist Nehe Reuben, opened a small home studio in Te Atatu. In 2004 they travelled to Europe, where they spent the next six months working in Germany, Switzerland and Holland. After she returned to New Zealand she spent a year and a half working at Art N Soul Tattoo in Whangarei. Then in 2008 she took over the day-to-day management of Artrageous Tattoo. "It was an established shop so it took people a while to realise Paul wasn't here any more. He'd been there for about ten years." Paul still works at the studio for a few days each month. "We're not the most well-known shop in the world. But Paul had developed a good reputation for quality work."

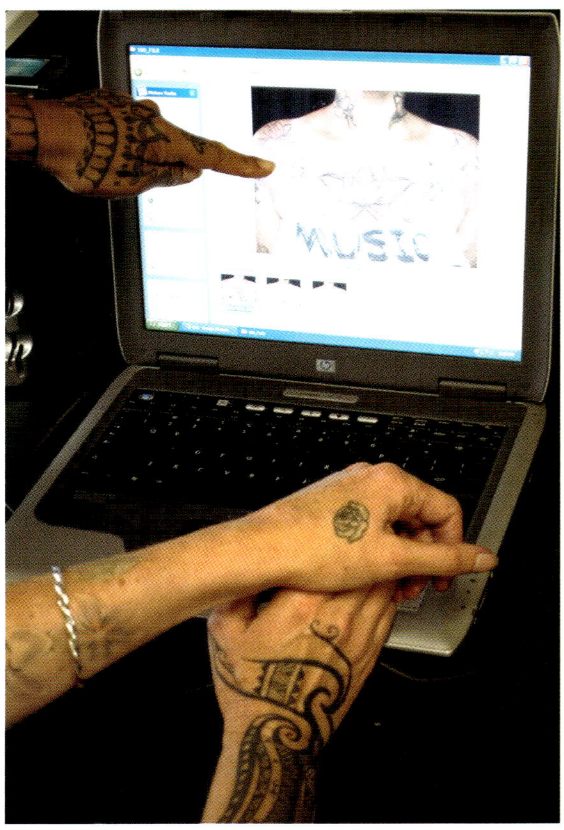

In Pip's view the industry has grown a lot in the time she's been working in it, especially over the last four or five years, and the people entering the industry are changing as well: "A lot of them are art school graduates these days, and now it's seen as a career option if you're an artist." With so many different styles of tattooing available, artists can specialise and be choosy about what work they do and don't do. And she finds New Zealand a good place to be a tattooist: "It's far more socially acceptable than it is in other countries. It's always been in our consciousness."

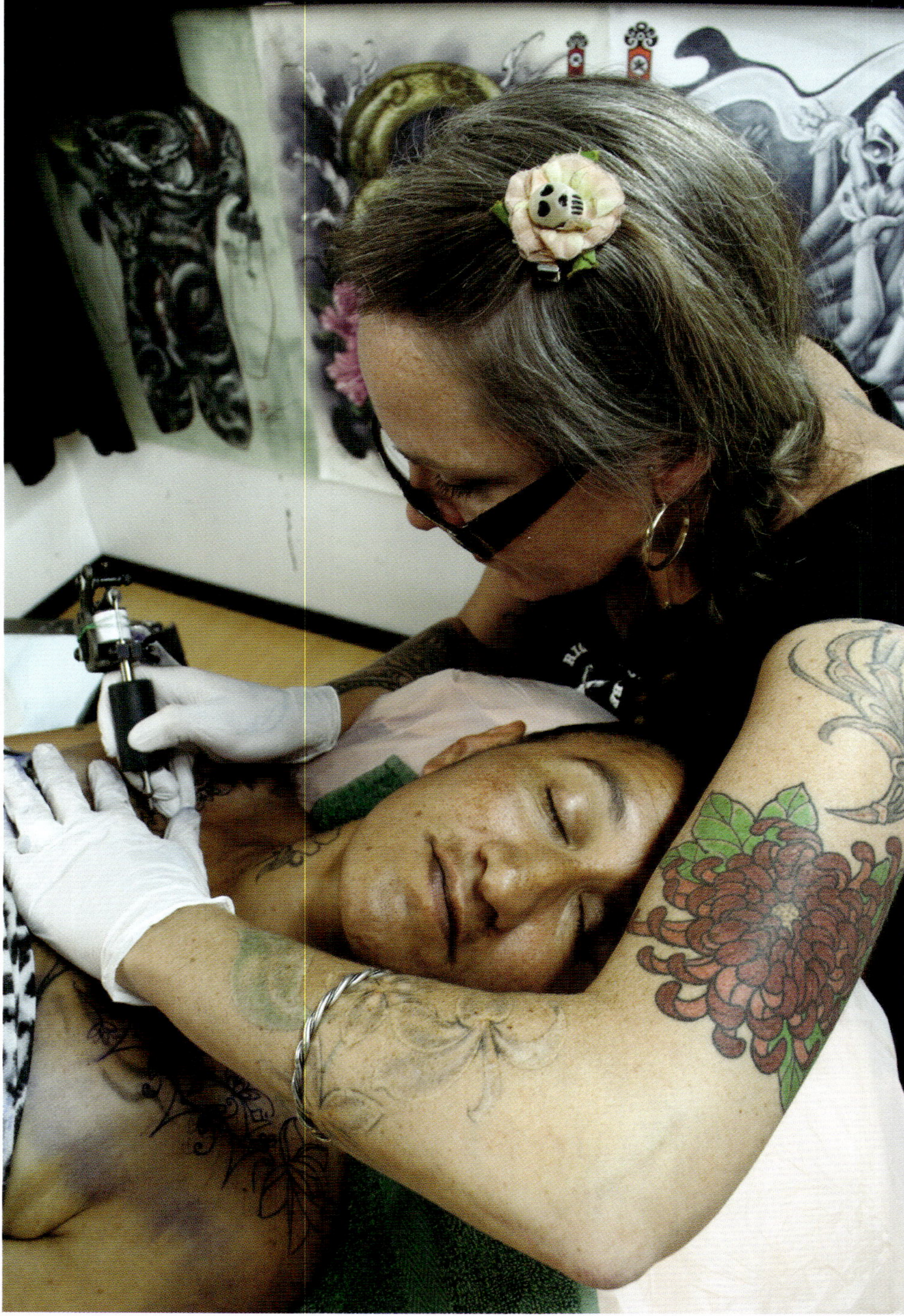

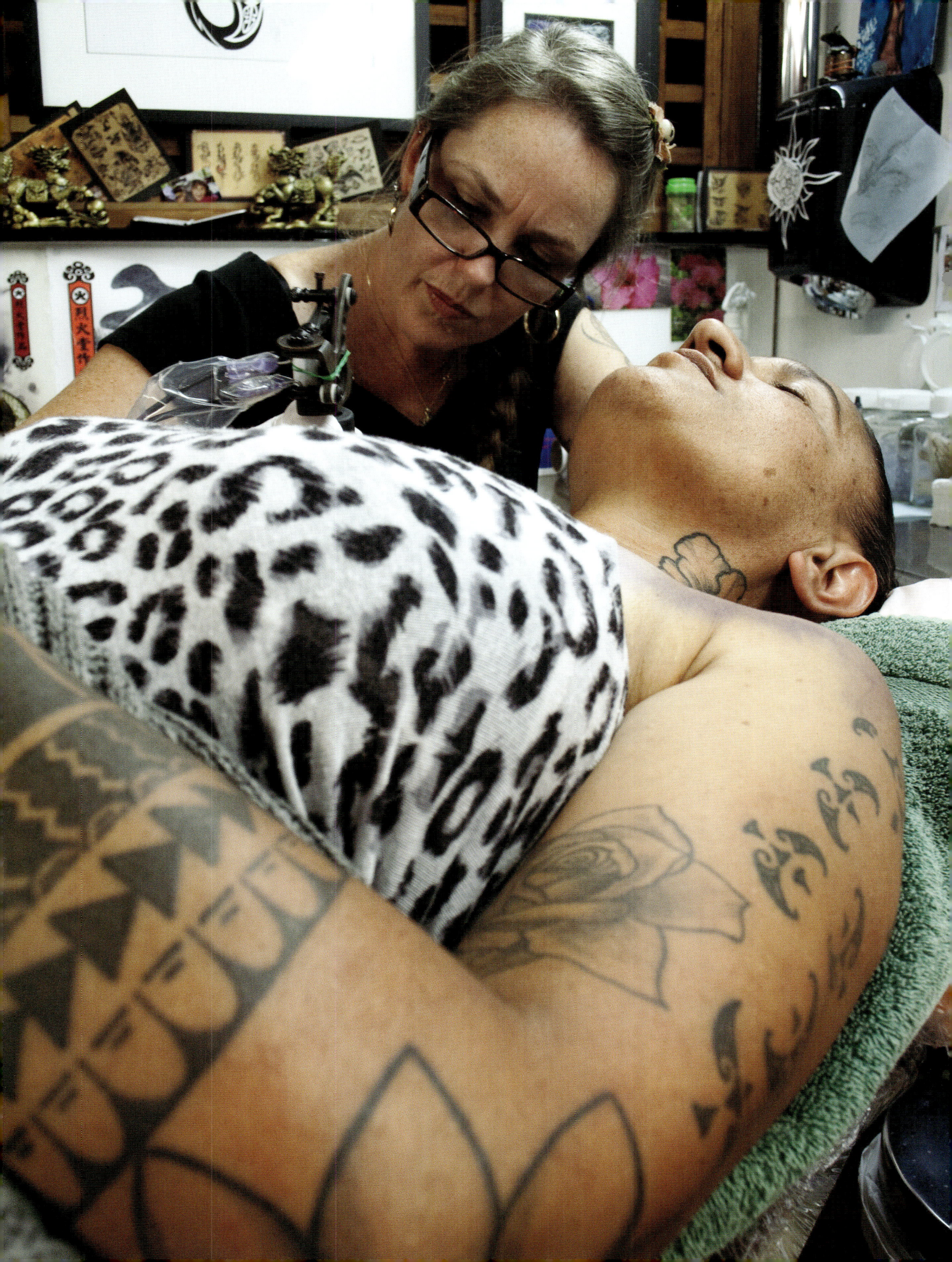

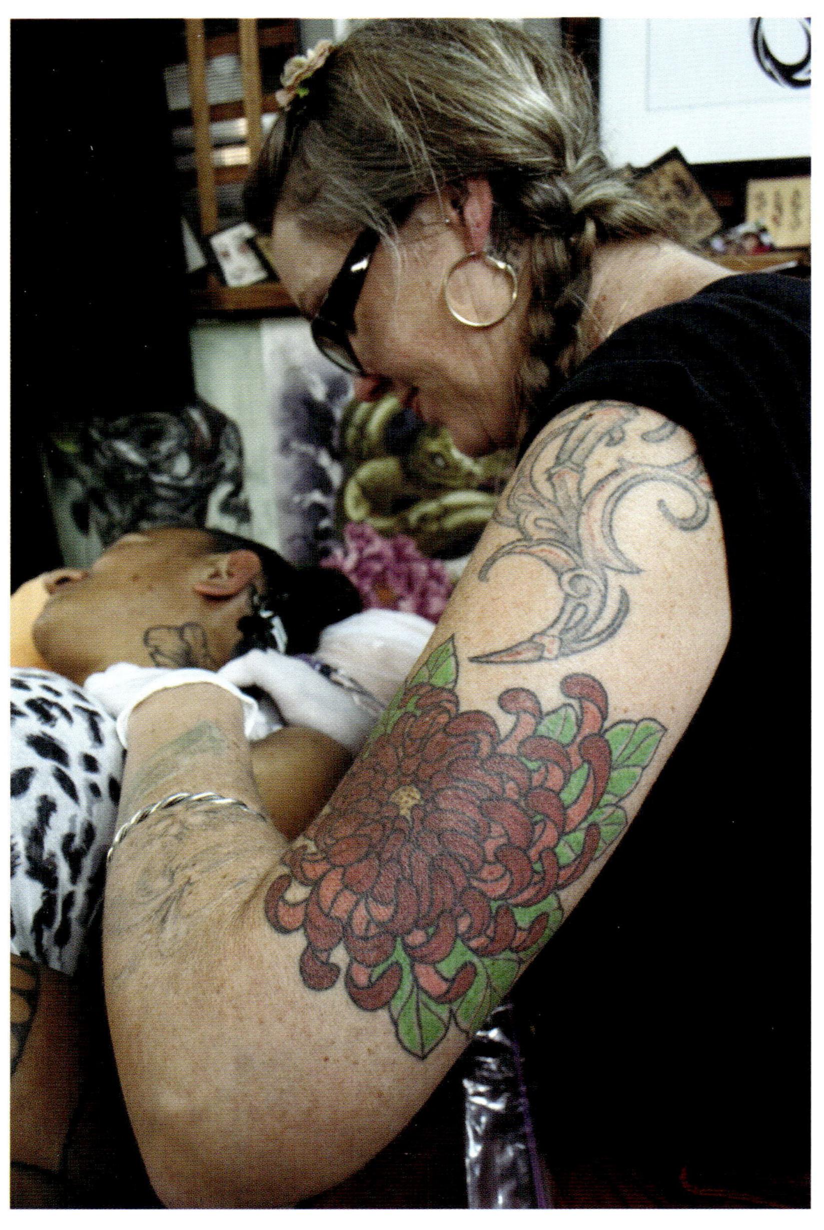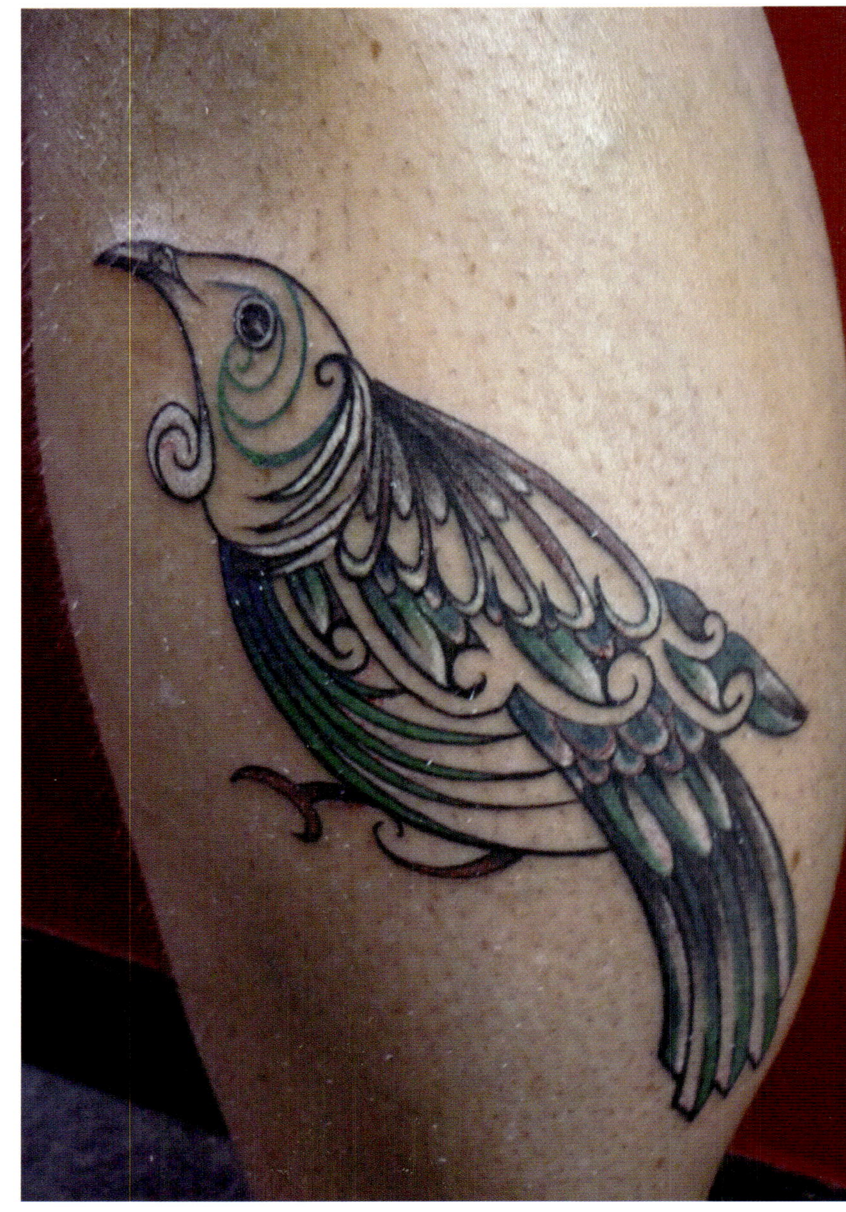

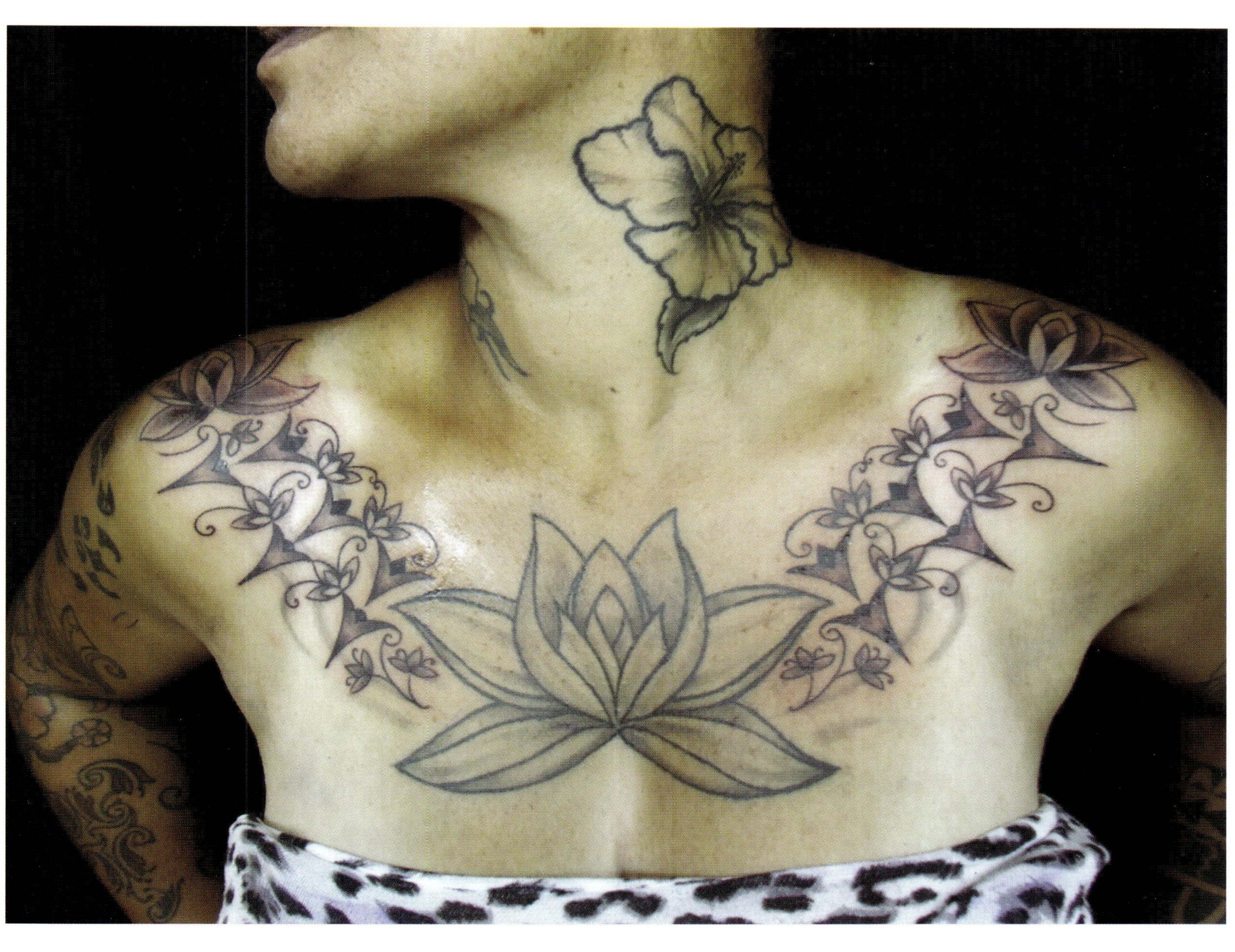

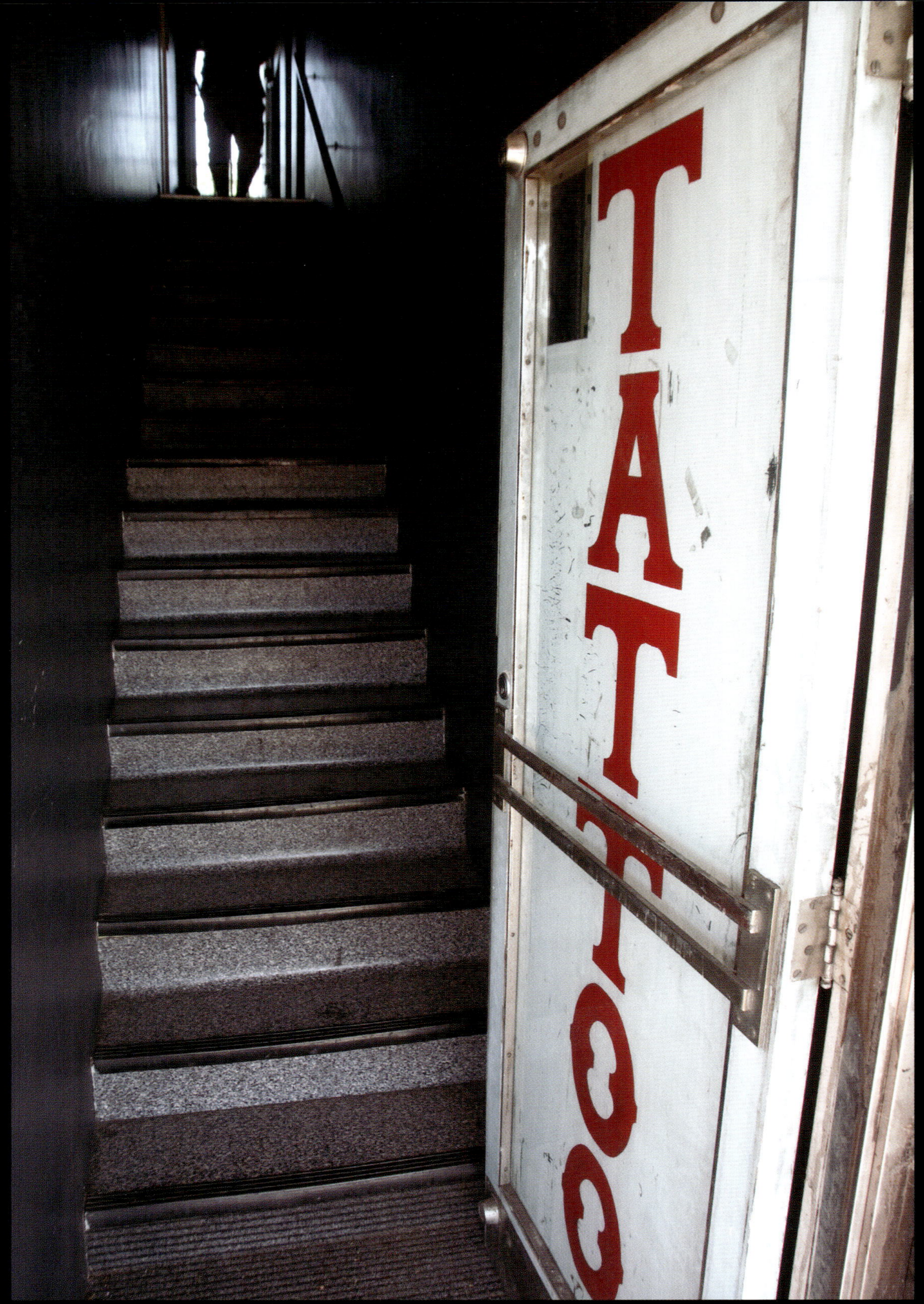

Chris Hoult is a photographer known for his haunting landscapes and social documentary work.
He has exhibited widely and published two books: *Home Free: Housetrucking in New Zealand*,
with Fiona Cunningham, and *Out West, a photographic journey through Auckland's West*.
Chris lives in Waima, Auckland with his partner and kids.

Steve Forbes is a freelance journalist who is also well known as a guitarist in bands including
The Kingites. Steve lives in New Lynn, Auckland with his partner and their young child.

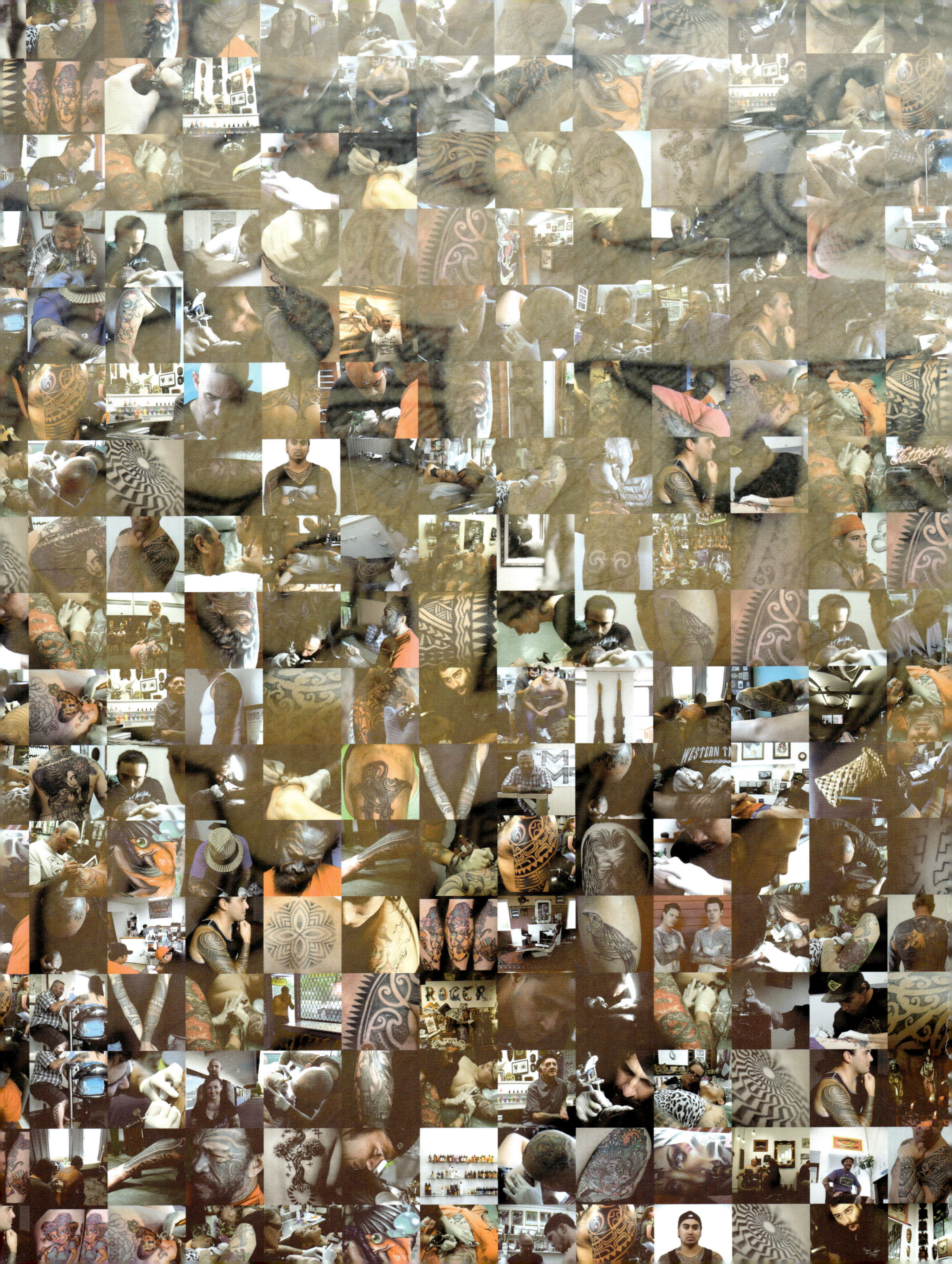